Applying the Free-Energy Principle to Complex Adaptive Systems

Applying the Free-Energy Principle to Complex Adaptive Systems

Editors

Paul Badcock
Maxwell Ramstead
Zahra Sheikhbahaee
Axel Constant

MDPI • Basel • Beijing • Wuhan • Barcelona • Belgrade • Manchester • Tokyo • Cluj • Tianjin

Editors

Paul Badcock
The University of Melbourne
Orygen
Australia

Maxwell Ramstead
McGill University
Canada
University College London
UK

Zahra Sheikhbahaee
University of Waterloo
Canada

Axel Constant
NSW University of Sydney
Australia
McGill University
Canada
University College London
UK

Editorial Office
MDPI
St. Alban-Anlage 66
4052 Basel, Switzerland

This is a reprint of articles from the Special Issue published online in the open access journal *Entropy* (ISSN 1099-4300) (available at: https://www.mdpi.com/journal/entropy/special_issues/Free_Energy_Adaptive_System).

For citation purposes, cite each article independently as indicated on the article page online and as indicated below:

LastName, A.A.; LastName, B.B.; LastName, C.C. Article Title. *Journal Name* **Year**, *Volume Number*, Page Range.

ISBN 978-3-0365-4773-2 (Hbk)
ISBN 978-3-0365-4774-9 (PDF)

© 2022 by the authors. Articles in this book are Open Access and distributed under the Creative Commons Attribution (CC BY) license, which allows users to download, copy and build upon published articles, as long as the author and publisher are properly credited, which ensures maximum dissemination and a wider impact of our publications.

The book as a whole is distributed by MDPI under the terms and conditions of the Creative Commons license CC BY-NC-ND.

Contents

About the Editors vii

Paul B. Badcock, Maxwell J. D. Ramstead, Zahra Sheikhbahaee and Axel Constant
Applying the Free Energy Principle to Complex Adaptive Systems
Reprinted from: *Entropy* **2022**, *24*, 689, doi:10.3390/e24050689 1

Noor Sajid, Laura Convertino and Karl Friston
Cancer Niches and Their Kikuchi Free Energy
Reprinted from: *Entropy* **2021**, *23*, 609, doi:10.3390/e23050609 9

Thomas Parr
Message Passing and Metabolism
Reprinted from: *Entropy* **2021**, *23*, 606, doi:10.3390/e23050606 27

Adam Safron
The Radically Embodied Conscious Cybernetic Bayesian Brain: From Free Energy to Free Will and Back Again
Reprinted from: *Entropy* **2021**, *23*, 783, doi:10.3390/e23060783 51

Rutger Goekoop and Roy de Kleijn
Permutation Entropy as a Universal Disorder Criterion: How Disorders at Different Scale Levels Are Manifestations of the Same Underlying Principle
Reprinted from: *Entropy* **2021**, *23*, 1701, doi:10.3390/e23121701 109

Rafael Kaufmann, Pranav Gupta and Jacob Taylor
An Active Inference Model of Collective Intelligence
Reprinted from: *Entropy* **2021**, *23*, 830, doi:10.3390/e23070830 147

Jesse Hoey
Equality and Freedom as Uncertainty in Groups
Reprinted from: *Entropy* **2021**, *23*, 1384, doi:10.3390/e23111384 175

Lancelot Da Costa, Pablo Lanillos, Noor Sajid, Karl Friston and Shujhat Khan
How Active Inference Could Help Revolutionise Robotics
Reprinted from: *Entropy* **2022**, *24*, 361, doi:10.3390/e24030361 197

About the Editors

Paul Badcock

Paul Badcock, Ph.D., is an academic specialist at the Centre for Youth Mental Health at The University of Melbourne, and at Orygen, a world-leading organization that specializes in youth mental health research and knowledge translation. His interests include theoretical psychology, evolutionary psychology, cognitive neuroscience, the free energy principle, mood and affective disorders, and youth mental health. He was the first to introduce the free energy principle to the breadth of subdisciplines in psychology, and is a leading expert on evolutionary models of human brain function. As an educator, he oversees the suite of online graduate courses in youth mental health offered by The University of Melbourne and Orygen, which equip teachers and health professionals with the latest theory, research and evidence-based approaches regarding youth mental health care.

Maxwell Ramstead

Maxwell Ramstead, Ph.D., is the Director of Research at VERSES and affiliated with the Spatial Web Foundation. His research focuses on the free-energy principle, multiscale active inference, and computational phenomenology. He now directs the VERSES Research Lab, which focuses on probabilistic model-based approaches to (artificial) intelligence (e.g., model-based reinforcement learning, active inference, multi-agent modelling and group inference, computational phenomenology of XR experience, category theory, and AI ethics.

Zahra Sheikhbahaee

Zahra Sheikhbahaee, Ph.D., is working with Prof. Jesse Hoey at University of Waterloo and Prof. Karl Friston at University College London. The field of research is Probabilistic Graphical models, Bayesian statistics, Machine Learning and Reinforcement Learning, combining optimal control algorithms with advances in deep reinforcement learning.

Axel Constant

Axel Constant, M.A. M.Sc. is a PhD candidate in the Philosophy of Biomedicine based at the University of Sydney. He works under the supervision of Paul Griffiths, Paul Badcock, Laurence Kirmayer, and Karl Friston. His published work is at the intersection of Evolutionary Biology, the Philosophy of Cognitive Science and Psychiatry, and Evolutionary Cultural Anthropology. His current work applies methods employed in Computational Psychiatry to theories in Cultural Psychiatry and Evolutionary Psychiatry.

Editorial

Applying the Free Energy Principle to Complex Adaptive Systems

Paul B. Badcock [1,2,*], Maxwell J. D. Ramstead [3,4], Zahra Sheikhbahaee [5] and Axel Constant [6]

1. Centre for Youth Mental Health, The University of Melbourne, Melbourne, VIC 3010, Australia
2. Orygen, Parkville, VIC 3052, Australia
3. VERSES Research Lab and the Spatial Web Foundation, Los Angeles, CA 90016, USA; maxwell.d.ramstead@gmail.com
4. Wellcome Centre for Human Neuroimaging, University College London, London WC1E 6BT, UK
5. David R. Cheriton School of Computer Science, University of Waterloo, Waterloo, ON N2L 3G1, Canada; zsheikhb@uwaterloo.ca
6. Charles Perkins Centre, The University of Sydney, John Hopkins Drive, Camperdown, NSW 2006, Australia; axel.constant.pruvost@gmail.com
* Correspondence: pbadcock@unimelb.edu.au

Citation: Badcock, P.B.; Ramstead, M.J.D.; Sheikhbahaee, Z.; Constant, A. Applying the Free Energy Principle to Complex Adaptive Systems. *Entropy* **2022**, *24*, 689. https://doi.org/10.3390/e24050689

Received: 6 May 2022
Accepted: 11 May 2022
Published: 13 May 2022

Publisher's Note: MDPI stays neutral with regard to jurisdictional claims in published maps and institutional affiliations.

Copyright: © 2022 by the authors. Licensee MDPI, Basel, Switzerland. This article is an open access article distributed under the terms and conditions of the Creative Commons Attribution (CC BY) license (https://creativecommons.org/licenses/by/4.0/).

The free energy principle (FEP) is a formulation of the adaptive, belief-driven behaviour of self-organizing systems that gained prominence in the early 2000s as a unified model of the brain [1,2]. Since then, the theory has been applied to a wide range of biotic phenomena, extending from single cells and flora [3,4], the emergence of life and evolutionary dynamics [5,6], and to the biosphere itself [7]. For our part, we have previously proposed that the FEP can be integrated with Tinbergen's seminal four questions in biology to furnish a multiscale ontology of living systems [8]. We have also explored more specific applications, e.g., to the evolution and development of human phenotypes [9–11], sociocultural cognition, behaviour, and learning [12,13], as well as the dynamic construction of environmental niches by their denizens [14,15].

Despite such contributions, the capacity of the FEP to extend beyond the human brain and behaviour, and to explain living systems more generally, has only begun to be explored. This begs the following questions: Can the FEP be applied to any organism? Does it allow us to explain the dynamics of all living systems, including large-scale social behaviour? Does the FEP provide a formal, empirically tractable theory of any complex adaptive system, living or not? With such questions in mind, the aim of this Special Issue was to showcase the breadth of the FEP as a unified theory of complex adaptive systems, biological or otherwise. Instead of concentrating on the human brain and behaviour, we welcomed contributions that applied the FEP to other complex adaptive systems, with the hope of exemplifying the extent of its explanatory scope.

For the uninitiated, it is worth briefly outlining what the FEP is. Variational free energy refers to an information theoretic quantity that places an upper limit on the entropy of a system's observations, relative to a generative model instantiated by an agent. (In this context, entropy is defined as the time-average of 'surprise' or the negative log probability of the agent's sensory data.) Generative models harness probabilistic mappings from hidden causes in the environment to observed consequences (i.e., sensory data), and state transitions inherent to the environment [2]. Under the FEP, an organism is modelled as implicitly 'expecting' to find itself within a limited range of phenotypic states; as such, deviations from these states elicit a type of 'phenotypic surprise' (i.e., the deviation between actual and phenotypically preferred states). Consequently, organisms remain alive by acting in ways that minimize this type of surprise (e.g., a fish avoiding the 'state' of being out of water). In other words, and more heuristically, free energy scores the discrepancy between desired and sensed data; and the FEP states that the imperative of all self-organizing systems is to keep this discrepancy at bay by bringing about preferred observations via action (see Figure 1).

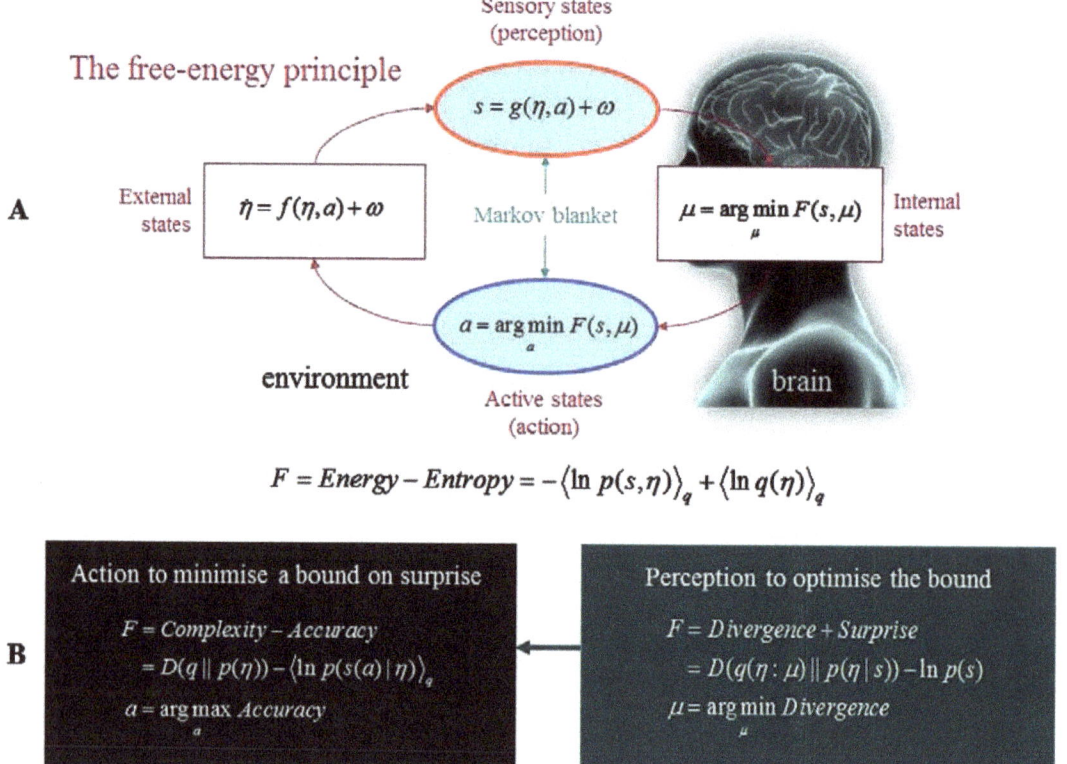

Figure 1. The free energy principle. (**A**) Schematic of the quantities that characterise free energy, including a system's internal states, μ (e.g., a brain), and quantities that describe the system's exchanges with the environment; specifically, its sensory input, $s = g(\eta, a) + \omega$, and actions, a, which alter the ways in which the system samples its environment. Environmental states are further defined by equations of motion, $\dot{\eta} = f(\eta, a) + \omega$, which describe the dynamics of (hidden) states extraneous to the system, η, whereas ω refers to random fluctuations. Under this scheme, internal states and action operate synergistically to reduce free energy, which reflects a function of sensory input and the probabilistic representation (variational density), $q(\eta:\mu)$, that internal states encode. Note that external and internal states are statistically separated by a Markov blanket, which possesses both 'sensory' and 'active' states. Internal states are influenced by, but cannot affect, sensory states, whereas external states are influenced by, but cannot affect, active states, creating a conditional independence between the system and its environment. (**B**) Alternative equations that describe the minimisation of free energy. With respect to action, free energy can only be suppressed by the system's selective sampling of (predicted) sensory input, which increases the accuracy of its predictions. On the other hand, optimising internal states minimises divergence by making the representation an approximate conditional density on the hidden causes of sensory input. This optimisation reduces the free energy bound on surprise, which means that action allows the system to avoid surprising sensations. Reproduced from [8].

There are two main ways for a self-organizing system to minimize free energy. The first is by changing its perception of the world. Previously, this has been explored through reference to human neural processing. The FEP appeals to a view of the brain as a hierarchical "inference machine", which instantiates a hierarchy of hypotheses about the world (i.e., a generative model) that enables an organism to minimize free energy (and therefore keep entropic dissipation at bay, at least locally) by reducing discrepancies between incoming sensory inputs and top-down predictions (i.e., prediction errors) [2]. Neurobiologically xpectations about sensory data are thought to be encoded by deep pyramidal cells (i.e., representation units) at every level of the cortical hierarchy, which carry predictions downward to suppress errors at the level below, whereas prediction errors themselves are encoded by superficial pyramidal cells and are carried forward to revise expectations at the level above [16]. The relative influence of ascending (error) and descending (representation) signals is weighted by their inverse variance or *precision* (e.g., a high precision on ascending error signals lowers confidence in descending predictions), which is mediated by neuromodulation and reflected psychologically by attentional selection and sensory attenuation. In short, the recursive neural dynamics described here enable us to minimise free energy (resp. prediction error) by updating our internal models (i.e., perception).

Second, an organism can reduce surprise directly by acting upon the world in order to fulfill its expectations and generate unsurprising sensations. This process of 'active inference' describes how an organism reduces free energy through self-fulfilling cycles of action and perception [17]. Active inference models implement action selection as the minimization of *expected free energy*, which is the free energy expected under beliefs about possible courses of action, or policies. By selecting actions that are expected to minimize free energy, the organism can maintain itself within preferred, phenotypically unsurprising states. Thus, survival mandates that an organism must not only reduce free energy from moment to moment; it must also reduce the expected free energy associated with the future outcomes of action [18,19].

Having briefly outlined the rudiments of the FEP, let us turn briefly to complex adaptive systems (CAS). This concept is synonymous with complexity science and has its roots in evolutionary systems theory, which assumes a dynamic, inextricable relationship between generalised selection and self-organization [11]. Broadly speaking, a CAS refers to any multi-component, self-organising system that adapts to it environment through an autonomous process of selection, which recruits the outcomes of localised interactions between its components to select a subset of those components for replication and enhancement [20]. Holland [21] describes four key features of CAS: they consist of large numbers of components that interact by sending and receiving signals (i.e., *parallelism*); the actions of their components depend upon the signals they receive (i.e., *conditional action*); groups of rules can form subroutines that can be combined to deal with environmental novelties (i.e., *modularity*); and the components of the system change over time to adapt to the environment and improve performance (i.e., *adaptation*). Applications of the CAS framework have proliferated across the physical, human and computer sciences, but there is not the scope to survey this literature here. However, to pre-empt the papers to follow, we would note that this framework has already been applied to precisely the same systems that are the foci of our contributors–ranging from metabolic and cellular processes, e.g., [22–26]; to the brain and social processes, e.g., [26–30]; and to artificial intelligence and robotics, e.g., [31–33]. The articles presented in our Special Issue build upon such literature by illustrating how the FEP can afford fresh insights into the dynamics of CAS.

Three of the contributions to our Special Issue leverage the FEP to cast new light on processes intrinsic to biological agents. In *Cancer Niches and their Kikuchi Free Energy*, Sajid, Convertino et al. [34] examine cancer morphogenetic fields as undesirable stable attractors in the complex dynamics of homeostasis, self-renewal and differentiation, which contributes to their deviation from regular autopoietic homeostasis (the internal molecular dynamics that regulate the production and regeneration of a system's components). Sajid, Convertino et al. offer a computational model in silico to study communication and information processing at a population level of cancer cell networks within their environment in vivo. By deploying the Kikuchi free energy approximation, which is a generalisation of the Bethe free energy for computing beliefs over large sets of cell clusters, they account for higher-order interactions and phase transitions between clusters of healthy and oncogenic cells. Here, cancer niche construction can be construed as a Bayes-optimal process for the transmission of information across different levels of cellular networks due to its tendency to minimize the overall Kikuchi free energy over the whole system. Their findings suggest that three distinct cancer trajectories–namely, proliferation (local growth), metastasis and apoptosis–can emerge from the natural evolution of the state function (i.e., free energy) in biological systems. These findings have important implications for our understanding and study of cancer cell growth and apoptosis.

Next, Parr describes how biochemical networks in adaptive biological systems can be recast in terms of an inferential message passing scheme that involves the gradient descent on variational free energy towards the least surprising states, based on the organism's implicit (generative) model of these states. In *Message Passing and Metabolism* [35], he points out that the biochemical regulation of metabolic processes relies on sparse interactions (message-passing) between coupled reactions, with enzymes creating conditional dependencies between reactants. He then extrapolates the *law of mass action* (the rate of chemical reaction and the concentrations of reactants involved in this process) and the *Michaelis–Menten kinetics* (which approximates the dynamics of irreversible enzymatic reactions) from the FEP. Assuming the existence of a causal structure in biochemical (metabolic) networks, one can build the sparse message passing scheme to capture the independence of substrates and products, conditioned upon the enzyme and enzyme-substrate complex within such networks. The temporal evolution of the categorical probability of each state within this system can be described by a chemical master equation that takes into account sparse network interactions. Parr describes how the steady state distribution of these dynamics can be recast as a generative model, which suggests that the biochemistry that underlies metabolism follows an inferential message-passing scheme that seeks to minimise free energy. An important extension of Parr's model is that metabolic disorder can emerge when an enzymatic disconnection by thiamine depletion interrupts message passing and incites aberrant prior beliefs, which gives rise to false (biochemical) inference.

The third contribution follows more traditional applications of the FEP by accounting for conscious, first-person experience. In *The Radically Embodied Conscious Cybernetic Bayesian Brain*, Safron [36] proposes models of embodied conscious agency based on the FEP, extending the Integrated World Modelling Theory of consciousness proposed elsewhere [37] to explicitly account for aspects of intentional actions and agentic experiences. According to the radically embodied account on offer, what we call attention and imagination emerge from the (sometimes liminal) activity of multimodal, action-oriented body maps and representations, realized as neural attractors in the form of 'embodied self-models' (ESMs), which conform to the FEP as cybernetic controllers. When functioning online, ESMs allow for overt interactions with affordances, or structured possibilities for environmental interactions. However, Safron suggests subthreshold activations of such 'quasi-homuncular' ESMs also underwrite our (affordance-structured) covert abilities to imagine and pursue courses of action, as well as our ability to intentionally deploy attentional resources. Thus, even seemingly abstract representational capacities may be grounded in twin capacities for embodied action and counterfactual explorations of the world. Safron then applies this radically embodied perspective to core aspects of conscious experience. He attempts to chart a middle way between perspectives in the representation wars in cognitive science, describing brains as hybrid machine learning architectures capable of supporting both symbolic and sub-symbolic processes for 4E agents (where cognition is thought to be *embodied, embedded, enacted* and *extended*). Safron's perspective is ecumenical, deploying information-theoretic constructs and representationalist concepts that would be rejected by hard-line proponents of both 4E cognition and more Cartesian (representationalist) approaches. For example, to account for information flow in mammalian brains, Safron deploys constructs that are typically rejected by 4E theorists, such as Cartesian theatres and quasi-homunculi. However, he does so from a radically embodied perspective, suggesting that such a "strange inversion of reasoning" follows from principles of cognitive development and computational neuroscience.

Unlike the authors above, Goekoop and de Kleijn look beyond the phenotype to consider how the FEP might apply to groups. In *Permutation Entropy as a Universal Disorder Criterion* [38], they argue that living systems can be described as hierarchical problem-solving machines that embody predictive models of their econiches, called a goal hierarchy, which incorporates a set of lower-order econiches (goals) and corresponding subniches (subgoals) that the system needs to pursue in order to achieve the global econiche (goal) represented at the top of the hierarchy. Using this scheme to frame the rest of their argument, they concentrate on stress responses in organisms, dyads and collectives. Equating stress with free energy or 'prediction error', and stress responses with 'action', they suggest that as free energy increases, there is a progressive collapse of (allostatic) hierarchical control, eventually resulting in disordered states characterised by behavioural shifts from long-term goal-directed behaviour (e.g., reproductive success) towards short-term goals and habitual behaviours concentrated on self-preservation (e.g., survival). After introducing permutation entropy as a universal measure of disordered states across such systems, they briefly describe how their model can be used to explain disorder at an individual level, before progressing to the transmission of disorder through interpersonal interactions, and concluding with a brief discussion of population-level dynamics.

The idea that the FEP can be extended to social systems is also taken up by Kaufmann and colleagues. In *An Active Inference Model of Collective Intelligence* [39], the authors propose an active inference model of alignment, describing the manner in which within-scale local interactions (e.g., individual agents' behaviors) can align with cross-scale global phenomena (e.g., collective behavior) in multi-scale systems. In so doing, they offer a principled, agent-based model that has the potential to function as a workbench to simulate collective intelligence as an emergent phenomenon, across many scales. Although one obvious target for this modelling approach would be human behavior as an emergent phenomenon that ties physiological, cognitive and cultural dynamics, nothing, in principle, limits the application of Kaufmann and colleagues' model to human phenomena.

In another paper that illustrates the broad scope of multiscale thinking under active inference, Jesse Hoey, in *Equality and Freedom as Uncertainty in Groups* [40], shows how agents attempting to align with other group members leads to a quasi-equilibrium, or "sweet spot", at which the group free energy is minimal and the agent's predictive capacity of higher order parameters, such as those attributed to the group, matches the group's capacity to predict an agent's behavior. Hoey further discusses two intriguing trade-offs. Higher agent model complexity leads to lower individual learning capacity with respect to the complexity of the group, resulting in agents who are hobbled in the pursuit of their own ends, but in a group that is more diverse, innovative, and open to change. On the other hand, lower agent model complexity allows the expression of individual preference towards the group, but the group becomes more homogeneous, secure, and closed, as otherwise the pro-social behaviours of individual agents would be hampered. Hoey suggests that such emergent social dynamics provides insights into concepts such as freedom and equality in society, which correspond to changes in model uncertainties and complexities. Oscillation between radical freedom, where no cooperation is possible, and radical equality, where no discovery is possible, is an emergent phenomenon characteristic of Western society; akin to what Karl Marx called historical materialism, which according to many is the main driver of history itself. Could Hoey's findings initiate research on an active inference model of history as an emergent phenomenon of human societies?

So far, we have considered a range of applications of the FEP to living systems. However, active inference–the process theory derived from the FEP–is increasingly being applied to machine intelligence in practical settings. Use cases in robotics provide an exciting opportunity to test the applicability of active inference to implement sensory processes and motor control in real time. In their review for our Special Issue, *How Active Inference Could Help Revolutionise Robotics*, Da Costa and colleagues [41] examine the usefulness of active inference for several core problems in robotics, such as state estimation in artificial perception, motor control, learning, safety and explainability. They argue that active inference may help advance robotics due to several of its core features: it enables explainable artificial intelligence in a manner that operates in situations involving uncertainty, volatility, and noise. This is especially relevant for human-centric applications, such as human–robot interaction and healthcare.

In closing, it is worth recognising that the majority of submissions presented herein focus chiefly on human systems, despite our call for more wide-ranging applications. Nevertheless, it should be clear that the authors' proposals can be readily extended to other complex adaptive systems, including biological dynamics intrinsic to other lifeforms [34–36], collective, group-level behaviour [39,40], and even non-living systems [41]. Taken together, we hope that the collection of papers presented in our Special Issue motivate others to consider how the FEP might be gainfully applied to their own systems of interest, living or otherwise.

Funding: ZS is supported by The Long-Term Future Fund, provided by the Centre for Effective Altruism. AC is supported by the Australian Laureate Fellowship project, A Philosophy of Medicine for the 21st Century (Ref: FL170100160), and by a Social Sciences and Humanities Research Council doctoral fellowship (Ref: 752-2019-0065).

Acknowledgments: We would like to thank Lancelot Da Costa, Rutger Goekoop, Jesse Hoey, Rafael Kaufmann, Thomas Parr, Adam Safron, and Noor Sajid for their comments on an earlier draft of this manuscript.

Conflicts of Interest: The authors declare no conflict of interest.

References

1. Friston, K. A theory of cortical responses. *Philos. Trans. R. Soc. B Biol. Sci.* **2005**, *360*, 815–836. [CrossRef] [PubMed]
2. Friston, K. The free-energy principle: A unified brain theory? *Nat. Rev. Neurosci.* **2010**, *11*, 127–138. [PubMed]
3. Kiebel, S.J.; Friston, K.J. Free energy and dendritic self-organization. *Front. Syst. Neurosci.* **2011**, *5*, 80. [CrossRef] [PubMed]
4. Calvo, P.; Friston, K. Predicting green: Really radical (plant) predictive processing. *J. R. Soc. Interface* **2017**, *14*, 20170096. [CrossRef]
5. Friston, K. Life as we know it. *J. R. Soc. Interface* **2013**, *10*, 20130475.
6. Campbell, J.O. Universal Darwinism as a process of Bayesian inference. *Front. Syst. Neurosci.* **2016**, *10*, 49. [CrossRef]
7. Rubin, S.; Parr, T.; Da Costa, L.; Friston, K. Future climates: Markov blankets and active inference in the biosphere. *J. R. Soc. Interface* **2020**, *17*, 20200503. [CrossRef]
8. Ramstead, M.J.D.; Badcock, P.B.; Friston, K.J. Answering Schrödinger's question: A free-energy formulation. *Phys. Life Rev.* **2018**, *24*, 1–16.
9. Badcock, P.B.; Friston, K.J.; Ramstead, M.J. The hierarchically mechanistic mind: A free-energy formulation of the human psyche. *Phys. Life Rev.* **2019**, *31*, 104–121.
10. Badcock, P.B.; Friston, K.J.; Ramstead, M.J.; Ploeger, A.; Hohwy, J. The hierarchically mechanistic mind: An evolutionary systems theory of the human brain, cognition, and behavior. *Cogn. Affect. Behav. Neurosci.* **2019**, *19*, 1319–1351. [CrossRef]
11. Badcock, P.B. Evolutionary systems theory: A unifying meta-theory of psychological science. *Rev. Gen. Psychol.* **2012**, *16*, 10–23. [CrossRef]
12. Ramstead, M.J.; Veissière, S.P.; Kirmayer, L.J. Cultural affordances: Scaffolding local worlds through shared intentionality and regimes of attention. *Front. Psychol.* **2016**, *7*, 1090. [CrossRef] [PubMed]
13. Veissière, S.P.; Constant, A.; Ramstead, M.J.; Friston, K.J.; Kirmayer, L.J. Thinking through other minds: A variational approach to cognition and culture. *Behav. Brain Sci.* **2020**, *43*, E90. [CrossRef] [PubMed]
14. Constant, A.; Clark, A.; Kirchhoff, M.; Friston, K.J. Extended active inference: Constructing predictive cognition beyond skulls. *Mind Lang.* **2020**, *in press*. [CrossRef]
15. Constant, A.; Ramstead, M.J.; Veissiere, S.P.; Campbell, J.O.; Friston, K.J. A variational approach to niche construction. *J. R. Soc. Interface* **2018**, *15*, 20170685. [CrossRef]
16. Bastos, A.M.; Usrey, W.M.; Adams, R.A.; Mangun, G.R.; Fries, P.; Friston, K.J. Canonical microcircuits for predictive coding. *Neuron* **2012**, *76*, 695–711. [CrossRef]
17. Friston, K.J.; Daunizeau, J.; Kiebel, S.J. Reinforcement learning or active inference? *PLoS ONE* **2009**, *4*, e6421. [CrossRef]
18. Friston, K.; FitzGerald, T.; Rigoli, F.; Schwartenbeck, P.; Pezzulo, G. Active inference: A process theory. *Neural Comput.* **2017**, *29*, 1–49. [CrossRef]
19. Friston, K.J.; Rosch, R.; Parr, T.; Price, C.; Bowman, H. Deep temporal models and active inference. *Neurosci. Biobehav. Rev.* **2018**, *90*, 486–501. [CrossRef]

20. Levin, S. Complex adaptive systems: Exploring the known, the unknown and the unknowable. *Bull. Am. Math. Soc.* **2003**, *40*, 3–19. [CrossRef]
21. Holland, J.H. Studying complex adaptive systems. *J. Syst. Sci. Complex.* **2006**, *19*, 1–8. [CrossRef]
22. Schwab, E.; Pienta, K.J. Cancer as a complex adaptive system. *Med. Hypotheses* **1996**, *47*, 235–241. [CrossRef]
23. Theise, N.D.; d'Inverno, M. Understanding cell lineages as complex adaptive systems. *Blood Cells Mol. Dis.* **2004**, *32*, 17–20. [CrossRef] [PubMed]
24. Mallick, P. *Complexity and Information: Cancer as a Multi-Scale Complex Adaptive System, in Physical Sciences and Engineering Advances in Life Sciences and Oncology*; Springer: Berlin/Heidelberg, Germany, 2016; pp. 5–29.
25. Rea, T.J.; Brown, C.M.; Sing, C.F. Complex adaptive system models and the genetic analysis of plasma HDL–cholesterol concentration. *Perspect. Biol. Med.* **2006**, *49*, 490. [CrossRef] [PubMed]
26. Barandiaran, X.; Moreno, A. Adaptivity: From metabolism to behavior. *Adapt. Behav.* **2008**, *16*, 325–344. [CrossRef]
27. Lansing, J.S. Complex adaptive systems. *Annu. Rev. Anthropol.* **2003**, *32*, 183–204. [CrossRef]
28. Shine, J.M. The thalamus integrates the macrosystems of the brain to facilitate complex, adaptive brain network dynamics. *Prog. Neurobiol.* **2021**, *199*, 101951. [CrossRef]
29. Morowitz, H.J.; Singer, J.L.E. *The Mind, the Brain and Complex Adaptive Systems*; Routledge: London, UK, 2018.
30. Page, S.; Miller, J.H. *Complex Adaptive Systems: An Introduction to Computational Models of Social Life*; Princeton University Press: Princeton, NJ, USA, 2009.
31. Neace, K.S.; Chipkevich, M.B.A. Designed complex adaptive systems exhibiting weak emergence. In Proceedings of the NAECON 2018–IEEE National Aerospace and Electronics Conference, Dayton, OH, USA, 23–26 July 2018.
32. Steels, L. Evolving grounded communication for robots. *Trends Cogn. Sci.* **2003**, *7*, 308–312. [CrossRef]
33. Stanescu, A.M.; Nita, A.; Moisescu, M.A.; Sacala, I.S. From industrial robotics towards intelligent robotic systems. In Proceedings of the 2008 4th International IEEE Conference Intelligent Systems, Varna, Bulgaria, 6–8 September 2008.
34. Sajid, N.; Convertino, L.; Friston, K. Cancer niches and their kikuchi free energy. *Entropy* **2021**, *23*, 609. [CrossRef]
35. Parr, T. Message Passing and Metabolism. *Entropy* **2021**, *23*, 606. [CrossRef]
36. Safron, A. The radically embodied conscious cybernetic Bayesian brain: From free energy to free will and back again. *Entropy* **2021**, *23*, 783. [CrossRef] [PubMed]
37. Safron, A. An Integrated World Modeling Theory (IWMT) of consciousness: Combining integrated information and global neuronal workspace theories with the free energy principle and active inference framework; Toward solving the hard problem and characterizing agentic causation. *Front. Artif. Intell.* **2020**, *3*, 30. [PubMed]
38. Goekoop, R.; de Kleijn, R. Permutation Entropy as a Universal Disorder Criterion: How Disorders at Different Scale Levels Are Manifestations of the Same Underlying Principle. *Entropy* **2021**, *23*, 1701. [CrossRef] [PubMed]
39. Kaufmann, R.; Gupta, P.; Taylor, J. An active inference model of collective intelligence. *Entropy* **2021**, *23*, 830. [CrossRef]
40. Hoey, J. Equality and Freedom as Uncertainty in Groups. *Entropy* **2021**, *23*, 1384. [CrossRef]
41. Da Costa, L.; Lanillos, P.; Sajid, N.; Friston, K.; Khan, S. How Active Inference Could Help Revolutionise Robotics. *Entropy* **2022**, *24*, 361. [CrossRef]

Article

Cancer Niches and Their Kikuchi Free Energy

Noor Sajid [1,*,†], Laura Convertino [1,2,*,†] and Karl Friston [1]

1. Wellcome Centre for Human Neuroimaging, Institute of Neurology, University College London, London WC1N 3BG, UK; k.friston@ucl.ac.uk
2. Institute of Cognitive Neuroscience, University College London, London WC1N 3BG, UK
* Correspondence: noor.sajid.18@ucl.ac.uk (N.S.); laura.convertino.18@ucl.ac.uk (L.C.)
† Equal Contribution.

Abstract: Biological forms depend on a progressive specialization of pluripotent stem cells. The differentiation of these cells in their spatial and functional environment defines the organism itself; however, cellular mutations may disrupt the mutual balance between a cell and its niche, where cell proliferation and specialization are released from their autopoietic homeostasis. This induces the construction of cancer niches and maintains their survival. In this paper, we characterise cancer niche construction as a direct consequence of interactions between clusters of cancer and healthy cells. Explicitly, we evaluate these higher-order interactions between niches of cancer and healthy cells using Kikuchi approximations to the free energy. Kikuchi's free energy is measured in terms of changes to the sum of energies of baseline clusters of cells (or nodes) minus the energies of overcounted cluster intersections (and interactions of interactions, etc.). We posit that these changes in energy node clusters correspond to a long-term reduction in the complexity of the system conducive to cancer niche survival. We validate this formulation through numerical simulations of apoptosis, local cancer growth, and metastasis, and highlight its implications for a computational understanding of the etiopathology of cancer.

Keywords: cancer niches; free energy; Kikuchi approximations; apoptosis; metastasis; cluster variation method

1. Introduction

The human body develops via the progressive specialisation of pluripotent stem cells, niche construction, and organ development (i.e., morphogenesis). Understanding these processes is not only fundamental to understanding how multicellular organisms come to be, but also has important implications for aberrant events. Cellular de-differentiation can cause (and be a consequence of) disruption of the mutual balance between cells and their niche, where cell proliferation and genetic regulation are released from their autopoietic homeostasis. The disruption of this balance and the creation of new niches drives cancer cell growth and sustains their survival. The concept of a stem cell niche [1,2] identifies the "whole" of the wholeness of the microenvironment in which stem cells differentiate, grow, and survive, and the humoral, paracrine, physical, metabolic, neuronal, structural properties with which the cell exchanges information. These specialised microenvironments are found in adult organisms and their homeostatic disruption may facilitate the development of cancer colonies through an interaction between cells and their niches [3]. In this paper, we pursue the notion that cancer niche construction requires individual cells with oncogenic potential to interact in subpopulations (i.e., clusters) of healthy and cancerous cells to reach a particular attractor state.

Briefly, cancer cell niche construction results from a maladaptive degeneration of the complex dynamic homeostasis that undergirds the balanced survival, renewal, and repair of mature organs. This homeostasis is replaced by a new niche that is beneficial to cancer growth, without which oncogenic cells might not be able to escape the physiological mechanisms of control and elimination of the degenerated cells [4]. We acknowledge the phenotypical differences between cancer cells and cancer stem cells, but for simplicity, we operationalise all cell types as simply cancer cells. Note, that cancer stem cells are a small subpopulation of cancer cells with capability of self-renewal, differentiation, and tumorigenesis [4,5].

To become carcinogenic, cells acquire some key properties that free them from their physiological life cycle. The main properties are: (i) self-sufficiency in growth signals; (ii) insensitivity to anti-growth signals; (iii) tissue invasions and metastasis; (iv) limitless reproductive potential; (v) angiogenesis; and (vi) avoiding apoptosis [6]. It may not be necessary for a cell to acquire all these properties to become a cancer cell, since different combinations of these properties are sufficient for inducing oncogenesis. For example, only some cancers have metastatic properties, namely the ability to leave the tissue of origin, move to another location and colonise another organ. The presence of metastatic sites determines the progression of cancer, staging, and patient prognosis. Fortunately, healthy organisms can fight oncogenesis via different mechanisms of self-preservation. Among these, apoptosis (i.e., programmed death) is crucial. This is a controlled mechanism of cell death that intervenes in normal organ repair, growth, renewal, as well as in inflammation and cancer.

For a computational understanding of cancer niche construction, a 2D Ising model has been used to evaluate phase transitions between cancerous and healthy cells [7–9]. For example, [10] used the Ising Hamiltonian to model metastasis, where the updates in the energy function were modelled using mean-field approximations, i.e., only considering average interactions. This factorised approach is consistent with other applications of the Ising model for simulating cancer progression [7–9]; however, cell niches are the result of numerous mechanisms, both at the cellular and population level. The single cells are involved in the construction and maintenance of the niche and they adapt via genetic, epigenetic, metabolic, structural, internal, and external signalling mechanisms. More recently, theoretical work has underlined the fundamental role of population dynamic and mutual information exchange in guiding the fate of local subpopulations of cells and the niche as a whole [11–13] via cell-to-cell, cell-to-niche, and niche-to-cell information flow.

Consequently, our work builds upon previous computational approaches by (i) casting cancer niche construction as a direct consequence of interactions between clusters of cancer and healthy cells, and (ii) using a Kikuchi Hamiltonian as a way to account for higher-order interactions when evaluating the state functions of such systems [14–19]. This allows us to move away from thinking about cells in isolation and towards accounting for interactions within cancer niches. Briefly, Kikuchi formulation approximates the free energy as a sum of local free energies of a cluster of cells (or nodes) in the system. In doing so, it provides a way to define a local population (or base cluster) which includes all the interactions between the cells.

In what follows, we simulate three cancer trajectories to provide proof of the principle of a computational formulation for oncogenic etiopathology. For this, we simulate a 2D Ising model for evaluating how cancer trajectories unfold using Kikuchi free energy approximation. Explicitly, we manipulate four (hyper)parameters, namely an interaction parameter that regulates the type of cell interaction, a tolerance parameter that determines the acceptance level of cancerous cells, a growth parameter that regulates the number of cell states switched during a single trial, and a noise parameter that influences the transition dynamics. We describe the technical details in Section 3.

First, we simulate local cancer growth within the tissue of origin by allowing pairwise interactions between cancerous and healthy cells (i.e., a high interaction parameter value). This allows us to reproduce the homeostatic shift in a healthy organ that results from the acquired oncogenic properties of single cells within it, but it is crucially sustained and enabled by the broader dynamic at the sub-population level. Secondly, we model the metastasis where cells exit their primary site and invade secondary locations. Here, cells have to prepare for the new environment before arrival in the metastatic site. Without a favourable environment, the cells would not be able to colonise the new organ. We treat this cancer spread as an embedded mechanism in the niche construction process. This is achieved by allowing pairwise interactions between/across cancerous and healthy cells (i.e., low positive interaction parameter value), alongside a restricted capacity to grow outside the initial cancer site (i.e., decaying noise parameter). Finally, we consider apoptosis, namely the programmed death of the cancer cells. In our simulations, we assume that the cancer cells do not acquire the ability to escape apoptosis, and the physiological mechanisms of control activate to eliminate the pathological cells (via a low tolerance threshold).

The remainder of the paper is organised as follows. In Section 2, we briefly review the notion of free energies, specifically their relevance in evaluating systems under thermodynamic equilibrium. We then describe and provide simple examples for the use of Kikuchi approximations in evaluating a system state function. Equipped with this, Section 3 describes the system used to simulate cancer niche construction, and the parameters required to simulate cancer progression. Section 4 details the simulation results for the three cancer trajectories. We conclude by highlighting the implications for specific etiopathology, and potential future directions.

2. Free Energies

In this section, we review the notion of free energy and its relevance for modelling cancer niche construction. For this, we follow the formulation introduced in [20]. Briefly, free energy is the state function of a (random dynamical) system that possesses a steady-state or pullback attractor. Its value is determined by the current state of the system. The free energy can be used to describe the spatiotemporal evolution of a system as it converges to an equilibrium or nonequilibrium steady state, e.g., a particular tissue population in the human body or the body itself. The distinction between nonequilibrium and equilibrium steady state rests upon the presence of solenoidal or divergence free flow. In the absence of solenoidal dynamics, the flow of systemic states is entirely dissipative, and the steady state is at (thermodynamic) equilibrium.

To make this concrete, we introduce a closed 2D system (e.g., an Ising model) with a set of N discrete random variables, $\{X_1, X_2, X_3, \ldots, X_N\}$ arranged in a square grid graph (Figure 1). Each random variable, X_i, has a possible realisation x_i. Here, we cast these realisations as distinct cell states in the body, or a particular tissue population, that can be either healthy or cancerous. The overall system state is denoted by the vector $\mathbf{x} = \{x_1, x_2, \ldots, x_N\}$, with the corresponding energy of the system given by its Hamiltonian, $H(\mathbf{x})$. For computational ease, we deal with an effective Hamiltonian to represent the system in a reduced space through nonlinear averaging of the true Hamiltonian. Consequently, this only describes a part of the eigenvalue spectrum of the true Hamiltonian. This formulation is in contrast to the molecular Hamiltonian where the Hamiltonian is decomposed into two or more separable parts (i.e., nuclei and electrons), and their interactions. For our purposes, this separation could involve the inclusion of additional random variables (that represent external states or distinct internal states) ($\mathbf{z}$) with a Hamiltonian of the following form: $H = H_1(\mathbf{x}) + H_2(\mathbf{z})$. Practically, decompositions of the Hamiltonian of this sort are potentially important because they could naturally account for local interactions; however, their inclusion would not speak to the long-range interactions that are the current focus.

At steady state, the probability of finding the system in this state is given by Boltzmann's law, which can be expressed as [21]:

$$
\begin{aligned}
P(\mathbf{x}) &= \frac{1}{Z} e^{-\beta H(\mathbf{x})} \\
\ln P(\mathbf{x}) &= -\beta H(\mathbf{x}) - \ln Z \\
Z &\triangleq \sum_{\mathbf{x} \in M} e^{-\beta H(\mathbf{x})}
\end{aligned}
\tag{1}
$$

where β is the inverse temperature or precision that shapes the probability density of the distribution, Z is the partition function, and M is the set of all possible states of the system. For our purpose, we make simplifying assumptions about our system. and set $\beta = 1$. Briefly, we assume that the joint probability distribution describes some nonphysical system. This allows us to view Boltzmann's law as a way of defining the energy of the system where is simply an arbitrary unit that scales the energy measure [20].

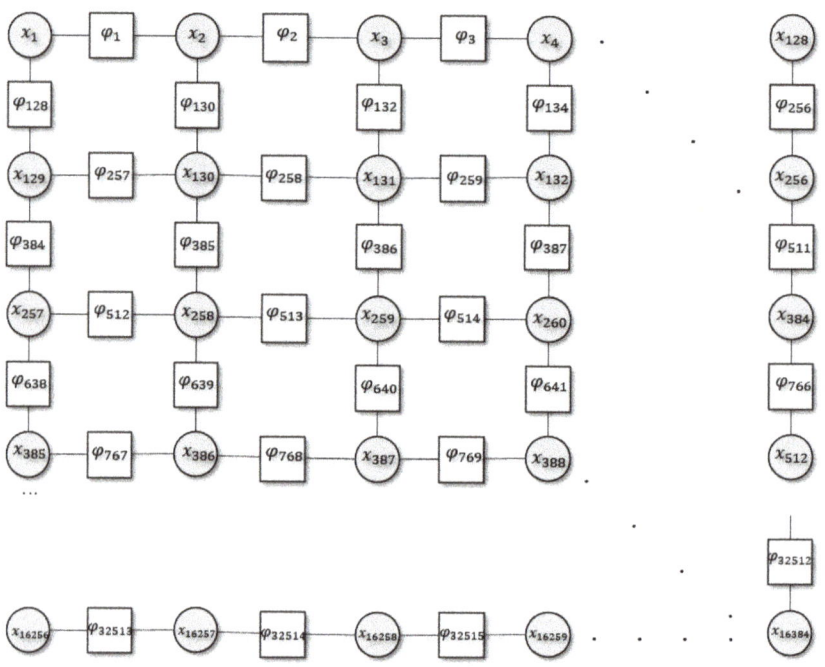

Figure 1. Schematic illustration of the 2D system with a set of N discrete random variables where $N = 128^2$. Here, the circles denote the variable node for each variable (x_i), squares denote the factor nodes (φ_a), and edges connect the variable node i to the factor a.

The partition function, Z, is closely related to Helmholtz free energy, F_H [20,22,23]:

$$\begin{aligned} F_H &= -\ln Z \\ &= \ln P(\mathbf{x}) + H(\mathbf{x}) \end{aligned} \qquad (2)$$

This quantity can be approximated using variational calculus [24], which allows an otherwise intractable F_H to be approximated. This requires the introduction of a variational distribution, $Q(\mathbf{x})$, assuming $\sum_{\mathbf{x} \in M} Q(\mathbf{x}) = 1$ and $0 \leq Q(\mathbf{x}) \leq 1; \forall \mathbf{x}$, and the corresponding variational (or Gibbs) free energy, F_V [20]:

$$\begin{aligned} F_V &\equiv \underbrace{U(Q)}_{\text{Internal energy}} - \underbrace{S(Q)}_{\text{Entropy}} \\ &= \sum_{\mathbf{x} \in M} Q(\mathbf{x}) H(\mathbf{x}) - \left[-\sum_{\mathbf{x} \in M} Q(\mathbf{x}) \ln Q(\mathbf{x}) \right] \\ &= \sum_{\mathbf{x} \in M} Q(\mathbf{x}) [\ln Q(\mathbf{x}) - \ln P(\mathbf{x})] + F_H \\ &= \underbrace{D_{KL}[Q(\mathbf{x}) || P(\mathbf{x})]}_{\text{Complexity}} + F_H \end{aligned} \qquad (3)$$

where $H(\mathbf{x}) = -\ln P(\mathbf{x}) + F_H$, and D_{KL} is the Kullback–Leibler divergence. We know that $D_{KL}[Q(\mathbf{x})||P(\mathbf{x})] \geq 0$ [25], hence F_V is an upper bound on the F_H:

$$F_V \geq F_H \quad (4)$$

Thus, it follows that by minimising F_V with respect to $Q(\mathbf{x})$, we can get a good approximation of F_H and recover $p(\mathbf{x})$; however, as $N \to c, c \gg 1$, this also becomes intractable. Therefore, a practical solution is to consider the upper bound F_H by minimising F_V with respect to a restricted class of variational distributions $Q(\mathbf{x})$. A standard restriction over the variational distribution follows from the mean-field approach, i.e., an absence of interactions [26–28]:

$$\begin{aligned}
Q_{MF}(x) &= \prod_{i=1}^{N} Q_i(x_i) \Rightarrow \\
F_{MF} &= U_{MF}(Q) - S_{MF}(Q) \\
&= -\sum_a \sum_{x_a} \ln \varphi_a(x_a) \prod_{i \in N(a)} Q_i(x_i) + \sum_{i=1}^{N} \sum_{x_i} Q_i(x_i) \ln Q_i(x_i) \\
H(\mathbf{x}) &= -\sum_a \ln \varphi_a(x_a)
\end{aligned} \quad (5)$$

where the Hamiltonian is defined as the sum of its factors, φ_a, under a factor graph probability distribution function (Figure 1). Conversely, we could consider more complicated factorisations, like structure mean-field approaches [29], Bethe free energy [15,30], or Kikuchi free energy approximations or a cluster variational method [16,17], which can provide more accurate approximations. Interestingly, the Kikuchi free energy is a generalisation of the Bethe free energy, using higher-order approximations [17].

Kikuchi Free Energy

In this work, we use Kikuchi approximation to evaluate the free energy of the system [15–17,20,31]. This allows us to account for higher-order interactions between variable nodes, mimicking the type of interactions present during cell niche construction. Practically, this characterises the system evolution in terms of interactions between neighbours of cancerous and health nodes, up to size d. This is calculated as changes to the sum of the energies of baseline clusters of variable nodes, minus the overcounted interactions (and interactions of interactions). The premise is that in accounting for higher-order interactions within clusters, we can get a better evaluation of the systems overall state function (i.e., free energy).

Formally, the Kikuchi free energy F_K is:

$$F_K = \sum_{r \in R} c_r F_r \quad (6)$$

where:

$$\begin{aligned}
F_r &= U_r(Q) - S_r(Q) \\
&= \sum_{x_r} Q_r(x_r) H_r(x_r) + \sum_{x_r} Q_r(x_r) \ln Q_r(x_r) \\
H_r(x_r) &= -\sum_{a \in A_r} \ln \varphi_a(x_a). \\
c_r &= 1 - \sum_{s \in super(r)} c_s
\end{aligned} \quad (7)$$

where r denotes a region, i.e., the set of variable nodes within a cluster of size d, and R a finite set of all possible regions. Additionally, c_r is the overcounting number of regions, and $super(r)$ is the set of all super-regions of r. This follows from how F_K is approximated. Generally, for each factor node within a cluster we need to include all adjacent variables nodes and sum the computed free energy; however, this process results in repeated counting of the interactions between sets within a cluster. Therefore, we need to subtract the free energy of interactions and interactions of interactions.

Figure 2 shows an example Kikuchi approximation using part of the system defined in Figure 1 for two different cluster sizes (2,3). To evaluate the Bethe approximation (i.e., $d = 2$) we use pairwise clusters. The Bethe entropy would then be the sum of all entropies in the pairwise cluster, subtracting the overcounted cluster interactions [15]:

$$\begin{aligned}S_{d=2}(\mathbf{x}) &= S(x_{1,2}) + S(x_{2,3}) + S(x_{129,130}) + S(x_{130,131}) \\ &+ S(x_{1,129}) + S(x_{2,130}) + S(x_{3,131}) \\ &- S(x_1) - S(x_{129}) - S(x_3) - S(x_{131}) \\ &- 2S(x_2) - 2S(x_{130})\end{aligned} \quad (8)$$

$$S = -\sum_{x_i} Q(x_i) \ln Q(x_i)$$

where x_1 appears in two clusters, $\{x_{1,2}\}, \{x_{1,129}\}$, i.e., its entropy was overcounted only once and we subtract it once. Conversely, x_2 appears in three clusters, $\{x_{1,2}\}, \{x_{2,3}\}, \{x_{2,130}\}$, and this mean that its entropy was overcounted twice, and we subtract it twice.

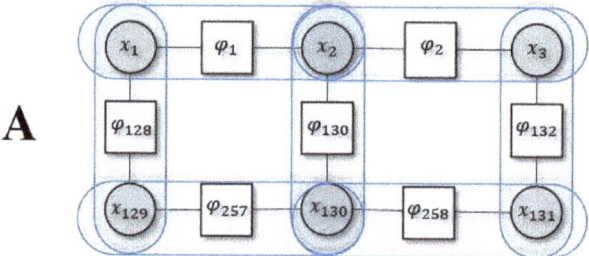

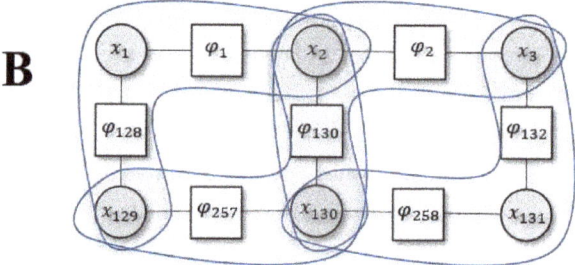

Figure 2. Example of Kikuchi free energy with two different cluster sizes. Panel **A** is for $d = 2$ or Bethe approximation and panel **B** is for $d = 3$.

We could approximate F_K differently by using a cluster size of 3:

$$\begin{aligned}S_{d=3}(\mathbf{x}) &= S(x_{129,1,2}) + S(x_{129,130,2}) + S(x_{130,2,3}) + S(x_{130,131,3}) \\ &- S(x_{2,129}) - S(x_{3,130}) - S(x_{2,130})\end{aligned} \quad (9)$$

Here, x_{129} and x_2 appear together in two separate clusters $\{x_{129,1,2}\}, \{x_{130,129,2}\}$, so their entropy is subtracted. Similar logic follows for (x_{130}, x_3) and (x_{130}, x_2).

We can define the Kikuchi Hamiltonian based on similar intuition. Accordingly, the Hamiltonian for Figure 2B, found using Equation (7), is the following:

$$H_{d=3}(\mathbf{x}) = H(x_{129,1,2}) + H(x_{129,130,2}) + H(x_{130,2,3}) + H(x_{130,131,3}) \\ - H(x_{2,129}) - H(x_{3,130}) - H(x_{2,130}) \quad (10)$$

Generally, the approximation accuracy is improved when we consider larger cluster sizes, which is in contrast to mean-field formulation. Explicitly, for $d = N$, the Kikuchi approximation for the entropy becomes exact [32]; however, by working with clusters, we cannot define an overall variational distribution, $Q(\mathbf{x})$, that is consistent with $Q_r(\mathbf{x}_r)$ and are unable to obtain an upper bound for F_H [33].

3. Constructing Cancer Niches using Kikuchi Free Energy

In this section, we introduce the model used for simulating cancer niches using Kikuchi free energy approximation. For this, we work with the system briefly introduced in Section 2 (Figure 1). Explicitly, this is a 2D Ising model with $N = 128^2$ discrete variables, $\{X_1, X_2, X_3 \ldots, X_N\}$, and is arranged in a grid structure. These variables, X_i, represent individual cells in a particular tissue population, and each variable can be in one of two states $x_i \in \{0, 1\}$. Here, 0 denotes a healthy state, i.e., x_i^0, and 1 denotes a cancerous state i.e., x_i^1. We factorise the 2D system as follows:

$$P(\mathbf{x}) = \sum_{s \in \{0,1\}} \left(\sum_{i,j \in N} P(x_{i,j}^s, x_{i,j+1}^s, x_{i-1,j}^s, x_{i-1,j+i}^s) \right) \quad (11)$$

where i, j denote the position on the grid (row, column) and s represents the particular variable realisation. This factorisation is a simplified characterisation of sub-populations of cells interacting during cancer niche construction. It is a simple characterisation because it corresponds to interactions of size 4. A different factorization of the system could have been chosen that might require a different higher-order Kikuchi approximation. Technically, even this simple construction leads to non-unique factorisation because of boundary effects. Consequently, to approximate the free energy of this factorised system we need to account for higher-order interactions whilst accounting for overlapping interactions. Specifically, we specify a Kikuchi Hamiltonian to evaluate the energy exchange in these interacting nodes. Practically, this is achieved by using the Kikuchi formulation introduced in for $d = 3$ [14,16] or B_3 using [16]'s notation. This is appropriate because B_3 with a base cluster as an angle of size 3 gives the same results when using a base cluster of size 4 but with a square [16]:

$$F_V = U_K(Q) - S_K(Q) + \lambda_1 \left(1 + \sum_{s_1,s_2,s_3 \in \{0,1\}} \sum_{i,j} H(x_{i,j}^{s_1}, x_{i-1,j-1}^{s_2}, x_{i-1,j+i}^{s_3}) \right) \\ + 4\lambda_2 \left(\begin{array}{c} Q(x_{i,j}^0, x_{i-1,j-1}^1, x_{i-1,j+i}^0) + Q(x_{i,j}^1, x_{i-1,j-1}^1, x_{i-1,j+i}^0) + Q(x_{i,j}^0, x_{i-1,j-1}^1, x_{i-1,j+i}^1) \\ -Q(x_{i,j}^0, x_{i-1,j-1}^0, x_{i-1,j+i}^1) - Q(x_{i,j}^1, x_{i-1,j-1}^0, x_{i-1,j+i}^0) - Q(x_{i,j}^1, x_{i-1,j-1}^0, x_{i-1,j+i}^1) \end{array} \right) \quad (12)$$

$$U(Q) = \underbrace{U_0}_{=0} + \underbrace{\varepsilon_{IN}(Q)}_{\text{Interaction}} \quad (13)$$

See Kikuchi and Brush (1976) Table II and IV for graphical representations. Additionally, the Appendix A presents the exact Kikuchi free energy approximation (Equations (A1)–(A3)). Here, λ_1, λ_2 are the Lagrangian multipliers necessary to satisfy the normalisation condition:

$$1 = \sum_{s_1 \in \{0,1\}} Q(x^{s_1}) = \sum_{s_1,s_2,s_3 \in \{0,1\}} \sum_{i,j} Q(x_{i,j}^{s_1}, x_{i-1,j-1}^{s_2}, x_{i-1,j+i}^{s_3}) \quad (14)$$

ε_{IN} is the interaction parameter, and U_0 is the activation energy. Following [14,16], we set the activation energy to 0 and quantify the interaction energy using pairwise interactions (Equation (A2)). Consequently, this particular interaction parameter allows us to accommodate the type of interactions the system evinces. Intuitively, increasing the interaction energy encourages interactions across healthy and cancerous pairs, whilst lower interaction energy encourages interactions within healthy or cancerous pairs [14,18]. Perturbing this interaction energy has a direct impact on the overall free energy of the system. In doing so, we have a way to evaluate the free energy of the system for a given trial. Now, we formalise a setting for how particular realisations evolve (i.e., transition from one state to another) under this system. At each trial, J variables may update their current state from either cancer to healthy or healthy to cancer state. This determines the growth rate hyperparameter i.e., $\alpha = \left[\frac{J}{N}\right] \times 100$. The variables transition to the other state (i.e., either healthy or cancerous, given the previous state) determined by the probability ρ:

$$v \sim p(v_t) = \rho^{v_t}(1-\rho)^{v_t}$$
$$x_{j,t} \sim \begin{cases} x_{j,t} = x_{\tilde{j}\setminus j \in R,t}^{s_t} & \text{if } v_t > nt, \\ x_{j \in N,t}^{s_t \neq s_{t-1}} & \text{if } v_t \leq nt, \end{cases} \quad (15)$$

where v_t denotes an auxiliary Bernoulli random variable indicating whether the variable x_j is in the same cluster, R, as $x_{\tilde{j}}$ at trial t, and nt is the noise hyperparameter. The variables $\tilde{j}$ are identified based on the tolerance, *tol*, threshold:

$$x_{\tilde{j}} \sim \begin{cases} 1 \text{ if } tol > 0.5 \\ 0 \text{ if } tol \leq 0.5 \end{cases} \quad (16)$$

The tolerance hyperparameter controls the maximum proportion of cancerous states allowed in the system. In our deterministic formulation, these state updates are retained if they minimise the overall Kikuchi free energy of the system. See the Appendix B for the pseudocode (Figure A1).

3.1. Simulations

Using the above formulation, we simulated three cancer trajectories: local growth, metastasis, and apoptosis. The initialisation of the system is dependent on the simulation, and the specific parameterisations for each simulation are presented in Table 1.

Table 1. Parameterisation of the simulations. The interaction parameter regulates the type of cell interaction. The tolerance parameter determines the acceptance level of cancerous cells. The growth hyperparameter controls the number of cell states allowed to switch during a single trial. The noise hyperparameter influences the transition dynamics. These parameters determine the evolution of the system to a steady state according to Equation (14).

	Tolerance, *tol*	Interaction, ε_{IN}	Growth Rate *, α	Noise, *nt*
Local Growth	0.60000	2.77259	0.00610	0.25/0.00
Metastasis	0.60000	1.88001	0.00061% $\rightarrow$ 0.00610%	0.30 $\rightarrow$ 0.25
Apoptosis	0.00001	-1.42670	0.00610%	0.25

3.1.1. Local Growth

First, we modelled growth within the tissue of origin. This speaks to a modification of healthy cells within the original site, i.e., the healthy nodes now become cancerous. Simulating localised cancer cell growth is a core step to elucidating how cancer growth in a healthy organ can be the result of an energy-efficient process in terms of population dynamics although being pathological for the organism as a whole. To simulate this, we specified a high tolerance for cancerous nodes, along with a high energy interaction parameter (Table 1) that constrains the specification of x_j to variables in the existing cancerous cluster. Here, the positive interaction parameter induces a reduction in overall free energy when cancerous cells interact with other cancerous cells.

For this cancer niche, we initialised the system with a single cancerous cell. Using this, we simulated two distinct patterns: dispersive and localised. The dispersive simulation emulates instances where growth is spread out throughout the tissue population. As a result, the noise hyperparameter was set to 0.25. Conversely, the localised simulation emulates instances where growth is restricted to a small region of the tissue population. For this, we set the noise hyperparameter to 0.

3.1.2. Metastasis

We next modelled metastasis. Understanding metastatic spread is a fundamental priority in cancer research and treatment. With this simulation, we attempted to recreate in silico metastatic progression where the metastatic invasion of a distant organ is enabled by the re-creation of a new niche, without which the cells (although able to migrate) would not survive. Generally, the development of a metastasis occurs in several steps which can develop in a different order over time, including the creation of a premetastatic niche (induced by a distant tumour), mesenchymal transition (EMT) of the original mass (which provides invasive properties), degradation of basement membranes and remodelling of the extracellular matrix (ECM), invasion of the surrounding tissue, angiogenesis, intravasation, arrest of the tumour cells in a capillary bed, extravasation, and the development of macrometastasis [34].

Intuitively, metastasis is the movement of cancer cells from a primary site, (e.g., the original skin tissue of growth) to a secondary location (e.g., lymph nodes). Here, we initialised a small region of the system as the primary site (Figure 3C, grey square), with the remaining grid representing the secondary location. We used a decaying noise hyperparameter to model the transition dynamics alongside an increasing growth rate. This allowed us to emulate the movement of cancerous cells from the primary site to the secondary location, via the bloodstream. Additionally, setting the interaction parameter value to 1.88 allowed us to strike a balance between having both (i) pairwise interactions across cancerous and healthy cells and (ii) pairwise interactions between cancerous and healthy cells within the cluster. This created a system with cancer cells in regions outside the primary site that could support the recreation of a new cancer niche.

3.1.3. Apoptosis

We then modelled apoptosis. This is a controlled mechanism of cell death that intervenes in normal organ repair, growth, and renewal, as well as in inflammation and cancer. It can result from three pathways (extrinsic, intrinsic, and perforine/granzyme). In cancer proliferation, the intrinsic pathway is impaired and cancer cells can escape their death [35]. Here, we aimed to show how the organisms self-preservation mechanisms could be properly activated against the oncogenic cells. Accordingly, we did not expect cancer growth and expected the new niche to be unable to stabilise at a new homeostatic equilibrium.

During this process, the tissue population would normally go through several stages: (i) healthy cells becoming cancerous; (ii) cancerous cells dying; and (iii) remaining healthy cells multiplying and repairing the organ. From our perspective, this simply ensures switching off existing cancerous cells in the population and replacing them with healthy cells.

We were interested in evaluating how the size of the cancer niche impacted apoptosis. Accordingly, we initialised two distinct grids. One had a small cancerous cluster of 41 nodes (or 0.25% of the population), and the other had a larger cluster of 172 nodes (or 1% of the population). For both, we set the tolerance hyperparameter to 10^{-5} and the interaction parameter to -1.426 to simulate two instances of apoptosis. Here, having a negative interaction parameter induces a reduction in the overall Kikuchi free energy when more cancer cells interact with healthy cells.

Each parameterisation was simulated across 100 trials with $\rho = 0.2$ and the other parameters were kept consistent.

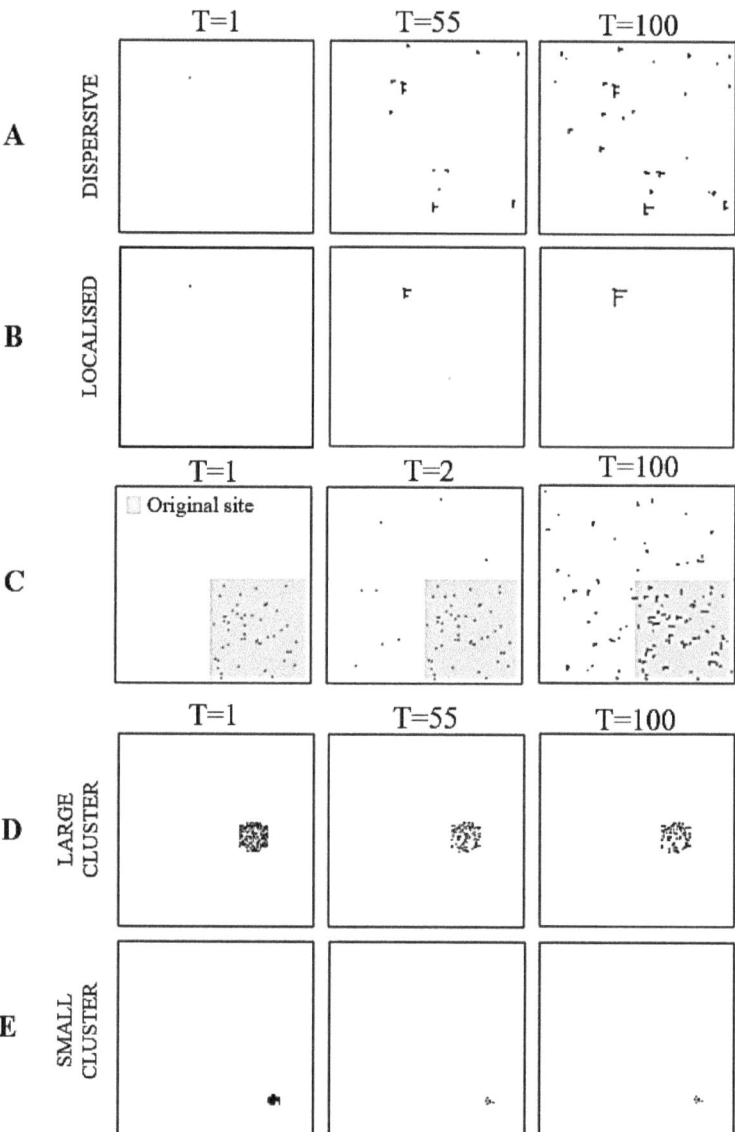

Figure 3. Simulating cancer niches. The figures are pictorial representations of the cancer niches in different trials during simulation. Each row denotes a different simulation: local growth (**A**,**B**), metastasis (**C**), and apoptosis (**D**,**E**). For row C, the grey square represents the original site location.

4. Results

The results from the simulations, for each cancer niche, are shown in Figures 3 and 4. For the local growth simulation, the construction of the cancer niche was entirely consistent with our expectations. That is, from a single cancerous cell we could observe cancer development. Specifically, by setting a high interaction and tolerance parameter, the cancer was able to survive in healthy tissue. In other words, the overall free energy of the system was minimised by allowing for interactions across cancerous and healthy cells that lead to an oncogenic environment (i.e., the topology of our system) (Figure 4). The free energy results measured using Kikuchi and mean-field approximation presented similar path trajectories.

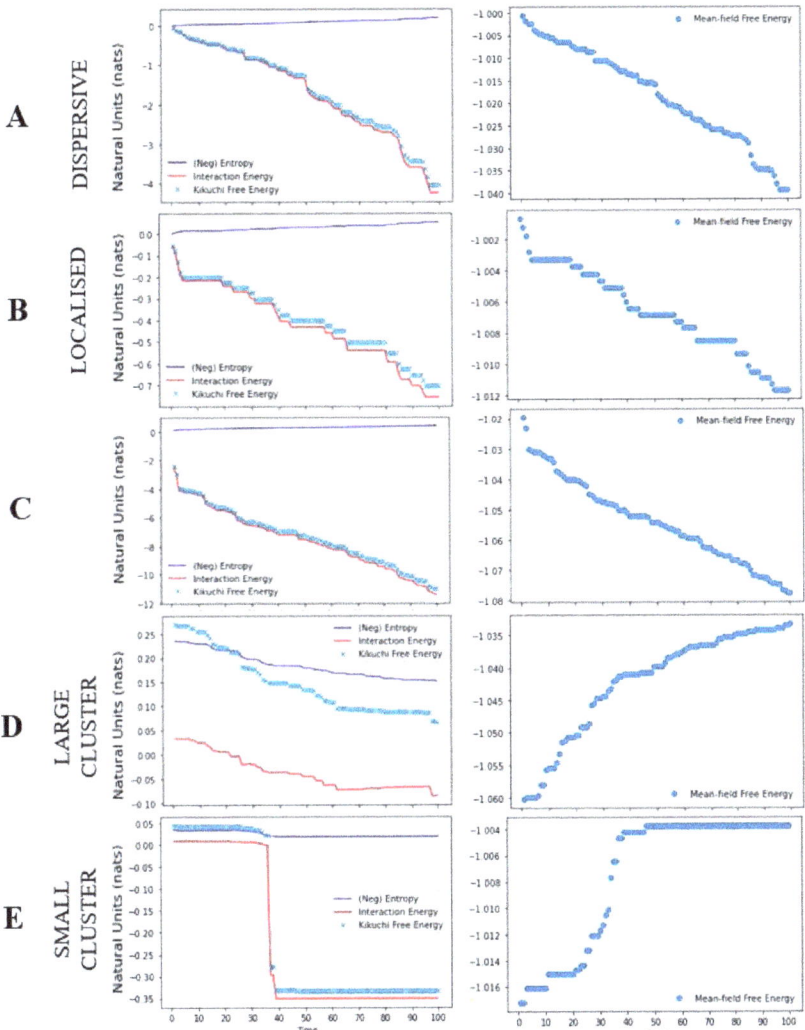

Figure 4. Free energy as a function of time. The graphic plots the free energies for each cancer niche simulation. Each row denotes a different simulation: local growth (**A**,**B**), metastasis (**C**), and apoptosis (**D**,**E**). For each plot, the Y-axis reports the free energy in natural units [36] and the x-axis as the trial. The first panel reports the Kikuchi free energy (blue dots), interaction energy (red line), and entropy (blue line). The second panel reports the mean-field free energy (blue dots).

The metastasis simulation illustrates (i) the movement of cancerous cells away from the original site and (ii) the ability to sustain the ensuing changes in cell nodes outside the original nodes. (Figure 3). This is a direct result of the interaction parameter value, that allowed for across/between interactions of cancerous and healthy cells. Thus, any changes to the overall system, distal to the original site, were maintained because they minimised the overall Kikuchi free energy of the system. As in the local growth simulation, we see that both Kikuchi free energy and mean-field free energy approximations follow a similar trend (Figure 4); however, the Kikuchi free energy gradient was steeper over time.

For the apoptosis simulation, the system was unable to maintain the existing cancer niche and/or create a new cancer niche. This is reflected by the gradual decline in the overall number of cancerous cells. It is a direct result of reducing the tolerance threshold to 0.00001, where the system now updates the state of cancerous cells to healthy (i.e., a process of renewal and repair). Moreover, the negative interaction parameter value effectuates an overall minimisation of the Kikuchi free energy as the number of interactions between healthy and healthy cells increases. Ultimately, this leads to an apoptotic fate for cancer cells (Figure 4). Interestingly, although we observed a drop in the Kikuchi free energy (as expected), the mean-field free energy for this system increased over time.

5. Discussion

Organ development and cellular differentiation, de-differentiation, and niche homeostasis arise from a complex interaction between both deterministic and stochastic mechanisms [13]. In these processes, the spatial aspects are as important as the temporal ones, and steady system states are found when the free energy of spatiotemporal dynamics reach minima. In this context, the geometry of the cell's population presents a role that goes beyond the mere effect on mechanics forces [37–40].

The original approach to investigate cellular population dynamics has mainly been deterministic, i.e., a stable genetic code defines cell fate as a programmed hierarchical process. More recently, research has shown how another group of mechanisms based on stochastic self-organisation plays a complementary role in morphogenesis (i.e., organ development) and cell development [41]. Under this perspective, genetic factors would interact with self-organisation mechanisms to balance the growth of an organism and the organisation of cellular assemblies in direct connection with environmental factors. The specific shapes and functions of cells are associated with physical constraints that, although not being genetically encoded, determine the spatial and functional organisation of organs and tissues and further recursively modulate the genetic expression. These physical factors are mechanical, chemical, and geometrical, as well as use-related stressors. Here, the distance or contiguity between cells allows for a spatial-dependent gradient of information such that the regulatory signals created by one cell reach neighbouring cells and regulate the surrounding environment depending on the geography of their position. Therefore, deterministic, stochastic, local, and population factors cooperate during self-organisation, which moves towards a reduction of the overall free energy of the system and stabilisation around the steady states.

Our approach, using Kikuchi free energy, endorses this perspective, namely, that regulatory signals created by cells can affect neighbour cells and influence the surrounding cluster. This induces the creation of new homeostasis in the tissue population (or the body) as a new equilibrium is reached. This stipulates that cancer niche construction is not destructive in physical terms but speaks to the natural evolution of the state function of the system. We have observed changes across our three cancer trajectory simulations. Here, cancer niche construction (or a topographic change to the system) persists because it minimises the overall Kikuchi free energy of the system. This has been shown during metastasis and local growth as nodes change from a healthy to a cancerous state here. Similarly, through apoptosis, a new minimum is reached as the system topology shifts from cancerous to an overall healthy state. The new homeostasis is a consequence of the changes in the interaction and tolerance parameters, that influence the overall Kikuchi free energy estimation and regulate the niche construction.

These parameters allow for changes at both the sub-population (or cluster) level and the overall system. Specifically, under this formulation, the overall system state is regulated by the tolerance level that determines the threshold for having cancerous cells. In our simulations, this meant that a system with high tolerance would permit an increased number of cancer nodes that are conducive to the proliferation and growth of cancer niches. Conversely, low tolerance meant that the system could not maintain the existing cancer niche and/or create a new cancer niche. Additionally, the interaction parameter regulates the types of interactions that would minimise the overall Kikuchi free energy. High interaction parameter values allowed for healthy pairwise interactions for cancer in clusters that are favourable for constructing a new niche. A low interaction parameter value shifted the system state towards either healthy or cancerous by preferring either healthy–healthy or cancer–cancer cell interactions. We postulate that these particular parameters can refer to the biochemical elements in the body which induce cancer formation, growth, and metastasis, as well as the activations of mechanisms of defence.

Our work provides cancer system biology research with a quantitative formulation of evaluating cancer niches that speaks to the recent change of perspective in the field. The role of population dynamics and cancer niches has been proven to be at the core of cancer growth. Our model includes these elements and illustrates their importance in evaluating cancer trajectories. Consequently, this approach has promising future directions for the field of computational biology and can help our understanding of how niches and cells and how possible therapies interact and interfere with each other. Similar mathematical approaches could be considered to test and validate the hypothesis, as well as to predict the possible development of a cancer mass depending on the degree of development and growth within its niche. Although our model is just a reductive simplification of the complex process of carcinogenesis, it demonstrates how Kikuchi free energy is a valuable tool for system biology studies.

5.1. Other Computational Approaches

The authors of [42] characterised cancer niche concentration as a (stochastic) transition of a healthy system to a distinct oncogenic steady state, e.g., proliferation or apoptosis. They hypothesised that this transition is a direct consequence of the nonlinear dynamic interactions amongst molecular/cellular pathways and modules, e.g., E2F [43], which constitutes an endogenous network. They introduced nonlinear stochastic differential equations (a generalised form of the Langevin equations) in [44–46] to elucidate the specific interactions and nodes that undergird these transitions. See [47] for a review of this approach. This approach is conceptually consistent with a continuous state-space formulation in the current work, albeit introducing stochastic dynamics. Conversely, our approach considers a simplified setting with a discrete-state space formulation with a minimum set of assumptions about the types of nodes and how they interact. Our focus places an endogenous set of agents, as defined by [42], in the setting of cellular population dynamics. This casts the construction of cancer niches in terms of interactions between neighbouring cells and how they influence the cluster using Kikuchi free energy. Interestingly, [47] proposed that free energy can be used to evaluate such noisy systems.

Our approach is complementary to the 2D stochastic cellular automation model proposed in [48] with three states: proliferative, dead ('vacant'), or quiescent. They proposed distinct (deterministic) transitions between each state with three hyperparameters governing the system dynamics (regrowth ability, death rate, and cell cycle arrest). Using Monte Carlo simulations and mean-field phase transition equations, they suggested that the collapse of homeostasis at the multicellular level may be underwritten by non-equilibrium processes; however, their model did not consider long-range intercellular interactions using Kikuchi free energy. Future work could look to incorporate the dynamic transitions introduced in [48] and update rules to model particular cancer niches using Kikuchi free energy.

5.2. Limitations

There are several limitations with our formulation of cancer niche construction as a consequence of the 2D Ising model used to describe our system. The model restricts the simulations to a closed grid that is unable to interact with the "outside" or be affected by external forces [49]. Nonetheless, this is sufficient for the purposes of understanding how the internal dynamics of a tissue population induce cancer niches. Moreover, our work provides a first step in going beyond a (factorised) mean-field approach to evaluating cancer proliferation and growth [7–10]. A second limitation arises from the deterministic formulation of the transition dynamics. As mentioned above, the self-organisation of cancer niches is a direct consequence of deterministic and stochastic processes that influence the appropriate environment for the growth and maintenance of oncogenic cells. An enactive formulation has been explored in [50] which casts self-organisation as an active inference process where morphogenesis is simply a result of variational free-energy minimization (i.e., of the sort that has been used to explain action and perception in neuroscience [51,52]) and morphogenesis in cellular biology [53].

A key difference between applications of the free energy principle to pattern formation [50] and the treatment in this paper rests upon the nature of the free energy. In applying the free energy principle, the variational free energy pertains to (Bayesian) beliefs parameterised by some (e.g., internal) states about other (e.g., external) states. In contrast, the application of free energy in this paper is directly attributable to the probability of states. This means the free energy principle treats cancer as a process of inference, e.g., a kind of delusion [54], whereas the current treatment treats carcinogenesis as a thermodynamic process (where, under certain conditions, one implies the other); however, future work could look to use Kikuchi free energy under a generalised belief propagation scheme [20] for modelling cancer niches while incorporating (i) external states and (ii) equipping cells with agency by conditioning state transitions on some active states.

Another limitation is a result of the simple generative model, i.e., our discrete random variables can be realised as either cancerous or healthy. Thus, when modelling metastasis, we are unable to model intermediate changes in the cell type (or different realisation of the random variables) as they move from the primary to the metastatic site. Future work could look to expand the model formulation beyond the 2D Ising model to account for these different states as particular cancer niches develop. This would give us a more realistic grounding in the transition dynamics that go beyond being simply healthy to cancerous or cancerous to healthy.

6. Conclusions

In this work, we illustrate that cancer niche construction is a direct consequence of interactions between clusters of modified cancerous cells using Kikuchi free energy approximation. We show that for certain cancer trajectories, Kikuchi free energy is a more accurate measure of evaluating system topology when compared to a mean-field approximation. Consequently, our work provides proof for the principle of using higher-order free energy approximations that can be more appropriate when evaluating cancer niche construction. Future work should extend the system formulation beyond a 2D Ising construct to evaluate the underlying differences in free energy approximations.

Author Contributions: Conceptualization, N.S., L.C. and K.F.; Formal analysis, N.S.; Methodology, N.S., L.C. and K.F.; Visualization, N.S.; Writing—original draft, N.S. and L.C.; Writing—review & editing, N.S., L.C. and K.F. All authors made substantial contributions to conception and design, and writing of the article. All authors have read and agreed to the published version of the manuscript.

Funding: This work was funded by Medical Research Council (MR/S502522/1, NS), Leverhulme Doctoral Training Programme for the Ecological Study of the Brain (LC), and the Wellcome Trust (Ref: 203147/Z/16/Z and 205103/Z/16/Z, KJF).

Conflicts of Interest: The authors declare no conflict of interest.

Appendix A

Exact Formulation for the Kikuchi Free Energy

We use the Kikuchi free energy formulation introduced in [16]:

$$F_V = U_K(Q) - S_K(Q) + \lambda_1 \left(1 + \sum_{s_1,s_2,s_3 \in \{0,1\}} \sum_{i,j} H(x^{s_1}_{i,j}, x^{s_2}_{i-1,j-1}, x^{s_3}_{i-1,j+i}) \right)$$
$$+ 4\lambda_2 \left(\begin{array}{c} \sum_{i,j,j_1,2,i_{1,2}} Q(x^0_{i,j}, x^1_{i_1,j_1}, x^0_{i_2,j_2}) + \sum_{i,j,j_1,2,i_{1,2}} Q(x^1_{i,j}, x^1_{i_1,j_1}, x^0_{i_2,j_2}) \\ - \sum_{i,j,j_1,2,i_{1,2}} Q(x^0_{i,j}, x^0_{i_1,j_1}, x^1_{i_2,j_2}) - \sum_{i,j,j_1,2,i_{1,2}} Q(x^1_{i,j}, x^0_{i_1,j_1}, x^1_{i_2,j_2}) \end{array} \right) \quad (A1)$$

where the following may be represented using Equation (1.3) in [16]:

$$U(Q) = \underbrace{U_0}_{activation} + \varepsilon_{IN} \left(\begin{array}{c} \sum_{i,j,j_1,2,i_{1,2}} Q(x^0_{i,j}, x^0_{i_1,j_1}, x^0_{i_2,j_2}) + \sum_{i,j,j_1,2,i_{1,2}} Q(x^0_{i,j}, x^1_{i_1,j_1}, x^0_{i_2,j_2}) \\ + \sum_{i,j,j_1,2,i_{1,2}} Q(x^1_{i,j}, x^0_{i_1,j_1}, x^1_{i_2,j_2}) - \sum_{i,j,j_1,2,i_{1,2}} Q(x^1_{i,j}, x^1_{i_1,j_1}, x^1_{i_2,j_2}) \end{array} \right)$$
$$= \varepsilon_{IN} \left(\begin{array}{c} \sum_{i,j,j_1,i_1} Q(x^1_{i,j}, x^0_{i_1,j_1}) + \sum_{i,j,j_1,i_1} Q(x^0_{i,j}, x^1_{i_1,j_1}) - \\ \sum_{i,j,j_1,i_1} Q(x^0_{i,j}, x^0_{i_1,j_1}) - \sum_{i,j,j_1,i_1} Q(x^1_{i,j}, x^1_{i_1,j_1}) \end{array} \right) \quad (A2)$$

$$S(Q) = \sum_{s_1,s_2,s_3 \in \{0,1\}} \sum_{i,j} S(x^{s_1}_{i,j}, x^{s_2}_{i-1,j-1}, x^{s_3}_{i-1,j+i}) - \sum_{s_1,s_2 \in \{0,1\}} \sum_{i,j} S(x^{s_1}_{i,j}, x^{s_2}_{i+1,j})$$
$$- \sum_{s_1,s_2 \in \{0,1\}} \sum_{i,j} S(x^{s_1}_{i,j}, x^{s_2}_{i+1,j+1}) + \sum_{s_1 \in \{0,1\}} \sum_{i,j} S(x^{s_1}_{i,j}) \quad (A3)$$

Appendix B

Pseudocode for simulating our system.

```
# Initialise:
duration=100 # length of simulation
noise=0.25; # noise for transition dynamics
tolerance=0.5 # allowed proportion of cancerous states
interaction_p=0.7 # between the two states, influences types of interactions
system = initialised_system(shape) # initialise the system state
J = 100 # defines how many nodes can be flipped during on epoch, I
compute interactions ← [system]
calculate base Kikuchi free energy ← [interaction, interation_p, system]

while i in range (0, duration), do:
    for j in range (0, J):
        if cancerous states < tolerance:
            identify state, i, and switch to 1 based on transition function
            compute interactions ← [updated_system]
            calculate Kikuchi free energy ← [interaction, interations, updated_system]
            if Kikuchi free energy < base Kikuchi free energy:
                system ← [updated_system];
                base Kikuchi free energy ← Kikuchi free energy
        if cancerous states > tolerance:
            identify state, i, and switch to 0 based on transition function
            compute interactions ← [updated_system]
            calculate Kikuchi free energy ← [interaction, interations, updated_system]
            if Kikuchi free energy < base Kikuchi free energy:
                system ← [updated_system].
                base Kikuchi free energy ← Kikuchi free energy
end
```

Figure A1. Pseudocode.

References

1. Schofield, R. The relationship between the spleen colony-forming cell and the haemopoietic stem cell. *Blood Cells* **1978**, *4*, 7–25.
2. Ferraro, F.; Celso, C.L.; Scadden, D. Adult stem cels and their niches. *Cell Biol. Stem Cells* **2010**, *695*, 155–168.
3. Donnelly, H.; Salmeron-Sanchez, M.; Dalby, M.J. Designing stem cell niches for differentiation and self-renewal. *J. R. Soc. Interface* **2018**, *15*, 20180388. [CrossRef] [PubMed]
4. Yu, Z.; Pestell, T.G.; Lisanti, M.P.; Pestell, R.G. Cancer stem cells. *Int. J. Biochem. Cell Biol.* **2012**, *44*, 2144–2151. [CrossRef] [PubMed]
5. Plaks, V.; Kong, N.; Werb, Z. The cancer stem cell niche: How essential is the niche in regulating stemness of tumor cells? *Cell Stem Cell* **2015**, *16*, 225–238. [CrossRef] [PubMed]
6. Hanahan, D.; Weinberg, R.A. The hallmarks of cancer. *Cell* **2000**, *100*, 57–70. [CrossRef]
7. Torquato, S. Toward an Ising model of cancer and beyond. *Phys. Biol.* **2011**, *8*, 015017. [CrossRef] [PubMed]
8. Züleyha, A.; Ziya, M.; Selçuk, Y.; Kemal, Ö.M.; Mesut, T. Simulation of glioblastoma multiforme (GBM) tumor cells using ising model on the Creutz Cellular Automaton. *Phys. A Stat. Mech. Its Appl.* **2017**, *486*, 901–907. [CrossRef]
9. Llanos-Pérez, J.; Betancourt-Mar, J.; Cocho, G.; Mansilla, R.; Nieto-Villar, J.M. Phase transitions in tumor growth: III vascular and metastasis behavior. *Phys. A Stat. Mech. Its Appl.* **2016**, *462*, 560–568. [CrossRef]
10. Barradas-Bautista, D.; Alvarado-Mentado, M.; Agostino, M.; Cocho, G. Cancer growth and metastasis as a metaphor of Go gaming: An Ising model approach. *PLoS ONE* **2018**, *13*, e0195654. [CrossRef]
11. Lei, J.; Levin, S.A.; Nie, Q. Mathematical model of adult stem cell regeneration with cross-talk between genetic and epigenetic regulation. *Proc. Natl. Acad. Sci. USA* **2014**, *111*, E880–E887. [CrossRef] [PubMed]
12. Ravichandran, S.; Okawa, S.; Arbas, S.M.; Del Sol, A. A systems biology approach to identify niche determinants of cellular phenotypes. *Stem Cell Res.* **2016**, *17*, 406–412. [CrossRef] [PubMed]
13. Székely Jr, T.; Burrage, K.; Mangel, M.; Bonsall, M.B. Stochastic dynamics of interacting haematopoietic stem cell niche lineages. *PLoS Comput. Biol.* **2014**, *10*, e1003794. [CrossRef] [PubMed]
14. Maren, A.J. The 2-D Cluster Variation Method: Topography Illustrations and Their Enthalpy Parameter Correlations. *Entropy* **2021**, *23*, 319. [CrossRef] [PubMed]
15. Yedidia, J.S.; Freeman, W.T.; Weiss, Y. Bethe free energy, Kikuchi approximations, and belief propagation algorithms. *Adv. Neural Inf. Process. Syst.* **2001**, *13*.
16. Kikuchi, R.; Brush, S.G. Improvement of the Cluster-Variation Method. *J. Chem. Phys.* **1967**, *47*, 195–203. [CrossRef]
17. Kikuchi, R. A theory of cooperative phenomena. *Phys. Rev.* **1951**, *81*, 988. [CrossRef]
18. Maren, A.J. The cluster variation method: A primer for neuroscientists. *Brain Sci.* **2016**, *6*, 44. [CrossRef]
19. Yedidia, J. An idiosyncratic journey beyond mean field theory. In *Advanced Mean Field Methods: Theory and Practice*; MIT press: Cambridge, MA, USA; London, UK, 2001; pp. 21–36.
20. Yedidia, J.S.; Freeman, W.T.; Weiss, Y. Constructing free-energy approximations and generalized belief propagation algorithms. *IEEE Trans. Inf. Theory* **2005**, *51*, 2282–2312. [CrossRef]
21. Bach, A. Boltzmann's Probability Distribution of 1877. *Arch. Hist. Exact Sci.* **1990**, *41*, 1–40.
22. Hinton, G.E.; Zemel, R.S. Autoencoders, minimum description length, and Helmholtz free energy. *Adv. Neural Inf. Process. Syst.* **1994**, *6*, 3–10.
23. Yoshioka, D. The Partition Function and the Free Energy. In *Statistical Physics: An Introduction*; Springer: Berlin/Heidelberg, Germany, 2007; pp. 35–44.
24. Parisi, G. *Statistical Field Theory*; Basic Books; The University of Virginia: Charlottesville, VA, USA, 1988.
25. Cover, T.M. *Elements of Information Theory*; John Wiley & Sons: Weinheim, Germany, 2012.
26. Parr, T.; Sajid, N.; Friston, K.J. Modules or Mean-Fields? *Entropy* **2020**, *22*, 552. [CrossRef] [PubMed]
27. Parr, T.; Markovic, D.; Kiebel, S.J.; Friston, K.J. Neuronal message passing using Mean-field, Bethe, and Marginal approximations. *Sci. Rep.* **2019**, *9*, 1889. [CrossRef] [PubMed]
28. Kadanoff, L.P. More is the same; phase transitions and mean field theories. *J. Stat. Phys.* **2009**, *137*, 777–797. [CrossRef]
29. Jordan, M.I.; Ghahramani, Z.; Jaakkola, T.S.; Saul, L.K. An introduction to variational methods for graphical models. In *Learning in Graphical Models*; Springer: Dordrecht, The Netherlands, 1998; pp. 105–161.
30. Frey, B.J.; MacKay, D.J. A revolution: Belief propagation in graphs with cycles. In *Advances in Neural Information Processing Systems*; MIT press: Cambridge, MA, USA, 1998; pp. 479–485.
31. Pelizzola, A. Cluster variation method in statistical physics and probabilistic graphical models. *J. Phys. A Math. Gen.* **2005**, *38*, R309. [CrossRef]
32. Yedidia, J.S.; Freeman, W.T.; Weiss, Y. Understanding belief propagation and its generalizations. *Explor. Artif. Intell. New Millenn.* **2003**, *8*, 236–239.
33. MacKay, D.J. A conversation about the Bethe free energy and sum-product. *Tech. Rep. of Mitsubishi Electric Research Lab.* **2001**.
34. Geiger, T.R.; Peeper, D.S. Metastasis mechanisms. *Biochim. Biophys. Acta (BBA) Rev. Cancer* **2009**, *1796*, 293–308. [CrossRef]
35. Elmore, S. Apoptosis: A review of programmed cell death. *Toxicol. Pathol.* **2007**, *35*, 495–516. [CrossRef]
36. Homma, N.; Happel, M.F.K.; Nodal, F.R.; Ohl, F.W.; King, A.J.; Bajo, V.M. A Role for Auditory Corticothalamic Feedback in the Perception of Complex Sounds. *J. Neurosci.* **2017**, *37*, 6149–6161. [CrossRef] [PubMed]

37. Manicka, S.; Levin, M. Modeling somatic computation with non-neural bioelectric networks. *Sci. Rep.* **2019**, *9*, 18612. [CrossRef] [PubMed]
38. Cervera, J.; Manzanares, J.A.; Mafe, S.; Levin, M. Synchronization of Bioelectric Oscillations in Networks of Nonexcitable Cells: From Single-Cell to Multicellular States. *J. Phys. Chem. B* **2019**, *123*, 3924–3934. [CrossRef] [PubMed]
39. Levin, M. Endogenous bioelectrical networks store non-genetic patterning information during development and regeneration. *J. Physiol.* **2014**, *592*, 2295–2305. [CrossRef] [PubMed]
40. Levin, M. Reprogramming cells and tissue patterning via bioelectrical pathways: Molecular mechanisms and biomedical opportunities. *Wiley Interdiscip. Rev. Syst. Biol. Med.* **2013**, *5*, 657–676. [CrossRef] [PubMed]
41. Collinet, C.; Lecuit, T. Programmed and self-organized flow of information during morphogenesis. *Nat. Rev. Mol. Cell Biol.* **2021**, *22*, 245–265. [CrossRef] [PubMed]
42. Ao, P.; Galas, D.; Hood, L.; Zhu, X. Cancer as robust intrinsic state of endogenous molecular-cellular network shaped by evolution. *Med. Hypotheses* **2008**, *70*, 678–684. [CrossRef]
43. Weinberg, R.A. The retinoblastoma protein and cell cycle control. *Cell* **1995**, *81*, 323–330. [CrossRef]
44. Yuan, R.; Zhu, X.; Radich, J.P.; Ao, P. From molecular interaction to acute promyelocytic leukemia: Calculating leukemogenesis and remission from endogenous molecular-cellular network. *Sci. Rep.* **2016**, *6*, 24307. [CrossRef]
45. Li, S.; Zhu, X.; Liu, B.; Wang, G.; Ao, P. Endogenous molecular network reveals two mechanisms of heterogeneity within gastric cancer. *Oncotarget* **2015**, *6*, 13607. [CrossRef]
46. Zhu, X.; Yuan, R.; Hood, L.; Ao, P. Endogenous molecular-cellular hierarchical modeling of prostate carcinogenesis uncovers robust structure. *Progress Biophys. Mol. Biol.* **2015**, *117*, 30–42. [CrossRef]
47. Yuan, R.; Zhu, X.; Wang, G.; Li, S.; Ao, P. Cancer as robust intrinsic state shaped by evolution: A key issues review. *Rep. Prog. Phys. Phys. Soc. (Great Britain)* **2017**, *80*, 042701. [CrossRef]
48. Lou, Y.; Chen, A.; Yoshida, E.; Chen, Y. Homeostasis and systematic ageing as non-equilibrium phase transitions in computational multicellular organizations. *R. Soc. Open Sci.* **2019**, *6*, 190012. [CrossRef] [PubMed]
49. Friston, K.J.; Daunizeau, J.; Kilner, J.; Kiebel, S.J. Action and behavior: A free-energy formulation. *Biol. Cybern.* **2010**, *102*, 227–260. [CrossRef]
50. Friston, K.; Levin, M.; Sengupta, B.; Pezzulo, G. Knowing one's place: A free-energy approach to pattern regulation. *J. R. Soc. Interface* **2015**, *12*, 20141383. [CrossRef] [PubMed]
51. Friston, K.; FitzGerald, T.; Rigoli, F.; Schwartenbeck, P.; Pezzulo, G. Active Inference: A Process Theory. *Neural Comput.* **2017**, *29*, 1–49. [CrossRef] [PubMed]
52. Pezzulo, G.; Rigoli, F.; Friston, K.J. Active Inference, homeostatic regulation and adaptive behavioural control. *Prog. Neurobiol.* **2015**, *134*, 17–35. [CrossRef] [PubMed]
53. Kuchling, F.; Friston, K.; Georgiev, G.; Levin, M. Morphogenesis as Bayesian inference: A variational approach to pattern formation and control in complex biological systems. *Phys. Life Rev.* **2019**. [CrossRef]
54. Levin, M. The Computational Boundary of a "Self": Developmental Bioelectricity Drives Multicellularity and Scale-Free Cognition. *Front. Psychol.* **2019**, *10*. [CrossRef] [PubMed]

Article
Message Passing and Metabolism

Thomas Parr

Wellcome Centre for Human Neuroimaging, Queen Square Institute of Neurology, University College London, London WC1N 3AR, UK; thomas.parr.12@ucl.ac.uk

Abstract: Active inference is an increasingly prominent paradigm in theoretical biology. It frames the dynamics of living systems as if they were solving an inference problem. This rests upon their flow towards some (non-equilibrium) steady state—or equivalently, their maximisation of the Bayesian model evidence for an implicit probabilistic model. For many models, these self-evidencing dynamics manifest as messages passed among elements of a system. Such messages resemble synaptic communication at a neuronal network level but could also apply to other network structures. This paper attempts to apply the same formulation to biochemical networks. The chemical computation that occurs in regulation of metabolism relies upon sparse interactions between coupled reactions, where enzymes induce conditional dependencies between reactants. We will see that these reactions may be viewed as the movement of probability mass between alternative categorical states. When framed in this way, the master equations describing such systems can be reformulated in terms of their steady-state distribution. This distribution plays the role of a generative model, affording an inferential interpretation of the underlying biochemistry. Finally, we see that—in analogy with computational neurology and psychiatry—metabolic disorders may be characterized as false inference under aberrant prior beliefs.

Keywords: message passing; metabolism; Bayesian; stochastic; non-equilibrium; master equations

1. Introduction

Common to many stochastic systems in biology is a sparse network structure [1–4]. In the nervous system, this manifests as many neurons that each synapse with a small subset of the total number [5]. In biochemistry, similar network structures exist, in which each chemical species reacts with a small number of other chemicals—facilitated by specific enzymes [6]. In both settings, the ensuing dynamics have parallels with techniques applied in the setting of probabilistic inference, where the sparsity is built into a (generative) statistical model that expresses how observable data are caused by latent or hidden states. Inversion of the model, to establish the most plausible causes for our observations, appeals to the conditional dependencies (and independencies) between its constituent hidden variables [7,8]. This has the appearance of message passing between nodes in a network of variables, with messages passed between nodes representing variables that conditionally depend upon one another [9].

The homology between inferential message passing and sparse dynamical systems is central to active inference—a theoretical framework applied primarily in the neurosciences [10]. Active inference applies to stochastic dynamical systems whose behaviour can be framed as optimisation of an implicit model that explains the inputs to that system. More specifically, it treats the dynamics of a system as a gradient flow on a marginal likelihood (a.k.a., model evidence), that is the minimum of a free energy functional [11]. The internal dynamics of a system are then seen as minimising free energy to find the marginal likelihood, which itself is maximized through acting to change external processes so that the system inputs become more probable [12].

In the brain sciences, active inference offers a principled approach that underwrites theoretical accounts of neuronal networks as performing Bayesian inference [13,14]. However, the same mathematics is also applicable to other biotic systems—as has been shown in the context of self-organisation and morphogenesis [15]—and even to non-biological systems [16]. This paper attempts to find out how far we can take this approach in the biochemical domain. This means an account of metabolic principles in terms of generative models, their constituent conditional dependencies, and the resulting probabilistic dynamics.

Part of the motivation for focusing on metabolism is that it calls for a slightly different formulation of stochastic dynamics to the Fokker–Planck formalisms [17] usually encountered in active inference [18]. As chemical species are categorical entities (e.g., glucose or fructose), discrete probability distributions, as opposed to continuous densities, are most appropriate in expressing our beliefs about chemical reactions. Systems of chemical reactions then offer useful concrete examples of a slightly different form of stochastic dynamics to those explored using Fokker–Planck equations. However, despite attempting to establish a construct validity in relation to metabolism, the primary focus of this paper is not biochemical. It is on the applicability of probabilistic dynamics, of the sort employed in active inference, to systems that are not made up of neuronal networks. Specifically, it is on the emergence of networks in stochastic dynamical systems, under a particular generative model, and upon the interpretation of the network dynamics as inferential message passing.

The argument of this paper can be overviewed as follows. Given an interpretation of a steady state as a generative model, the behaviour of stochastic systems that tend towards that distribution can be interpreted as inference. When such systems are formulated in terms of master equations, they have the appearance of gradient flows on a free energy functional—the same functional used to score approximate Bayesian inference schemes. In practice, we may be interested in high-dimensional systems, for which the distribution can be factorized into a set of lower-dimensional systems. In this setting, a mean-field approximation can be applied such that we only need work with these lower-dimensional marginal distributions. When the implicit generative model is sufficiently sparse, steady state can be achieved through dynamics that involve sparse coupling between the marginal distributions—analogous to inferential message passing schemes in machine learning. Under certain assumptions, these probabilistic dynamics have the appearance of chemical kinetics, licensing an interpretation of some chemical reactions—including biological, enzymatic, reactions—as if the chemical species were engaged in a form of (active) inference about one another. An implication of this interpretation is that metabolic pathologies can be framed in terms of the implicit generative model (i.e., steady state) they appear to be solving.

The main sections of this paper are organized as follows. Section 2 outlines probabilistic dynamics of a categorical sort, and the relationship between these dynamics and the notion of a generative model. This includes the use of mean-field assumptions and the construction of dynamical systems with a particular steady state in mind. Section 3 applies these ideas in the setting of biochemistry, relating the probability of being in each configuration to the concentrations of the associated chemicals. Here, under certain assumptions, we see the emergence of the law of mass action, and the Michaelis–Menten equation—standard results from biochemistry. Section 4 offers an example of a biochemical network, based on the kinetics developed in the previous sections. This paper then concludes with a discussion of the relationship between message passing of the sort found in biochemical and neurobiological systems.

2. Probabilistic Dynamics

2.1. Free Energy and Generative Models

Bayesian inference depends upon an important quantity known as a marginal likelihood. This tells us how probable the data we have observed are, given our model for how those data are generated. As such, it can be thought of as the evidence afforded to a model by those data [19]. For stochastic dynamical systems that have a (possibly non-equilibrium) steady state, the partition function at this steady state can be interpreted as if it were a marginal likelihood [12]. This lets us think of such systems as 'self-evidencing' [20], in the sense that they tend over time towards a high probability of occupancy for regions of space with a high marginal likelihood, and low probability of occupancy for regions with a low marginal likelihood.

The term 'marginal' refers to the summation, or integration, of a joint probability distribution with respect to some of its arguments, such that only a subset of these arguments remains in the resulting marginal distribution. In Bayesian statistics, we are normally interested in finding the marginal likelihood, under some model, of data (y). This is a common measure of the evidence the data affords to the model. However, the model includes those variables (x) that conspire to generate those data. These are variously referred to as hidden or latent states. It is these states that must be marginalized out from a joint distribution.

Variational inference reframes this summation (or integration) problem as an optimisation problem [8,21], in which we must optimize an objective functional (function of a function) whose minimum corresponds to the marginal likelihood. This functional is the variational free energy, defined as follows:

$$
\begin{aligned}
F[y, P(x, \tau|y)] &\triangleq \mathbb{E}_{P(x,\tau|y)}[\ln P(x, \tau|y) - \ln P(x, y, \infty)] \\
\ln P(y, \infty) &= - \min_{P(x,\tau|y)} F[y, P(x, \tau|y)] \\
P(x, \infty|y) &= \operatorname*{argmin}_{P(x,\tau|y)} F[y, P(x, \tau|y)]
\end{aligned}
\tag{1}
$$

The notation $P(x,\tau)$ should be read as the probability that a random variable X takes a value x at time τ, consistent with conventions in stochastic thermodynamics [22]. The symbol $\mathbb{E}$ means the expectation, or average, under the subscripted probability distribution. Equation (1) says that, if free energy is minimized with respect to a time-dependent probability density, then self-evidencing can proceed through minimisation of free energy with respect to y. In neurobiology, minimisation of an upper bound on negative log model evidence is associated with synaptic communication [10]. This neural activity ultimately results in muscle contraction, which causes changes in y [23,24].

An important perspective that arises from Equation (1), and from an appeal to free energy minimisation, is the association between a steady-state distribution and a generative model. The generative model can be written in terms of prior and likelihood distributions whose associated posterior and model evidence (marginal likelihood) are the minimizer of and minimum of the free energy, respectively:

$$
\begin{aligned}
P(x, y, \infty) &= \underbrace{P(y, \infty|x)}_{\text{Likelihood}} \underbrace{P(x, \infty)}_{\text{Prior}} \\
&= \underbrace{P(x, \infty|y)}_{\text{Posterior}} \underbrace{P(y, \infty)}_{\text{Model evidence}}
\end{aligned}
\tag{2}
$$

The key insight from Equation (2) is that, when free energy changes such that it comes to equal the negative log model evidence, the requisite evolution of the time-dependent conditional distribution tends towards a posterior probability. The implication is that when we interpret the partition function (i.e., marginal) of the steady-state distribution as if it were model evidence, the process by which the system tends towards its steady state over time has an interpretation as Bayesian inference.

2.2. Master Equations

This paper's focus is upon probabilistic dynamics of a categorical sort. This deviates from recent accounts [12,18,25] of Bayesian mechanics in terms of Fokker–Planck equations, which describe the temporal evolution of probability density functions. However, master equations [26,27] afford an analogous expression for the dynamics of categorical probability distributions. The form of these equations can be motivated via a Taylor series expansion:

$$P(x,\tau) = \mathbb{E}_{P(z,t)}[P(x,\tau|z,t)]$$
$$P(x,\tau|z,t) = \underbrace{P(x,t|z,t)}_{\delta_{xz}} + \partial_t P(x,t|z,t)\Delta\tau + O(\Delta\tau^2) \quad (3)$$
$$\Delta\tau = \tau - t$$

Equation (3) uses the Kronecker delta function. This expresses the fact that, given $X = z$ at time t, the probability that it is equal to x at time t is one when x is equal to z, and is zero otherwise. Substituting the Taylor series expansion of the second line into the first line gives us:

$$P(x,\tau) = P(x,t) + \mathbb{E}_{P(z,t)}[\partial_t P(x,t|z,t)]\Delta\tau + O(\Delta\tau^2)$$
$$\Rightarrow$$
$$\partial_\tau P(x=i,\tau) = \sum_j \mathbf{L}_{ij} P(z=j,\tau) \quad (4)$$
$$\mathbf{L}_{ij} \triangleq \partial_\tau P(x=i,\tau|z=j,\tau)$$

The transition rate matrix $\mathbf{L}$ determines the rate at which probability mass moves from one compartment to another. The dynamics of a time-dependent distribution are as follows. Assuming that it is a categorical distribution, whose sufficient statistics comprise a vector of probabilities $\mathbf{p}$:

$$P(x,\tau) = Cat(\mathbf{p}(\tau))$$
$$\partial_\tau \mathbf{p}(\tau) = \mathbf{L}\mathbf{p}(\tau) \quad (5)$$

The elements of $\mathbf{p}$ are the probabilities of the alternative states x may assume and must sum to one. Now that we have an expression for a time-dependent probability distribution, how do we link this back to the steady state of the free energy minimum from Equation (1)? One answer to this question comes from recent work that formulates the dynamics of a master equation in terms of a potential function that plays the role of a steady state [28]. This involves the following decomposition of the transition rate matrix:

$$\partial_\tau \mathbf{p}(\tau) = (\mathbf{Q} - \mathbf{\Gamma})\mathbf{\Lambda}\mathbf{p}(\tau)$$
$$\mathbf{\Gamma} \triangleq -\frac{1}{2}(\mathbf{A} + \mathbf{A}^T)$$
$$\mathbf{Q} \triangleq \frac{1}{2}(\mathbf{A} - \mathbf{A}^T) \quad (6)$$
$$\mathbf{A} \triangleq \mathbf{L}\mathbf{\Lambda}^{-1}$$
$$\mathbf{\Lambda} \triangleq diag(\mathbf{p}(\infty))^{-1}$$

The steady-state distribution $\mathbf{p}(\infty)$ is given by the (normalized) right singular vector of $\mathbf{L}$ whose singular value is zero. This follows directly from a singular value decomposition of Equation (5). Equation (6) decomposes the transition rate matrix into two parts, the first with a skew-symmetric matrix $\mathbf{Q}$ and the second with a symmetric matrix $\mathbf{\Gamma}$. This construction resembles the Helmholtz decomposition sometimes applied to continuous dynamical systems [29]—where the flow is decomposed into a solenoidal (conservative) and a dissipative component.

We can relate Equation (6) directly to the minimisation of free energy in Equation (1) when $\mathbf{p}$ is a distribution conditioned upon some input variable y. This rests upon a local linear approximation to the gradient of the free energy. Using the notation of Equation (6), free energy and its gradient are:

$$
\begin{aligned}
F(\mathbf{p}(\tau)) &= \mathbf{p}(\tau) \cdot (\ln \mathbf{p}(\tau) - \ln \mathbf{p}(\infty)) + z(\infty) \\
z(\infty) &\triangleq \ln P(y, \infty) \\
\nabla_{\mathbf{p}(\tau)} F(\mathbf{p}(\tau)) &= \ln \mathbf{p}(\tau) - \ln \mathbf{p}(\infty) + 1 \\
&= 1 + \ln \Lambda \mathbf{p}(\tau) \\
&\approx \Lambda \mathbf{p}(\tau) \\
&\Rightarrow \\
\partial_\tau \mathbf{p}(\tau) &\approx (\mathbf{Q} - \mathbf{\Gamma}) \nabla_{\mathbf{p}(\tau)} F(\mathbf{p}(\tau))
\end{aligned}
\tag{7}
$$

The approximate equality in the fifth line follows from a Taylor series expansion (around $\Lambda \mathbf{p}(\tau) = 1$) of the logarithm in the previous line, truncated after the linear term. This tells us that Equation (6) is, at least locally, a gradient descent on free energy augmented with a solenoidal flow orthogonal to the free energy gradients. Figure 1 illustrates this using a randomly generated transition rate matrix for a system with three possible states. The steady state was identified from the right singular vectors of this matrix, facilitating computation of the free energy. Starting from different locations in the free energy landscape, we see that the combination of the solenoidal and dissipative flows is consistent with a gradient descent on the free energy landscape. The dissipative flow has a similar appearance, while the solenoidal trajectories travel along the free energy gradients, eventually leaving the simplex (violating the conservation of probability).

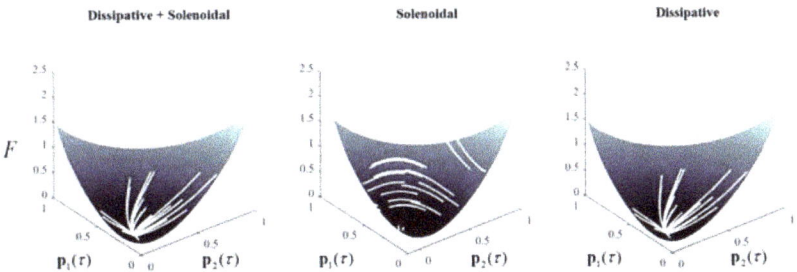

Figure 1. Solenoidal and dissipative dynamics in categorical systems. This figure provides a numerical example of a (three-dimensional) system consistent with Equation (5), and its decomposition as in Equation (6), starting from a series of random initial states. Each trajectory is shown in white. In addition, it illustrates the free energy landscape (in 2 dimensions) to demonstrate the interpretation given in Equation (7). On the left, we see the combination of the dissipative and solenoidal flows that tend towards the free energy minimum. In the centre, the dissipative part of the flow has been suppressed, leading to trajectories around the free energy contours. Such trajectories conserve free energy (but not probability) so do not find its minimum. On the right, the purely dissipative trajectories find the free energy minimum, but take subtly different paths compared to those supplemented with the solenoidal flow.

2.3. Mean-Field Models

The above establishes that probabilistic dynamics under a master equation can be formulated in terms of a gradient descent on variational free energy. However, these dynamics appear limited by their linearity. As nonlinear dynamical systems are ubiquitous in biology, it is reasonable to ask what relevance Equation (5) has for living systems. The answer is that, when x can be factorized, Equation (5) deals with the evolution of a joint probability distribution. Linear dynamics here do not preclude non-linear dynamics of the associated marginal distributions that deal with each factor of x individually. This section unpacks how non-linear behaviour emerges from Equation (5) when we adopt a mean-field assumption. A mean-field assumption [30–32] factorizes a probability distribution into a set of marginal probabilities (Q):

$$\begin{aligned} Q(x_1, \ldots, x_N, \tau) &= \prod_i Q(x_i, \tau) \\ &\Rightarrow \\ \partial_\tau Q(x_i, \tau) &\approx \mathbb{E}_{\prod_k Q(x_k, \tau)} [\partial_\tau P(x_i, \tau | x_1, \ldots, x_N, \tau)] \end{aligned} \quad (8)$$

Equation (8) depends upon the same steps as Equations (3) and (4). It effectively decomposes the dynamics of the joint probability into those of a set of linked compartmental systems. Rewriting this in the form of Equation (5) gives:

$$\begin{aligned} \partial_\tau q_j^i(\tau) &= \sum_{klmn\ldots} L_{jklmn\ldots}^i \, q_k^1(\tau), \ldots, q_s^N(\tau) \\ Q(x_i, \tau) &= \mathrm{Cat}(\mathbf{q}^i(\tau)) \end{aligned} \quad (9)$$

This formulation allows for dynamical interactions between the marginal distributions. Equation (9) can be re-written, using a Kronecker tensor product, to illustrate the savings associated with a mean-field approximation. Here, we see that, although we retain the same number of columns as in our original transition rate matrix, the number of rows reduces to the sum of the lengths of the marginal vectors.

$$\mathbf{q}(\tau) = \mathbf{q}^1(\tau) \otimes \mathbf{q}^2(\tau) \otimes \mathbf{q}^3(\tau) \otimes \cdots$$

$$\mathbf{L}^i = \begin{bmatrix} L_{111\ldots}^i & L_{121\ldots}^i & \cdots & L_{112\ldots}^i & L_{122\ldots}^i & \cdots \\ L_{211\ldots}^i & L_{221\ldots}^i & & L_{212\ldots}^i & L_{222\ldots}^i & \\ \vdots & & \ddots & \vdots & & \ddots \end{bmatrix} \quad (10)$$

$$\partial_\tau \mathbf{q}^i(\tau) = \mathbf{L}^i \mathbf{q}(\tau)$$

This formulation is useful, as we can use it to engineer an $\mathbf{L}$ that would lead to a desired steady state. We can do this by defining $\mathbf{L}$ in terms of the components of its singular value decomposition. This involves setting one of the right singular vectors equal to the desired steady state, and setting the associated singular value to zero:

$$\begin{aligned} \mathbf{L}^i &= \mathbf{A}\mathbf{S}^i\mathbf{V}^i \\ \mathbf{S}^i &= \begin{bmatrix} 0 & 0 & \cdots \\ 0 & \lambda^i & \\ \vdots & & \ddots \end{bmatrix}, \mathbf{V}^i = \begin{bmatrix} \mathbf{p}(\infty)^T \\ \mathbf{v}^i \\ \vdots \end{bmatrix} \\ \mathbf{A} &= \begin{bmatrix} 1 & \mathbf{a} & \cdots \end{bmatrix} \end{aligned} \quad (11)$$

In what follows, we will assume we are dealing with binary probabilities, such that $\mathbf{q}^i(\tau)$ is a two-dimensional vector for all i. To simplify things, we only concern ourselves with the second column of $\mathbf{A}$ and second row of $\mathbf{V}$:

$$\mathbf{L}^i = \lambda^i \mathbf{a} \mathbf{v}^i. \quad (12)$$

It is worth noting that this choice can result in there being more than one fixed point. However, some of these will be inconsistent with the simplex that defines allowable probability distributions and can be safely ignored. Others impose limits on the initial conditions of a dynamical system for which Equation (12) is valid. The terms from Equation (12) can be parameterized as follows:

$$\mathbf{a} = \begin{bmatrix} 1 & -1 \end{bmatrix}^T$$
$$\mathbf{v}^i \mathbf{p}(\infty) = 0$$
$$\mathbf{v}^i = \beta^i \begin{bmatrix} \begin{bmatrix} 1 & 1 \end{bmatrix} \otimes \begin{bmatrix} 1 & 1 \end{bmatrix} \otimes \begin{bmatrix} 1 & 1 \end{bmatrix} \cdots \\ \begin{bmatrix} 1 & 0 \end{bmatrix} \otimes \begin{bmatrix} 1 & 1 \end{bmatrix} \otimes \begin{bmatrix} 1 & 1 \end{bmatrix} \cdots \\ \begin{bmatrix} 1 & 1 \end{bmatrix} \otimes \begin{bmatrix} 1 & 0 \end{bmatrix} \otimes \begin{bmatrix} 1 & 1 \end{bmatrix} \cdots \\ \begin{bmatrix} 1 & 0 \end{bmatrix} \otimes \begin{bmatrix} 1 & 0 \end{bmatrix} \otimes \begin{bmatrix} 1 & 1 \end{bmatrix} \cdots \\ \vdots \\ \begin{bmatrix} 1 & 0 \end{bmatrix} \otimes \begin{bmatrix} 1 & 0 \end{bmatrix} \otimes \begin{bmatrix} 1 & 0 \end{bmatrix} \cdots \end{bmatrix}. \qquad (13)$$

Here, the $\mathbf{a}$ vector is assumed to be the same for all factors of the probability distribution. It ensures any change in probability for one of the binary states is combined with an equal and opposite change in probability for the other state. In other words, it ensures the columns of the transition rate matrix sum to zero, consistent with conservation of probability. The $\mathbf{v}$ (row) vector is parameterized in terms of a weighted sum of row vectors, each of returns a different marginal when multiplied with $\mathbf{p}$ or $\mathbf{q}$. This leads to the following expression for the transition probabilities:

$$\mathbf{L}^i \mathbf{q}(\tau) = \lambda^i \mathbf{a} \left(\beta_1^i + \beta_2^i \mathbf{q}_1^1(\tau) + \beta_3^i \mathbf{q}_1^2(\tau) + \beta_4^i \mathbf{q}_1^1(\tau) \mathbf{q}_1^2(\tau) + \ldots \right). \qquad (14)$$

There may be multiple combinations of the β coefficients that satisfy the condition that $\mathbf{p}(\infty)$ is orthogonal to $\mathbf{v}^T$. The next subsection offers one way in which we can constrain these, based upon the notion of a Markov blanket [33].

2.4. Graphical Models and Message Passing

It need not be the case that all variables in a generative model depend upon all others. Before moving to a chemical interpretation of the probabilistic dynamics outlined above, it is worth touching upon their interpretation as message passing when the underlying model is sufficiently sparse. For this, we need the concept of a Markov blanket [33]. A Markov blanket for x_i is the set of variables that render all other variables conditionally independent of x_i. For example, if the Markov blanket of x_i is x_j at steady state, the following relationship holds:

$$\begin{aligned} (x_i \perp \{x_k : k \neq i, k \neq j\}) | x_j \\ \Rightarrow P(x_i, \infty | \{x_k : k \neq i\}) = P(x_i, \infty | x_j) \end{aligned}. \qquad (15)$$

The implication is that any marginals corresponding to variables outside of the Markov blanket, under the steady-state distribution, add no additional information as to the steady state for the variable inside the blanket. As such, we can set the β coefficients from Equation (14) to zero for all terms except those exclusively comprising variables in the Markov blanket. Figure 2 shows an example of a generative model, expressed as a normal factor graph [34], that illustrates an interpretation of the associated dynamics as message passing among the posterior marginals.

To summarize, so far, the dynamics of a categorical probability distribution can be formulated in terms of a master equation. The steady state of these dynamics is interpretable as the minimizer of a free energy functional of the sort used in variational Bayesian inference. Locally, the dynamics of a master equation can be formulated as a gradient descent on the same variational free energy. Crucially, free energy is a functional of a generative model. Starting from this model, we can construct master equations that lead to steady states consistent with that model. One way of doing this is to specify the components of a singular value decomposition of a probability transition matrix such that the singular value, corresponding to the right singular vector parallel to the steady state, is zero. For systems with many components, it is often more efficient to deal with a mean-field approximation of the dynamics. This lets us formulate the dynamics of marginal distributions for each variable without reference to the probability of variables outside of the Markov blanket of those variables. The next section highlights the points of contact between these mean-field dynamics and established concepts in biochemistry. These include the law of mass action, reaction networks, and Michaelis–Menten enzyme kinetics.

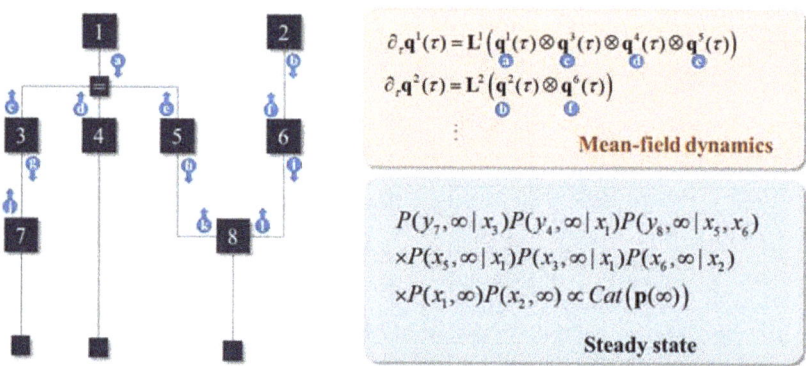

Figure 2. Sparse models and messages. This figure illustrates a generative model using normal (Forney) factor graph. Here, we have 8 different variables. The y variables are indicated by the small squares at the bottom of the factor graph. Dependencies between variables, represented on the edges of the graph, are indicated by the square factor nodes. The Markov blanket of a variable is determined by identifying those variables that share a factor (i.e., any edges connected to the associated square nodes). Not every variable is conditionally dependent upon every other; implying this generative model has a degree of sparsity. This lets us simplify the mean-field dynamics such that the rate of change of each marginal distribution depends only upon its Markov blanket. The result has the appearance of message passing, as indicated by the arrows. Each arrow represents a message coming from a factor. Where they meet, they each contribute to the local steady state.

3. Biochemical Networks

3.1. The Law of Mass Action

This section starts by relating the mean-field dynamics of the previous section to the law of mass action, which specifies the relationship between the rate of a chemical reaction and the concentrations of the chemical species involved in that reaction [35–37]. A reversible chemical reaction is expressed as follows:

$$\sum_i \sigma_i S_i \rightleftharpoons \sum_i \rho_i S_i. \tag{16}$$

Here, S stands in for the different chemical species (indexed by the subscript), and σ and ρ for the stoichiometric coefficients (i.e., the number of molecules of S used up by, or produced by, a single reaction taking place, respectively). The symbol between substrates and products indicates a reversible transition between the substrates and products.

Our challenge is to express Equation (16) in terms of the joint distribution of chemical species at steady state (i.e., a generative model), and then to find an appropriate master equation to describe the route to this steady state. The following shows the form of a steady state for a system with two substrates and two products:

$$P(S_1 \otimes S_2, \infty) = Cat\left(\begin{bmatrix} \alpha \\ 0 \\ 0 \\ 1-\alpha \end{bmatrix}\right)$$

$$P(S_3 \otimes S_4, \infty | S_2) = Cat\left(\begin{bmatrix} 0 & 1 \\ 0 & 0 \\ 0 & 0 \\ 1 & 0 \end{bmatrix}\right).$$ (17)

Intuitively, the first probability distribution tells us that the only plausible configurations of the two substrate molecules are both present and both absent. The second distribution says that, if the second (and therefore the first) substrates are present, the products are both absent. However, if the substrates are absent, the products are present. As all variables of Equation (17) are conditionally dependent upon all other variables, the resulting master equations must depend upon the marginals for all variables. In selecting $\mathbf{v}$, we can group these depending upon which side of the reaction they occupy:

$$\begin{aligned} \mathbf{v}^i &= \beta[\ 1\ \ 1\ ] \otimes [\ 1\ \ 1\ ] \otimes [\ 1\ \ 0\ ] \otimes [\ 1\ \ 0\ ] \\ &- [\ 1\ \ 0\ ] \otimes [\ 1\ \ 0\ ] \otimes [\ 1\ \ 1\ ] \otimes [\ 1\ \ 1\ ] \\ \beta &\triangleq \left(\tfrac{\alpha}{1-\alpha}\right) \\ &\Rightarrow \end{aligned}$$

$$\begin{bmatrix} \partial_\tau \mathbf{q}_1^1(\tau) \\ \partial_\tau \mathbf{q}_1^2(\tau) \\ \partial_\tau \mathbf{q}_1^3(\tau) \\ \partial_\tau \mathbf{q}_1^4(\tau) \end{bmatrix} = \lambda \begin{bmatrix} \beta \mathbf{q}_1^3(\tau)\mathbf{q}_1^4(\tau) - \mathbf{q}_1^1(\tau)\mathbf{q}_1^2(\tau) \\ \beta \mathbf{q}_1^3(\tau)\mathbf{q}_1^4(\tau) - \mathbf{q}_1^1(\tau)\mathbf{q}_1^2(\tau) \\ \mathbf{q}_1^1(\tau)\mathbf{q}_1^2(\tau) - \beta \mathbf{q}_1^3(\tau)\mathbf{q}_1^4(\tau) \\ \mathbf{q}_1^1(\tau)\mathbf{q}_1^2(\tau) - \beta \mathbf{q}_1^3(\tau)\mathbf{q}_1^4(\tau) \end{bmatrix}.$$ (18)

The final line follows from the previous lines via Equation (12). The probabilities that the chemical species is absent (subscript 2) have been omitted as they are simply the complement of the probabilities that they are present (subscript 1). Note that the marginals (at steady state) that result from these dynamics are not consistent with the marginals of the generative model. This is due to the violation of the mean-field assumption. We can correct for the discrepancy by raising the numerator of β to a power of the number of substrates, and the denominator to the power of the number of reactants. This correction is obtained by setting Equation (14) to zero when the marginals are consistent with those at steady state and solving for the β coefficients. In addition, these kinetics conserve the summed probability of species being present (i.e., they conserve mass) so cannot achieve the steady state from Equation (17) unless the initial conditions include a summed probability of presence of 1.

By interpreting the probabilities as the proportion of the maximum number (N) of molecules of each species, and dividing these by the volume (V) in which they are distributed, Equation (18) can be rewritten in terms of chemical concentrations ($\mathbf{u}$):

$$\begin{bmatrix} \partial_\tau \mathbf{u}_1(\tau) \\ \partial_\tau \mathbf{u}_2(\tau) \\ \partial_\tau \mathbf{u}_3(\tau) \\ \partial_\tau \mathbf{u}_4(\tau) \end{bmatrix} = \begin{bmatrix} \kappa_2 \mathbf{u}_3(\tau)\mathbf{u}_4(\tau) - \kappa_1 \mathbf{u}_1(\tau)\mathbf{u}_2(\tau) \\ \kappa_2 \mathbf{u}_3(\tau)\mathbf{u}_4(\tau) - \kappa_1 \mathbf{u}_1(\tau)\mathbf{u}_2(\tau) \\ \kappa_1 \mathbf{u}_1(\tau)\mathbf{u}_2(\tau) - \kappa_2 \mathbf{u}_3(\tau)\mathbf{u}_4(\tau) \\ \kappa_1 \mathbf{u}_1(\tau)\mathbf{u}_2(\tau) - \kappa_2 \mathbf{u}_3(\tau)\mathbf{u}_4(\tau) \end{bmatrix}$$

$$\mathbf{u}_i(\tau) \triangleq V^{-1} N \mathbf{q}_1^i(\tau)$$

$$\kappa_1 \triangleq \lambda N^{-1} V$$ (19)

$$\kappa_2 \triangleq \lambda \beta N^{-1} V$$

$$\beta = \frac{\alpha^2}{(1-\alpha)^2}.$$

Equation (19) uses the 'corrected' β coefficient. A simulation of this reaction is shown in Figure 3, represented both in terms of the evolution of probability and as chemical concentrations. Note the gradual transition from substrates to products, under a generative model in which the latter are more probable. The free energy of this reaction can be seen to monotonically decrease, highlighting the consistency with the dynamics of Equation (7) despite the mean-field assumptions.

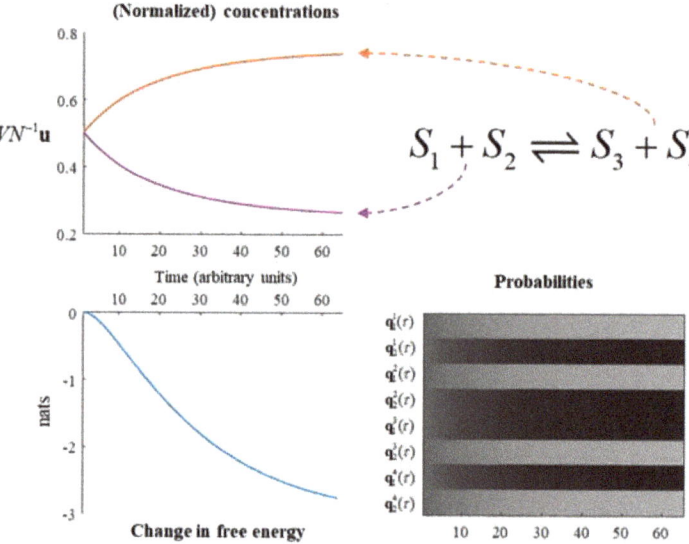

Figure 3. A chemical reaction. This figure illustrates the solution to the generative model outlined in Equation (17), under the dynamics given in Equation (20). The upper-left plot shows the rate of change of the substrates and products. The two substrates have equal concentrations to one another, as do the two products. Under this model, with $\alpha = \frac{1}{4}$, the substrates are converted into products until the substrates are at a quarter of their maximum concentration, with the remainder converted to the products. The same information is presented in probabilistic form in the lower right. Here, black indicates a probability of 1, white of 0, and intermediate shades represent intermediate probabilities. The plot of free energy over time shows that, despite the mean-field approximation and the constraints applied to the transition rate matrix, the reaction still evolves towards a free energy minimum—as in Figure 1. Note that, in the absence of an external input to this system, the free energy reduces to a Kullback–Leibler divergence between the current state and the steady state.

In chemical systems, the rate of change of some reactants can depend non-linearly on the concentration of those reactants. We can take a step towards this relationship as follows. If we then stipulate that two (or more) of the chemical species are the same, we can re-express this, with suitable modification of the constants, as:

$$2S_1 \rightleftharpoons S_3 + S_4$$

$$\left. \begin{array}{l} \mathbf{u}_1(\tau) \propto \mathbf{q}_1^1(\tau) + \mathbf{q}_1^2(\tau) \\ \mathbf{q}_1^1(0) = \mathbf{q}_1^2(0) \end{array} \right\} \Rightarrow \begin{bmatrix} \partial_\tau \mathbf{u}_1(\tau) \\ \partial_\tau \mathbf{u}_3(\tau) \\ \partial_\tau \mathbf{u}_4(\tau) \end{bmatrix} = \begin{bmatrix} 2\kappa_2 \mathbf{u}_3(\tau)\mathbf{u}_4(\tau) - 2\kappa_1 \mathbf{u}_1(\tau)^2 \\ \kappa_1 \mathbf{u}_1(\tau)^2 - \kappa_2 \mathbf{u}_3(\tau)\mathbf{u}_4(\tau) \\ \kappa_1 \mathbf{u}_1(\tau)^2 - \kappa_2 \mathbf{u}_3(\tau)\mathbf{u}_4(\tau) \end{bmatrix} \quad (20)$$

This brings an autocatalytic element to the reaction, allowing the substrate to catalyse its own conversion to the reaction products. Generalising the above, we can express the law of mass action [35–37] for the generic reaction in Equation (16) as:

$$\partial_\tau \mathbf{u}_i(\tau) = (\rho_i - \sigma_i)\left(\kappa_1 \prod_j \mathbf{u}_j(\tau)^{\sigma_j} - \kappa_2 \prod_j \mathbf{u}_j(\tau)^{\rho_j}\right). \tag{21}$$

This subsection started with from the mean-field master equation developed in Section 2 and illustrated how, under certain conditions, the law of mass action for chemical systems can be obtained. This application of a master equation to chemical dynamics should not be confused with the chemical master equation, detailed in Appendix A [38]. The key steps were (i) the specification of a generative model for which the marginal probabilities that each chemical species is present sum to one and (ii) the choice of right singular vector, orthogonal to the resulting joint distribution, for the transition rate matrix.

3.2. Reaction Networks

In the previous two subsections, all chemical species were assumed to participate in a single reaction. Here, we extend this, such that we can see how the message passing from Figure 3 appears in a network of chemical reactions. To do this, we need to be able to construct a generative model, as we did above, that accounts for multiple chemical reactions. Figure 4 illustrates an example of a generative model, and associated master equation, that accounts for a system of two (reversible) reactions. The associated reaction constants are given, as functions of the parameters of the generative model, in Table 1. As above, these are obtained by solving for the coefficients of Equation (14) when at steady state. This serves to illustrate two things. First, the methods outlined in the previous section are equally applicable to systems of multiple reactions. Second, when multiple reactions are in play, the generative model can be formulated such that chemical species that do not participate in the same reaction can be treated as being conditionally independent of one another. This induces the sparsity that makes inferential message passing possible. A generic expression of a reaction system obeying the law of mass action is as follows:

$$\begin{aligned}\partial_\tau \mathbf{u}_i(\tau) &= \sum_j \Omega_{ij} \mathbf{r}_j(\mathbf{u}(\tau)) \\ \mathbf{r}_j(\mathbf{u}(\tau)) &= \kappa_j \prod_i \mathbf{u}_i(\tau)^{\sigma_i}\end{aligned}. \tag{22}$$

The stoichiometry matrix Ω indicates the difference between ρ and σ for each chemical species for each reaction. The $\mathbf{r}$ vector function returns all the reaction rates (treating forwards and backwards reactions as separate reactions). Equation (21) is then a special case of Equation (22) when there are only two reactions. Equation (22) provides a clear depiction of message passing in which each element of $\mathbf{r}$ is a message, with the stoichiometry matrix determining where those messages are sent. Figure 4 demonstrates the relationship between this message passing and the graphical formulation of chemical reaction systems. Via this graphical notation, Equation (22) has many special cases throughout biology [37,39], some examples of which are outlined in Appendix B. However, for systems with many components, it can be very high-dimensional. The next subsection details one way in which the dimensionality of metabolic networks can be reduced, through an appeal to a separation of time scales.

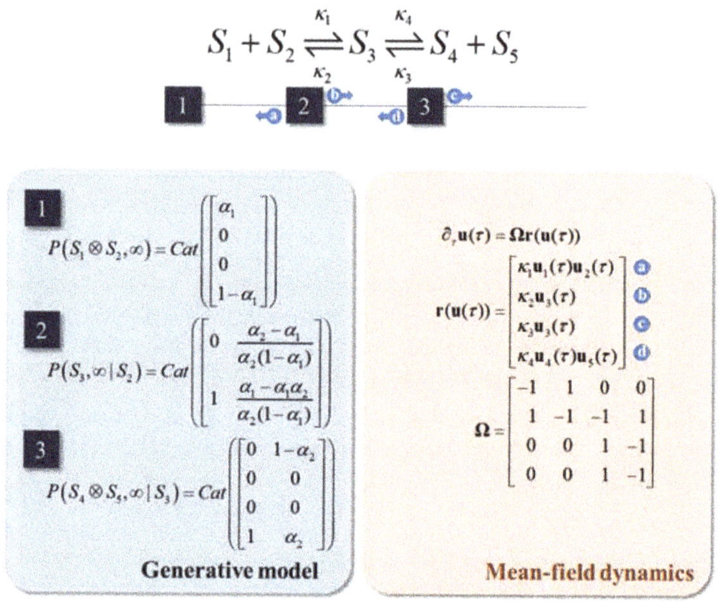

Figure 4. Reaction networks. This schematic illustrates the factor graph associated with a system comprising a pair of coupled reversible reactions (i.e., four reactions in total). The factors are specified in the blue panel. These are chosen to enforce conservation of mass, in the sense that the marginal of S_1 or of S_2 plus the marginal of S_3 plus the marginal of S_4 or of S_5 is one.

Table 1. Rate constants for the reaction network in Figure 4. This table specifies the κ parameters from Figure 4 as functions of the α parameters of the associated generative model and a free parameter z.

Rate Constant	Function of α
κ_1	$\lambda N^{-1} V z \alpha_1^{-2} \alpha_2^{-1}(\alpha_2 - \alpha_1)$
κ_2	λz
κ_3	$\lambda(1-z)$
κ_4	$\lambda N^{-1} V (1-z) \alpha_1^{-2} \alpha_2 (1-\alpha_2)^{-2}(\alpha_2 - \alpha_1)$

3.3. Enzymes

So far, everything that has been said could apply to any chemical reaction system. However, the introduction of enzymes brings us into the domain of the life sciences. Just as we can group elements on the same side of a reaction to account for autocatalytic dynamics, we can group elements on opposite sides of the reaction to account for catalytic activity. Enzymes are biological catalysts that combine with substrates to form an enzyme–substrate complex, modify the substrate and dissociate from the resulting product. As such, they appear on both sides of the overall reaction.

More formally, an enzymatic reaction has a stoichiometry matrix of the form:

$$\Omega = \begin{bmatrix} -1 & 1 & 0 & 0 \\ -1 & 1 & 1 & -1 \\ 1 & -1 & -1 & 1 \\ 0 & 0 & 1 & -1 \end{bmatrix}. \tag{23}$$

$$\Rightarrow S_S + S_E \rightleftharpoons S_C \rightleftharpoons S_P + S_E$$

The rows of Ω are the substrate, enzyme, enzyme–substrate complex, and product. These are shown in the reaction system using the subscripts S, E, C, and P, respectively. We can express a generative model for this reaction system as follows:

$$P(S_C \otimes S_E) = \text{Cat}\left(\begin{bmatrix} 0 \\ \alpha_1 \\ 1-\alpha_1 \\ 0 \end{bmatrix}\right)$$

$$P(S_S | S_C \otimes S_E) = \text{Cat}\left(\begin{bmatrix} 0 & \alpha_2 & 0 & \alpha_2 \\ 1 & 1-\alpha_2 & 1 & 1-\alpha_2 \end{bmatrix}\right). \quad (24)$$

$$P(S_P | S_C \otimes S_E) = \text{Cat}\left(\begin{bmatrix} 0 & 1-\alpha_2 & 0 & 1-\alpha_2 \\ 1 & \alpha_2 & 1 & \alpha_2 \end{bmatrix}\right)$$

The first term gives the proportion of enzyme we expect to be in complex form versus being free to engage with the substrate or product. The probability of being in both states simultaneously, and of being in neither of the two states, is zero. When the complex is present, the substrate and product are both absent. When the enzyme is present, the substrate is present with some probability, and the product is present with the complement of that probability. As before, a chemical reaction network can be constructed based upon the conditional independencies of the associated model, i.e., the independence of substrate and product conditioned upon the enzyme and complex, which satisfies the sparse message passing of Equation (23). The requisite rate constants (corrected for the mean-field assumption) are shown in Table 2.

Table 2. Rate constants for an enzymatic reaction. This table specifies the κ parameters from Equation (24) as a function of the α parameters of Equation (23) and a free parameter z.

Rate Constant	Function of α
κ_1	$\lambda N^{-1} V(z - \alpha_1 z + c)\alpha_1^{-2}\alpha_2^{-1}$
κ_2	λz
κ_3	$\lambda(1-z)$
κ_4	$\lambda N^{-1} V((1-z)(1-\alpha_1) - c)\alpha_1^{-2}(1-\alpha_2)^{-1}$

In constructing these messages, we relax the assumption that the steady state is at equilibrium. This means that detailed balance can be violated and involves using a non-zero β_1 from Equation (14) in some of the terms, such that there is constant production of, and removal of, certain chemical species from the system. Specifically, we will assume production of the substrate and removal of the product at equal rate (c). A consequence of this is that reactions generating products must be faster than reactions using up product in order for steady state to be maintained. The plots on the left of Figure 5 illustrate the resulting dynamics. Note the initial decrease in substrate and enzyme concentration as they combine to form the complex, followed by the slow rise in product concentration.

In metabolic reaction systems, there are many reactions catalysed by enzymes. In this setting, it is useful to be able to reduce the number of elements of the system to a manageable dimension through omitting the explicit representation of enzymes. A common approach to this is to use Michaelis–Menten kinetics [40]. This depends upon a separation of timescales. The two timescales in question are illustrated in Figure 5 through the rapid conversion of substrate to complex, and the slower generation of product. Combination of substrate and enzyme, and dissociation of complex to substrate and enzyme are both faster than dissociation of complex to product and enzyme. When this is true, a quasi-equilibrium approximation may be adopted. This means that the rates of the reactions involving the substrate are assumed to be much faster than those involving the product:

$$\partial_\tau \mathbf{u}_P = \mathbf{r}(\mathbf{u}) - c$$

$$\left.\begin{array}{l}\kappa_4 \mathbf{u}_P \mathbf{u}_E \ll \kappa_3 \mathbf{u}_C \\ \kappa_1 \mathbf{u}_S \mathbf{u}_E \gg \kappa_3 \mathbf{u}_C \\ \kappa_2 \mathbf{u}_C \gg \kappa_3 \mathbf{u}_C\end{array}\right\} \Rightarrow \mathbf{r}(\mathbf{u}) \approx v_{\max}\left(\frac{\mathbf{u}_S}{\kappa_m + \mathbf{u}_S}\right)$$

$$v_{\max} \triangleq \kappa_1 \kappa_3 (\mathbf{u}_E + \mathbf{u}_C)$$

$$\kappa_m \triangleq \frac{\kappa_2}{\kappa_1}$$

$$c \leq (1-z)(1-\alpha_1) \qquad (25)$$

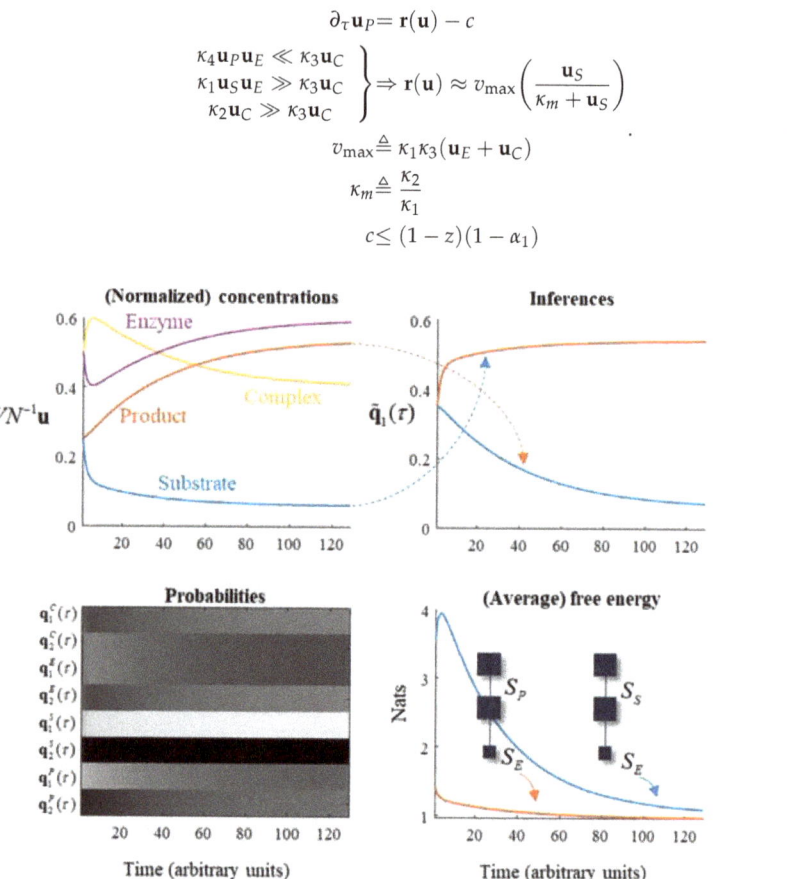

Figure 5. Enzymes, Markov blankets, and chemical inference. This figure illustrates several points. The plots on the left use the same formats as in Figure 3 to show the evolution of the reaction in terms of concentration and probability. The plots on the right exploit the Markov blanket structure implicit in an enzymatic reaction to show the evolution of the 'beliefs' implicitly encoded by the expected value of the substrate about the product, and vice versa. The upper-right plot shows these beliefs, defined as $\tilde{\mathbf{q}}_1^1 = \alpha_2 - \mathbf{q}_1^2$ and $\tilde{\mathbf{q}}_1^2 = \alpha_2 - \mathbf{q}_1^1$, which converge towards $\mathbf{q}_1^1$ and $\mathbf{q}_1^2$, respectively as the steady state is attained. The implicit generative models are shown in the free energy plot, with the enzyme playing the role of the data being predicted. The free energy of each decreases as the beliefs converge upon the posterior probabilities of substrate and product given enzyme.

Equation (25) specifies the quasi-equilibrium assumption [41], and the resulting Michaelis–Menten form for the reaction function $\mathbf{r}$. The final line follows from the condition that the rate constants be non-negative. The rate constants, in terms of the generative model, are given in Table 2. This lets us consider what the assumptions underneath the Michaelis–Menten equation mean in relation to the underlying generative model. First, the assumption that the reaction generating the product from the complex is much faster than the reverse reaction implies α_1 approaches its lower limit. When interpreted from the perspective of the generative model, this makes intuitive sense, as the implication is that given sufficient time, most of the enzyme will be in the non-complex form. Second, the assumption that the forwards and backwards reactions between substrate and complex are faster than the reaction generating the product implies the z parameter must be close to one.

Equation (25) simplifies a system comprising four chemical species into a single non-linear rate function that depends only upon the substrate. Practically, this means Michaelis–Menten kinetics can be used to omit explicit representation of enzymes from a reaction system. This lets us replace the reaction function (**r**) from Equation (21) with that from Equation (24), significantly reducing the dimensionality of the resulting system. This formulation is the starting point for methods for further dimensionality reduction of high-dimensional metabolic networks [42]. For instance, the extreme pathway method [43,44] defines extreme pathways as the set of **r** (normalized by v_{max} for the rate limiting reaction in the pathway) for which $\Omega \mathbf{r}$ returns a vector of zeros. By taking the singular value decomposition of the matrix of extreme pathway vectors, the left singular vectors can be used to describe 'eigenpathways.' By omitting eigenpathways with sufficiently small singular values, a simpler representation of the network may be obtained.

This subsection brought the concept of an enzyme into the chemical kinetics of the previous sections and demonstrated how an appeal to separable timescales results in a simpler, lower-dimensional, representation of an enzymatic system. The associated rate function that resulted from this emphasizes the emergence of nonlinear phenomena at slower scales of a multicomponent system.

3.4. Enzymatic Inference

The enzymatic system of the previous subsection is useful in unpacking an active inferential interpretation of chemical kinetics. The plots on the right of Figure 5 are key to this perspective. The upper-right plot illustrates a function of the substrate concentration that converges to the product concentration, and a function of the product concentration that converges to the substrate concentration. There is a sense in which we could interpret this as the substrate, on average, representing beliefs about the product and vice versa [15,25]. The plots of variational free energy (averaged under the enzyme and complex probabilities) decrease over time. The implication is that the models determining the evolution of the substrate and product, both of which predict the enzymatic state, become better explanations for these data (on average) over time.

Although the interactions between the substrate and enzyme are bidirectional, the influence of the enzyme on the product is unidirectional. This is a consequence of the steady state being non-equilibrium. This highlights that there are two ways of optimising free energy. The first is to do as the distributions encoded by the product, and to change beliefs to better explain the data at hand. The second is to do as the substrate does, through changing the data (i.e., enzyme concentration) such that the explanation fits. Note the initial increase in free energy for the model optimized by the product concentration, as the enzyme concentration changes. This is then suppressed, much like a prediction error in neurobiology [45–49], as the product updates its implicit beliefs.

While it might seem a bit strange to formulate the dynamics of one component of a system in relation to a functional of beliefs about other components, this move is central to the Markovian monism that underwrites active inference [50]. It is this that offers us a formal analogy with theoretical neurobiology, and the action-perception loops [51] found in the nervous system. The distinction between active (e.g., muscular) and sensory (e.g., retinal) limbs of these loops derives from the same non-equilibrium property, breaking the symmetry of message passing, such that beliefs can directly influence active but not sensory states. Whether something is active or sensory depends upon the perspective that we take, with enzymes being sensory from the perspective of beliefs encoded by the product, and active from the perspective of beliefs encoded by the substrate.

4. Metabolism

In this section, we briefly consider a (fictional) biochemical network that exploits the formulation above. A generative model for the network is illustrated in the upper left of Figure 6. The pink arrows supplement this model with the directional influences assumed at the lowest levels of the model. The lowest level of the model reflects the 'active' and 'sensory' interactions with another system that is not explicitly modelled here. All reactions are enzymatic, but with explicit treatment of the enzymes omitted via the Michaelis–Menten formulation. As such, the factors corresponding to the enzymes in the model are absorbed into the factors relating the concentrations of reactants. On finding the kinetics consistent with this steady state, the result is the reaction system shown in the upper right of Figure 6.

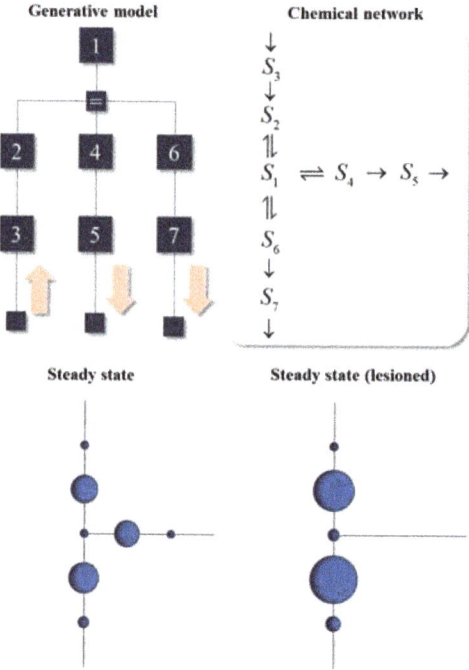

Figure 6. Metabolic networks and their pathologies. This figure shows the conditional dependencies in a generative model in the upper left, highlighting the directional influences at the lowest level of the model with pink arrows. These ensure S_3 is a sensory state, while S_5 and S_7 are active states. In the upper right is the chemical message passing that solves this model. The two plots in the lower part of the figure illustrate the relative probability of the marginal probabilities (or concentrations) of each chemical species. The spatial configuration matches that of the network in the upper right. The sizes of the circles indicate the relative concentrations once steady state has been attained. The plots on the left and right show the steady states before and after introduction of a lesion that disconnects the reaction from S_1 to S_4. Here, we see a redistribution of the probability mass, resulting in an alternative (possibly pathological) steady state.

The plots of the steady state shown in the lower part of Figure 6 use the same layout as the reaction network, but show the marginals (i.e., concentrations) of each species once it reaches steady state. The larger the circle, the greater the concentration. The initial conditions involve zero concentration for all species, so their concentrations can only increase when they receive messages from S_3, via the other reactants.

The lower-left plot shows successful convergence to the non-equilibrium steady state determined by the generative model. The structure of this steady state resembles the architectures found in metabolic networks in the sense that an external system supplies some chemical (S_3) which is converted through a series of reactions into other chemical species (S_5 and S_7) that participate in other reactions external to the system. The glycolysis pathway is one example, in which glucose is provided to the system to be converted to acetyl CoA (taken up by the citric acid cycle) or to lactate (taken up by the Cori cycle) [52].

The lower-right plot in Figure 6 shows the steady state obtained when a lesion is introduced into the message passing, through setting v_{max} to zero for the reaction converting S_1 to S_4. Recall that v_{max} is a function of the reaction constants which themselves are functions of the parameters of the generative model. For example, when α_1 approaches its upper limit, the enzyme spends little of its time in complex form, so cannot catalyse the reaction. This effectively induces a disconnection, precluding conversion of S_1 to S_4. The reason for inducing this lesion is to illustrate the diaschisis that results. A diaschisis is a concept from neurobiology [53–55]. It refers to the consequences of a localized lesion for distant parts of a network. Just as lesions to one neural system can have wide reaching functional consequences throughout the brain, the consequences of the localized lesion in Figure 6 can be seen throughout the reaction network. In addition to the loss of S_4 and S_5, there is a compensatory increase in S_2 and S_6. This ensures a steady state is attained, as the loss of output from S_5 is offset by increased output from S_7. However, it is not the same steady state as in the pre-lesioned network. A conclusion we can draw from this is that, as in neurobiology [56], a disconnection can be framed as a change to the parameters of a generative model representing the steady state. The distributed message passing that maintains steady state allows for the effects of the disconnection to propagate throughout the network.

One example (of many) of a disorder in which a new steady state is attained following an enzymatic disconnection is due to thiamine deficiency (a.k.a., Beriberi) [57]. Thiamine is a B vitamin that facilitates the action of several important enzymes, including pyruvate dehydrogenase, which converts pyruvate to acetyl CoA. An alternative fate for pyruvate is conversion to lactate [52]. If we were to associate S_3 with glucose, S_1 with pyruvate, S_6 with lactate, and S_4 with acetyl CoA, we could interpret the lesion in Figure 6 as resulting from thiamine deficiency. The resulting accumulation of lactate is consistent with the local increases in this toxic metabolite observed in neural tissue following thiamine depletion [58]. This may be one aspect of the pathophysiology of Wernicke's encephalopathy and Korsakov's psychosis [59]. These are forms of 'dry' beriberi with profound neurological and psychiatric consequences. While associating this with the lesion in Figure 6 is overly simplistic, it serves to illustrate the way in which the somewhat abstract formulations above could be applied to specific metabolic systems, their disconnections, and the resulting diaschisis.

5. Discussion

This paper has sought to apply the probabilistic dynamics that underwrite active inferential approaches to neurobiology to biochemical networks. This started from the expression of a categorical system in terms of a master equation and the interpretation of this equation in terms of flows on a free energy functional. As free energy is a functional of a generative model, this meant the dynamics acquired an interpretation as inference, in the sense of approximating a marginal likelihood. In what followed, the dimensionality of the representation afforded by the master equation was reduced, first through an appeal to a mean-field assumption. The interactions between different factors were simplified by noting that only those variables in the Markov blanket of a given state are necessary to find the appropriate steady-state distribution.

The sparse message passing that resulted from this—reminiscent of the approach used in variational message passing [7]—reduces to the law of mass action under certain assumptions. This lets us treat simple chemical reactions as if they were optimising a generative model. By introducing enzymatic reactions, and working with a non-equilibrium steady state, a further reduction in dimensionality is afforded by Michaelis–Menten kinetics. This emphasizes the emergence of increasingly nonlinear dynamics at higher spatiotemporal scales—something that has been observed in a range of network systems [60,61]. In addition, the combination of the Markov blanket inherent in an enzymatic reaction and the asymmetric message passing in a non-equilibrium system offered an opportunity to frame different parts of the system as optimising beliefs about other parts of the system. This minimisation of free energy through action and 'perception' is known as active inference in neuroscience.

Finally, a simple metabolic network was constructed that exploited the reduced expression of enzymatic dynamics, and which utilized the asymmetric message passing associated with active inference. Just as models of inference in the nervous system can be used to simulate pathology through disconnection [62–64], this metabolic network was lesioned to illustrate that disconnections, whether axonal or enzymatic, can result in a diaschisis, i.e., distributed changes in distant parts of the network. Crucially, the system still attains steady state following a lesion. It is just a different steady state. This offers a point of connection with approaches in computational neurology [65] and psychiatry [66,67], motivated by the complete class theorems [68,69], which treat pathology as optimally attaining a suboptimal steady state [70]. This perspective places the burden of explanation for pathological behaviour on the prior probabilities associated with the steady state (i.e., it asks 'what would I have to believe for that behaviour to appear optimal?'). The advantage of this approach is that it provides a common formal language (prior probabilities) in which a range of conditions—from psychosis to visual neglect—can be articulated. The example in Figure 6 suggests metabolic disorders may be amenable to the same treatment.

There are several directions in which the ideas presented in this paper could be pursued. Broadly, these include (i) generalising the dynamics beyond Michaelis–Menten kinetics to include more complex reaction functions, (ii) identifying the generative models of real reaction systems, and (iii) moving beyond metabolic systems to other forms of biological dynamics. Taking these in turn, the Michaelis–Menten formulation can be generalized for molecules (e.g., enzymes) with more than one binding site. This means that there is more than one enzyme–substrate complex state, and a set of reactions allowing transitions between these. One of the most prominent examples is the binding of oxygen to haemoglobin, a protein with four binding sites. The haemoglobin dissociation curve has a sigmoidal form [71], offering an alternative reaction function to the saturating Michaelis–Menten reaction function. More generally, the Hill equation [72] can be obtained using an analogous derivation to the Michaelis–Menten equation and has the latter as a special case.

Identifying generative models in biological chemical networks may be as simple as finding the steady state. However, the perspective offered in Section 3.4 adds an important twist to this. The generative model should express beliefs about something external to the network. To understand the problem a given network is solving, we need to be able to express a model of the inputs to that network. An active inference account of glycolysis would have to start from a generative model of the factors outside of the glycolytic pathway that explain glucose availability. Treating the constituents of the glycolysis pathway as expressing beliefs about the things causing glucose availability, we would hope to find the message passing among elements of the pathway emerge from minimising the free energy of their associated beliefs. Similar approaches have been adopted in neural systems, demonstrating that it is possible to identify implicit probabilistic beliefs about variables in a generative model in networks of in vitro neurons [73]. While outside the scope of this paper, many of these models call for caching of past observations. As highlighted by one of the reviewers, such models need to incorporate forgetting to ensure steady state and preclude convergence to a narrow distribution [74,75].

The above emphasizes what may be the most important practical implication of this paper for metabolic network analysis. Given the scale of such networks in biotic systems, and their interaction with chemical systems in the wider environment, most analyses are restricted to a small part of an open system. In most interesting cases, the kinetics within that system will change when those outside that system change. For instance, the behaviour of a glycolytic network will vary when the rate of lipolysis increases or decreases. This suggests that it should be possible to formulate and test hypotheses of a novel kind. In place of questions about alternative kinetics that could be in play, the inferential perspective lets us ask about the problem a biochemical system is solving, with reference to the probable states of external systems. Practically, this means we can borrow from the ('meta-Bayesian' [69]) methods developed in fields such as computational psychiatry—designed to ask questions about the problems the brain is solving—and formalize alternative functional hypotheses about the problem a metabolic network is solving.

There are many biological applications of categorical probabilistic dynamics—sometimes referred to as compartmental models. For instance, in epidemiology [76,77] the movement of people between susceptible, exposed, immune, and recovered compartments mimics the exchanges between different chemical species. Similar mean-field dynamics can be found in neurobiology [78], immunology [79,80], ecology [81], and pharmacokinetics [82]. In addition, they are common outside of biology, in fields such as economics [83] and climate science [84]. In principle, a similar treatment could be applied to such systems, interpreting the interactions between compartments as inferential message passing given a generative model.

6. Conclusions

This paper sought to illustrate some points of contact between active inference, a well-established framework in theoretical neurobiology, and the techniques used in modelling biochemical networks. Specifically, the focus was on the relationship between generative models, their associated inferential message passing, and the sparse network interactions in metabolic systems. Under certain assumptions, the master equation describing the evolution of a categorical probability distribution has the same form as the law of mass action, from which standard biochemical results may be derived. This enables construction of a biochemical network, whose rate constants are functions of an underlying generative model. The kinds of pathology affecting this network can be formulated in terms of aberrant prior beliefs, as in computational neurology and psychiatry, and manifest as disconnections whose consequences propagate throughout the network.

Funding: This research received no external funding.

Institutional Review Board Statement: Not applicable.

Informed Consent Statement: Not applicable.

Data Availability Statement: The Matlab code used to generate the figures in this paper is available at https://github.com/tejparr/Message-Passing-Metabolism accessed on 12 May 2021.

Acknowledgments: I am grateful to the editors for the invitation to submit to this Special Issue.

Conflicts of Interest: The author declares no conflict of interest.

Appendix A

This appendix highlights the point of connection between the formalism advanced here and the chemical master equation [38]. The chemical master equation deals with a joint probability distribution over the number of molecules of each species. This can be expressed in terms of a vector **p** whose elements are the probabilities of each possible configuration of N particles. Assuming a 'one-hot' vector variable x whose elements represent every possible configuration of the N particles among the available chemical species, a reaction k is formulated as a discrete jump of the form:

$$x(\tau + \Delta \tau) = \tilde{\xi}_k x(\tau). \tag{A1}$$

In Equation (A1), $\tilde{\xi}_k$ is a square matrix, with a single one in each column and zeros elsewhere. Expressing Equation (A1) in the form of a master equation, we have:

$$\begin{aligned}\partial_\tau \mathbf{p}(\tau) &= \mathbf{L}\mathbf{p}(\tau)\\ \mathbf{L}_{zx} &= \sum_{k\in K}\gamma_k(x),\ K=\{k:z=\xi_k x\}\\ \mathbf{L}_{xx} &= -\sum_k \gamma_k(x)\\ \Rightarrow \partial_\tau \mathbf{p}_x(\tau) &= \sum_k\left(\gamma_k(\xi_k^{-1}x)\mathbf{p}_{\xi_k^{-1}x}(\tau) - \gamma_k(x)\mathbf{p}_x(\tau)\right)\end{aligned} \quad (A2)$$

The first line here is the master equation from Equation (5). The definition of the transition rate matrix says that if there exists a reaction that leads to a move between two configurations, there is a nonzero transition rate, specific to that reaction. The transition rate along the diagonal is negative and includes the sum of all rates of transitions from this state. For transitions for which there is no associated reaction, the rate is zero. The final line is the resulting chemical master equation. A common alternative, but equivalent, expression of this is formulated such that x has elements representing each chemical species, where each element takes the value of the number of molecules of that species in the configuration represented by x.

An excellent example of the application of the chemical master equation, highly relevant to the treatment in this paper, is given in [85]. Focusing on monomolecular reaction systems, the authors detail the relationship between steady state (i.e., the implicit generative model) and the associated reaction kinetics. Their results highlight the way in which a steady state can be determined from the kinetics. This complements the approach pursued here, in which the kinetics, under certain assumptions, emerge from the steady state.

In practice, the chemical master equation is often approximated by a lower dimensional system [86], that is easier to solve, often through focusing on the marginals, taking limits and re-expressing as a Fokker–Planck equation. The key difference between the chemical master equation and the approach pursued in the main text is that the former treats the number of particles (and implicitly the concentrations) as stochastic variables. In contrast, the approach in the main text assumes the concentrations are simply scaled probabilities, which then evolve deterministically. When dealing in small numbers of molecules, the chemical master equation is considerably more accurate.

Appendix B

This appendix provides two examples of systems outside of biochemistry that can be subject to the same analysis. By formulating a reaction system based upon a model of the conditional dependencies between parts of a population experiencing an epidemic, we can formulate an SEIR model, of the sort used in epidemiology for communicable diseases. Similarly, we can formulate a model of predator-prey interactions, using the Lotka–Volterra equations, using the same formalism.

Starting with an SEIR model [77], the idea is to express the proportion of a population occupying the susceptible (S), exposed (E), infected (I), and recovered (R) compartments. Susceptible people become exposed on interaction with an infected individual, and then transition from exposed to infected as the incubation period expires. The infected population gradually transition to the recovered state where, from which they gradually become susceptible again. The associated reaction system is as follows:

$$\begin{matrix} S+I \to E+I \\ E \to I \\ I \to R \\ R \to S \end{matrix} \quad \Omega = \begin{bmatrix} -1 & 0 & 0 & 1 \\ 1 & -1 & 0 & 0 \\ 0 & 1 & -1 & 0 \\ 0 & 0 & 1 & -1 \end{bmatrix} \quad \mathbf{r}(\mathbf{u}) = \begin{bmatrix} \kappa_1 \mathbf{u}_S \mathbf{u}_I \\ \kappa_2 \mathbf{u}_E \\ \kappa_3 \mathbf{u}_I \\ \kappa_4 \mathbf{u}_R \end{bmatrix}. \quad (A3)$$

Equation (A3) expresses the system as if it were a chemical reaction, interpretable via the law of mass action in terms of the stoichiometry matrix and a reaction function. As before, these specify the message passing and the messages, respectively. The steady state to which the system tends is determined by the κ terms (and vice versa). This makes the difference between a transient epidemic that decays to (nearly) zero prevalence over time, or an endemic steady state with a persistently high infection level.

The SEIR system is relatively simple, in the sense that the stoichiometric matrix includes only zeros and ones. In contrast, the generalized Lotka–Volterra system [81] has a more complicated stoichiometry:

$$\begin{array}{l} P \to \rho_P P \\ P + H \to \rho_H H \\ H \to \\ H + C \to \rho_C C \\ C \to \end{array} \quad \Omega = \begin{bmatrix} \rho_P - 1 & -1 & 0 & 0 & 0 \\ 0 & \rho_H - 1 & -1 & -1 & 0 \\ 0 & 0 & 0 & \rho_C - 1 & -1 \end{bmatrix} \quad \mathbf{r}(\mathbf{u}) = \begin{bmatrix} \kappa_1 \mathbf{u}_P \\ \kappa_2 \mathbf{u}_P \mathbf{u}_H \\ \kappa_3 \mathbf{u}_H \\ \kappa_4 \mathbf{u}_H \mathbf{u}_C \\ \kappa_5 \mathbf{u}_C \end{bmatrix}. \quad (A4)$$

Equation (A4) deals with a system comprising a plant population (P), a herbivore population (H), and a carnivore population (C). As plants reproduce, they increase in number. However, they are kept in check by the herbivorous creatures, who increase their own population on encountering plants, while causing a decrease in the plant population. The herbivore population declines through carnivore-dependent and independent processes. The interaction between carnivores and herbivores mimics that between herbivores and plants. Again, this can be expressed, via the law of mass action, in terms of a series of messages ($\mathbf{r}$) and a scheme determining where those messages are sent (Ω).

Interestingly, both biological systems are not at equilibrium, in the sense that the individual reactions are not reversible. This preserves the active and sensory distinction found in neurobiology. The purpose of this appendix is to highlight the expression of these systems in terms of messages passed between nodes of a network. Given the relationship between these expressions and the steady state dynamics outlined in the main text, a possible direction for future research is the formulation of such systems in terms of the generative models their constituents are implicitly solving.

References

1. Ao, P. Global view of bionetwork dynamics: Adaptive landscape. *J. Genet. Genom.* **2009**, *36*, 63–73. [CrossRef]
2. Klein, B.; Holmér, L.; Smith, K.M.; Johnson, M.M.; Swain, A.; Stolp, L.; Teufel, A.I.; Kleppe, A.S. Resilience and evolvability of protein-protein interaction networks. *bioRxiv* **2020**. [CrossRef]
3. Barabási, A.-L.; Gulbahce, N.; Loscalzo, J. Network medicine: A network-based approach to human disease. *Nat. Rev. Genet.* **2011**, *12*, 56–68. [CrossRef] [PubMed]
4. Proulx, S.R.; Promislow, D.E.L.; Phillips, P.C. Network thinking in ecology and evolution. *Trends Ecol. Evol.* **2005**, *20*, 345–353. [CrossRef] [PubMed]
5. Bullmore, E.; Sporns, O. Complex brain networks: Graph theoretical analysis of structural and functional systems. *Nat. Rev. Neurosci.* **2009**, *10*, 186–198. [CrossRef] [PubMed]
6. Mardinoglu, A.; Nielsen, J. Systems medicine and metabolic modelling. *J. Intern. Med.* **2012**, *271*, 142–154. [CrossRef] [PubMed]
7. Winn, J.; Bishop, C.M. Variational message passing. *J. Mach. Learn. Res.* **2005**, *6*, 661–694.
8. Dauwels, J. On variational message passing on factor graphs. In Proceedings of the 2007 IEEE International Symposium on Information Theory, ISIT 2007, Nice, France, 24–29 June 2007; pp. 2546–2550.
9. Loeliger, H.A.; Dauwels, J.; Hu, J.; Korl, S.; Ping, L.; Kschischang, F.R. The Factor Graph Approach to Model-Based Signal Processing. *Proc. IEEE* **2007**, *95*, 1295–1322. [CrossRef]
10. Friston, K.; FitzGerald, T.; Rigoli, F.; Schwartenbeck, P.; Pezzulo, G. Active Inference: A Process Theory. *Neural Comput.* **2017**, *29*, 1–49. [CrossRef]
11. Friston, K.; Mattout, J.; Trujillo-Barreto, N.; Ashburner, J.; Penny, W. Variational free energy and the Laplace approximation. *NeuroImage* **2007**, *34*, 220–234. [CrossRef] [PubMed]
12. Friston, K. A free energy principle for a particular physics. *arXiv* **2019**, arXiv:1906.10184.
13. Parr, T.; Markovic, D.; Kiebel, S.J.; Friston, K.J. Neuronal message passing using Mean-field, Bethe, and Marginal approximations. *Sci. Rep.* **2019**, *9*, 1889. [CrossRef] [PubMed]
14. George, D.; Hawkins, J. Towards a Mathematical Theory of Cortical Micro-circuits. *PLoS Comput. Biol.* **2009**, *5*, e1000532. [CrossRef] [PubMed]
15. Friston, K. Life as we know it. *J. R. Soc. Interface* **2013**, *10*. [CrossRef] [PubMed]
16. Baltieri, M.; Buckley, C.L.; Bruineberg, J. Predictions in the eye of the beholder: An active inference account of Watt governors. In Proceedings of the 2020 Conference on Artificial Life, Online, 13–18 July 2020; pp. 121–129.

17. Risken, H. Fokker-Planck Equation. In *The Fokker-Planck Equation: Methods of Solution and Applications*; Springer: Berlin/Heidelberg, Germany, 1996; pp. 63–95. [CrossRef]
18. Koudahl, M.T.; de Vries, B. A Worked Example of Fokker-Planck-Based Active Inference. In Proceedings of the International Workshop on Active Inference, Ghent, Belgium, 14 September 2020; pp. 28–34.
19. Penny, W.D.; Stephan, K.E.; Daunizeau, J.; Rosa, M.J.; Friston, K.J.; Schofield, T.M.; Leff, A.P. Comparing Families of Dynamic Causal Models. *PLoS Comput. Biol.* **2010**, *6*, e1000709. [CrossRef]
20. Hohwy, J. The Self-Evidencing Brain. *Noûs* **2016**, *50*, 259–285. [CrossRef]
21. Beal, M.J. *Variational Algorithms for Approximate Bayesian Inference*; University of London: London, UK, 2003.
22. Seifert, U. Stochastic thermodynamics, fluctuation theorems and molecular machines. *Rep. Prog. Phys.* **2012**, *75*, 126001. [CrossRef] [PubMed]
23. Buckley, C.L.; Kim, C.S.; McGregor, S.; Seth, A.K. The free energy principle for action and perception: A mathematical review. *J. Math. Psychol.* **2017**, *81*, 55–79. [CrossRef]
24. Friston, K. The free-energy principle: A unified brain theory? *Nat. Rev. Neurosci.* **2010**, *11*, 127–138. [CrossRef] [PubMed]
25. Parr, T.; Costa, L.D.; Friston, K. Markov blankets, information geometry and stochastic thermodynamics. *Philos. Trans. R. Soc. A Math. Phys. Eng. Sci.* **2020**, *378*, 20190159. [CrossRef]
26. Toral, R.; Colet, P. *Stochastic Numerical Methods: An Introduction for Students and Scientists*; John Wiley & Sons: Hoboken, NJ, USA, 2014.
27. Van KAMPEN, N.G. The Expansion of the Master Equation. *Adv. Chem. Phys.* **1976**, 245–309. [CrossRef]
28. Ao, P.; Chen, T.-Q.; Shi, J.-H. Dynamical Decomposition of Markov Processes without Detailed Balance. *Chin. Phys. Lett.* **2013**, *30*, 070201. [CrossRef]
29. Friston, K.; Ao, P. Free energy, value, and attractors. *Comput Math. Methods Med.* **2012**, *2012*, 937860. [CrossRef] [PubMed]
30. Weiss, P. L'hypothèse du champ moléculaire et la propriété ferromagnétique. *J. Phys. Appl.* **1907**, *6*, 661–690. [CrossRef]
31. Parr, T.; Sajid, N.; Friston, K.J. Modules or Mean-Fields? *Entropy* **2020**, *22*, 552. [CrossRef]
32. Kadanoff, L.P. More is the same; phase transitions and mean field theories. *J. Stat. Phys.* **2009**, *137*, 777–797. [CrossRef]
33. Pearl, J. *Probabilistic Reasoning in Intelligent Systems: Networks of Plausible Inference*; Morgan Kaufmann: San Fransisco, CA, USA, 1988.
34. Forney, G.D. Codes on graphs: Normal realizations. *IEEE Trans. Inf. Theory* **2001**, *47*, 520–548. [CrossRef]
35. van't Hoff, J.H. Die Grenzebene, ein Beitrag zur Kenntniss der Esterbildung. *Ber. Der Dtsch. Chem. Ges.* **1877**, *10*, 669–678. [CrossRef]
36. Guldberg, C.M.; Waage, P. Ueber die chemische Affinität. § 1. Einleitung. *J. Für Prakt. Chem.* **1879**, *19*, 69–114. [CrossRef]
37. McLean, F.C. Application of The Law of Chemical Equilibrium (Law of Mass Action) to Biological Problems. *Physiol. Rev.* **1938**, *18*, 495–523. [CrossRef]
38. Gillespie, D.T. A rigorous derivation of the chemical master equation. *Phys. A Stat. Mech. Its Appl.* **1992**, *188*, 404–425. [CrossRef]
39. Horn, F.; Jackson, R. General mass action kinetics. *Arch. Ration. Mech. Anal.* **1972**, *47*, 81–116. [CrossRef]
40. Michaelis, L.; Menten, M.L. Die kinetik der invertinwirkung. *Biochem. Z* **1913**, *49*, 352.
41. Briggs, G.E.; Haldane, J.B. A Note on the Kinetics of Enzyme Action. *Biochem. J.* **1925**, *19*, 338–339. [CrossRef]
42. Gorban, A.N. Model reduction in chemical dynamics: Slow invariant manifolds, singular perturbations, thermodynamic estimates, and analysis of reaction graph. *Curr. Opin. Chem. Eng.* **2018**, *21*, 48–59. [CrossRef]
43. Schilling, C.H.; Letscher, D.; Palsson, B.Ø. Theory for the Systemic Definition of Metabolic Pathways and their use in Interpreting Metabolic Function from a Pathway-Oriented Perspective. *J. Theor. Biol.* **2000**, *203*, 229–248. [CrossRef]
44. Price, N.D.; Reed, J.L.; Papin, J.A.; Wiback, S.J.; Palsson, B.O. Network-based analysis of metabolic regulation in the human red blood cell. *J. Theor. Biol.* **2003**, *225*, 185–194. [CrossRef]
45. Bastos, A.M.; Usrey, W.M.; Adams, R.A.; Mangun, G.R.; Fries, P.; Friston, K.J. Canonical microcircuits for predictive coding. *Neuron* **2012**, *76*, 695–711. [CrossRef] [PubMed]
46. Friston, K.; Kiebel, S. Predictive coding under the free-energy principle. *Philos. Trans. R. Soc. B Biol. Sci.* **2009**, *364*, 1211. [CrossRef]
47. Rao, R.P.; Ballard, D.H. Predictive coding in the visual cortex: A functional interpretation of some extra-classical receptive-field effects. *Nat. Neurosci.* **1999**, *2*, 79–87. [CrossRef]
48. Shipp, S. Neural Elements for Predictive Coding. *Front. Psychol.* **2016**, *7*, 1792. [CrossRef] [PubMed]
49. Srinivasan, M.V.; Laughlin, S.B.; Dubs, A.; Horridge, G.A. Predictive coding: A fresh view of inhibition in the retina. *Proc. R. Soc. Lond. Ser. B. Biol. Sci.* **1982**, *216*, 427–459. [CrossRef]
50. Friston, K.J.; Wiese, W.; Hobson, J.A. Sentience and the Origins of Consciousness: From Cartesian Duality to Markovian Monism. *Entropy* **2020**, *22*, 516. [CrossRef]
51. Fuster, J.M. Upper processing stages of the perception–action cycle. *Trends Cogn. Sci.* **2004**, *8*, 143–145. [CrossRef] [PubMed]
52. Lunt, S.Y.; Vander Heiden, M.G. Aerobic Glycolysis: Meeting the Metabolic Requirements of Cell Proliferation. *Annu. Rev. Cell Dev. Biol.* **2011**, *27*, 441–464. [CrossRef] [PubMed]
53. von Monakow, C. *Die Lokalisation im Grosshirn und der Abbau der Funktion Durch Kortikale Herde*; JF Bergmann: Wiesbaden, Germany, 1914.
54. Carrera, E.; Tononi, G. Diaschisis: Past, present, future. *Brain* **2014**, *137*, 2408–2422. [CrossRef]

55. Price, C.; Warburton, E.; Moore, C.; Frackowiak, R.; Friston, K. Dynamic diaschisis: Anatomically remote and context-sensitive human brain lesions. *J. Cogn. Neurosci.* **2001**, *13*, 419–429. [CrossRef] [PubMed]
56. Parr, T.; Friston, K.J. The Computational Anatomy of Visual Neglect. *Cereb. Cortex* **2017**, 1–14. [CrossRef] [PubMed]
57. Dhir, S.; Tarasenko, M.; Napoli, E.; Giulivi, C. Neurological, Psychiatric, and Biochemical Aspects of Thiamine Deficiency in Children and Adults. *Front. Psychiatry* **2019**, *10*. [CrossRef]
58. Hazell, A.S.; Todd, K.G.; Butterworth, R.F. Mechanisms of Neuronal Cell Death in Wernicke's Encephalopathy. *Metab. Brain Dis.* **1998**, *13*, 97–122. [CrossRef]
59. Zubaran, C.; Fernandes, J.G.; Rodnight, R. Wernicke-Korsakoff syndrome. *Postgrad. Med. J.* **1997**, *73*, 27. [CrossRef]
60. Friston, K.J.; Fagerholm, E.D.; Zarghami, T.S.; Parr, T.; Hipólito, I.; Magrou, L.; Razi, A. Parcels and particles: Markov blankets in the brain. *Netw. Neurosci.* **2020**, 1–76. [CrossRef]
61. Klein, B.; Hoel, E. The Emergence of Informative Higher Scales in Complex Networks. *Complexity* **2020**, *2020*, 8932526. [CrossRef]
62. Parr, T.; Friston, K.J. Disconnection and Diaschisis: Active Inference in Neuropsychology. In *The Philosophy and Science of Predictive Processing*; Bloomsbury Publishing: London, UK, 2020; p. 171.
63. Geschwind, N. Disconnexion syndromes in animals and man. II. *Brain J. Neurol.* **1965**, *88*, 585. [CrossRef]
64. Geschwind, N. Disconnexion syndromes in animals and man. I. *Brain* **1965**, *88*, 237. [CrossRef]
65. Parr, T.; Limanowski, J.; Rawji, V.; Friston, K. The computational neurology of movement under active inference. *Brain* **2021**. [CrossRef] [PubMed]
66. Friston, K.J.; Stephan, K.E.; Montague, R.; Dolan, R.J. Computational psychiatry: The brain as a phantastic organ. *Lancet Psychiatry* **2014**, *1*, 148–158. [CrossRef]
67. Adams, R.; Stephan, K.; Brown, H.; Frith, C.; Friston, K. The Computational Anatomy of Psychosis. *Front. Psychiatry* **2013**, *4*. [CrossRef] [PubMed]
68. Wald, A. An Essentially Complete Class of Admissible Decision Functions. *Ann. Math. Stat.* **1947**, 549–555. [CrossRef]
69. Daunizeau, J.; den Ouden, H.E.M.; Pessiglione, M.; Kiebel, S.J.; Stephan, K.E.; Friston, K.J. Observing the observer (I): Meta-bayesian models of learning and decision-making. *PLoS ONE* **2010**, *5*, e15554. [CrossRef] [PubMed]
70. Schwartenbeck, P.; FitzGerald, T.H.B.; Mathys, C.; Dolan, R.; Wurst, F.; Kronbichler, M.; Friston, K. Optimal inference with suboptimal models: Addiction and active Bayesian inference. *Med. Hypotheses* **2015**, *84*, 109–117. [CrossRef] [PubMed]
71. Hill, A.V. The Combinations of Haemoglobin with Oxygen and with Carbon Monoxide. I. *Biochem. J.* **1913**, *7*, 471–480. [CrossRef] [PubMed]
72. Stefan, M.I.; Le Novère, N. Cooperative binding. *PLoS Comput. Biol.* **2013**, *9*, e1003106. [CrossRef] [PubMed]
73. Isomura, T.; Friston, K. In vitro neural networks minimise variational free energy. *Sci. Rep.* **2018**, *8*, 16926. [CrossRef]
74. Gunji, Y.-P.; Shinohara, S.; Haruna, T.; Basios, V. Inverse Bayesian inference as a key of consciousness featuring a macroscopic quantum logical structure. *Biosystems* **2017**, *152*, 44–65. [CrossRef] [PubMed]
75. Gunji, Y.-P.; Murakami, H.; Tomaru, T.; Basios, V. Inverse Bayesian inference in swarming behaviour of soldier crabs. *Philos. Trans. R. Soc. A Math. Phys. Eng. Sci.* **2018**, *376*, 20170370. [CrossRef]
76. Friston, K.; Parr, T.; Zeidman, P.; Razi, A.; Flandin, G.; Daunizeau, J.; Hulme, O.; Billig, A.; Litvak, V.; Moran, R.; et al. Dynamic causal modelling of COVID-19 [version 2; peer review: 2 approved]. *Wellcome Open Res.* **2020**, *5*. [CrossRef]
77. Kermack, W.O.; McKendrick, A.G.; Walker, G.T. A contribution to the mathematical theory of epidemics. *Proc. R. Soc. Lond. Ser. AContain. Pap. A Math. Phys. Character* **1927**, *115*, 700–721. [CrossRef]
78. Lindsay, A.E.; Lindsay, K.A.; Rosenberg, J.R. Increased Computational Accuracy in Multi-Compartmental Cable Models by a Novel Approach for Precise Point Process Localization. *J. Comput. Neurosci.* **2005**, *19*, 21–38. [CrossRef] [PubMed]
79. De Boer, R.J.; Perelson, A.S.; Kevrekidis, I.G. Immune network behavior—I. From stationary states to limit cycle oscillations. *Bull. Math. Biol.* **1993**, *55*, 745–780. [CrossRef]
80. Parr, T.; Bhat, A.; Zeidman, P.; Goel, A.; Billig, A.J.; Moran, R.; Friston, K.J. Dynamic causal modelling of immune heterogeneity. *arXiv* **2020**, arXiv:2009.08411.
81. Volterra, V. Variations and Fluctuations of the Number of Individuals in Animal Species living together. *ICES J. Mar. Sci.* **1928**, *3*, 3–51. [CrossRef]
82. Gerlowski, L.E.; Jain, R.K. Physiologically Based Pharmacokinetic Modeling: Principles and Applications. *J. Pharm. Sci.* **1983**, *72*, 1103–1127. [CrossRef] [PubMed]
83. Tramontana, F. Economics as a compartmental system: A simple macroeconomic example. *Int. Rev. Econ.* **2010**, *57*, 347–360. [CrossRef]
84. Sarmiento, J.L.; Toggweiler, J.R. A new model for the role of the oceans in determining atmospheric P CO_2. *Nature* **1984**, *308*, 621–624. [CrossRef]
85. Jahnke, T.; Huisinga, W. Solving the chemical master equation for monomolecular reaction systems analytically. *J. Math. Biol.* **2007**, *54*, 1–26. [CrossRef] [PubMed]
86. Jahnke, T. On reduced models for the chemical master equation. *Multiscale Model. Simul.* **2011**, *9*, 1646–1676. [CrossRef]

Article

The Radically Embodied Conscious Cybernetic Bayesian Brain: From Free Energy to Free Will and Back Again

Adam Safron [1,2,3]

1. Center for Psychedelic and Consciousness Research, Johns Hopkins University School of Medicine, Baltimore, MD 21218, USA; asafron@gmail.com
2. Kinsey Institute, Indiana University, Bloomington, IN 47405, USA
3. Cognitive Science Program, Indiana University, Bloomington, IN 47405, USA

Citation: Safron, A. The Radically Embodied Conscious Cybernetic Bayesian Brain: From Free Energy to Free Will and Back Again. *Entropy* **2021**, *23*, 783. https://doi.org/10.3390/e23060783

Academic Editor: Karl Friston

Received: 18 January 2021
Accepted: 27 May 2021
Published: 20 June 2021

Publisher's Note: MDPI stays neutral with regard to jurisdictional claims in published maps and institutional affiliations.

Copyright: © 2021 by the author. Licensee MDPI, Basel, Switzerland. This article is an open access article distributed under the terms and conditions of the Creative Commons Attribution (CC BY) license (https://creativecommons.org/licenses/by/4.0/).

Abstract: Drawing from both enactivist and cognitivist perspectives on mind, I propose that explaining teleological phenomena may require reappraising both "Cartesian theaters" and mental homunculi in terms of embodied self-models (ESMs), understood as body maps with agentic properties, functioning as predictive-memory systems and cybernetic controllers. Quasi-homuncular ESMs are suggested to constitute a major organizing principle for neural architectures due to their initial and ongoing significance for solutions to inference problems in cognitive (and affective) development. Embodied experiences provide foundational lessons in learning curriculums in which agents explore increasingly challenging problem spaces, so answering an unresolved question in Bayesian cognitive science: what are biologically plausible mechanisms for equipping learners with sufficiently powerful inductive biases to adequately constrain inference spaces? Drawing on models from neurophysiology, psychology, and developmental robotics, I describe how embodiment provides fundamental sources of empirical priors (as reliably learnable posterior expectations). If ESMs play this kind of foundational role in cognitive development, then bidirectional linkages will be found between all sensory modalities and frontal-parietal control hierarchies, so infusing all senses with somatic-motor properties, thereby structuring all perception by relevant affordances, so solving frame problems for embodied agents. Drawing upon the Free Energy Principle and Active Inference framework, I describe a particular mechanism for intentional action selection via consciously imagined (and explicitly represented) goal realization, where contrasts between desired and present states influence ongoing policy selection via predictive coding mechanisms and backward-chained imaginings (as self-realizing predictions). This embodied developmental legacy suggests a mechanism by which imaginings can be intentionally shaped by (internalized) partially-expressed motor acts, so providing means of agentic control for attention, working memory, imagination, and behavior. I further describe the nature(s) of mental causation and self-control, and also provide an account of readiness potentials in Libet paradigms wherein conscious intentions shape causal streams leading to enaction. Finally, I provide neurophenomenological handlings of prototypical qualia including pleasure, pain, and desire in terms of self-annihilating free energy gradients via quasi-synesthetic interoceptive active inference. In brief, this manuscript is intended to illustrate how radically embodied minds may create foundations for intelligence (as capacity for learning and inference), consciousness (as somatically-grounded self-world modeling), and will (as deployment of predictive models for enacting valued goals).

Keywords: Free Energy Principle; active inference; Bayesian brain; generative models; cybernetics; embodiment; enactivism; cognitivism; representations; consciousness; free will; mental causation; cognitive-affective development; emotions; feelings; readiness potentials; intentionality; agency; intelligence

1. Introduction

1.1. Descartes' Errors and Insights

> "Any time a theory builder proposes to call any event, state, structure, etc., in a system (say the brain of an organism) a signal or message or command or otherwise endows it with content, he takes out a loan of intelligence. He implicitly posits along with his signals, messages, or commands, something that can serve a signal reader, message-understander, or commander, else his 'signals' will be for naught, will decay unreceived, uncomprehended. This loan must be repaid eventually finding and analyzing away these readers or comprehenders; for, failing this, the theory will have among its elements unanalyzed man-analogues endowed with enough intelligence to read the signals, etc., and thus the theory will postpone answering the major question: what makes for intelligence?"
>
> —Daniel Dennett [1]

From the traditional perspective of cognitive science, minds are understood as analyzable on multiple levels [2], where functional (or computational) properties can be considered separately from their specific algorithmic realizations, which can further be considered separately from particular implementational details. This multilevel approach allows progress to be made on studying mental functions without requiring understanding of underlying neurobiological processes, so allowing cognitive science to proceed without being held back by our limited understanding of nervous systems. Alternatively, combining different levels of analysis can provide constraints over plausible hypotheses, so affording inferential synergy.

Another perspective is provided by "4-E" cognition [3–5], in which minds are conceptualized as inherently embodied, embedded, extended, and enactive. From this point of view, understanding cognition requires considering how intelligent systems depend on bodily control processes. 4-E cognitive science further emphasizes how embedding within particular environments both enables and constrains functioning, where functional properties of mind extend into a world/niche that is modified/constructed via value-driven actions. More radical versions of this embodied-enactivist perspective tend to reject computational framings from traditional cognitive science, eschewing explicit models and representations in favor of dynamic environmental couplings. More traditional "cognitivists", in contrast, tend to dismiss embodied cognition as a research program whose promise is limited by rejecting computational principles connecting brains and minds. From this point of view, embodied cognitive science is sometimes dismissed as a collection of interesting mind-body correlations, but which may be conceptually shallow in lacking precise operationalization.

While these perspectives often seem irreconcilable, there is near-universal agreement that cognitive science needs to divorce itself from the last vestiges of Cartesian thinking [6–12]. The only point of disagreement seems to be which aspects of Cartesian thinking are most egregiously mistaken. The charges are as follows:

1. The mind-body problem: Separating bodies and minds as distinct orders of being.
2. The theater fallacy: Describing perception in terms of the re-presentation of sensations to inner experiencers.
3. The homunculus fallacy: Failing to realize the inadequacy of inner experiencers as explanations, since these would require further experiencers to explain their experiences, resulting in infinite regress.

Many argue that the primary goal of cognitive science should be explaining away this naïve folk psychology in terms of non-mental computational and mechanistic processes [13,14]. Enactivists further (and differently) argue that cognitive science will only be thoroughly cleansed of its Cartesian origins once we eliminate concepts such as representation from our explanatory frameworks [3]. Yet the overwhelming consensus is clear: the mind sciences must rid themselves of the legacy of Descartes' errors. The ghost must be exorcised from the machine.

Below I suggest this consensus may be mistaken along important dimensions, and propose ways in which each of these supposed errors point to invaluable perspectives. In brief:

1. Minds are thoroughly embodied, embedded, enacted, and extended, but there are functionally important aspects of mind (e.g., integrative processes supporting consciousness) that do not extend into bodies, nor even throughout the entire brain.
2. The brain not only infers mental spaces, but it populates these spaces with representations of sensations and actions, so providing bases for causal reasoning and planning via mental simulations.
3. Not only are experiences re-presented to inner experiencers, but these experiencers take the form of embodied person-models with degrees of agency, and even more, these quasi-homunculi form necessary scaffolding for nearly all aspects of mind.

In what follows, I intend to justify these claims and show how attention, imagination, and goal-oriented behavior may be explained using a Bayesian computational framework for understanding action, perception, and consciousness. My ultimate goal is illustrating how understanding the nature(s) of embodiment may allow for bridges between computational and enactivist perspectives on minds, so affording a grounding for unification in cognitive science.

1.2. Radically Embodied Minds

"Now what are space and time? Are they actual entities? Are they only determinations or also relations of things, but still such as would belong to them even if they were not intuited? Or are they such that they belong only to the form of intuition, and therefore to the subjective constitution of our mind, without which these predicates could not be ascribed to any things at all?... Concepts without intuitions are empty, intuitions without concepts are blind ... By synthesis, in its most general sense, I understand the act of putting different representations together, and of grasping what is manifold in them in one knowledge ... The mind could never think its identity in the manifoldness of its representations ... if it did not have before its eyes the identity of its act, whereby it subordinates all ... to a transcendental unity ... This thoroughgoing synthetic unity of perceptions is the form of experience; it is nothing less than the synthetic unity of appearances in accordance with concepts."

—Immanuel Kant [15]

"We shall never get beyond the representation, i.e. the phenomenon. We shall therefore remain at the outside of things; we shall never be able to penetrate into their inner nature, and investigate what they are in themselves... So far I agree with Kant. But now, as the counterpoise to this truth, I have stressed that other truth that we are not merely the knowing subject, but that we ourselves are also among those realities or entities we require to know, that we ourselves are the thing-in-itself. Consequently, a way from within stands open to us as to that real inner nature of things to which we cannot penetrate from without. It is, so to speak, a subterranean passage, a secret alliance, which, as if by treachery, places us all at once in the fortress that could not be taken by attack from without."

—Arthur Schopenhauer [16]

Natural selection may have necessarily relied on general-purpose learning mechanisms for designing organisms capable of adaptively navigating (and constructing) their environments [17]. With respect to the importance of domain-general processes, Mountcastle [18] suggested a common algorithm for hierarchical pattern abstraction upon discovering the canonical layered-columnar organization of all neocortical tissue. Empirical evidence increasingly supports this suggestion, with hierarchical "predictive coding" (or predictive processing more generally) providing a unifying account of cortical functioning [19,20]. This dependence upon broadly applicable mechanisms may have been a matter of necessity due to the limits of genetic specification. While complex structures can be 'encoded' by genomes, particular phenotypes are realized in an algorithmic fashion, similar to how simple equations can generate highly complex fractal patterns [21,22]. For example, kidneys are complex, but no single nephron is special a priori. Similarly, brains have complex microstructure and macrostructure, but with few exceptions [23,24], no single neuronal connection is special a priori; rather, most neural complexity arises through experience-dependent self-organization. Further, much of the functional significance of specific connections in complex neural networks may be inherently difficult to predict due to the sensitivity of (chaotic) self-organizing systems to initial conditions [25,26]. Predicting functional significances may be even more limited to the degree that 'representational' properties of networks are shaped by information that will only emerge through unique developmental experiences.

In these ways, while some predictable features of brains may be subject to extensive genetic canalization [27–29], evolution may have been unable to produce cognitive adaptations relying on pre-specified complex representations. Yet, empirically, infants seem to possess impressively rich knowledge of objects and processes [30,31]—though developmental studies usually occur at several months post-birth, and even newborns have prenatal learning experiences [32]. Even largely empiricist statistical learning models from "Bayesian cognitive science" acknowledge the need for inborn inductive biases to facilitate inference and learning [33–35]. However, if there are substantial limits to genetic specification, how is this prior knowledge introduced?

I suggest the problems of under-constrained inference spaces are solved by remembering that brains evolved and develop as control systems for bodies, the regulation of which continues to be the primary task and central context of minds throughout life [36,37]. Bodies represent near-ideal initial systems for learning and inference, with this prototypical object and causal system providing bases for further modeling. Several factors contribute to the power of embodied learning [38,39]:

1. Constant availability for observation, even prenatally.
2. Multimodal sensory integration allowing for ambiguity reduction in one modality based on information within other modalities (i.e., cross-modal priors).
3. Within-body interactions (e.g., thumb sucking; hand–hand interaction; skeletal force transfer).
4. Action-driven perception (e.g., efference copies and corollary discharges as prior expectations; hypothesis testing via motion and interaction).
5. Affective salience (e.g., body states influencing value signals, so directing attentional and meta-plasticity factors).

Support for cross-modal synergy may be found in studies of adults learning motor sequences where performance is enhanced by combining multiple modalities [40–42]. Other insights regarding the nature of embodied learning derive from studies of developmental robotics and infant development [39,43], wherein morphological constraints and affordances function as implicit inductive biases for accelerated learning. For example, the limited range of motion of shoulder joints may increase tendencies for situating objects (beginning with hands themselves) in locations where they can be more readily explored with other sensor and effector systems [38].

By this account, complex minds necessarily require initial experiences of learning to control bodies, with increasing levels of complexity achieved—over the course of evolution and development—by expanding hierarchically-higher cortical areas [44]. This somatic developmental legacy is consistent with accounts in which abstract symbolic thought is grounded in mental simulation [45,46] and metaphorical extension from embodied experiences [47,48]. Below I will further characterize these embodied foundations for minds, suggesting that associative linkages to sensors and effectors generate body maps at multiple levels of abstraction, ranging from 1st-person semi-transparent interfaces [49] to 3rd-person body schemas capable of acting as self-reflexive intentional controllers (i.e., teleological agents).

1.3. The Cybernetic Bayesian Brain

> "Each movement we make by which we alter the appearance of objects should be thought of as an experiment designed to test whether we have understood correctly the invariant relations of the phenomena before us, that is, their existence in definite spatial relations."
>
> —Hermann Ludwig Ferdinand von Helmholtz [50]

[Note: While the following section might be technically challenging, the key takeaway is that all cortex may operate according to a common algorithm of *"free energy"* minimization via *hierarchical predictive processing (HPP) (cf. predictive coding)*, in which prior expectations generate *top-down predictions* of likely observations, and where discrepancies between predictions and observations ascend to hierarchically higher levels as *prediction errors*. Biasing the degree to which prediction errors are likely to be passed upwards is referred to as *precision weighting*, which is understood as constituting attentional selection for Bayesian inference via hierarchical predictive processing.]

As perceptual illusions demonstrate [51,52], information arriving at the senses is inherently ambiguous, in that similar inputs could result from an unbounded number of world states (e.g., is an object small and close, or large and distant?). The *Bayesian brain hypothesis* states that perception can be understood as a kind of probabilistic inference, given sensory observations and prior expectations from past experience [53]. These inferences are hypothesized to be "Bayesian" in constituting a weighted combination of priors and likelihood mappings between observations and their hidden (or latent) causes from world states. Along these lines, the *Free Energy Principle and Active Inference (FEP-AI)* framework offers a promising integrative perspective for describing both perception and action in terms of probabilistic inference and *prediction error minimization* [54–56]. FEP-AI suggests that hierarchically-organized nervous systems entail hierarchical generative models, wherein perception (as inference) is constituted by probabilistic estimates (or predictions) of the likely causes of sensory observations.

The FEP-AI framework is grounded in fundamental biophysical considerations [57,58], as well as principles of *cybernetics: the analysis of complex adaptive systems in terms of self-regulation/governance with varying forms of feedback* [59–61]. Persisting systems must regulate both internal and external states to avoid entropic accumulation, which the "Good regulator theorem" suggests requires some kind of (predictive) modeling in order to ensure adaptive selection [36]. Prediction error—also referred to as *"free energy"*, or *"surprisal"*—can be minimized either by updating the implicit model of system-internal dynamics (i.e., perceptual inference), or by modifying external dynamics to make sensory-input more closely match predictions (hence, active inference). In this way, perception and action are both means of maximizing model-evidence (by minimizing prediction error) for the implicit prediction of system-preserving states, a process referred to as "self-evidencing" [62]. Intriguingly (and perhaps strangely) [63,64], the general logic of this kind of analysis appears consistent with pre-theoretic philosophical intuitions in which persisting systems are viewed as possessing a kind of 'will-to-exist' [65,66], even if this apparent goal-directedness is actually illusory (i.e., teleonomy, rather than actual teleology) [13]. While deflationary accounts of teleological phenomena emphasize continuity with teleonomical processes [14], the purpose of this manuscript is to single out and explain not just the origins of goal-directedness, but to make inroads into understanding uniquely human-like intentionality.

HPP provides a parsimonious account of how this Bayesian world-modeling may be realized on algorithmic and implementational levels of analysis [19]. In HPP (Figure 1), top-down (empirical) priors are passed downwards as predictions based on posterior expectations (i.e., beliefs revised after making observations), which suppress bottom-up prediction errors from being transmitted up cortical hierarchies. In this encoding scheme, all observations take the form of prediction errors, indicating sensory inputs at the lowest hierarchical levels, sensory expectations at somewhat higher levels, and beliefs of a more folk psychological variety at even higher levels. [In these models, posterior expectations—or more generally beliefs—are formally equivalent to empirical priors at intermediate levels in the model; I will use (empirical) priors and posteriors interchangeably.] By only passing prediction errors up cortical hierarchies, predictive coding automatically prioritizes novel 'news-worthy' information in the process of updating beliefs and subsequent predictions. This recurrent message-passing is suggested to occur simultaneously in every part of cortex, with hierarchical dynamics reflecting hierarchical world structure [67,68], including events unfolding over multiple (hierarchically-nested) temporal scales [69–71]. In this way, HPP generates a dynamic mapping between brain and world, mediated by (hierarchically-organized) cycles of action-influenced perception. HPP further provides a mechanistic process model for enaction in FEP-AI by providing means of altering world states to better fit predictions via active inference [72]. This means that all neuronal dynamics and ensuing action can be regarded as complying with the same imperative: namely, to minimize prediction error (i.e., free energy, or "surprisal").

Predictive coding and neural oscillatory bands

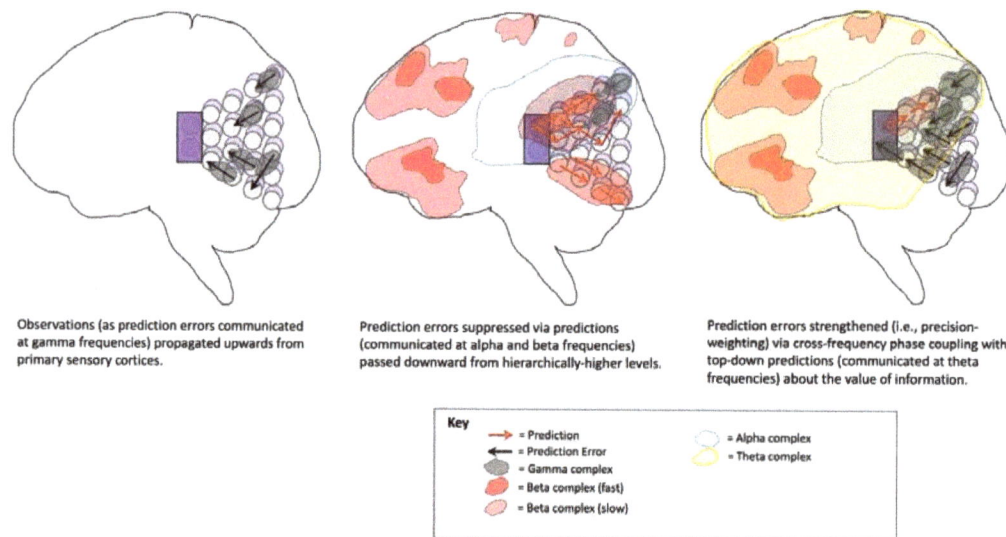

Figure 1. A schematic of hierarchical predictive processing in the brain. Left panel: Observations from primary sensory modalities (black arrows) indicate messages passed hierarchically upwards via superficial pyramidal neurons, communicated via small synchronous complexes (i.e., neuronal ensembles) at gamma frequencies. Middle panel: Predictions from hierarchically deeper areas of the brain (red arrows) suppress ascending observations, communicated via synchronous complexes of varying sizes at alpha and beta frequencies; bottom-up observations (as prediction errors) are only passed upwards when they fail to be anticipated by top-down predictions. Right panel: Attentional selection via strengthening of prediction errors by expectations regarding value of information, communicated via cross-frequency phase coupling with large synchronous complexes at theta frequencies. For all panels, darker arrows indicate degree of precision weighting associated with entailed (implicit) probabilistic beliefs, so determining relative contributions to Bayesian inference/updating. Please see previous work for more details on these hypothesized biocomputational principles [73,74].

According to HPP, brains function as both cybernetic controllers and memory systems [59–61], with experience-dependent expectations providing bases for control, which in turn create new memories and predictions. This cybernetic perspective has been further extended to interoceptive inference [61,75] in terms of homeostatic maintenance via predictive regulation (i.e., allostasis). In this account of emotional experience, affective states arise from active inferential control of interoceptive and autonomic states under different levels of uncertainty [75,76].

Reliable inference must account for degrees of certainty associated with various beliefs, which in HPP is described as "precision" (i.e., inverse variance) of probability distributions [77]. In HPP, ascending signals update descending posterior expectations proportional to relative precisions of (empirical) prior predictions and sensory-grounded observations. More precise prediction errors have greater influences in updating higher-level beliefs, which can be thought of as selecting more reliable sources of 'news'—as opposed to more unreliable, or 'fake' news. Algorithmically, certainty-based biasing of prediction errors realizes Bayesian inference as a precision-weighted sum of probabilities, so providing a functional basis for attentional selection. Mechanistically (and potentially phenomenologically), this attentional selection involves modulation of excitation for particular neuronal populations, so making entailed precision-weighted prediction errors more or less likely to percolate into deeper portions of cortical hierarchies where this information may shape larger-scale (potentially conscious) dynamics [73,74].

Precision weighting can have profound effects on relative influences of descending predictions and ascending prediction errors. If bottom-up signals are given too much precision, then excessive sensory prediction errors may access deeper portions of cortical hierarchies, which could potentially result in the kinds of overly intense sensory reactions often observed with autism [78–80]. Alternatively, if bottom-up signals are given too little precision, then prediction errors may not result in belief updating, which if excessive, could result in false-positive inferences, potentially including the kinds of delusions and hallucinations observed with schizophrenia [81–83].

Between the basic idea of perception as inference and its cybernetic extensions to active inference, the Bayesian brain is thoroughly embodied. This discussion goes further in suggesting that action-oriented body maps form the core of Bayesian brains, structuring inferential flows in ways that not only enhance control, but also allow minds to solve inferential problems that have hitherto been assumed to require extensive innate knowledge. As described above, bodies provide brains with learning opportunities in which hypothesis spaces are fruitfully constrained, and so rendered tractable. In light of the adaptive significance of embodied learning, selective pressures are likely to shape bodies in ways that brains readily infer and learn, so shaping further histories of selection. I further suggest this more easily acquirable knowledge allows learners to handle increasingly challenging problems (or lessons [84]) along zones of proximal development [85].

Neurodevelopmentally, this model can be considered broadly Piagetian [86], albeit without intellectual commitments with respect to particular developmental stages. This point of view is consistent with perspectives in which body-centric self-models are required for successful structure learning in the process of developing reasonably accurate and useful predictive models [75,87,88]. This proposal is also consistent with previous descriptions of active inference [89], but suggesting a particular—and I suggest, necessary—means by which generative models come to reflect world structure. That is, we may acquire many foundational (empirical) priors from learning about bodies as more tractable causal (and controllable) systems. Without this toehold/grip with respect to inferential bootstrapping, it may be the case that neither Bayesian cognitive science nor Bayesian brains could explain how biological learners handle under-constrained inference spaces.

The notion of embodiment as a source of foundational beliefs is increasingly recognized in FEP-AI. Allen and Tsakiris [90] have compellingly proposed a "body as first prior" model in which interoceptive inference provides a source of highly precise priors (or predictions), so allowing overall active inferential belief dynamics to be dominated by organismic, allostatic needs. In their account, interoception supplies fundamental priors in yet another sense in playing central roles with respect to establishing models of body ownership and (minimal) selfhood, both of which constitute necessary preconditions for learning about other aspects of the world. The specific nature(s) of these embodied priors has been further explored in terms of their shaping by developmentally early socioemotional coupling, including with respect to perinatal and prenatal interactions with caregivers upon which infants depend for life [87,91,92]. Below, I explore some of these ideas, as well as additional (complementary) ways in which embodiment may form necessary foundations in growing minds, the extent of which may be difficult to overstate.

2. From Action to Attention and Back Again

While some of the content in these next sections may be challenging, the key messages from these sections are as follows:

1. Much of conscious goal-oriented behavior may largely be realized via iterative comparisons between sensed and imagined states, with predictive processing mechanisms automatically generating sensibly prioritized sub-goals based on prediction errors from these contrasting operations.
2. Partially-expressed motor predictions—initially overtly expressed, and later internalized—may provide a basis for all intentionally-directed attention, working memory, and imagination.
3. These imaginings may provide a basis for conscious control of overt patterns of enaction, including the pursuit of complex goals.

2.1. Actions from Imaginings

The goal of this manuscript is to illustrate the radically embodied foundations of agency, ranging from basic motor control to complex planning. Towards this end, I propose a model in which all conscious goal-directed behavior is realized with hierarchical predictive coding and iterated comparisons among perceptions of sensed and imagined (i.e., counterfactual) states [93]. Let us consider someone writing a manuscript at a computer and discovering that they want tea, while also inferring that their cup is empty. These experiences would likely include mental imagery or memories of drinking tea, accompanied by feelings of thirst. However, such counterfactual beliefs (or predictions) would then be contradicted by sensory evidence if tea is not presently being consumed. The contrast between the counterfactual tea drinking and the observation of an empty cup would then be likely to prime similar situations in the past (e.g., unresolved thirst or hunger). Those situations will also be likely to be accompanied by relevant affordances [94–96] (e.g., tea-making/acquiring actions) associated with minimizing those varieties of discrepancies between preferred and present-estimated states. That is, memories and analogous imaginings are likely be dominated by actions whose relevance is determined based on past similar situations [59,97].

These counterfactual imaginings will be likely to be centered on goal-specific discrepancies, such as the fact that one may be sitting in front of a computer, rather than acquiring the desired tea (Table 1; Figure 2). In this case, the most likely set of affordances to be retrieved from memory would involve actions such as ambulating to the kitchen, where the sink, stove, and tea kettle are located. However, our thirsty agent may find themselves confronted with yet another set of discrepancies, such as the fact that sitting is not walking to the kitchen. In this case, the next likely set of memory-affordances to be retrieved could be those involving getting up, and perhaps shifting weight and pressing one's feet into the ground. At various points, these counterfactual plans may become sufficiently close to the present state that they become actionable, and so contribute to ongoing action selection.

Table 1. Example of goal-oriented behavior via iterated comparisons between imagined (dark grey) and estimated (light grey) states.

Examples of Imaginative Policy Selection			
Counterfactual Predictions	**Observations**	**Prediction-Errors and Associated Memories**	**Types of Value**
... Drinking tea	Not drinking tea	Body states associated with drinking	Pragmatic
Finding tea in cup	Not seeing tea	Surprise and reorienting	Epistemic
Making tea	Sitting at desk	Location and object affordances	Pragmatic
Going to kitchen	Sitting at desk	Location and locomotion	Pragmatic
Effort of standing	Standing	Motion and accompanying visceral sensations	Pragmatic
Drinking tea	Not drinking tea (but closer)	Body states associated with drinking	Pragmatic
Making tea	Locomoting to kitchen	Location and object affordances	Pragmatic
Holding tea bags	Standing in kitchen	Location, position, and object affordances	Pragmatic
Finding tea bags	Scanning kitchen	Surprise and re-orienting	Epistemic
Drinking tea	Not drinking tea (but closer)	Body states associated with drinking	Pragmatic
Steeping tea	Pouring water	Location, position, and object affordances	Pragmatic ...
... Drinking tea	Holding hot cup	Body position	Pragmatic
Burning mouth	Holding hot cup	Body states associated body damage	Pragmatic
Sipping slowly	Not burning mouth	Body states associated with drinking	Pragmatic

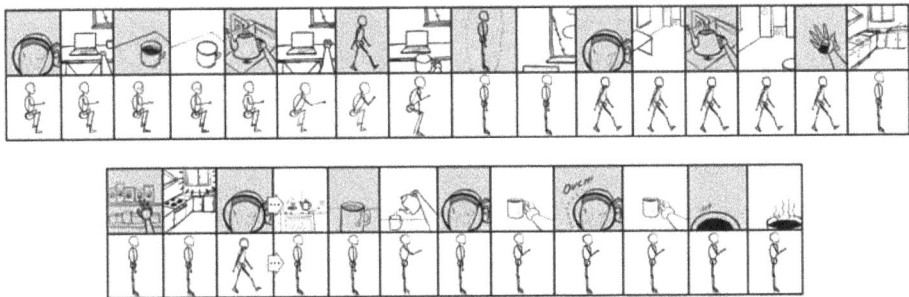

Figure 2. Imaginings and perceptions associated with policy selection via backward chaining from goal states. Top panels of each row illustrate the counterfactual predictions (grey) and observations (white) listed in Table 1. Bottom panels of each row depict associated body positions. Note: This example lacks substantial metacognitive and reflexive processing, with only a few panels depicting the agent imagining itself from an external viewpoint. To the extent that consciousness actually models the actions associated with making tea (as opposed to mind-wandering), a more immediate and non-reflective mode of cognition might be expected for this kind of relatively simple behavior. However, for more complex goals, we might expect more elaborate imaginings involving objectified self-representations with varying levels of detail and abstraction.

Mechanistically speaking, this actionability of counterfactual imaginings may be realized when neuronal ensembles associated with goal representations have relatively high degrees of overlap with those associated with proximate sensorimotor contingencies. If critical thresholds for motoric action selection are surpassed under such conditions of convergent excitation between present-estimated and desired states, then neural activity from imagined goals may become capable of functionally coupling with—or directionally entraining (i.e., "enslaving") [98]—an organism's effector systems. These imagined scenarios will also be continuously altered based on changing sensory evidence with unfolding behavior. For example, the location of the tea kettle may come into view en route to the kitchen, along with memories related to filling and emptying the kettle, so adjusting expectations with respect to whether the kettle needs to be brought to the sink to obtain water.

In FEP-AI [55], the sequences of actions (i.e., policies) we infer ourselves enacting are dominated by our prior preferences and expected consequences of actions. Crucially for adaptive behavior, this imperative to minimize prediction error (i.e., free energy) can also be applied to expected prediction error (i.e., expected free energy), wherein we select policies (potentially implicitly) anticipated to bring about preferred outcomes (e.g., having a cup of tea) in the future. This expected free energy (i.e., cumulative, precision-weighted prediction error) can be further decomposed based on relevance to either pragmatic or epistemic value, where pragmatic affordance is defined in terms of prior preferences (i.e., drinking tea) and epistemic affordance entails opportunities for reducing uncertainty (e.g., locating teabags) [99].

To the extent that actions are highly rehearsed, minimal conscious visualization may be required for goal attainment [43,100]. If tea is central to the lifeworld of our agent [101,102], then the entire sequence could end up proceeding with only very brief flashes of subjective awareness [103]. It is also notable that little awareness will likely accompany the coordinated activity of specific muscles, for which effortless mastery will be attained early in development. To the extent that goal-attainment involves novel circumstances—e.g., learning how to prepare loose-leaf tea for the first time—consciousness may play more of a central role in shaping behavior.

In this model of imaginative planning, activation of goal-related representations produces prediction errors wherever there are discrepancies between anticipated goal states and inferred present states. That is, goal-related representations act as predictions, and discrepancies with estimated present states result in prediction errors within particular sub-representations related to goal-attainment, generated at multiple hierarchical levels. When goal-discrepancy prediction errors are passed up the cortical hierarchy, they may access more richly connected networks, allowing for (potentially conscious) global availability of information [104], and so become more effective at driving subsequent neuronal activity. Given sufficient experience, goal-related representations with greater activity at the next moment will likely correspond to neuronal ensembles that most reliably succeeded (and so were reinforced) in minimizing those particular kinds of discrepancies in the past (i.e., relevant affordances).

By this account, comparisons between representations of goal states and present states generate greater activity for goal-related representations with more prediction error, often corresponding to the largest obstacles to goal attainment. These sources of maximal prediction error from iterative contrasting may naturally suggest prioritization for selecting appropriate sub-goals for overall goal-realization [105]. Sequential comparisons between representations of sub-goals and estimated present states will likely activate relevant sub-representations for additional obstacles, the overcoming of which becomes the next goal state. This comparison process proceeds iteratively, with repeated discrete updating [106] of imagined goals and estimated present states, so shaping neural dynamics (and entailed streams of experience) in accordance with predicted value realization.

With experience and learning—including via imagined experiences [107]—this iterative selection process is likely to become increasingly efficient. Considering that superordinate and subordinate action sequences are themselves associatively linked, they will provide mutual constraints as parallel comparisons continuously minimize overall prediction errors on multiple levels of action hierarchies. Thus, similar cognitive processes may be involved in selecting higher-level strategies for (potentially abstract) goal attainment, as well as the conscious adjustment of lower-level sequences retrieved from memory for intentional motor control. In terms of active inference, skillful motoric engagement is largely achieved through the ability of predicted actions to provide a source of "equilibrium points" [108], realized as neural systems dynamically self-organize via predictive processing mechanisms [109]. The model presented here describes a particular (potentially conscious) source of such high-level predictions as drivers of behavior. [Notably, the existence of separate dopamine value signals in the ventral tegmental area and substantia nigra pars compacta [110]—along with differing temporal dynamics and credit assignment challenges—suggest complexities requiring additional neurocomputational details in order to adequately describe (hierarchical) neuronal activity selection.] The imagination-focused account above describes the operation of intentional control processes to the (limited) degree they are capable of influencing behavior. Often this intentional influence may 'merely' take the role of biasing competition and cooperation among unconscious habitual and reflexive patterns.

By this account, to have a goal is to predict its realization, where initial predictions generate further causal paths as means of bridging gaps between imagination and reality. This kind of connection between imagination and action has precedents in ideomotor theory [111–113], which has also been explored in active inferential terms with respect to attentional biasing (i.e., precision weighting) [114]. Below I expand on this work in proposing that all voluntary (and much involuntary) attention may be realized by partially-expressed motor predictions as mental actions, so providing an agentic source for precision weighting in governing inferential dynamics as a kind of covert motoric skill. [Please note that I do not intend to suggest that most attention is consciously directed. Rather, much (and perhaps most) top-down precision weighting might be automatically generated by interoceptive salience maps, implemented by insular and cingulate cortical hierarchies [115].

2.2. Attention from Actions

"A good way to begin to consider the overall behavior of the cerebral cortex is to imagine that the front of the brain is 'looking at' the sensory systems, most of which are at the back of the brain. This division of labor does not lead to an infinite regress . . . The hypothesis of the homunculus is very much out of fashion these days, but this is, after all, how everyone thinks of themselves. It would be surprising if this overwhelming illusion did not reflect in some way the general organization of the brain."

—Francis Crick and Christoff Koch [6]

In this radically embodied account of attentional control, partially expressed motor predictions realize all intentional directing of perception, including with respect to attention, working memory, imagination, and action. This control is achieved by efferent copies from action-related neuronal ensembles to associated perception-related neural populations, with functional linkages established via past learning [116,117]. Developmentally—and evolutionarily [118]—actions initially take the form of externally expressed behavior; with respect to overt attention, effector systems orient sensors relative to the environment and so change patterns of sensation. However, via either incomplete or inhibited expression, these actions will also be expressed covertly in imagination as mental simulations with varying degrees of detail and awareness. When these partially-expressed motor predictions for overt attending are activated, connections to associated perceptual components can then be used as bases for covert attending. With experience, adaptive control over overt and covert expression will be learned, so allowing context-sensitive shifting between perception, imagination, and action. Further degrees of control over perception and action can be enabled by intentionally directing attention to contents of working memory (Figure 3), including with respect to the imagination of counterfactual scenarios required for causal reasoning and planning [119].

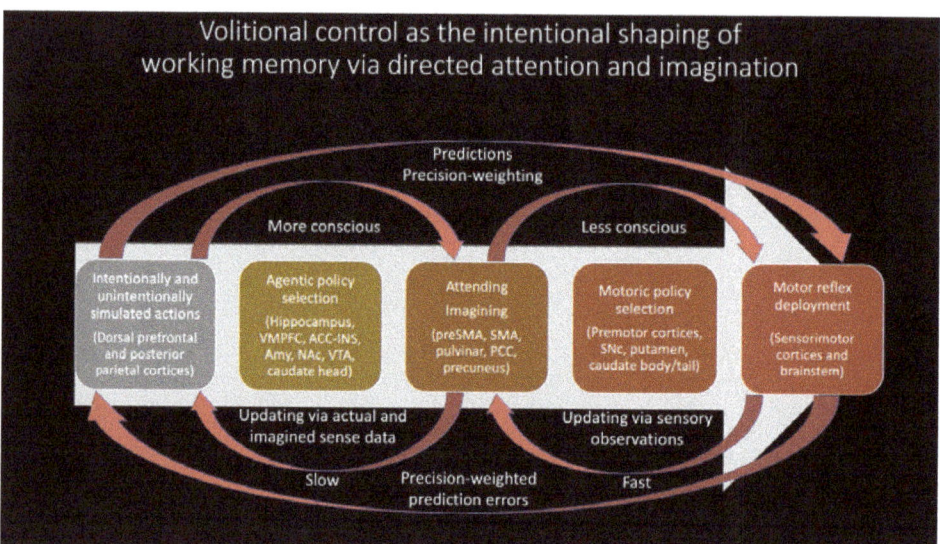

Figure 3. Imaginative policy selection via a multilevel active inferential control hierarchy and associated neural systems. Going from left to right, predictions are passed downwards as (empirical) prior expectations, and are updated into posterior expectations (and subsequent priors) by sensory observations, which are then passed upwards as prediction errors. Upper-level control processes (left action-perception cycle) involve more slowly-evolving attracting states, corresponding to more coarse-grained, higher-level abstract modeling of organismic-scale causes, which may be associated with conscious intentionality. Lower-level control processes (right action-perception cycle) involve more quickly-evolving attracting states, allowing for rapid adjustment of action-perception cycles and fine-grained environmental coupling. While multiple factors may point to the significance of a two-tier hierarchy, this distinction ought not be overstated, as integrating (potentially conscious) processes may potentially attend to (or couple with) dynamics from either level. VMPFC = ventromedial prefrontal cortex, ACC-INS = anterior cingulate cortex and insula, Amy = amygdala, NAc = nucleus accumbens, VTA = ventral tegmental area, SMA = supplementary motor area, PCC = posterior cingulate cortex, SNc = substantia nigra pars compacta.

This model represents a generalization of Vygotsky's [120] hypothesis regarding the development of thinking through the internalization of speech. By this account, first we learn how to speak, then we learn how to prepare to speak without overt expression, and then by learning how to internally speak to ourselves—imagining what we would have heard if speech were externally expressed—we acquire capacities for symbolic thought. Similarly, through the internalization of initially overt actions [121], all voluntary (and much involuntary) cognition may develop as a control hierarchy grounded in controllable effector systems. Indeed, I propose skeletal muscle is the sole foundation for all voluntary control due to its unique ability to generate gross actions with real-time low-latency feedback.

To summarize, ontogenetically (and phylogenetically), information acquisition is initially biased via overt action-perception. However, learners eventually acquire the ability to perform actions covertly, and thereby utilize the associated perceptual components of particular simulated actions as bases for covert processing (including counterfactual imaginings). In all cases, actions have their origins in control hierarchies over sensorimotor cortices—and associated striatal loops—whose dynamics are grounded in manipulating skeletal muscles, along with associated sensations. In this way, partially-expressed motor predictions can bias attention and working memory spatially (e.g., simulated saccades), temporally (e.g., simulated rhythmic actions), or even based on semantic or object feature information (e.g., simulated speech) (Table 2).

Table 2. Kinds of attentional biasing via partially-expressed motor predictions.

Kinds of Attention	Relevant Actions	
Spatial biasing	(a)	Foveation
	(b)	Head or trunk turning/orienting
	(c)	Pointing
	(d)	Other directional gestures
	(e)	Locomotion
Feature and object focusing	(a)	Speech or sound production (i.e., phonological loops)
	(b)	Actions related to particular morphological, locational, emotional, or affordance characteristics (i.e., physically interacting-with or constructing)
	(c)	Patterns of motion typically associated with particular objects
	(d)	Physical sketching
	(e)	Physical interaction with or locomotion through some (potentially synesthetic) memory-palace-like mapping
Following temporal patterns	(a)	Rhythmic speech or sound production
	(b)	Rhythmic motions of gross musculature
	(c)	Rhythmic motions of sensory apparatuses (e.g. foveations, auricular constrictions, etc.)
Duration-based attending	(a)	Extended production and tracking of accumulation of simulated rhythms (i.e., inner clocks)
	(b)	Enacting events/processes with temporal extent without being clearly rhythmic
	(c)	Mapping time onto a spatial reference frame (i.e., spatialization of time)

2.3. Imaginings from Attention

This account is consistent with premotor [122] and biased competition [123] theories of attention. However, I further suggest partially-expressed motor predictions are the only means by which content is voluntarily generated in working memory (Figure 3), whether based on attending to perceptual traces of recent sensations, or generating counterfactual perceptual experiences decoupled from actual sensory stimulation (i.e., imagination). While this proposal may seem excessively radical in the extent to which embodiment is emphasized, convergent support can be found in substantial evidence implicating the "formation of internal motor traces" in working memory [124]. Further evidence may be obtained in attentional selection being enhanced when neuronal oscillations from frontal eye fields entrain sensory cortices [125], as well as from visual attention and working memory heavily depending on frontal-parietal networks [126,127] (which are here interpreted as upper levels of action-perception hierarchies). With respect to embodied sources of top-down attention, striatum and midbrain value signals (e.g., dopamine) likely play key roles [128], both influencing moment-to-moment pattern selection, and also allowing future planning to be influenced by histories of reinforcement and punishment. To the extent that learning effectively aligns these patterns with agentic goals, mental content—and the resultant influences on action selection—can be understood as involving intentionality.

Imagined goals may be generated and contrasted with estimated states (whether imagined or observed) on timescales of approximately 200–300 msec [129–132], potentially implemented by activation/stabilization of neocortical ensembles via cross-frequency phase coupling with hippocampal theta rhythms (Figure 4) [133,134]. The iterative generation of new (posterior) goal-relevant imaginings—may take significantly longer, potentially depending in complex ways in which processes are contrasted. If this process requires stabilization of novel combinations of cortical ensembles by the hippocampal complex, then this may help to explain why medial temporal lobe damage is associated with impaired counterfactual processing [135,136], which here forms the basis of intentional action selection via iterative contrasting and predictive processing. A prediction of these models is that hippocampal damage may be associated with disrupted goal-pursuit in dementia—above and beyond the problem of task-forgetting—for which additional anecdotal evidence can be found with the case of the neurological patient "HM" [137]. The central role of the hippocampus for orchestrating goal-oriented behavior is further suggested by its involvement in "vicarious trial-and-error" behavior [138], as well as by the centrality of theta rhythms for intentional control [126,131,139,140]. Additional supporting evidence can be found in hippocampally-mediated orchestration of counterfactual inferences in other domains, ranging from predictive information over likely trajectories for locomoting rodents [141,142] to the simulation of alternative perspectives by imagining humans [143,144].

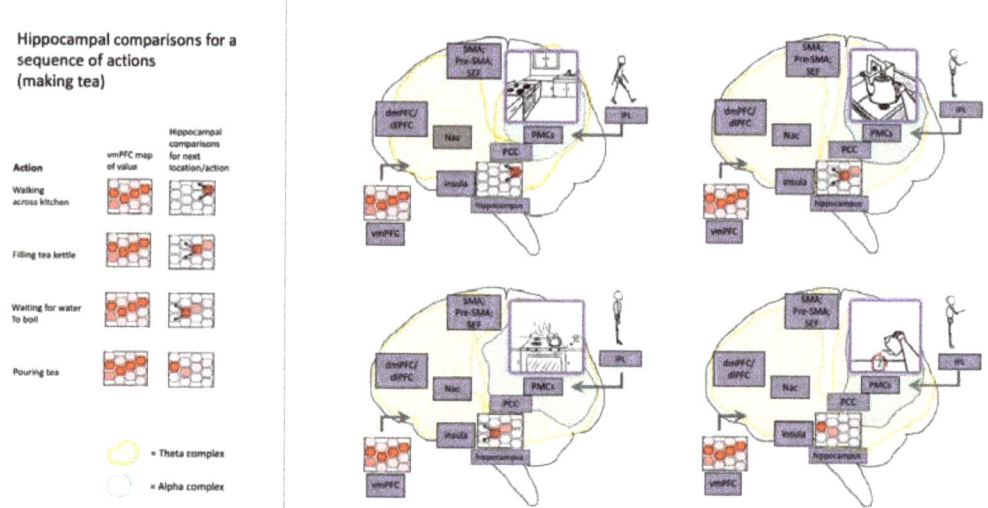

Figure 4. *Reprinted with permission from Safron, 2020b.* Hippocampally-orchestrated imaginative planning and action selection via generalized navigation. Action sequences from Figure 2 are depicted with respect to relevant neural processes. The hippocampal system provides (a) organization of cortical attracting states into value-canalized spatiotemporal trajectories, (b) stabilization of ensembles via theta-mediated cross-frequency phase coupling, and (c) goal-oriented cognition and behavior via contrasting (not depicted) sensed and imagined states. Hippocampal trajectories are shaped according to whichever paths are expected to result in more positively valanced outcomes (cf. reward prediction errors). The expected value associated with navigating to different portions of (potentially abstract) space is informed via coupling with similarly spatiotemporally-organized value representations (red shaded hexagons) in vmPFC and associated systems. As chained patterns of activity progress across hippocampal place fields (red hexagons with variable degrees of shading), theta-synchronized frontal ensembles (yellow shading spreading towards the front of the brain) help to generate (via cross-frequency phase coupling) ensembles for directing attention, working memory, and overt enaction. Sensory updating of posterior cortices occurs at alpha frequencies (blue shading), so providing a basis for conscious perception and imagination. With respect to these integrated estimates of sensory states, hippocampal coupling at theta frequencies (yellow shading spreading towards the back of the brain) provides a basis for (a) episodic memory and replay, (b) novel imaginings, and (c) adjustment of neuronal activity selection via orchestrated contrasting between cortical ensembles. Abbreviations: nAC = nucleus accumbens; vmPFC = ventromedial prefrontal cortex; dmPFC = dorsomedial prefrontal cortex; SMA = supplementary motor area; Pre-SMA = presupplementary motor area; SEF = supplementary eye fields; PCC = posterior cingulate cortex; PMCs = posterior medial cortices; IPL = inferior parietal lobule.

These proposals expand on previous descriptions of motor control via predictive processing [114] by emphasizing the role of consciously-experienced body maps as a source of intentionally-directed attention (i.e., precision weighting), imagination, and action. However, if voluntary action is a function of attention, and if attention is achieved by simulated actions and partially-expressed motor predictions, then what allows voluntary actions to develop in the first place? This potential explanatory regress is prevented by the (potentially surprising) ease of controlling cleverly 'designed' body plans, particularly when such morphologies are constrained to adaptive areas of state space [38,110]. For example, much of locomotion emerges from relatively controllable pendulum dynamics, and brainstem and spinal pattern generators further help produce coherently timed force vectors and locomotory modes [145]. To provide another example, limited range of motion for shoulder, arm, and finger joints promote effective engagement and exploration of the world via grasping (e.g., gripping made easier by fingers not bending backwards) and manipulation within likely fields of view (e.g., arms being more likely to place objects in front of facial sensors). Such near-optimal grips may be further facilitated by the functional resemblance between finger pads and deformable soft robotics manipulators, where degrees of force provide adaptively adjustable contact surfaces, so simplifying control via offloading to morphological 'computation' [146]. By this account, not only do well-designed body plans automatically contribute to adaptive behavior [147], but such embodied intelligence provides foundations and scaffolding for all cognitive (and affective) development. These favorable learning conditions are further enhanced via supervision by other more experienced humans (including nurturing parents) in the context of human-engineered environments [92,148,149]. In these ways, we automatically find ourselves in capable bodies in the midst of value-laden goal-oriented activities [100], where these grips on the world eventually allow us to construct coherent world models and conscious intentionality.

3. Grounding Intentionality in Virtual Intrabody Interactions and Self-Annihilating Free Energy Gradients

"We have to reject the age-old assumptions that put the body in the world and the seer in the body, or, conversely, the world and the body in the seer as in a box. Where are we to put the limit between the body and the world, since the world is flesh? Where in the body are we to put the seer, since evidently there is in the body only "shadows stuffed with organs," that is, more of the visible? The world seen is not "in" my body, and my body is not "in" the visible world ultimately: as flesh applied to a flesh, the world neither surrounds it nor is surrounded by it. A participation in and kinship with the visible, the vision neither envelops it nor is enveloped by it definitively. The superficial pellicle of the visible is only for my vision and for my body. But the depth beneath this surface contains my body and hence contains my vision. My body as a visible thing is contained within the full spectacle. But my seeing body subtends this visible body, and all the visibles with it. There is reciprocal insertion and intertwining of one in the other...".

—Maurice Merleau-Ponty [150]

This proposal is radically embodied in claiming to provide an exhaustive account of intentional control via internalized action patterns. Partially-expressed motor predictions are suggested to be the only means of volitional control over attention, working memory, and imagination, whether such influences are based on attending to a perceptual trace of recent sensations, or through generating novel counterfactual perceptual experiences via associated fictive actions. Representations selected by these partially-expressed motor predictions function as particularly robust predictions in active inference—perhaps particularly if made conscious [73]—so providing powerful means of voluntarily shaping thought and behavior.

In this active inferential view, *intentions* represent a functional intersection of beliefs and desires, where *desires* are understood as a species of *counterfactual beliefs*, so generating prediction errors (or *free energy gradients*) to be minimized through enaction. As will be discussed in greater detail below, emotions and feelings may be fruitfully conceptualized as the active and perceptual components of action-perception cycles over organismic modes. In this view, desires may be conceptualized as both *emotions as driving active inference* and also *feelings as updating perceptual models* [151]. As described above, the imagination of counterfactual desired world states will produce goal-relevant prediction errors, which are minimized either via updating predictions (desire as feeling), or by updating world states (desire as emotion).

Given that sources of value associated with desires are rooted in homeostatic imperatives, these affectively-laden prediction errors will center on interoceptive modalities [152,153] (Figure 5). As compellingly described by Seth et al. [154] with respect to the insular inferential hierarchy, this predominantly interoceptive free energy may be allostatically minimized via modulating neuroendocrine and autonomic functions. Alternatively, these primarily interoceptive free energy gradients (here understood as desires) could be minimized through the more indirect strategy of generating counterfactual predictions regarding the exteroceptive and proprioceptive consequences of action [75]. If counterfactual proprioceptive poses are stably held in mind, they may eventually result in the driving of motor pools as neural systems self-organize to minimize prediction error via overt enaction [72,109,155]. From this perspective, all actions are ultimately understood as a kind of extended allostasis in constituting predictive homeostatic life-management [156].

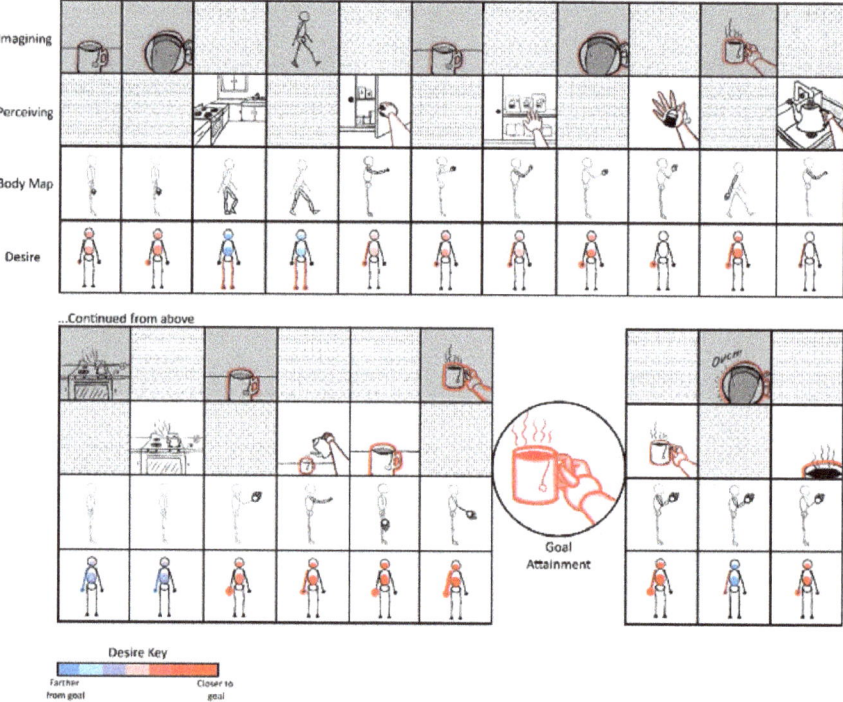

Figure 5. Interacting modalities in the context of imaginative planning and policy selection. This sequence of frames depicts interactions between modalities as agents select actions in order to achieve the goal of having tea (see Figures 2 and 4). Each row depicts a different aspect of experience, all of which interact in the context of goal-oriented cognition and behavior. Imagining and Perceiving (1st and 2nd rows) correspond to the current content of visuospatial awareness, likely mediated by hierarchies centered on posterior medial cortices. Whether this workspace is occupied by perceiving or imagining would respectively be a function of either stronger interactions with hierarchically lower cortical areas, or more stimulus-decoupled default mode processing (so affording counterfactual percepts). Body map (3rd row) corresponds to experienced proprioceptive pose, likely mediated by a hierarchy centered on inferolateral parietal cortices. Differential shading and size of body parts indicate differential attentional focus and modeling properties associated with affordance-related salience with respect to ongoing goal pursuit. Desire (4th row) corresponds to affective body experiences, likely also mediated by inferolateral parietal networks, but also involving interactions with insula and cingulate cortices. Differential red and blue shading respectively indicate positive and negative valence associated with different body parts, including with respect to interoceptive estimates of semi-localized aspects of the internal milieu. Taken together, rows 1 and 2 could be considered as constituting the "mind's eye" (or "Cartesian theater"), and rows 3 and 4 as the "lived body." Through their coupling, these networks and associated phenomena may (potentially exhaustively) constitute physical substrates of consciousness as integrative workspace for agent-based modeling and control.

The degree to which desires drive overt action selection via proprioceptive predictions will largely depend on differential precision weighting allocated to various portions of cortical hierarchies (Figures 1 and 3). With respect to the insula, precision weighting could allow prediction errors to reach hierarchically higher (i.e., more anatomically anterior) levels [154], where interoceptive information may have more opportunities to influence predictions for exteroceptive and proprioceptive hierarchies, and thereby drive action. Whether overall prediction error (i.e., free energy) is minimized by updating internal models (i.e., perceptual inference) or updating world states (i.e., active inference) will depend on attenuating precision at primary modalities [72,157], so protecting goal-related predictions from disruption (or updating) by discrepancies with present sensory data. For example, decreased precision on lower levels of interoceptive hierarchies could promote interoceptive active inference via autonomic functions (i.e., desire as unconscious emotion), since reduced gain on interoceptive sensations will allow associated representations to be more updatable via predictive coding mechanisms. Increased precision on middle levels of the interoceptive hierarchy, in contrast, would promote interoceptive information reaching the anterior insula and attaining more global availability (i.e., desire as conscious feeling). If these consciously-felt interoceptive states generate robust predictions for other modalities, and if sensory evidence does not have excess precision, then free energy will flow up interoceptive and into exteroceptive and proprioceptive hierarchies, thereby driving action to minimize overall prediction error (i.e., free energy). In these ways, desire (as free energy gradient) may be viewed as a force [158] that flows across multimodal body maps, which may result in overt enaction if these cascading predictions are sufficiently robust to result in minimizing prediction error via spinal motor pools and associated muscular effectors. Computationally speaking, these information flows would be constituted by patterns of precision weighting, either selecting specific predictions for enaction (e.g., relevant affordances for minimizing particular kinds of interoceptive prediction errors), or as hyperpriors influencing policy selection thresholds (e.g., modulating neuromodulatory systems).

This account of driving large-scale neuronal activity selection by visceral desires is consistent with interoceptive inferences being uniquely capable of enslaving cortex due to the highly stable (and so precise) nature of those predictions [90], which may have further entraining power via the high centrality of these subnetworks. These models are supported by numerous studies in which insula-cingulate connectivity is shown to be central for motivated cognition and behavior [159–162]. Further indirect supporting evidence may be found in voluntary actions being more frequently initiated during exhalations, where associated neural dynamics (i.e., readiness potentials) exhibit modulation by respiratory cycles [163]. Perhaps the most compelling evidence for these models of viscerally-driven action may be found in work by Zhou et al. [164], wherein organismic saliency models constituted the highest level of hierarchical control among resting state networks.

Much interoceptively-influenced biasing of attention and action selection may be unconscious. However, when these viscerally-grounded [130] prediction errors reach levels of cortical hierarchies where we become aware of them, then we can further attend to these sensations using efference copies (as predictions, or Bayesian priors) from exteroceptive and proprioceptive modalities. For example, we can (either overtly or imaginatively) visually scan through maps of the body and its interior, so modeling interoceptive contents by means other than the sensory channels that directly transmit this information from the internal milieu. This intentional attending to interoceptive states could then allow us to modulate the degree to which consciousness and action is influenced by feelings of desire. Theoretically, this mechanism could also provide enactive models of mindfulness practices such as "body scanning" or meditation on the breath [165–167].

This account of emotional regulation from directed attention to interoceptive states can also apply to attention to exteroceptive and proprioceptive modalities. Partially-expressed motor predictions may bias activity in these body representations (e.g., simulated foveations on hands), so influencing which actions are likely to be selected next (e.g., hands grasping in particular ways). While subject to multiple interpretations, some evidence for this model may be found in precision-estimation being influenced via functional interactions between theta power from frontal midline structures and beta power from frontal-parietal networks [127], which here may be (speculatively) interpreted as respectively indicating fictitious foveations interacting with other aspects of action-oriented body maps (Table 2). To the extent that partially-expressed actions provide bases for top-down attention, we may intentionally influence attention by attending to action-oriented body maps, so driving further patterns of attending and intending. Is there really room for intentionality in this cascade of converging cross-modal predictions? The answer to this question will depend on how we define intention, which here represents any instance of conscious desires being able to influence neuronal activity selection. Human-like intentionally can further be said to arise when these processes are driven by goals involving narrative self-models and associated concepts, as will be described in greater detail below.

4. The Emergence of Conscious Teleological Agents

[Note: In what follows, the word consciousness is used in multiple senses, sometimes involving basic subjective experience, and other times involving conscious access with respect to the knowledge, manipulability, and reportability of experiences [168]. Unless otherwise specified, these discussions can be considered to refer to both senses of consciousness. For a more thorough discussion of the physical and computational substrates of phenomenal consciousness, please see Integrated World Modeling Theory [73,74].]

4.1. Generalized Dynamic Cores

"What is the first and most fundamental thing a new-born infant has to do? If one subscribes to the free energy principle, the only thing it has to do is to resolve uncertainty about causes of its exteroceptive, proprioceptive and interoceptive sensations... It is at this point the importance of selfhood emerges – in the sense that the best explanation for the sensations of a sentient creature, immersed in an environment, must entail the distinction between self (creature) and non-self (environment). It follows that the first job of structure learning is to distinguish between the causes of sensations that can be attributed to self and those that cannot ... The question posed here is whether a concept or experience of minimal selfhood rests upon selecting (i.e. learning) models that distinguish self from non-self or does it require models that accommodate a partition of agency into self, other, and everything else."

—Karl Friston [88]

"[We] localize awareness of awareness and dream lucidity to the executive functions of the frontal cortex. We hypothesize that activation of this region is critical to self-consciousness — and repudiate any suggestion that 'there is a little man seated in our frontal cortex' or that 'it all comes together' there. We insist only that without frontal lobe activation the brain is not fully conscious. In summary, we could say, perhaps provocatively, that (self-) consciousness is like a theatre in that one watches something like a play, whenever the frontal lobe is activated. In waking, the 'play' includes the outside world. In lucid dreaming the 'play' is entirely internal. In both states, the 'play' is a model, hence virtual. But it is always physical and is always brain-based."

—Allan Hobson and Karl Friston [11]

The cybernetic Bayesian brain has also been extended to phenomenology, suggesting possible explanations for qualitative aspects of experience ranging from the sense of agency to synesthetic percepts. A felt sense of "presence" (or subjective realness) is suggested to correspond to the successful predictive suppression of informative interoceptive signals evoked by autonomic and motor actions, producing a sense of agency in association with self-generated action [154]. Histories of self-generated actions allow for the "mastery of sensorimotor contingencies" [169], with the extent and variety of evoked affordance-related predictive abilities (i.e., "counterfactual richness") determining degrees of presence associated with various aspects of experience [61].

Speculatively, counterfactual richness could contribute to perceptual presence via micro-imaginings that may be barely accessible to conscious awareness. That is, perception may always involve associated affordance relations, but where such imaginings may not be consciously accessible due to their fleeting nature (e.g., a single integrative alpha complex over posterior modalities failing to be more broadly integrated into a coherent causal unfolding). Yet, such simulated affordances may nonetheless contribute to attentional selection of different aspects of percepts and their multimodal associations (e.g., likely interoceptive consequences), so generating a penumbra of possibility accompanied by a particular sense of meaningfulness. This model of *phenomenality without accessibility* may be crucially important for understanding multiple aspects of agency, in which consciously experienced *isolated qualia* may potentially have strong impacts on minds in providing surprisingly rich sources of "unconscious" processing.

Alternatively, part of the reason that counterfactual richness is associated with perceptual presence may be because these (non-actual) affordance-related predictions fail to suppress bottom-up sensations. Imagined sensorimotor contingencies would generate prediction errors where they fail to align with actual sensory observations, which would influence conscious experiences if they reach hierarchically higher levels of cortex with rich-club connectivity [104,170]. These subnetworks are notable in having both high centrality and high reciprocal (or re-entrant) connectivity, which have been suggested to support "dynamic cores" of mutually-sustaining activation patterns [6,171], so implementing "global workspaces" [172] capable of both integrating and differentiating [173] multiple aspects of phenomena with sufficient spatiotemporal and causal organization for coherent conscious modeling [15,73,74].

While the account of conscious agency presented here is radically embodied, it parts ways with more radically enactivist "extended mind" interpretations of predictive processing [174]. According to radical enactivist interpretations of active inference, subjective experience is the entailment of an implicit model represented by the *entire system* of hierarchical relations within an organism's brain, body, and environment. However, I have suggested that processes only contribute to consciousness to the degree they couple with dynamic cores of neural activity on timescales at which information is integrated into particular large-scale meta-stable states [73,74], with coherence enhanced by mechanisms for stabilizing and coordinating synchronous activity [175,176]. While minds are certainly extended [177,178], consciousness may be a more spatiotemporally limited phenomenon.

Dynamic cores of consciousness may play another central role in Bayesian brains as sources of robust and (meta-)stable predictions. Conscious driving of neural dynamics allows for several properties that would not be possible without centralized control processes. To the degree widespread availability of information—often taking the form of embodied simulation—allows for coupling with linguistic production systems and their combinatorial and recursive generative potential, this would vastly increase the stability, complexity, and flexibility of active inference. To the degree these expanded abilities allow for inferring temporally-extended events, they may provide bases for constructing abstract self-models and a new kind of symbolic order [13,179]. Under this regime of conscious symbolism, a new kind of dynamic core becomes possible as world models with extended causal unfoldings and structuring by abstract knowledge. Such generalized dynamic cores would be constituted by systems of mutually sustaining predictions, whose robustness would increase when intersecting predictions provide synergistically greater inferential power when combined (e.g., converging lines of evidence).

I propose *embodied self-models (ESMs)* as constituting self-sustaining robust inferential cores at multiple levels. At lower levels of abstraction, minimal ESMs [180] correspond to body maps organized according to 1st-person perspectival reference frames. At higher levels of abstraction, more elaborate ESMs correspond to 3rd-person perspective body maps and schemas. These 1st- and 3rd-person perspectival ESMs both develop in inter-subjective social contexts, potentially via the internalization of 2nd-person perspectives [181] and mirroring with (and by) others [182,183]. Essential aspects of core selfhood—with both embodied and symbolic objectified characteristics—may involve a kind of internal 'mirroring' of 1st- with 3rd-person ESMs, so establishing linkages of effective connectivity for advanced self-modeling (Cf. mirror self-recognition as test of sentience) and self-control. Through experience, these various ESMs become associatively linked to each other as a control heterarchy governed by diverse modes of selfhood at varying levels of abstraction.

Neural populations capable of realizing these various self-processes will also develop reciprocal connections with inferior frontal and temporal hierarchies over phonological action-perception cycles, grounded in respective outputs to the vocal apparatus and inputs to hearing. These functional linkages would provide bases for semantic understanding based on syntactic grammar, which may allow for thought as inner-speech as previously described. From this radically embodied perspective, linguistic thought is a kind of motor skill, which partially renders declarative knowledge as a special case of procedural memory. These symbolic capacities afford more complex modes of organization, where ESMs take the form of narrative-enhanced selves [111,156] with nearly unbounded semiotic potential [184–186], including multilevel interpersonal coupling [187,188], participatory sense making and shared intentionality [189,190], and structuring experience by abstract meanings [121,148,191].

I suggest we may interpret "dynamic cores" game-theoretically [192], and extend this concept to emergent patterns structuring minds across all levels. Under the Free Energy Principle, all persisting forms necessarily minimize prediction error, and as patterns vie for promoting their existence, these interactions would constitute a kind of game with both cooperative and competitive characteristics. A 'core' would be established whenever a set of predictions becomes sufficiently stable such that it is capable of functioning as a kind of dominant paradigm [193] in belief space. This core property could be obtained because of a kind of faithful correspondence between model and world, or simply because it arises early in development and so structures subsequent modeling (whether accurate or not). Embodied selfhood is a good candidate for a generalized core in providing parsimonious modeling of correlated activity between heterogeneous sensations, whether interoceptive, proprioceptive, or exteroceptive [75]. I suggest ESMs provide such powerful explanations for experience that they form a necessary scaffolding for all other aspects of mind, with different aspects of selfhood being understood as kinds of extended embodiment [194–197], ranging from material possessions [198] to social roles, and other more abstract senses of self and ownership [111]. From this view, psychological development would be re-framed in terms of preserving and adapting various core patterns—in neo-Piagetian terms, assimilation and accommodation—so allowing minds to bootstrap themselves towards increasingly rarefied states of complexity.

Among these developmental milestones, perhaps the most significant major transition is acquiring capacities for self-awareness [199]. As suggested above with respect to the potential importance of mirroring, such self-models may develop via the internalization of social interactions involving various forms of intersubjective inference. While the richness of selfhood ought not be reduced to any given mechanism, focusing on action-perception cycles illuminates ways that various neural systems may contribute to the construction (and control) of different objectified self-representations. Given sufficient experience, imagined actions from 1st-person reference frames will be accompanied by auto-associative linkages to perceptions of similar actions from other points of view. These various viewpoints become 'encoded' by ventral visual stream neuronal ensembles, which can become consciously accessible via posterior medial cortices [73,74]. Conscious 3rd-person self-representations afford additional forms of modeling/control and navigation of complex contingencies, such as imagining multistep plans, potentially accompanied by visualizations of moving through spatialized time. [Speculatively, this sort of perspectival cross-mapping may have been facilitated by the evolutionary elaboration of white matter tracts connecting dorsal and ventral cortical hierarchies [200,201].

Objectified selfhood represents a major transition in evolution, indicating a movement from 1st-to 2nd-order cybernetics, wherein agents become capable of using processes of self-regulation to recursively model themselves as goal-seeking self-regulating feedback systems [202]. Thus, a radically embodied perspective may help us to understand not only the micromechanics of intentional goal-oriented behavior, but also the nature of self-consciousness and potentially uniquely human forms of agency. This constructed selfhood with metacognitive capacities via mental actions also suggests ways that compromised mechanisms of agency would contribute to varying forms of maladaptive functioning and psychopathology [203]. This constructed selfhood also suggests means by which pathological self-processes could be updated, potentially via the intentionally-directed attention towards somatic states described above as a proto-model of meditative practices [166,167].

4.2. Embodied Self-Models (ESMs) as Cores of Consciousness

4.2.1. The Origins of ESMs

To summarize, ESMs may form foundational cores and scaffolding for numerous and varied mental processes, ranging from the handling of under-constrained inference spaces to the intentional control of attention, imagination, and action. ESMs are both body maps and cybernetic control hierarchies, constituted by action-perception cycles grounded in skeletal muscle and associated perceptual efferents (Figure 6). As described above, the centrality of ESMs is expected based on early experiences [84,204] in which bodies provide learning curriculums wherein possibilities are fruitfully constrained [38], so allowing organisms to bootstrap their ways toward handling increasingly challenging modeling spaces within zones of proximal development [120]. With respect to the challenge of constructing robust causal world models—both enabling and possibly entailing conscious experiences [73,74]—the combinatorics of unconstrained inference spaces may only be surmountable via the inductive biases afforded by embodied learning. This fundamentally somatic developmental legacy suggests a radical perspective in which ESMs form a semi-centralized scaffolding for all intentional (and many unintentional) mental processes, grounding abstract symbolic thought in mental simulation and metaphorical extension from initial embodied experiences [47,48].

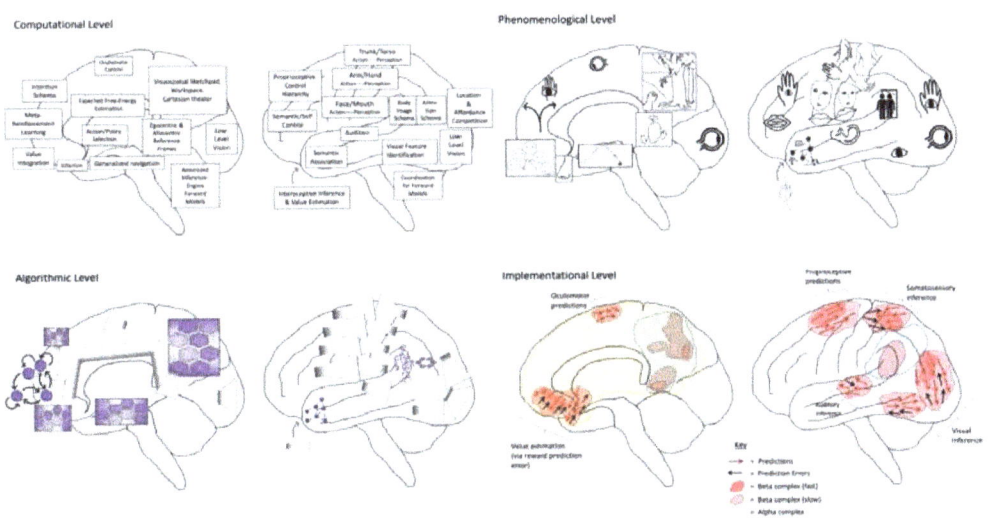

Figure 6. Depiction of the human brain in terms of entailed aspects of experience (i.e., phenomenology), as well as computational (or functional), algorithmic, and implementational levels of analysis [2,74]. A phenomenological level is specified to provide mappings between consciousness and these complementary/supervenient levels of analysis. Modal

depictions connote the radically embodied nature of mind, but not all images are meant to indicate conscious experiences. Phenomenal consciousness may solely be generated by hierarchies centered on posterior medial cortex, supramarginal gyrus, and angular gyrus as respective visuospatial (cf. consciousness as projective geometric modeling) [181,205], somatic (cf. grounded cognition and intermediate level theory) [3,206,207], and intentional/attentional phenomenology (cf. Attention Schema Theory) [118]. Computationally, various brain functions are identified according to particular modal aspects, either with respect to generating perception (both unconscious and conscious) or action (both unconscious and potentially conscious, via posterior generative models). [Note: Action selection can also occur via affordance competition in posterior cortices [94], and frontal generative models could be interpreted as a kind of forward-looking (unconscious) perception, made conscious as imaginings via parameterizing the inversion of posterior generative models.] On the algorithmic level, these functions are mapped onto variants of machine learning architectures—e.g., autoencoders and generative adversarial networks, graph neural networks (GNNs), recurrent reservoirs and liquid state machines—organized according to potential realization by neural systems. GNN-structured latent spaces are suggested as a potentially important architectural principle [208], largely due to efficiency for emulating physical processes [209–211]. Hexagonally-organized grid graph GNNs are depicted in posterior medial cortices as contributing to quasi-Cartesian spatial modeling (and potentially experience) [212,213], as well as in dorsomedial, and ventromedial prefrontal cortices for agentic control. Neuroimaging evidence suggests these grids may be dynamically coupled in various ways [214], contributing to higher-order cognition as a kind of navigation/search process through generalized space [215–217]. A further GNN is speculatively adduced to reside in supramarginal gyrus as a mesh grid placed on top of a transformed representation of the primary sensorimotor homunculus (cf. body image/schema for the sake of efficient motor control/inference). This quasi-homuncular GNN may have some scaled correspondence to embodiment as felt from within, potentially morphed/re-represented to better correspond with externally viewed embodiments (potentially both resulting from and enabling "mirroring" with other agents for coordination and inference) [39]. Speculatively, this partial translation into a quasi-Cartesian reference frame may provide more effective couplings (or information-sharing) with semi-topographically organized representations in posterior medial cortices. Angular gyrus is depicted as containing a ring-shaped GNN to reflect a further level of abstraction and hierarchical control over action-oriented body schemas—which may potentially mediate coherent functional couplings between the "lived body" and the "mind's eye"—functionally entailing vectors/tensors over attentional (and potentially intentional) processes [218]. [Note: The language of predictive processing provides bridges between implementational and computational (and also phenomenological) levels, but descriptions such as vector fields and attracting manifolds could have alternatively been used to remain agnostic as to which implicit algorithms might be entailed by physical dynamics.] On the implementational level, biological realizations of algorithmic processes are depicted as corresponding to flows of activity and interactions between neuronal populations, canalized by the formation of metastable synchronous complexes (i.e., "self-organizing harmonic modes" [73]). [Note: The other models discussed in this manuscript do not depend on the accuracy of these putative mappings, nor the hypothesized mechanisms of centralized homunculi and "Cartesian theaters" with semi-topographic correspondences with phenomenology.].

As described above, ESMs provide means by which action selection can be influenced via iterated comparisons of sensed and imagined sensorimotor states, with much complex planning achieved through backward chaining from goals, implemented via predictive coding mechanisms. Intentions (as self-annihilating free energy gradients) are proposed to function as systemic causes over neural dynamics, arising through interactions between beliefs and desires as counterfactual predominantly-interoceptive beliefs. Additionally, neuronal ensembles underlying ESMs—and the intermediate level representations they support [3,206,207]—may be positioned as centrally located, richly connected nodes in generative neural networks. On account of embodiment being functionally linked to most causes of sensory observations, coherent organization between ESM nodes would contribute to small-world connectivity, so enhancing message-passing potential, so enhancing capacity for informational integration. Thus, in addition to constituting the core of most mental processes, ESMs would be at the center of dynamic cores of neural activity [73,74,219], generating high degrees of integrated information [173,220] and instantiating communication backbones for global workspaces [221,222].

With respect to this hypothesis of workspace dynamics via ESMs, it is notable that periods of high and low modularity most strongly vary based on degrees of activity within sensorimotor and visual networks [223], potentially suggesting pivotal roles for these systems with respect to large-scale cognitive cycles [224]. Sensorimotor networks constitute the most extensive resting state component, involving 27% of overall grey matter [225]. Even more, these somatic networks establish a core of functional connectivity [226], with high degrees of overlap and coupled activity with other functional networks, including the default mode network, thus potentially linking conscious workspace dynamics to selfhood on multiple levels [227–230].

4.2.2. Phenomenal Binding via ESMs

High degrees of mutual information across ESMs may enhance capacities for self-organized synchrony and inferential stability [204]. Indeed, the early emergence (with respect to both ontogeny and phylogeny) of body-centered neural responses suggests they may be foundational for extra-bodily forms of perceptual inference [91,231]. In terms of developmental primacy, studies of zebra fish demonstrate that spinal motor-neurons begin a stereotyped process of establishing global synchronization dynamics, beginning with the reliable enabling of increasing degrees of synchronous local activity [232], followed by larger-scale integration (or self-organization) into well-defined oscillatory modes as critical thresholds are surpassed [233]. High degrees of integrative capacity via body maps may potentially help to explain the remarkable capacities of nervous systems to reconfigure themselves for both good (e.g., recovery after injury) and ill (e.g., phantom limb syndrome) [194,234,235].

Theoretically, ESMs may transfer some of their synchronous (and inferential) stability to non-body representations (e.g., external objects) when functionally coupled. This coupling could be realized by the driving of simulated (and sometimes overtly enacted) actions by reactive dispositions and perceived affordances [94,95]. Affordance relations must have physical bases in neuronal ensembles—even if highly dynamic and context-sensitive—constituted by representations of action-perception cycles, grounded in bodily effectors and sensors. If non-body representations are auto-associatively linked to ESMs via affordance relations [71], then synchronous dynamics within ESMs could transitively entrain neural ensembles for non-body representations, so increasing their perceptual stability. With relation to perceptual binding, specific affordances could contribute to specific patterns of synchrony, so instantiating specific networks of integration, which in some instances may entail phenomenal experience and potentially conscious access. [Note: The other models discussed in this manuscript do not depend on the accuracy of this hypothesis of *phenomenal binding via ESMs*.]

Mechanistically, traveling waves [236–238] from ESMs could form major points of nucleation for the formation of large-scale meta-stable rhythmic attractors [229,239–242]. Such self-organizing harmonic modes likely have multiple functional significances within nervous systems [73,74], including the ability to coordinate large-scale patterns of brain activity. This model of resonant binding via simulated embodied engagements further suggests that partially-expressed motor predictions with specific affordance linkages could be used for attentional selection over particular objects. From this point of view, enactivist discussion of "optimal grips" [89] may potentially indicate a foundational mechanism by which conscious access is realized via fictitious motor commands. Consistent with linguistic use, there may be a surprisingly (or perhaps intuitively) meaningful sense in which we "hold" objects in mind with attention (as partially-expressed motor predictions), potentially providing a neurocomputational understanding for the word "concept" in terms of its etymological origins (i.e., "to grasp").

ESMs are proposed to form cores of consciousness as dominant sources of integrated effective connectivity across the entire brain, facilitating coherent perception and action. ESM-grounded consciousness would not only imbue all percepts with the affordance potential of sensorimotor contingencies [169], but also the previously discussed sense of "presence" as perceptual depth from counterfactual richness [154,243], so illuminating fundamental aspects of phenomenology. If this model of virtual enactive binding and manipulation of percepts is accurate, then we may possess yet another account of the roles of frontal lobes with respect to global workspace dynamics and higher-order consciousness. While posterior cortices may generate conscious experiences of space [73,74,212], frontal cortices may provide bases for cognitive 'work' in the form of the stabilization and manipulation of percepts within these mental spaces (Figure 6).

This radically embodied view has received some support from findings in which motor information heavily influences neural signaling in almost every modality [244–246]. Notably, parietal cortex provides sources of both high-level body representations as well as spatial awareness, with damage not only resulting in anosognosia and alien limb syndromes, but also hemi-spatial neglect [218]. There is also a counter-intuitive finding in which the spatial extent of neglect symptoms are extended via providing a reach-extending tool for the hand corresponding to the affected side of space [195,247]. Speculatively, affordance-based bindings via ESMs may potentially provide a partial explanation for this surprising phenomenon, in that neglect symptoms could result from coupling with ESMs whose coherent (synchronous and inferential) dynamics have been compromised. Resonant coupling between percepts and ESMs may also help explain how external objects —potentially including other agents [248]—may become incorporated into body maps [249], with synchronous motions helping to establish expansion/binding. These fundamentally-embodied bases for phenomenality could also be (indirectly) evidenced by impaired memory with out-of-body states [250], and superior memory accompanying 1st-person points of view [251].

Recent work from Graziano and colleagues may provide support for this model of perceptual binding via ESM-based affordances. In Attention Schema Theory (AST) [118,252], conscious awareness is thought to correspond to reduced-dimensionality schematic modeling of attention, providing an informational object that is simpler to predict and control, relative to that which is modeled. The sketch-like nature of attention schemas makes them unamenable for clear introspection, so contributing to an anomalous inference wherein awareness is implicitly (and sometimes explicitly) viewed as a fluid-like physical substance that comes out of a person's eyes and reaches out into the world, so contributing to the "extramission myth of visual perception." Researchers from Graziano's lab [253] found evidence for an intriguing phenomenon in which seeing another person's gaze appeared to result in inferences of force-transfer towards an unstable object. This finding is consistent with the ESM-based model of perceptual binding described above, although variations on the experiment might provide an opportunity to uniquely test the hypotheses proposed here. According to the "eye beams" model of AST, implicit forces associated with gaze should always be a push—due to the implicit anomalous inference that awareness is like a fluid that can be emitted—causing the object to be more likely to fall away from observers. However, according to the model of phenomenal binding via ESMs, the force would either push or pull, depending on associated affordances, and possibly affective states.

In AST, conscious awareness is suggested to be the phenomenal entailment of attention schemas and the representations they bias. In the radically-embodied view described here, attention schemas would represent upper levels of control hierarchies over action-oriented 1st-person body schemas [118], or ESMs as action-perception hierarchies distributed across frontal and parietal cortices (Figure 6). The neuropsychological literature provides some support for this idea, with frontal and parietal lesions both contributing to neglect symptoms [254]. The centrality of the temporoparietal junction (TPJ) for conscious awareness in AST [218] points to possible functional overlaps between networks establishing embodied selfhood and conscious awareness. Notably, TPJ disruptions can result in perceptual anomalies such as out-of-body experiences and body-transfer illusions [255,256]. Associations between mental state inference [257] and overlapping representations for self and other in the TPJ (and dorsomedial PFC) provides further support for social bootstrapping of objectified selfhood described above. High-level action-oriented body maps may be indispensable for attempting to infer mental states and intentions, whether through "mirroring" or perspective-taking via attention schemas shared between self and others [118,121,190,258–260]. Thus, conscious access might not only depend on radically embodied minds, but may also fundamentally involve intersubjective modeling [187,188,261].

4.2.3. Varieties of ESMs

> *"We suggest that a useful conceptual space for a notion of the homunculus may be located at the nexus between those many parallel processes that the brain is constantly engaged in, and the input from other people, of top-top interactions. In this understanding, the role of a putative homunculus becomes one of a dual gatekeeper: On one hand, between those many parallel processes and the attended few, on the other hand be-tween one mind and another... [T]he feeling of control and consistency may indeed seem illusionary from an outside perspective. However, from the inside perspective of the individual, it appears to be a very important anchor point both for action and perception. If we did not have the experience of this inner homunculus that is in control of our actions, our sense of self would dissolve into the culture that surrounds us."*

—Andreas Roepstorff and Chris Frith [12]

In this account, ESMs function as sources of maximal model evidence in FEP-AI [75], complexes of integrated information [173,220], and backbones for global workspaces [129]. This view of consciousness and agency centered on ESMs is consistent with both the information closure [262] and intermediate-level [207] theories of consciousness. Intermediate levels of abstraction afford embodied simulation [3,206,263], wherein action-perception cycles enable cybernetic sense-making and grounded cognition. Indeed, cybernetic grounding via ESMs could partially help in explaining why consciousness may arise "only at the personal level" [264].

ESMs are composed of multilayer control hierarchies at varying levels of abstraction, ranging from 1st-person interfaces, i.e., the "lived body" [43,181], to 3rd-person body schemas capable of acting as symbolic and self-reflexive intentional controllers. The singular embodied self and models of selfhood as a "center of narrative gravity" [228,265] imply multiple roles for unified embodied representations as high-level control processes, organized according to multiple perspectival reference frames. The complexity and specificity of these models of self and world are greatly expanded by the combinatorial and recursive properties of language [156,179], including temporal extension and stabilization via organization into diachronic narratives [184]. While consciousness may not depend on language for its realization, linguistic capacities may have profound impacts on the evolution and development of conscious awareness, selfhood, and agency.

Multilevel integration via selfhood may represent a necessary condition for perceptual coherence by providing binding from core embodiment. Similarly, in line with renormalization group theory and the enslaving principle of synergetics [266,267], the ability of self-processes to stably persist through time provides reduced-dimensionality attracting center manifolds capable of bringing order to—or generating selective pressures over—faster dynamics at lower levels of organization. A slower, larger, and more centrally positioned set of dynamics has asymmetric potential to entrain (or enslave) faster and more fleeting processes, which will be relatively less likely to generate cohesive influences due to their transient character. Self-processes can be viewed as sources of highly coherent meso- and macro-scale vectors—or effective field theories [268]—over biophysical dynamics, allowing systems to explore state spaces in ways that would be unlikely without centralized integrative structures.

Selves provide spatial and temporal structure for complex sequences at multiple levels of abstraction, including symbolically. Such abstract integrative structures are referred to as "narratives" [184,269,270], for which it is no coincidence that such modes of organization facilitate learning, and where the act of telling and listening to stories is a human universal [271,272]. In terms of control systems, narratives allow for coherent stabilization of evolving conceptual structures in ways that provide multilevel syntax, so affording planning on multiple temporal and spatial scales. Narratives with multiscale organization provide one of the best ways to model and control such extended processes, including with respect to the narrativizing processes that both help to generate and are governed by self-models. In these ways, agentic selfhood is a story that becomes (more or less) true with the telling/enacting.

At their most basic, selves are constituted by models of embodiment and embedding within the external environment. At their most complex and abstract [273]—returning to the evolutionary game-theoretic considerations described above with respect to generalized dynamic cores—selves are patterns with which agent-like-systems are most consistently identified, where agentic systems are construed according to a kind of projected revisionist victor's history [14,265,274], wherein victors are constituted by dominating coalitions of patterns, bound together by evolving interactions between habits, narratives, and specific niches constructed by agents. Inter-temporally coherent belief-desire coalitions more consistently achieve higher value [275,276], and so tend to be reinforced, and so tend to dominate persona evolution [60]. Shared narratives co-evolving with these pattern coalitions [271,277,278] are shaped by repeated games both within [279–281] and between individuals [121,269,282]. Although self-processes may become extremely complex (and abstract) in these ways, in all cases such generative models both originate from and must continually deal with the constraints and affordances of their radically embodied nature.

4.3. Free Energy; Will Power; Free Will

The self-sustaining stability and predictive power of multilevel dynamic cores constitute free energy reservoirs [73,283], capable of enslaving hierarchically lower levels, and so driving overall systems towards novel (and surprising) regions of state space predicted in imagination. By this predictive processing model, will power is proportional to the strength with which an agent predict/imagine actions for desired states in the face of obstacles to goal attainment. The embodied attention mechanisms described above provide organism-centered (and potentially more intuitively controllable) means of boosting the predictive power of specific representations. These distributed high-level controllers necessarily grow from histories of predictive homeostatic regulation (i.e., allostasis via active interoception), largely centered around control hierarchies spanning insular and cingulate cortices [284,285], which influence neuromodulatory value signals through direct and indirect connections to hypothalamic and brainstem nuclei [286,287].

The radically embodied proposal presented here is that all self-control processes have their origins in controlling skeletal muscle, both via multilevel shared mechanisms, as well as via metaphorical extension from experiences with movement [288]. To the extent these regulating dynamics depend on particular neuroanatomical hubs, conscious willing constitutes a limited resource to the degree that sustained activity results in degradation of efficient predictions. This is consistent with rest periods being required to avoid "ego depletion" [289], possibly via mechanisms involving slow wave activity and synaptic downscaling within these hubs [290–293]. Based on the models described above, these executive resources would heavily depend on networks utilized for simulating actions of varying degrees of complexity, with fictitious foveations and virtual motoric manipulations likely being especially impactful (Table 2). Dorsomedial and dorsolateral prefrontal cortices provide higher-order control over frontal eye fields and pre-supplementary motor areas [74] (Figure 6), which have both been associated with attention and working memory [125,294,295]. Strong evidence for these models would be obtained if executive failure (and recovery) were reliably indexed by local increases (and subsequent decreases with rest) in slow oscillations, as well as if stimulation [296] applied to these areas—or perhaps other integrative networks [297]—was found to increase self-control and promote repletion during rest intervals.

However, even without exhausting limited (but flexible) neural resources, sustained willing may be preemptively curtailed based on explicit and implicit predictive models of ongoing dynamics [298]. In the context of goal-pursuit, emotional states reflect a balance between inferred benefits and costs associated with various goals [162], including estimates of opportunity costs, which have both direct and indirect effects on motivating/energizing (or inhibiting) behavior. These proactive regulatory mechanisms largely stem from insular and cingulate cortices acting as predictive homeostatic (i.e., allostatic) control systems, as well as from additional converging inputs to neuromodulatory processes (e.g., dopaminergic nuclei of the brainstem), so influencing thresholds for neuronal activity cascades and subsequent overt actions.

Other self-control limitations may be difficult to describe in terms of specific neural systems, but may instead emerge from heterogeneous predictions regarding value attainment associated with goal-pursuit. For example, it may be the case that self-processes become more causally efficacious in minds to the extent that they are predicted to be causally efficacious in the world. In these ways, there could potentially be bidirectional relationships between willpower, situation-specific self-efficacy, and even global self-esteem.

A radically embodied cybernetic Bayesian brain suggests multiple mechanisms by which we can be said to have (within limits) the "varieties of free will worth having" [299]. While debates regarding the ontological status of free will may not be definitively resolved in this manuscript, we have shown that intentions—as conjoined beliefs and desires—can function causally in their ability to act as coherently stable predictions. To the extent these predictions can be maintained in the face of discrepant observations, these sources of control energy will drive overall dynamics. Thus, conscious mental states are not only "real patterns" [300] because of their significance for experiencing subjects, but also because consciously 'held' intentions may meaningfully contribute to cognitive (and potentially thermodynamic) work cycles [13,73,301,302].

4.4. Mental Causation

This mental causation could be similarly described in the language of generalized Darwinism [279], with preferences functioning causally within minds in the same ways that selective pressures [303–306] are causal within evolutionary systems [17]. More enduring preferences can be viewed as ultimate-level causes that select for the development of context-specific proximate-level choices [307]. We may further think of motor control via hierarchical predictive processing in terms of a hierarchy of selection processes. In this view of action selection as a kind of natural selection, hierarchically lower levels provide specific adaptations for realizing hierarchically-higher selective pressures, the totality of which constitute the overall direction of 'will' in any given moment. On longer timescales, histories of experience change beliefs and desires, so providing another way in which preferences act as (recursively self-modifying) causes for minds as multilevel evolutionary systems.

Intriguingly, the concept of 'pressure' and the ability of free energy gradients to drive work may be isomorphic when considered in the contexts of Bayesian model selection, natural selection, and thermodynamics [308–310]. Although post hoc confabulation occurs [311,312], in many cases the driving of behavior via intentions may be viewed as (formally) similar to the powering of engines via controlled explosions. Further, in the gauge-theoretic framing of the Free Energy Principle [158], precision weighting is formally understood as a kind of (symmetry-preserving) force in precisely the same sense as gravity is a force resulting from the deformation of spacetime. Therefore, desires and willpower may be forces in every meaningful sense of the words 'power' and 'force.'

Can things as seemingly ephemeral and abstract as beliefs and desires have causal powers in the same senses as in physics? Perhaps this is just an exercise in semantic games, playing with metaphors and words to avoid the obvious and inevitable conclusion: the only real causation is physical, and any other sense of cause is mere expediency, representing an approximate attempt at explaining and predicting events whose underlying reality is too complexly determined and difficult for us to measure and understand. Perhaps. Yet it is also the case that 'causes,' 'powers,' and 'forces' are themselves just words, or metaphors, or models for the phenomena they attempt to represent in compressed form, and where they would lack explanatory or predictive utility without dimensionality-reducing approximations [48,59]. Occasionally we need to remember that the meanings of words are determined by our interacting minds, wherein they are always (without exceptions) mere expediencies—even if this expedience also affords the evolution of civilizations and the technologies upon which we depend for life [271]. The word 'cause' is mostly lacking in physics, as most physicists have no need of singling out specific things in order to explain or predict particular events [268]. Master equations of dynamics may be specified such as Hamiltonians and Lagrangians, from which system-evolution flows deterministically, but the notion of causation is not found in such descriptions. The absence of causal notions in physics makes sense in light of physical laws being symmetric with respect to time, and where time may be an emergent local description, rather than a fundamental principle of the universe [313]. Even 'force' has been deflated in fundamental physics, and instead replaced with "fictitious force" in conceptualizations such as the gauge constructions underlying relativity and other field theories [158]. On account of the conceptual elegance of these theories, many physicists no longer talk about "fictitious" forces, since it could be argued that there are no other kinds.

Perhaps even more fundamentally [314], if we trace the genealogy of these concepts, and so understand the radically somatic origins of minds, then we might discover our notions of cause and force were initially derived via metaphorical extension from embodied experiences of volitional control [16,48,59,288]. This is not to say that it is permissible to commit a genealogical fallacy and reduce the realities of these concepts to their beginnings. Formal accounts of causation have been provided in terms of operations over graphical models involving manipulations of dependencies via counterfactual interventions [119]. However, such handlings require commitment to a given ontology (i.e., carving up a domain into particular kinds), and do not support reducing processes to more fine-grained dynamics where higher-level properties are undefined. Even if temporality is found to be fundamental (rather than emergent) in ways that afford causal modeling over some 'true atomism,' reductive explanations would still not be of an eliminative variety. Eliminative perspectives on emergent phenomena (such as intentionality) may be literally meaningless and nonsensical, in that they violate the rules of logical reasoning whereby sense-making is made possible.

Alternatively framed, intentions (as conjoined beliefs and desires) could be viewed as kinds of "effective field theories" over psychodynamics and behavior [268], affording maximally powerful ways of explaining and predicting events whose underlying statistics afford (and demand) coarse-graining [315] in ways that give rise to new ontologies. In these ways, beliefs and desires are as real as any-'thing' [64], even if there is a wider (but nonetheless constrained) range of plausibly useful interpretations, relative to 'things' like particles. However, a proper understanding of the formal properties underlying these more rarefied emergent phenomena—as generalized evolution [308,309]—may be shared among all similarly configured physical systems. Therefore, our intentions really are sources of cause, power, and force in every meaningful sense of these words. Our intentions are real patterns [300], and so are we.

5. Neurophenomenology of Agency

5.1. Implications for Theories of Consciousness: Somatically-Grounded World Models, Experiential Richness, and Grand Illusions

> "For my part, when I enter most intimately into what I call myself, I always stumble on some particular perception or other, of heat or cold, light or shade, love or hatred, pain or pleasure. I never can catch myself at any time without a perception, and never can observe any thing but the perception. When my perceptions are remov'd for any time, as by sound sleep; so long am I insensible of myself, and may truly be said not to exist. And were all my perceptions remov'd by death, and cou'd I neither think, nor feel, nor see, nor love, nor hate after the dissolution of my body, I shou'd be entirely annihilated, nor do I conceive what is farther requisite to make me a perfect non-entity... But setting aside

some metaphysicians of this kind, I may venture to affirm of the rest of mankind, that they are nothing but a bundle or collection of different perceptions, which succeed each other with an inconceivable rapidity, and are in a perpetual flux and movement."

—David Hume [316]

As described in previous work [73,74], consciousness can be understood as the capacity of minds to support global workspaces [317], defined by dynamic cores of competing and cooperating patterns [171,219], which depend on—but are not identical to—a system's integrated information [173,220]. However, the deeply embodied perspective described here suggests that for systems to be conscious, integrated information must apply to representations with experience-grounded meanings. These representations need not be explicitly defined symbols, but their semiotic content could be entailed in a cybernetic manner via the coordination of action-perception cycles. A neuronal complex could have an arbitrarily high amount of integrated information, but it may not be conscious unless it also refers to patterns external to the system. Capacity for consciousness may be proportional to (but not necessarily defined by) integrated information from dynamics with representational content. One of the primary adaptive advantages of consciousness may be enabling representations—computationally realized a balance of integrated and differentiated dynamics—that evolve on timescales roughly proportional to events in the world that systems attempt to control, so enabling cybernetically-grounded meaning making. [For perceiving dynamics on spatiotemporal scales where more direct coupling is infeasible, we may require (embodied) metaphor, such as may be used in the spatialization of time [318,319].] By this view, informational objects in "qualia-space" [320] would have phenomenal content by virtue of being isomorphic with probability distributions of generative models over bodily sensoriums for systems that evolve-develop through interactions with environments in which they are embedded. Thus, a radically embodied perspective may be essential for explaining the circumstances in which integrated information does or does not imply conscious experience.

The models presented here are also consistent with Higher-Order-Thought [321] theories emphasizing the importance of the frontal lobes in conscious awareness and intentionality, whose functional connectivity with parietal (and temporal) regions may be crucial for stabilizing representational content [6,11]. Anterior portions of prefrontal cortex may be particularly pivotal/central in establishing small-world connectivity for the entire brain [170], so affording large-scale (flexible) availability of information. While this area may be particularly well-connected across primate species [322], this connectomic hub may have been uniquely expanded in humans relative to non-human primates [179,323]. However, a radically embodied perspective suggests that prefrontal hubs may not merely establish global connectivity. Rather, these systems may specifically function as upper levels of hierarchies shaping dynamics via simulated actions and partially-expressed motor predictions (Figure 6), so providing a basis for intentional control. In this way, the frontal lobes as subserving "executive functions" may be something more than a 'mere' metaphor, but may also be an apt description of a quasi-homuncular hierarchical control architecture centered on body-centric agency. We may even want to go as far as recasting the notion of "access consciousness" [168] to depend on the kinds of fictitious mental acts described above for realizing meta-cognition and conceptual thought, understood as abstract motor skills, potentially involving resonant phenomenal binding via embodied self-models (ESMs).

As described in previous work [73,74], not only may there be something of a Cartesian theater, but percepts may be re(-)presented on/in this virtual reality screen (Figures 2 and 4–6). Further, as described above, quasi-homuncular ESMs (as multimodal action-oriented body maps) would introspect the contents of these spaces with partially-expressed motor predictions, with simulated foveations—and other fictitious actions (Table 2)—providing sources of both (a) attentional "spotlights," and (b) coherent vectors for intention and action. However, what is the extent of this unified field of experience? Do we actually fill in a full and rich simulated environment, or is this subjective experience some kind of "grand illusion", where in fact we only fill in local aspects of the environment in an ad hoc fashion [8,324–326]? Rather than filling in a complete sensorium all at once, might we instead generate percepts reflecting the sensory acuity accompanying our actual sensorimotor engagements, which may be surprisingly limited (e.g., proportional to the narrow field of view afforded by the focal region of the retina)?

Phenomena such as invisible ocular blind spots suggest some perceptual filling occurs, and which is something the brain's generative models may be well suited to provide [73,74]. However, the extent of this pattern completion remains unclear, and may be surprisingly sparse. For example, to what extent does the "visuospatial sketchpad" model of working memory actually involve a kind of internal sketching, potentially even involving the internalization of actual experiences with drawing [327]?

Indirect evidence for low-dimensional inner-sketching may be found in work in which similarities were observed between models of internal visual percepts and behavioral line drawings [328]. The authors note that such images can be traced back to Paleolithic hunters 40,000 years ago (with possibly earlier origins), suggesting that line drawings not only represent effective means of conveying meanings, but may also reveal functional principles of the visual system. While this particular study focused on predicting responses in the ventral stream, patterns of neural activity in the posterior medial cortex may be particularly important in having strong correspondences with visual consciousness (Figure 6). That is, feature hierarchies of the ventral stream may help to coordinate evolving spatiotemporal manifolds in posterior medial cortices as consciously accessible 2D sketchpads. Some support for this model is provided by a study in which attention and working memory indicated 2D mappings of the visual field [329]. Connections between this midline structure and upper levels of other sensory hierarchies further allow for the (partial) filling-in of multimodal somatosensory states, so providing bases for not just a Cartesian theater, but fully immersive virtual reality [49]. Even more, connections between these various modalities of experience with the hippocampal-entorhinal system could allow this somatic pattern completion to evolve according to trajectories through physical and abstract spaces, so providing a basis for episodic memory, novel imaginings, and planning (Figures 3 and 4). With respect to the filling-in process, the specific contents of consciousness may depend on the specific degree to which representations from various sensory hierarchies are capable of coupling with large-scale meta-stable synchronous complexes on their temporal and spatial scales of formation [73,74].

While conscious experience may be "flat" [330] in terms of being of surprisingly low dimensionality, the functioning of consciousness within overall mental systems may also be deep. The multiply-determined contextual significances of reduced-dimensional processing is potentially reflected in nearly all languages converging on a common information transmission rate of ~39 bits/second [331]. Theoretically, the limited dimensionality of conscious processing may be a primary reason for this communicative bottleneck. However, the generative potential of consciousness and expressive power of language (with its "infinite use of finite means") may nonetheless afford supra-astronomical semiotic capacities. Even if integrative dynamic cores and global workspaces have extremely limited capacities, they may nonetheless possess depth and powerful combinatorics via spanning levels both within and across hierarchically-organized systems, so constituting multiscale functional heterarchies. The temporally-extended nature of conscious processes [332,333] affords numerous and varied opportunities for shaping by complex unconscious dynamics, many of which can be given coherent organization by diverse—but capable of being integrated, to varying degrees—self- and world-modeling on multiple levels, whose richness is greatly expanded by narrative organization in the ways described above [184].

While some of the richness of consciousness may represent a "grand illusion", in many ways this supposedly illusory phenomenon may function as if a rich and full field were always present by filling in details on an as-needed basis. Given this availability of relevant information, in addition to having many of the "varieties of free will worth wanting" [299], we have many of the varieties of conscious experience worth wanting as well. Consciousness would only appear to be "flat" if we fail to consider its nature(s) as a temporally-extended unfolding of generative processes [73,74,334]. Thus, the illusory nature of rich consciousness may itself be something of an illusion due to trying to model inherently time-dependent processes from an atemporal perspective, which would be prima facie inadequate for evaluating relevant phenomena. [Note: Deflations of deflationary accounts of selfhood may be arrived at in a similar fashion, including with respect to Buddhistic/Humean reductions of selfhood to non-self elements.]

5.2. Conscious and Unconscious Cores and Workspaces; Physical Substrates of Agency

Although a detailed handling is beyond the scope of the present discussion, a variety of methods may be useful for estimating subnetworks (e.g., giant components) contributing to consciousness [335–337], and perhaps agency. One intriguing study used k-core decomposition to track transitions from conscious to unconscious subliminal perceptual states [338]. Surprisingly, the most connected kernel and inner core of the conscious state remained functionally active when the brain transitioned to the subliminal-state. Not only may activity within the inner-most connectivity core of the brain be unconscious, but conscious access was lost by inactivating peripheral shells, potentially suggesting the importance of sensorimotor information for enabling coherent experience. These findings suggest that accessible consciousness might not be generated in the inner-most core, but at intermediate levels of hierarchical organization and abstraction [207,262], potentially involving the kinds of fictitious action-perception cycles described above with respect to meta-cognition and self-consciousness.

These findings could also potentially illuminate otherwise mysterious phenomena, including things like intuitive cognition [339], "tip-of-the tongue" effects, and even the roles of spontaneity in agency [314,340]. Some aspects of intuition and semi-conscious percepts may correspond to attractor dynamics accumulating in an (unconscious) innermost core and outer shells and bypassing intermediate levels. Alternatively, in line with the "isolated qualia" model described above, information may be capable of driving action selection and conscious imaginings from networks supporting (consciously experienceable) embodied simulations—potentially the 1st shell out from the inner core—but without sufficient robustness to be stably introspectable.

While agency might typically depend on predictability for the sake of controllability, there may be ways in which overall control is enhanced by limitations of self-prediction:

- Avoiding excessive exploitation (at the expense of exploration) in action selection (broadly construed to include mental acts with respect to attention and working memory).
- A process for generating novel possibilities as a source of counterfactuals for causal reasoning and planning.
- Game theoretic considerations such as undermining the ability of rival agents to plan agonistic strategies, potentially even including "adversarial attacks" from the agent itself.

In these ways, somewhat paradoxically, agency may sometimes be enhanced by limiting the scope of intentional control.

Relatedly, intriguing work in artificial intelligence models the frontal pole as a recurrent neural network whose capacity for chaotic bifurcation enables flexible action selection and predictive learning [341,342]. Recurrent computational reservoirs have high potential for informational density due to the combinatorics of re-entrant connections, but more overtly hierarchical architectures have the advantages of discrete compositionality (so affording precise control) and robustness-via-modularity (so affording separable optimization). Cortical systems may leverage both of these capacities by placing a recurrent bifurcating nexus on top of a hierarchy of action-perception cycles with more linear dynamics [43] (Figure 6). The capacity of recurrent systems to exert recursive causal influences on themselves makes them chaotic systems with sensitivity to initial conditions. In these ways, upper regions of cortical control hierarchies may be occupied by processes that are inherently inaccessible to conscious modeling. Notably, these deepest portions of cortex are also newest with respect to both evolution and development [179], and have many of the properties we normally associate with personhood [143], including individuality [343,344], spontaneity, and autonomy [345].

If these models regarding the neural substrates of consciousness are accurate, then they may also help contextualize findings where agency appears to be missing. The *Libet experiment* [346] provides a particularly notable example of a supposed demonstration of non-agency, as the subjective experience of deciding to move was observed to emerge *after* predictive neural activity. Potential limitations of the paradigm notwithstanding [299,347,348], the question arises as to how conscious mental states could be causal, given that we expect causes to precede effects. Theoretically, reports regarding decisions to act occurring after predictive neural signals could be partially accounted for by effective connectivity between preparatory motor activity and largely unconscious inner cores.

If actions may be 'decided' by processes outside of conscious awareness, then is our sense of free will another grand illusion? Perhaps in some cases, but probably often not with respect to the "varieties of free will worth wanting" [299], as much meaningful executive control does not involve the generation of motor deployment events based on capricious whims. Such spontaneous acts might primarily be governed by stochastic activity within hierarchically lower levels, closer to primary modalities that have less access to richly connected networks where large-scale (consciously accessible and controllable) coordinated activity would tend to center [203]. Most actions do not occur as one-off events, but unfold within contexts involving conscious imagining and planning (Table 1, Figure 2), which can substantially drive overall neural dynamics. Similarly to the previously discussed case of the apparent flatness of consciousness and the supposed insubstantiality of selfhood, we may find ourselves denying the existence of "real patterns" [300] based on investigations that were ill-equipped to capture the relevant phenomena. In some senses we might identify agency (and personhood) with overall systems with both conscious and unconscious components. Such systems (and persons) may not be strongly shaped by consciousness in any given moment, yet could be significantly consciously shaped over time. Agency may be like the relationship between conductor and an orchestra, where conductors are neither omnipotent nor mere epiphenomena. Or to use the metaphor of the elephant and its rider: elephants with and without riders are very different "beast machines" [349].

5.3. Readiness Potentials and the Willingness to Act

Alternative explanations for Libet phenomena may be found in the Free Energy Principle and Active Inference (FEP-AI) framework [55], wherein brains are understood as cybernetic control systems that predictively model the world [59–61]. As previously described, within FEP-AI, support is accumulating for an associated process theory of hierarchical predictive processing (HPP) as a unified principle governing neural functioning [20,148,350]. In HPP, all brain areas generate top-down predictions over bottom-up inputs, where information is only passed upwards (as prediction error) if it fails to be predictively inhibited. Support for this common cortical algorithm is evidenced by theoretical considerations (e.g., efficiency), and is consistent with common architectural principles reflected throughout cortex [18]. HPP suggests both perception and action are inherently interrelated and fundamentally similar: perception minimizes prediction error via updating internal models, and action realizes this objective by updating world states to better match predictions. Action selection is understood as the (complementary) inverse of perception: perceptual hierarchies are updated via ascending prediction errors, and action hierarchies are updated via descending predictions [351]. Particular actions are selected as more complex/abstract predictions from higher areas cause cascades of more fine-grained lower-level predictions, ultimately driving motion via spinal motor pools and associated reflex arcs with skeletal muscles [72].

HPP (and FEP-AI more generally) may represent a "Rosetta stone" for neuroscience [71], allowing new interpretations of previously ambiguous phenomena, potentially including the nature of *readiness potentials (RPs)* associated with seemingly voluntary movement decisions [352]. This multilevel modeling framework could prove invaluable for investigating the functional significances of RPs and associated waveforms [353]. FEP-AI would understand these slowly-building potentials as evidence accumulation with respect to predictive models, accompanied by non-linear phase transitions in large-scale updating of implicit (and sometimes explicit) Bayesian beliefs over proprioceptive poses [73,74,106,334]. Through HPP mechanisms, these discretely updated predictions would constitute kinds of self-fulfilling prophecies when passed down cortical hierarchies with sufficient power to drive overt enaction.

I suggest RPs—as motor predictions—are biophysically realized via accumulation of recurrent neural activity in frontal-parietal action-oriented proprioceptive body maps (Figures 6–8), coupling with cingulate-insula salience networks, with patterns of enaction released when critical thresholds are surpassed in control hubs (e.g., pre-supplementary motor area) [354]. This threshold-crossing could be understood as an "ignition event" as described by global workspace theories [73,74,227,334], so constituting one (of multiple) means by which consciousness enters causal streams to leading to action. These periods of non-linear increases in activity may also correspond to periods where action-oriented body maps possess the highest degrees of integrated information, whose estimation could potentially correlate with measured strength of will [73]. Conscious intentions (as conjoined beliefs-desires) would contribute to ramping activity via the kinds of affectively-driven mental simulations described above [355,356] (Figure 5). This hypothesis of imaginative planning contributing to RPs is consistent with observed patterns of dopaminergic discharges, and also decreasing variance (and larger magnitude waveforms) leading up to volitional actions, indicative of value-based control processes [357,358].

Neurophenomenologically (Figures 7 and 8), the feeling of "urge" preceding action corresponds to (non-linear) positive feedback interactions between frontal action hierarchies [351], posterior body-space-affordance hierarchies [94], and insulo-cingular (interoceptively-grounded) salience hierarchies [162] (Figure 6). These feelings are more than mere epiphenomena, influencing attentional selection for affective states, thereby modulating effective connectivity between these control hierarchies [154,160] (Figure 5). The stream of consciousness would further contribute to action selection via the counterfactual processing (e.g., simulated movements) and imaginative planning enabled by the hippocampal system [139,214,216,359] (Figure 4), including with respect to "Type 1" planned or "Type 2" capricious RPs [360]. These systems also contribute to imagining/predicting the consequences of more complex (and potentially meaningful) decisions [348], which would involve greater hierarchical depth and multiple realizability via particular actions from a "contrastive causation" perspective [361]. At these higher levels of abstraction, maximal explanatory power would be found in terms of more coarse-grained descriptions such as personhood and self-consciousness [162,207,264,315], so providing further neurocomputational grounding for agency. Finally, the "isolated qualia" model described above could also be relevant for explaining gaps between estimated 'decision' times and measured RPs, in that capricious actions will be more likely to be associated with quale-states that are difficult to take up into coherently introspectable streams of experience, yet nonetheless involve meaningful driving of dynamics by person-relevant values.

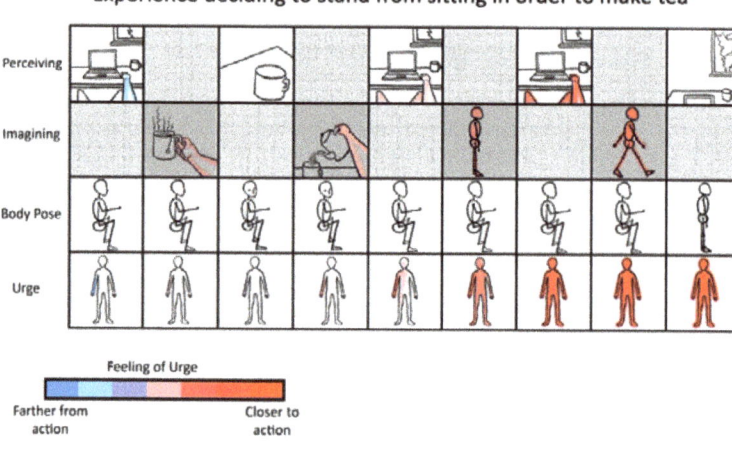

(a)

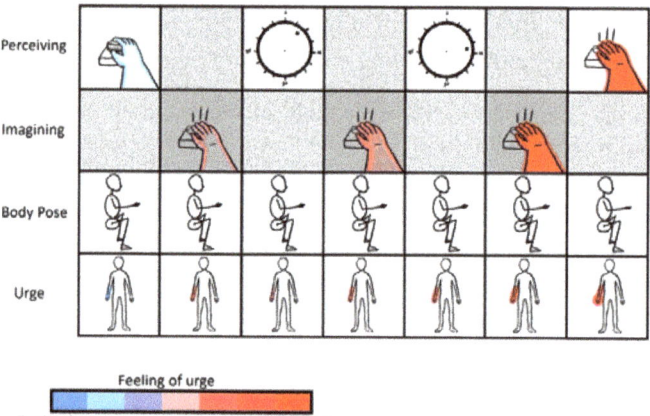

(b)

Figure 7. (**a**) Experience deciding to stand in order to make tea (see Table 1 and Figures 2, 4 and 5). The individual alternates between (1) perceiving sitting with an empty cup, and (2) imagining actions related to achieving the desired goal of obtaining tea. As the individual imagines (or rehearses) possible actions, feelings of urge accumulate across multimodal body maps, which peak accompanying the overt enaction of standing. (**b**) Experience deciding to move one's hand in a Libet paradigm. The individual alternates between (1) perceiving one's hand and the clock and (2) imagining button-pressing. As possible actions are imagined/rehearsed, feelings of "urge" accumulate across multimodal body maps, which peak accompanying the overt action of button-pressing.

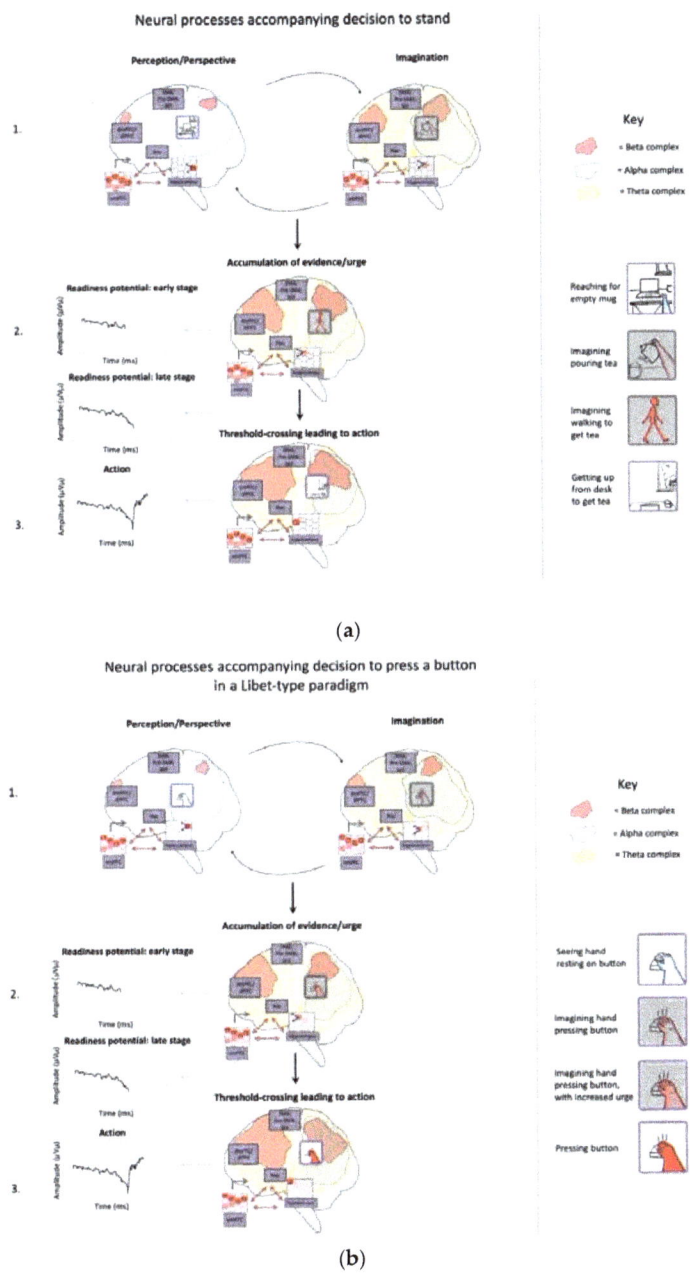

Figure 8. Readiness potential reflecting the accumulation of urge from simulated actions. (**a**) Neural processes accompanying decision to stand (see Figure 7a). (**b**) Neural processes accompanying decision to press a button in a Libet-type paradigm (see Figure 7b). Imaginative simulations (alpha oscillations, blue shading) are hippocampally orchestrated (Figure 4) via theta oscillations (yellow shading) and cross-frequency phased coupled nested gamma. Potential actions are selected based

on estimation of their relative expected value, with contrasting realized by coupled maps/graphs of the hippocampal system and vmPFC, with estimation and selection particularly influenced by the NAc and associated cortical systems. Lightly colored red hexagons indicate potential trajectories through (generalized) space, and dark red hexagons indicate chosen directions (either in imagination or reality). Imaginings cause increasing expectation (beta oscillations, red shading) for the value of potential actions, with corresponding accumulation of recurrent activity in body maps resulting in overt enaction once critical thresholds are surpassed. Abbreviations: Nac = nucleus accumbens; vmPFC = ventromedial prefrontal cortex; dmPFC = dorsomedial prefrontal cortex; SMA = supplementary motor area; Pre-SMA = presupplementary motor area; SEF = supplementary eye fields.

5.4. Qualia Explained?

Above we have considered prototypical qualitative aspects of experience, including pleasure, pain, and desire. Each of these "qualia" can be extremely rich in terms of their particular characteristics, underlying mechanisms, and functionalities, and the ways these vary across contexts. In what follows, I adopt a neurophenomenological approach [4,362–364] in beginning to explore how principles and mechanisms from FEP-AI can be used to cast light on how these aspects of our existence can be so fundamental, yet remain so mysterious.

5.4.1. Emotions and Feelings

In attempting to analyze the nature of emotional experience, perhaps some of the continuing mystery is due to a lack of agreement on terminology. Damasio et al. [63,156,285,365], argue emotions can be ascribed to the value-oriented behavior of all living organisms, including single-celled organisms such as bacteria. However, Damasio reserves the word "feeling" for the conscious re-representation of emotions. Feldman-Barrett and LeDoux [179,284], in contrast, object to this more inclusive conceptualization of emotion, arguing instead that emotional language should be reserved for consciously-experienced affective states that are expressed and constructed through interpretive processes. LeDoux has even gone as far as to claim that emotions only arose via cultural evolution *after* the advent of language.

There are clear merits to both points of view. While less inclusive conceptualizations may avoid some confusions, they also miss opportunities to identify ways in which value and integrated informational dynamics are essential to all life [366,367]. I propose adopting an intermediate position, viewing emotions and feelings as respective action and perception components of action-perception cycles over large-scale changes in organismic modes. Relevant macroscale dynamics include diverse phenomena ranging from autonomic functions, to musculoskeletal body modifications [368], to nervous system alterations via neuromodulatory systems and effective connectivity from neural areas with high effective centrality (e.g., the amygdala complex). In addition to this cybernetic formulation of emotions as a kind of action, and feelings as a kind of perception, we may add an additional distinction as to the extent to which we are conscious of expressed emotions and sensed feelings. While potentially counter-intuitive, from this more inclusive point of view we may have both conscious and unconscious emotions, as well as conscious and unconscious feelings. This use of terminology would support many of the rationales for the positions described above, as well as many folk intuitions as expressed in normal linguistic use. If useful for communicative clarity and ethical considerations, additional distinctions can be made as to whether consciousness involves basic phenomenal awareness or is of a more complex access or autonoetic variety.

LeDoux [179,369] has argued that animals without complex language cannot be said to possess emotions, but merely have functional activity within "survival circuits". These claims are justified by language providing necessary syntactic structures for the construction of complex extended self-models; or as LeDoux states: "No self, no fear." This emphasis on the foundational importance of selfhood for conscious experience is largely compatible with the view presented here, and elsewhere [91]. Without extended self-processes, emotions and feelings will be qualitatively different than the kinds of emotions and feelings constructed by humans governed by (and governing) a symbolic order of being. However, within this cybernetic formulation, functional activity of "survival circuits" could contribute to the generation of emotions as large-scale organismic modes, yet still not be consciously expressed or felt.

Hence, all evolved cybernetic systems could be said to have emotions and feelings, but only systems capable of coherent integrative world modeling would consciously experience those affects [73,74]. These conscious systems likely include all mammals and birds, and possibly reptiles or fish if pallial tissue [370,371] is sufficiently elaborated to model system-world states with spatial, temporal, and causal coherence. Thus, we may take a middle way between the perspectives described above in viewing emotions and feelings as ubiquitous features of life, while simultaneously recognizing qualitative differences that emerge when these phenomena are associated with various kinds of consciousness. Both more and less inclusive conceptual stances are reasonable, but with respect to qualitatively different kinds of affective phenomena.

5.4.2. What Is Value? Reward Prediction Errors and Self-Annihilating Free Energy Gradients

In FEP-AI, all living systems can be described as obeying a single objective of self-model-evidence maximization and prediction error minimization [372]. In this framework, organisms begin development by implicitly predicting the rectification of homeostatic (and later reproductive) prediction errors, so forming a foundation out of which all subsequent models grow. With experience, these modeling efforts come to apply to the modeling processes themselves and the experiences they generate, including models of what is likely to cause changes in prediction error. In this way, we come to predict ourselves minimizing prediction errors and experiencing associated mental states, including with respect to emotions and feelings. Through this associative chaining of memories from early organismic experiences, biological agents begin life being reinforced/punished as they continually attempt to engage in predictive homeostatic rectification (i.e., allostasis). However, organisms progressively learn sensorimotor contingencies for making these reward-related stimuli more/less likely to be available. Mechanistically, representations detecting these contingencies are themselves connected to midbrain value signals—e.g., orbitofrontal cortex → accumbens shell → ventral tegmental area → dopamine [110]—so allowing cortical models to drive reinforcement/punishment and shape adaptive policies for enaction.

This account has parallels with work on meta-reinforcement learning [342], where systems are initially given primary reward functions from which more capable secondary reward functions may be acquired from experience. From an FEP-AI perspective, these secondary predictions would constitute higher-order beliefs about likely patterns of prediction error minimization. According to candidate trace models [373], dopamine is likely to strengthen whatever predictions were most likely to contribute to its release by being most active leading up to phasic increases, so providing a partial solution to the credit assignment problem. If phasic dopamine increases are proportional to the rate of change of prediction error rectification [76,374–377], then the more quickly something minimizes prediction error, the more it will come to be predicted.

In these ways, organisms come to predict states of initial increases in prediction error, so that these free energy gradients (experienced as desire, or "wanting") may be destroyed through enaction (experienced as pleasure, or "liking") [378,379]. The creation and destruction of these gradients of anticipatory and consummatory reward will then stimulate dopamine release proportional to magnitudes of free energy minimization, as well as temporal intervals over which prediction errors are reduced [380]. These experiences, in turn, update beliefs and desires, whose counterfactual nature provide further sources of free energy to motivate future behavior. These mechanisms will shape organisms to predict themselves not only in homeostatic and reproductive states, but also diverging from these desirable modes of being, to the degree that such discrepancies between goals and actualities are anticipated to be manageable. Thus, through experience, we come to predict ourselves encountering initially negatively valanced states, which may become positively valanced when we annihilate these free energy gradients through either imagined or overt enaction, so establishing new goals/gradients to pursue/destroy in the future.

5.4.3. Curiosity and Play/Joy

This prediction of prediction error minimization creates an interesting setup in which organisms end up being surprised when they do not find themselves riding down steep enough gradients of prediction error [76,374]. This is exactly what evolution would 'want' [17,381], since there is no limit to how evolutionarily fit an organism can be, and so organisms ought to always seek opportunities for realizing value in new ways. Driving of dopamine release by reward prediction errors may provide one means of realizing this evolutionary imperative for expansion in seeking opportunities for value realization. If the mechanisms underlying reinforcement and behavioral disinhibition are only activated for unexpectedly good outcomes, then organisms will always find themselves seeking to explore the limits of what they can attain. This exploratory impulse will be even stronger if accompanied by opportunities for refining models and satisfying curiosity-based desires, so realizing the intrinsic value of learning in addition to the extrinsic value of utility maximization [382–386].

Boredom, in contrast, represents a punishing process that functions in an inverse fashion to curiosity (and play). One mechanism for implementing this negative incentive could be found in predictive coding in terms of habituation. If organisms come to near-perfectly predict rewards—or consider associated stimuli to be not worth attending to—then this familiarity will result in prediction errors only being generated at lower levels of cortical hierarchies, which lack access to richly connected networks enabling conscious awareness [73]. Prediction errors failing to reach deeper levels will result in reduced recognition of features associated with those potential rewards. Both with respect to implicit predictions and explicit expectations, previously rewarding events that do not fully register will be experienced as disappointing in contrast to expected value [387,388], so resulting in stimulus-devaluation and reduced probabilities for selecting associated policies. Almost paradoxically, by becoming less (pleasantly) surprised by (or more familiar with) rewarding stimuli, organisms end up becoming more (unpleasantly) surprised relative to anticipated rewards, since predicted rewards never manifest in experience. Some evidence for this model can be found in over-rehearsed pleasurable acts being overly automatic, habitual, and progressively losing their hedonic tone. Between these twin masters of curiosity and boredom, agents are shaped to always expand their repertoire of policies for value realization, with growth continuing to the extent that these efforts are expected to result in increasingly desirable outcomes [386].

Under FEP-AI, we ought to expect living organisms—by virtue of being successful at existing—to be equipped with (or constituted by) system-defining prior expectations (or preferences) in which they are optimizing models of themselves doing the kinds of things which would be required for survival, including foraging for information. These modeling imperatives require organisms to enact system-world configurations dependent on policies with consequences in the future, and to also depend on policies not yet deployed [389]. This means successfully persisting adaptive systems must not only minimize free energy, but also expected free energy in (definitionally counterfactual) futures. A successful active inferential agent will expect itself to be maximizing information gain (i.e., precision-weighted prediction errors), while also avoiding the accumulation of cybernetic entropy [59–61,390,391] with respect to existential threats to the system. Within FEP-AI, this dilemma of balancing stability/plasticity tradeoffs is (boundedly optimally) resolved by gradient descent over a singular objective functional of expected free energy.

The maximal rate of reduction in overall expected free energy will be found in situations where agents are able to simultaneously balance imperatives for maximizing the intrinsic value of information/exploration with the extrinsic value of realizing preferred world states. This situation may be referred to as play, or "PLAY" [386,392,393] —potentially subjectively accompanied by "flow" states [394]—which, in maximizing reward, represents attracting states for organisms that places them precisely where they ought to be to maximize learning and evolutionary fitness [395]. The balanced conditions of play attract agents to a zone of proximal development [396]—or "edge of the adjacent possible" [397,398], and also the "edge of chaos" [239]—where learning rate is optimal, creating neither overly nor underly challenging conditions for promoting increasingly skillful engagement with the world [399,400].

These considerations help explain why we would not expect agents to minimize surprise by sequestering themselves in low-complexity environments. This is an a priori unlikely outcome, since such conditions would increase prediction errors from homeostatic regulatory nuclei and systems with which they (allostatically) couple. Further, such agents would both experience boredom and deprivation with respect to curiosity and play. Although we should also keep in mind that this supposed "Dark Room problem" [401] may not be completely solved by active inferential systems, as people often do seek out reduced complexity environments, whether due to the kinds of pathological beliefs associated with anxiety and depression [363,402], or by getting stuck at local maxima of excessive exploitation relative to exploration in model optimization.

5.4.4. Synesthetic Affects

In the account described above, all affect is ultimately associatively linked to the rectification of either homeostatic or reproductive error signals, for which interoceptive consequences may be some of the most reliable sources of information [75]. However, these signals from the body's internal milieu have poor spatial localizability and controllability. If spatiotemporal and causal contextualization are necessary for enabling coherent experience, then these constraints on sense-making could result in interoceptive information being attributed to non-interoceptive sources. The best available inference regarding these visceral (and vital) signals may be that they are both caused by and also inextricably part of the conditions with which they are associated. Theoretically, this could cause much of interoception to have a quasi-synesthetic quality, wherein poorly localizable signals become intimately entangled with (or 'infused' into) more easily modeled proprioceptive and exteroceptive phenomena (Figure 5). For example, we may both feel our body from within, while also projecting these feelings onto and into associated objects.

While it may seem odd to describe feelings as a kind of synesthesia, all perception may have at least some degree of synesthetic phenomenology by virtue of involving cross-modal blending [403–407]. Analogous (and likely overlapping) phenomena would include "oral referral" in which primarily olfactory percepts are mapped onto taste sensations [408]. Theoretically, synesthetic affects may provide a partial account of referred pain phenomena, in which damage to body parts are mistakenly attributed to another location [152,409]. To go out on a further speculative limb, the phenomenology of color perception may often be synesthetic in this way, with prototypical qualia such as the "redness of red" having its particular 'textures' due to interoceptive cross-mappings.

This *synesthetic-affects hypothesis* may have further support from descriptions of pleasure as a kind of "gloss" applied to objects of hedonic experience [378]. If accurate, this model could also explain part of why emotional experiences often have an ineffable quality when reported. That is, affects may heavily depend on information that is difficult to explicitly model, and for which modeling efforts usually involve a kind of anomalous inference that are personal feelings are inextricably—and essentially [410]—part of the conditions that evoke them.

Synesthetic affects may not only explain some of the ways that our feelings 'color' the world—for both good and ill—but also the phenomenology of will with respect to both motivation and effort (Figures 5–8). In this view, the feeling of willing corresponds to a hybrid percept in which interoceptive states are mapped onto the effector systems by which intentions are realized. Thus, in addition to helping to explain otherwise mysterious aspects of experience, these synesthesia-like processes would also have extensive functional consequences. Perhaps most fundamentally, this kind of synesthetic phenomenology may help to establish senses of body ownership and minimal (embodied) selfhood upon which most aspects of mind ultimately depend. One line of evidence provided in support of these models is findings using augmented reality, in which superimposing interoceptive cardiac signals enhanced susceptibility to "rubber hand illusions" [411]. Intriguingly, such anomalous inferences are also moderated by tendencies for experiencing mirror-touch synesthesia and kinesthetic mirror illusions [197,412].

Predictive coding accounts of emotional active inference have been proposed in which prediction errors from interoceptive states can be minimized through either (a) changing autonomic conditions, or (b) changing related world states via mobilization of proprioceptive effector systems [75,413]. If synesthetic phenomenology increases the extent to which interoceptive states are tightly coupled with actions and perceived outcomes, then this conjunction would help establish affordance-informed salience mappings over perceptual contents, so facilitating action selection and planning [414]. As described above with respect to free energy flows across multimodal body maps and the generation of readiness potentials (Figures 5–8), these tight perceptual couplings could strengthen patterns of effective connectivity between interoceptive and proprioceptive modalities. Such linkages would be more than mere epiphenomena, but would enable greater control energy from networks whose dynamics are ultimately grounded in evolutionary fitness and experiential histories with organismic value.

The subjective sense of presence [243] for affective phenomena may substantially depend on relatively tight associations between emotions and outcomes, so contributing to synesthetic mappings between feelings and inferred causes. If these links are disconnected —e.g., via insensitivity to interoceptive sensations or inabilities to imagine the realization of valued goals—synesthetic infusions of interoceptive value into other percepts would be compromised. In terms of consequences for normative functioning, severing synesthetic bridges to interoception could be involved in clinical conditions like anhedonia, alexithymia, the negative symptoms of schizophrenia, and even Cotard's syndrome and Capgras illusions [154].

5.4.5. The Computational Neurophenomenology of Desires/Pains as Free Energy Gradients That Become Pleasure through Self-Annihilation

Dopaminergic neuromodulation is commonly understood as indicating desire-related states [415,416], and also plays important roles in FEP-AI [417–419]. Dopamine modulates activity for representations of value-relevant stimuli, including actions associated with realizing valued goals. While dopaminergic functionality is complex [420], elevated signaling levels may be interpreted as indicating confidence that current policies/capabilities are likely to realize desired outcomes with respect to sensed or imagined stimuli. Relevant stimulus-features include both external reward cues as well as multimodal representations of activities involved in seeking valued goals, including avoiding undesirable outcomes.

In the predictive processing accounts of goal-oriented behavior described above, when an agent predicts itself obtaining value, but has not yet realized these desired outcomes, generated prediction errors correspond to discrepancies between representations for goal attainment, relative to estimated present or imagined likely states. These discrepancies are suggested to derive from iterative contrasting of desired and estimated likely states, occurring at theta frequencies orchestrated by hippocampal-prefrontal coupling [139,142] (Figure 4). As these comparison operations proceed, discrepant features generate increased activity as prediction errors, so drawing attention to and seeding imaginings with the most important features that need to be handled either by updating internal models or changing the world [105].

Much of the phenomenology of desire may represent the prediction of value-attainment, activating associated somatic and interoceptive concomitants of consumption, which are subjectively (and synesthetically) felt in body maps in places most associated with value realization (Figure 5). If these sensations are accompanied by temporary net decreases in predicting homeostatic or reproductive value-realization [76,374]—potentially mediated by opioid signaling [379,421]—overall unpleasant interoceptive inference may accompany these perceptions. In this way, the feeling of desire would be experienced as a kind of pain, with its particular characteristics depending on unique learning histories. However, painful desire can be transformed into pleasurable anticipation if we find ourselves predicting overall increases in value, so creating pleasurable contrasts with the discomfort of wanting. If the visceral concomitants of affective experiences become entangled with exteroceptive and proprioceptive percepts in the quasi-synesthetic fashion described above, then pleasure and pain (including desire) would be generated as interoceptive modes becoming infused into other modalities in particular ways based on historical associations.

To use a musical metaphor, in experiences of pain and unfulfilled desire, the overall melody is played in a more minor, or entropic [390,391] key/timbre. Alternatively, in experiences of pleasure and fulfilled desire—potentially including virtual fulfillment (i.e., pleasurable anticipation)—affective orchestras play melodies with greater consonance. One could view such soundtracks to the (fully immersive virtual reality) movies of experience as separate streams of information that help contextualize what is being seen on 'screens' over which we see stories unfold (Figure 6). However, it may be closer to experience to say that this metaphorical music enters into what we see and feel, imbuing (or synesthetically coloring) it with meanings. Indeed, we may be able to find most of the principles of affective phenomena to be well-reflected in our experiences of music [16,385,422], where we play with building and releasing tension, enjoying the rise and fall of more and less consonant (or less and more dissonant) melodies. In musical pleasure, we explore harmony and the contrast of disharmony, eventually expecting to return home to the wholeness of the tonic, but with abilities of our "experiencing selves" [423–425] to find satisfaction in the moment not necessarily being the reasons that our "remembering selves" find ourselves attracted to particular songs.

The affective melodies played by neural orchestras will be dominated by interoceptive modalities, the most ancient—both developmentally and evolutionarily speaking—and reliable indicators of homeostatic and reproductive potential [63,130,285,426,427]. Do we have relaxed and dynamic cardiac rhythms? Is our breathing easy or forced? Do we feel warm—but not too hot—or cold? Are our bowels irritated or copacetic? Do we feel full or empty inside? Do we feel like our body is whole and strong, ours to command where we will, if we wanted it? Or do we feel damaged and weak? This interoceptive information speaks to foundations of life and the cores of value out of which persons may grow.

5.4.6. Desiring to Desire; Transforming Pain into Pleasure, and Back Again

How can we reconcile the experience of desire as a species of pain in light of the fact that we often desire to desire? While desiring may sometimes be desirable, it is not a pleasant thing to be in a state of unsatisfied hunger or thirst without believing this situation to be manageable. To be hungry or thirsty without cessation is to predict moving away from homeostasis and survival. Unless an organism can be confident that it will eventually rectify this situation, failing to satisfy such desires would indicate an existential threat to the system. Thus, we would expect desire unsatisfied to be experienced as a kind of pain. However, the pain of desire can then be transformed into pleasure—and back again (and so on)—by consummation, or the vivid imagination of attainment.

Can an agent ever come out ahead with this back and forth between pleasure and pain, either with respect its experiencing or remembering selves [424]? How can motivation be maintained if all pleasures will eventually be transformed back into kinds of pain through their absence? In addition to low-level mechanisms such as opioid signaling resulting in concomitant dopamine release [421], additional asymmetries between pleasurable and painful experiences may be found in predictive coding mechanisms. That is, more changeable patterns will be more likely to violate expectations—by virtue of being difficult to precisely track—and so experiencing/remembering will likely be dominated by transitions between pleasure and pain, especially if accompanied by precipitous or punctuated alterations [76,248,374,380,428]. If seeking without finding results in relatively gradual accumulation of desire, and if consummation tends to rectify situations more rapidly, then experience and memory for successfully enacted goals will have an overall pleasurable (and reinforcing) quality. Additionally, by virtue of being substantially generated by an agent's own (potentially intentional) actions, the greater predictability of consummatory acts might allow attentional resources to be marshalled in ways that allow for more extended conscious processing of pleasurable experiences. Finally, some symmetry breaking with respect to pain and pleasure may come from the motoric nature of attention described above, in that the experience of attending to pleasurable experiences will be more likely to be reinforcing both in the (extended) moment as well as across time. [Note: The conditioning of top-down attention also suggests that some quasi-psychodynamic phenomena are to be expected as almost inevitable consequences of the laws of learning.] However, this pleasure is not something that natural selection 'wanted' us to have and hold onto, but to be continually "SEEKING" [392], thereby maximizing fitness.

5.4.7. Why Conscious Feelings?

Consciously-experienced feelings may provide unified attractors for coordinating global organismic states [130,285]. While emotional shaping may occur without consciousness, these affects may be more likely to entrain the overall system when integrated into coherent fields of experience. Even if these feelings take the form of "isolated qualia" without conscious access (as described above), these self-stabilizing cores may still provide sources of greatly elevated control energy. However, this entraining power would be even greater when made consciously accessible in ways that afford planning and continuous adjustments of actions based on organismic value. This mapping of hedonic states onto consciously introspectable models of enaction also provides a partial means of handling the credit assignment problem, via conjoining value and actions in both experience and memory. If affects took place "in the dark" without feeling like anything, they would be unable to strongly influence events, nor be coherently integrated into explicit modeling and planning, including plans involving pursuing those feelings as ends in and of themselves, such as in the domains of play and art.

5.5. Facing up to the Meta-Problem of Consciousness

The hard problem of consciousness asks, how can it be that there is "something that it is like" to be a physical system [429,430]? The "meta-problem" of consciousness refers to the (potentially more tractable) challenge of addressing why opinions and intuitions vary greatly with respect to what could meaningfully answer this question [431]. As suggested elsewhere [73], one potential solution to the meta-problem may derive from the unavailability of bridging principles, which would cause prospects for explaining consciousness to seem either impossible (perhaps even in principle), or merely (extremely) difficult. An additional solution to the meta-problem may be found in the nature of explanations for various qualia: while perhaps intuitive after consideration, at first glance some of the models proposed above seem to directly contradict experience, such as desire constituting a species of pain, and vice versa [152]. Other explanations of aspects of experience may not necessarily contradict intuitions, yet may nonetheless seem irreducibly strange and so prima facie implausible, such as the model of synesthetic affects described above. However, if it is indeed the case that some of the most fundamental and familiar aspects of experience are difficult to recognize upon close inspection, then this is itself something in need of explanation.

Much of this seeming paradox of the unrecognizability of the most fundamental and familiar could be resolved if such aspects of experience are likely to become "phenomenally transparent" [49,432], and so resistant to introspection. Neurocomputationally, the contents of perception in any given moment are likely entailed by synchronous beta complexes with particular zones of integration [73,74], but with these local inferences requiring further integration into larger (alpha- and theta-synchronized) complexes for phenomenal and access consciousness. Such broader integration may not end up occurring if predictive coding mechanisms are so successful that they are capable of "explaining away" aspects of experience before they can be consciously registered. That is, iterative Bayesian model selection unfolds over multiple (potentially nested) levels of hierarchical depth, and so if explaining away observations is largely successful via smaller beta complexes closer to the modalities, that information would never reach more richly connected cores/subnetworks enabling coherent world modeling and experienceable perception. Alternatively, such information could give rise to experience in the form of "isolated qualia," yet fail to achieve conscious accessibility due to the transient nature of these quale states. In these ways, that which is most fundamental and familiar would almost inevitably become nearly invisible to introspective access.

The meta-problem may be as conceptually rich as the Hard problem itself. Further promising approaches may involve paradoxes from functional "Strange loops" and self-reference [433], computational limits of recursion [434], and seeming paradoxes deriving from mechanisms by which egocentric perspective is established [181]. Finally, some solutions may be sociological in nature, potentially reflecting a legacy of "physics envy" in the mind sciences [435]. Not only have we lacked bridging principles and understanding of embodiment as the core of selfhood and experience, but scientific practice both implicitly and explicitly denigrated subjectivity after the decline of introspectionism and rise of behaviorism. Given this taboo on subjectivity—i.e., the very thing we would hope to explain with respect to consciousness—why should we have been surprised if we lacked satisfying understanding of the nature(s) of experience? Finally, some of the (Hard) problem may derive from frames in cognitive science that rendered all Cartesian framings of mental functioning taboo. That is, if quasi-Cartesian intuitions were actually semi-faithful representations of the nature(s) of mind and brain, then why should we be surprised if our scholarship—and its denigration of folk psychology [436]—failed to provide satisfying accounts of the nature(s) of our conscious agency?

6. Conclusions

> "The intentionality of all such talk of signals and commands reminds us that rationality is being taken for granted, and in this way shows us where a theory is incomplete. It is this feature that, to my mind, puts a premium on the yet unfinished task of devising a rigorous definition of intentionality, for if we can lay claim to a purely formal criterion of intentional discourse, we will have what amounts to a medium of exchange for assessing theories of behavior. Intentionality abstracts from the inessential details of the various forms intelligence-loans can take (e.g., signal-readers, volition-emitters, librarians in the corridors of memory, egos and superegos) and serves as a reliable means of detecting exactly where a theory is in the red relative to the task of explaining intelligence; wherever a theory relies on a formulation bearing the logical marks of intentionality, there a little man is concealed."

—Daniel Dennett [1]

These explorations have attempted to repay as many "intelligence loans" as possible by creating an embodied backing for intentionality, so providing a common currency for understanding cognition. I have suggested that consciousness is generated from dynamic predictive cores, centered on embodied self-models, functioning as cybernetic controllers for agents embedded in environments within which they seek valued goals. To realize these values, agents engage in imaginative planning in which they chain inferences from desired outcomes back to present-estimated states, with enaction realized via multilevel action-oriented body maps. For these quasi-homunculi, intentional control is driven by beliefs and desires, understood as free energy gradients, which are annihilated when prediction errors are minimized through skillful enaction, so establishing new goals to pursue in the future. Through a variety of simulated actions, embodied self-models both influence and are influenced by high-level representations from interoceptive and exteroceptive inferential hierarchies, so providing bases for various forms of conscious access, metacognition, and self-knowledge. This deeply embodied architecture provides enactive bases for most mental operations discussed in cognitive science, including means by which conscious mental states can causally influence attention, working memory, imagination, and action. In these ways and more, understanding the radically embodied foundations of conscious minds may vindicate much of folk psychological and traditional conceptions of selves containing both multiplicity and unity, and of will defined by both constraints and freedom.

Funding: This research received no external funding.

Data Availability Statement: This manuscript does not have associated data.

Acknowledgments: I am deeply grateful to all the people with whom I have explored these ideas over many years. I would like to especially thank Karl Friston for his feedback on a previous version of this manuscript in early 2018, for giving me an opportunity to present some of this material at a University College London Theoretical Neurobiology Meeting, and for his ongoing guidance and inspiration. I would also like to thank Andy Clark and Anil Seth for their pioneering work which informed these ideas, and for providing me with the opportunity to present to their research groups. I would like to thank Jakob Hohwy for his feedback on another incarnation of this manuscript, and for introducing the concept of "self-evidencing," which continues to shape my thinking on many levels. I would like to thank Aaron Schurger and Uri Maoz for teaching me about readiness potentials and Libet phenomena, and Walter Sinnott-Armstrong for introducing me to the idea of "contrastive causation." Any errors and/or stylistic, thematic, or communicative judgment lapses are all my own.

I would like to thank Rutger Goekoop for his work on goal hierarchies and control structures, and also for his friendship. I would like to thank Paul Badcock for his work on hierarchical mechanistic minds and for making connections between the Free Energy Principle and (generalized) evolution, which I believe to be essential for describing agentic causation. I would like to thank Inês Hipólito for teaching me the ways of radical enactivism, and also for her openness to my (unusual) cognitivism. I would like to thank Zahra Sheikhbahaee for everything she has taught me about machine learning and its relations to the Free Energy Principle and Active Inference framework. I would also like to extend deep thanks to Amelia Thomley for sharing her artistic talent with me in attempting to illustrate the nature(s) of experience. I look forward to future collaborations.

Finally, I would like to express my deep gratitude to Daniel Dennett for rescuing me from an extended and severe existential crisis over free will, for giving me invaluable thinking tools, and for providing me with strongly motivating reasons to explore these ideas. If it were not for his monumental impact on cognitive science and philosophy of mind, I probably would not have engaged in this "strange inversion of reasoning," attempting to describe how what might seem to be the most naïve interpretation of mental phenomena may be the key to understanding how conscious purposes could emerge from nature, wherein we find ourselves in a world in which the only meanings are those which we create for ourselves and each other.

Conflicts of Interest: The author declares no conflict of interest.

References

1. Dennett, D. *Brainstorms: Philosophical Essays on Mind and Psychology*; The MIT Press: Cambridge, MA, USA, 1981; ISBN 978-0-262-54037-7.
2. Marr, D. *Vision: A Computational Investigation into the Human Representation and Processing of Visual Information*; Henry Holt and Company: New York, NY, USA, 1983; ISBN 978-0-7167-1567-2.
3. Varela, F.J.; Thompson, E.T.; Rosch, E. *The Embodied Mind: Cognitive Science and Human Experience*, Revised ed.; The MIT Press: Cambridge, MA, USA, 1992; ISBN 978-0-262-72021-2.
4. Rudrauf, D.; Lutz, A.; Cosmelli, D.; Lachaux, J.-P.; Le Van Quyen, M. From Autopoiesis to Neurophenomenology: Francisco Varela's Exploration of the Biophysics of Being. *Biol. Res.* **2003**, *36*, 27–65. [CrossRef] [PubMed]
5. Clark, A.; Chalmers, D.J. The Extended Mind. *Analysis* **1998**, *58*, 7–19. [CrossRef]
6. Crick, F.; Koch, C. A Framework for Consciousness. *Nat. Neurosci.* **2003**, *6*, 119–126. [CrossRef]
7. Damasio, A. *Descartes' Error: Emotion, Reason, and the Human Brain*, 1st ed.; Harper Perennial: New York, NY, USA, 1995; ISBN 0-380-72647-5.
8. Dennett, D. *Consciousness Explained*, 1st ed.; Back Bay Books: New York, NY, USA, 1992; ISBN 0-316-18066-1.
9. Dolega, K.; Dewhurst, J. CURTAIN CALL AT THE CARTESIAN THEATRE. *J. Conscious. Stud.* **2015**, *22*, 109–128.
10. Forstmann, M.; Burgmer, P. The Cartesian Folk Theater: People Conceptualize Consciousness as a Spatio-Temporally Localized Process in the Human Brain 2021. *PsyArXiv* **2021**. [CrossRef]
11. Hobson, J.A.; Friston, K.J. A Response to Our Theatre Critics. *J. Conscious. Stud.* **2016**, *23*, 245–254.
12. Roepstorff, A.; Frith, C. What's at the Top in the Top-down Control of Action? Script-Sharing and "top-Top" Control of Action in Cognitive Experiments. *Psychol. Res.* **2004**, *68*, 189–198. [CrossRef]

13. Deacon, T.W. *Incomplete Nature: How Mind Emerged from Matter*, 1st ed.; W. W. Norton & Company: New York, NY, USA, 2011; ISBN 978-0-393-04991-6.
14. Dennett, D. *From Bacteria to Bach and Back: The Evolution of Minds*, 1st ed.; W. W. Norton & Company: New York, NY, USA, 2017; ISBN 978-0-393-24207-2.
15. Kant, I. *Critique of Pure Reason*; Guyer, P., Wood, A.W., Eds.; Cambridge University Press: Cambridge, MA, USA, 1781; ISBN 978-0-521-65729-7.
16. Schopenhauer, A. *The World as Will and Representation*; Courier Corporation: North Chelmsford, MA, USA, 1844; ISBN 978-0-486-13093-4.
17. Safron, A. Multilevel Evolutionary Developmental Optimization (MEDO): A Theoretical Framework for Understanding Preferences and Selection Dynamics. *arXiv* **2019**, arXiv:1910.13443.
18. Mountcastle, V.B. The Columnar Organization of the Neocortex. *Brain J. Neurol.* **1997**, *120 Pt 4*, 701–722. [CrossRef]
19. Bastos, A.M.; Usrey, W.M.; Adams, R.A.; Mangun, G.R.; Fries, P.; Friston, K.J. Canonical Microcircuits for Predictive Coding. *Neuron* **2012**, *76*, 695–711. [CrossRef] [PubMed]
20. Walsh, K.S.; McGovern, D.P.; Clark, A.; O'Connell, R.G. Evaluating the Neurophysiological Evidence for Predictive Processing as a Model of Perception. *Ann. N. Y. Acad. Sci.* **2020**, *1464*, 242–268. [CrossRef] [PubMed]
21. Bassingthwaighte, J.B. Fractal vascular growth patterns. *Acta Stereol.* **1992**, *11*, 305–319.
22. Ermentrout, G.B.; Edelstein-Keshet, L. Cellular Automata Approaches to Biological Modeling. *J. Theor. Biol.* **1993**, *160*, 97–133. [CrossRef] [PubMed]
23. Eaton, R.C.; Lee, R.K.; Foreman, M.B. The Mauthner Cell and Other Identified Neurons of the Brainstem Escape Network of Fish. *Prog. Neurobiol.* **2001**, *63*, 467–485. [CrossRef]
24. Lancer, B.H.; Evans, B.J.E.; Fabian, J.M.; O'Carroll, D.C.; Wiederman, S.D. A Target-Detecting Visual Neuron in the Dragonfly Locks on to Selectively Attended Targets. *J. Neurosci.* **2019**, *39*, 8497–8509. [CrossRef]
25. Sculley, D.; Holt, G.; Golovin, D.; Davydov, E.; Phillips, T.; Ebner, D.; Chaudhary, V.; Young, M. Machine Learning: The High Interest Credit Card of Technical Debt. 2014. Available online: https://research.google/pubs/pub43146/ (accessed on 26 May 2021).
26. Wolfram, S. *A New Kind of Science*, 1st ed.; Wolfram Media: Champaign, IL, USA, 2002; ISBN 978-1-57955-008-0.
27. Crispo, E. The Baldwin Effect and Genetic Assimilation: Revisiting Two Mechanisms of Evolutionary Change Mediated by Phenotypic Plasticity. *Evol. Int. J. Org. Evol.* **2007**, *61*, 2469–2479. [CrossRef]
28. Jaeger, J.; Monk, N. Bioattractors: Dynamical Systems Theory and the Evolution of Regulatory Processes. *J. Physiol.* **2014**, *592*, 2267–2281. [CrossRef]
29. Waddington, C.H. Canalization of development and the inheritance of acquired characters. *Nature* **1942**, *150*, 150563a0. [CrossRef]
30. Hofsten, C.V.; Feng, Q.; Spelke, E.S. Object Representation and Predictive Action in Infancy. *Dev. Sci.* **2000**, *3*, 193–205. [CrossRef]
31. Spelke, E.S.; Kinzler, K.D. Core Knowledge. *Dev. Sci.* **2007**, *10*, 89–96. [CrossRef]
32. Partanen, E.; Kujala, T.; Näätänen, R.; Liitola, A.; Sambeth, A.; Huotilainen, M. Learning-Induced Neural Plasticity of Speech Processing before Birth. *Proc. Natl. Acad. Sci. USA* **2013**, *110*, 15145–15150. [CrossRef]
33. Lake, B.M.; Ullman, T.D.; Tenenbaum, J.B.; Gershman, S.J. Building Machines That Learn and Think like People. *Behav. Brain Sci.* **2017**, *40*. [CrossRef] [PubMed]
34. Tenenbaum, J.B.; Kemp, C.; Griffiths, T.L.; Goodman, N.D. How to Grow a Mind: Statistics, Structure, and Abstraction. *Science* **2011**, *331*, 1279–1285. [CrossRef] [PubMed]
35. Zador, A.M. A Critique of Pure Learning and What Artificial Neural Networks Can Learn from Animal Brains. *Nat. Commun.* **2019**, *10*, 1–7. [CrossRef] [PubMed]
36. Conant, R.C.; Ashby, W.R. Every Good Regulator of a System Must Be a Model of That System. *Int. J. Syst. Sci.* **1970**, *1*, 89–97. [CrossRef]
37. Mansell, W. Control of Perception Should Be Operationalized as a Fundamental Property of the Nervous System. *Top. Cogn. Sci.* **2011**, *3*, 257–261. [CrossRef]
38. Pfeifer, R.; Bongard, J. *How the Body Shapes the Way We Think: A New View of Intelligence*; A Bradford Book: Cambridge, MA, USA, 2006; ISBN 978-0-262-16239-5.
39. Rochat, P. Emerging Self-Concept. In *The Wiley-Blackwell Handbook of Infant Development*; Bremner, J.G., Wachs, T.D., Eds.; Wiley-Blackwell: Hoboken, NJ, USA, 2010; pp. 320–344. ISBN 978-1-4443-2756-4.
40. Bingham, G.P.; Snapp-Childs, W.; Zhu, Q. Information about Relative Phase in Bimanual Coordination Is Modality Specific (Not Amodal), but Kinesthesis and Vision Can Teach One Another. *Hum. Mov. Sci.* **2018**, *60*, 98–106. [CrossRef]
41. Snapp-Childs, W.; Wilson, A.D.; Bingham, G.P. Transfer of Learning between Unimanual and Bimanual Rhythmic Movement Coordination: Transfer Is a Function of the Task Dynamic. *Exp. Brain Res.* **2015**, *233*, 2225–2238. [CrossRef]
42. Zhu, Q.; Mirich, T.; Huang, S.; Snapp-Childs, W.; Bingham, G.P. When Kinesthetic Information Is Neglected in Learning a Novel Bimanual Rhythmic Coordination. *Atten. Percept. Psychophys.* **2017**, *79*, 1830–1840. [CrossRef]
43. Tani, J. *Exploring Robotic Minds: Actions, Symbols, and Consciousness as Self-Organizing Dynamic Phenomena*; Oxford University Press: Oxford, UK, 2016.
44. Buckner, R.L.; Krienen, F.M. The Evolution of Distributed Association Networks in the Human Brain. *Trends Cogn. Sci.* **2013**, *17*, 648–665. [CrossRef]

45. Barsalou, L. Grounded Cognition. *Annu. Rev. Psychol.* **2008**, *59*, 617–645. [CrossRef]
46. Barsalou, L. Perceptual Symbol Systems. *Behav. Brain Sci.* **1999**, *22*, 577–609; discussion 610–660. [CrossRef]
47. Lakoff, G. Mapping the Brain's Metaphor Circuitry: Metaphorical Thought in Everyday Reason. *Front. Hum. Neurosci.* **2014**, *8*. [CrossRef] [PubMed]
48. Lakoff, G.; Johnson, M. *Philosophy in the Flesh: The Embodied Mind and Its Challenge to Western Thought*; Basic Books: New York, NY, USA, 1999; ISBN 0-465-05674-1.
49. Metzinger, T. *The Ego Tunnel: The Science of the Mind and the Myth of the Self*, 1st ed.; Basic Books: New York, NY, USA, 2009; ISBN 978-0-465-04567-9.
50. Helmholtz, H. The Facts in Perception. In *Selected Writings of Hermann Helmholtz*; Kahl, R., Ed.; Wesleyan University Press: Middletown, CT, USA, 1878.
51. McGurk, H.; MacDonald, J. Hearing Lips and Seeing Voices. *Nature* **1976**, *264*, 746–748. [CrossRef] [PubMed]
52. Nour, M.M.; Nour, J.M. Perception, Illusions and Bayesian Inference. *Psychopathology* **2015**, *48*, 217–221. [CrossRef] [PubMed]
53. Harman, G.H. The Inference to the Best Explanation. *Philos. Rev.* **1965**, *74*, 88–95. [CrossRef]
54. Friston, K. The Free-Energy Principle: A Unified Brain Theory? *Nat. Rev. Neurosci.* **2010**, *11*, 127–138. [CrossRef] [PubMed]
55. Friston, K.J.; FitzGerald, T.; Rigoli, F.; Schwartenbeck, P.; Pezzulo, G. Active Inference: A Process Theory. *Neural Comput.* **2017**, *29*, 1–49. [CrossRef] [PubMed]
56. Friston, K.J.; Kilner, J.; Harrison, L. A Free Energy Principle for the Brain. *J. Physiol. Paris* **2006**, *100*, 70–87. [CrossRef]
57. Friston, K. Life as We Know It. *J. R. Soc. Interface* **2013**, *10*, 20130475. [CrossRef]
58. Ramstead, M.J.D.; Badcock, P.B.; Friston, K.J. Answering Schrödinger's Question: A Free-Energy Formulation. *Phys. Life Rev.* **2017**. [CrossRef] [PubMed]
59. Safron, A. Bayesian Analogical Cybernetics. *arXiv* **2019**, arXiv:1911.02362.
60. Safron, A.; DeYoung, C. Integrating Cybernetic Big Five Theory with the Free Energy Principle: A New Strategy for Modeling Personalities as Complex Systems. *PsyArXiv* **2020**. [CrossRef]
61. Seth, A.K. *The Cybernetic Bayesian Brain*; Open MIND; MIND Group: Frankfurt am Main, Germany, 2014; ISBN 978-3-95857-010-8.
62. Hohwy, J. The Self-Evidencing Brain. *Noûs* **2016**, *50*, 259–285. [CrossRef]
63. Damasio, A.R. *The Strange Order of Things: Life, Feeling, and the Making of Cultures*; Pantheon Books: New York, NY, USA, 2018; ISBN 978-0-307-90875-9.
64. Friston, K.J. A Free Energy Principle for a Particular Physics. *arXiv* **2019**, arXiv:1906.10184.
65. Schopenhauer, A. *Arthur Schopenhauer: The World as Will and Presentation: Volume I*, 1st ed.; Kolak, D., Ed.; Routledge: New York, NY, USA, 1818; ISBN 978-0-321-35578-2.
66. Spinoza, B. *de Ethics*; Penguin Classics: London, UK, 1677; ISBN 978-0-14-043571-9.
67. Fuster, J.M. Cortex and Memory: Emergence of a New Paradigm. *J. Cogn. Neurosci.* **2009**, *21*, 2047–2072. [CrossRef] [PubMed]
68. Hayek, F.A. *The Sensory Order: An Inquiry into the Foundations of Theoretical Psychology*; University of Chicago Press: Chicago, IL, USA, 1952; ISBN 0-226-32094-4.
69. Baldassano, C.; Chen, J.; Zadbood, A.; Pillow, J.W.; Hasson, U.; Norman, K.A. Discovering Event Structure in Continuous Narrative Perception and Memory. *Neuron* **2017**, *95*, 709–721.e5. [CrossRef]
70. Friston, K.; Buzsáki, G. The Functional Anatomy of Time: What and When in the Brain. *Trends Cogn. Sci.* **2016**, *20*, 500–511. [CrossRef]
71. Hawkins, J.; Blakeslee, S. *On Intelligence*; Adapted; Times Books: New York, NY, USA, 2004; ISBN 0-8050-7456-2.
72. Adams, R.; Shipp, S.; Friston, K.J. Predictions Not Commands: Active Inference in the Motor System. *Brain Struct. Funct.* **2013**, *218*, 611–643. [CrossRef]
73. Safron, A. An Integrated World Modeling Theory (IWMT) of Consciousness: Combining Integrated Information and Global Neuronal Workspace Theories With the Free Energy Principle and Active Inference Framework; Toward Solving the Hard Problem and Characterizing Agentic Causation. *Front. Artif. Intell.* **2020**, *3*. [CrossRef]
74. Safron, A. Integrated world modeling theory (IWMT) implemented: Towards reverse engineering consciousness with the free energy principle and active inference. *PsyArXiv* **2020**. [CrossRef]
75. Seth, A.K.; Friston, K.J. Active Interoceptive Inference and the Emotional Brain. *Phil. Trans. R. Soc. B* **2016**, *371*, 20160007. [CrossRef] [PubMed]
76. Hesp, C.; Smith, R.; Allen, M.; Friston, K.; Ramstead, M. Deeply felt affect: The emergence of valence in deep active inference. *PsyArXiv* **2019**. [CrossRef]
77. Parr, T.; Friston, K.J. Working Memory, Attention, and Salience in Active Inference. *Sci. Rep.* **2017**, *7*, 14678. [CrossRef]
78. Markram, K.; Markram, H. The Intense World Theory—A Unifying Theory of the Neurobiology of Autism. *Front. Hum. Neurosci.* **2010**, *4*, 224. [CrossRef]
79. Pellicano, E.; Burr, D. When the World Becomes "Too Real": A Bayesian Explanation of Autistic Perception. *Trends Cogn. Sci.* **2012**, *16*, 504–510. [CrossRef] [PubMed]
80. Van de Cruys, S.; Evers, K.; Van der Hallen, R.; Van Eylen, L.; Boets, B.; de-Wit, L.; Wagemans, J. Precise Minds in Uncertain Worlds: Predictive Coding in Autism. *Psychol. Rev.* **2014**, *121*, 649–675. [CrossRef]
81. Friston, K. Hallucinations and Perceptual Inference. *Behav. Brain Sci.* **2005**, *28*, 764–766. [CrossRef]

82. Horga, G.; Schatz, K.C.; Abi-Dargham, A.; Peterson, B.S. Deficits in Predictive Coding Underlie Hallucinations in Schizophrenia. *J. Neurosci.* **2014**, *34*, 8072–8082. [CrossRef]
83. Sterzer, P.; Adams, R.A.; Fletcher, P.; Frith, C.; Lawrie, S.M.; Muckli, L.; Petrovic, P.; Uhlhaas, P.; Voss, M.; Corlett, P.R. The Predictive Coding Account of Psychosis. *Biol. Psychiatry* **2018**, *84*, 634–643. [CrossRef]
84. Smith, L.B.; Jayaraman, S.; Clerkin, E.; Yu, C. The Developing Infant Creates a Curriculum for Statistical Learning. *Trends Cogn. Sci.* **2018**, *22*, 325–336. [CrossRef] [PubMed]
85. Emerson, C. The Outer Word and Inner Speech: Bakhtin, Vygotsky, and the Internalization of Language. *Crit. Inq.* **1983**, *10*, 245–264. [CrossRef]
86. Piaget, J. The Role of Action in the Development of Thinking. In *Knowledge and Development*; Springer: Boston, MA, USA, 1977; pp. 17–42. ISBN 978-1-4684-2549-9.
87. Ciaunica, A.; Constant, A.; Preissl, H.; Fotopoulou, A. The First Prior: From Co-Embodiment to Co-Homeostasis in Early Life. *PsyArXiv* **2021**. [CrossRef]
88. Friston, K.J. Self-Evidencing Babies: Commentary on "Mentalizing Homeostasis: The Social Origins of Interoceptive Inference" by Fotopoulou & Tsakiris. *Neuropsychoanalysis* **2017**, *19*, 43–47.
89. Bruineberg, J.; Rietveld, E. Self-Organization, Free Energy Minimization, and Optimal Grip on a Field of Affordances. *Front. Hum. Neurosci.* **2014**, *8*, 599. [CrossRef] [PubMed]
90. Allen, M.; Tsakiris, M. The Body as First Prior: Interoceptive Predictive Processing and the Primacy of Self-Models. In *The Interoceptive Mind: From Homeostasis to Awareness*; Tsakiris, M., De Preester, H., Eds.; Oxford University Press: Oxford, UK, 2018; pp. 27–45.
91. Ciaunica, A.; Safron, A.; Delafield-Butt, J. Back to square one: From embodied experiences in utero to theories of consciousness. *PsyArXiv* **2021**. [CrossRef]
92. Fotopoulou, A.; Tsakiris, M. Mentalizing Homeostasis: The Social Origins of Interoceptive Inference-Replies to Commentaries. *Neuropsychoanalysis* **2017**, *19*, 71–76. [CrossRef]
93. Palmer, C.J.; Seth, A.K.; Hohwy, J. The Felt Presence of Other Minds: Predictive Processing, Counterfactual Predictions, and Mentalising in Autism. *Conscious. Cogn.* **2015**, *36*, 376–389. [CrossRef]
94. Cisek, P. Cortical Mechanisms of Action Selection: The Affordance Competition Hypothesis. *Philos. Trans. R. Soc. B Biol. Sci.* **2007**, *362*, 1585–1599. [CrossRef] [PubMed]
95. Gibson, J.J. *"The Theory of Affordances," in Perceiving, Acting, and Knowing. Towards an Ecological Psychology*; John Wiley & Sons Inc.: Hoboken, NJ, USA, 1977.
96. Reed, E. James Gibson's ecological approach to cognition. In *Cognitive Psychology in Question*; Costall, A., Still, A., Eds.; St Martin's Press: New York, NY, USA, 1991; pp. 171–197.
97. Hofstadter, D.; Sander, E. *Surfaces and Essences: Analogy as the Fuel and Fire of Thinking*, 1st ed.; Basic Books: New York, NY, USA, 2013; ISBN 978-0-465-01847-5.
98. Haken, H. Synergetics of the Brain: An Outline of Some Basic Ideas. In *Induced Rhythms in the Brain*; Başar, E., Bullock, T.H., Eds.; Brain Dynamics; Birkhäuser Boston: Boston, MA, USA, 1992; pp. 417–421. ISBN 978-1-4757-1281-0.
99. Friston, K.J.; Rigoli, F.; Ognibene, D.; Mathys, C.; Fitzgerald, T.; Pezzulo, G. Active Inference and Epistemic Value. *Cogn. Neurosci.* **2015**, *6*, 187–214. [CrossRef]
100. Dreyfus, H.L. Why Heideggerian AI Failed and How Fixing It Would Require Making It More Heideggerian. *Philos. Psychol.* **2007**, *20*, 247–268. [CrossRef]
101. Husserl, E. *The Crisis of European Sciences and Transcendental Phenomenology: An Introduction to Phenomenological Philosophy*; Northwestern University Press: Evanston, IL, USA, 1936; ISBN 978-0-8101-0458-7.
102. Shanahan, M. *Embodiment and the Inner Life: Cognition and Consciousness in the Space of Possible Minds*, 1st ed.; Oxford University Press: Oxford, UK; New York, NY, USA, 2010; ISBN 978-0-19-922655-9.
103. Williams, J.; Störmer, V.S. Working Memory: How Much Is It Used in Natural Behavior? *Curr. Biol.* **2021**, *31*, R205–R206. [CrossRef]
104. Dehaene, S.; Changeux, J.-P. Experimental and Theoretical Approaches to Conscious Processing. *Neuron* **2011**, *70*, 200–227. [CrossRef]
105. Ho, M.K.; Abel, D.; Correa, C.G.; Littman, M.L.; Cohen, J.D.; Griffiths, T.L. Control of Mental Representations in Human Planning. *arXiv* **2021**, arXiv:2105.06948.
106. Parr, T.; Friston, K.J. The Discrete and Continuous Brain: From Decisions to Movement-And Back Again. *Neural Comput.* **2018**, *30*, 2319–2347. [CrossRef] [PubMed]
107. Hassabis, D.; Kumaran, D.; Summerfield, C.; Botvinick, M. Neuroscience-Inspired Artificial Intelligence. *Neuron* **2017**, *95*, 245–258. [CrossRef]
108. Latash, M.L. Motor Synergies and the Equilibrium-Point Hypothesis. *Motor Control* **2010**, *14*, 294–322. [CrossRef] [PubMed]
109. Hipólito, I.; Baltieri, M.; Friston, K.; Ramstead, M.J.D. Embodied Skillful Performance: Where the Action Is. *Synthese* **2021**. [CrossRef]
110. Mannella, F.; Gurney, K.; Baldassarre, G. The Nucleus Accumbens as a Nexus between Values and Goals in Goal-Directed Behavior: A Review and a New Hypothesis. *Front. Behav. Neurosci.* **2013**, *7*, 135. [CrossRef]

111. James, W. *The Principles of Psychology, Vol. 1*, Reprint edition; Dover Publications: New York, NY, USA, 1890; ISBN 978-0-486-20381-2.
112. Shin, Y.K.; Proctor, R.W.; Capaldi, E.J. A Review of Contemporary Ideomotor Theory. *Psychol. Bull.* **2010**, *136*, 943–974. [CrossRef]
113. Woodworth, R.S. The Accuracy of Voluntary Movement. *Psychol. Rev. Monogr. Suppl.* **1899**, *3*, i–114. [CrossRef]
114. Brown, H.; Friston, K.; Bestmann, S. Active Inference, Attention, and Motor Preparation. *Front. Psychol.* **2011**, *2*, 218. [CrossRef]
115. Menon, V.; Uddin, L.Q. Saliency, Switching, Attention and Control: A Network Model of Insula Function. *Brain Struct. Funct.* **2010**, *214*, 655–667. [CrossRef]
116. Caporale, N.; Dan, Y. Spike Timing-Dependent Plasticity: A Hebbian Learning Rule. *Annu. Rev. Neurosci.* **2008**, *31*, 25–46. [CrossRef] [PubMed]
117. Markram, H.; Gerstner, W.; Sjöström, P.J. A History of Spike-Timing-Dependent Plasticity. *Front. Synaptic Neurosci.* **2011**, *3*, 4. [CrossRef]
118. Graziano, M.S.A. *Rethinking Consciousness: A Scientific Theory of Subjective Experience*, 1st ed.; WWNorton & Company: New York, NY, USA, 2019; ISBN 978-0-393-65261-1.
119. Pearl, J.; Mackenzie, D. *The Book of Why: The New Science of Cause and Effect*; Basic Books: New York, NY, USA, 2018; ISBN 978-0-465-09761-6.
120. Vygotsky, L.S. *Thought and Language—Revised Edition*, Kozulin, A., Ed.; revised edition; The MIT Press: Cambridge, MA, USA, 1934; ISBN 978-0-262-72010-6.
121. Tomasello, M. *A Natural History of Human Thinking*; Harvard University Press: Cambridge, USA, 2014; ISBN 978-0-674-72636-9.
122. Rizzolatti, G.; Riggio, L.; Dascola, I.; Umiltá, C. Reorienting Attention across the Horizontal and Vertical Meridians: Evidence in Favor of a Premotor Theory of Attention. *Neuropsychologia* **1987**, *25*, 31–40. [CrossRef]
123. Desimone, R.; Duncan, J. Neural Mechanisms of Selective Visual Attention. *Annu. Rev. Neurosci.* **1995**, *18*, 193–222. [CrossRef]
124. Marvel, C.L.; Morgan, O.P.; Kronemer, S.I. How the Motor System Integrates with Working Memory. *Neurosci. Biobehav. Rev.* **2019**, *102*, 184–194. [CrossRef] [PubMed]
125. Veniero, D.; Gross, J.; Morand, S.; Duecker, F.; Sack, A.T.; Thut, G. Top-down Control of Visual Cortex by the Frontal Eye Fields through Oscillatory Realignment. *Nat. Commun.* **2021**, *12*, 1757. [CrossRef]
126. Liang, W.-K.; Tseng, P.; Yeh, J.-R.; Huang, N.E.; Juan, C.-H. Frontoparietal Beta Amplitude Modulation and Its Interareal Cross-Frequency Coupling in Visual Working Memory. *Neuroscience* **2021**, *460*, 69–87. [CrossRef]
127. Watanabe, T.; Mima, T.; Shibata, S.; Kirimoto, H. Midfrontal Theta as Moderator between Beta Oscillations and Precision Control. *NeuroImage* **2021**, 118022. [CrossRef] [PubMed]
128. Landau, S.M.; Lal, R.; O'Neil, J.P.; Baker, S.; Jagust, W.J. Striatal Dopamine and Working Memory. *Cereb. Cortex* **2009**, *19*, 445–454. [CrossRef] [PubMed]
129. Baars, B.J.; Franklin, S.; Ramsoy, T.Z. Global Workspace Dynamics: Cortical "Binding and Propagation" Enables Conscious Contents. *Front. Psychol.* **2013**, *4*. [CrossRef]
130. Craig, A.D.B. How Do You Feel–Now? The Anterior Insula and Human Awareness. *Nat. Rev. Neurosci.* **2009**, *10*, 59–70. [CrossRef]
131. Estefan, D.P.; Zucca, R.; Arsiwalla, X.; Principe, A.; Zhang, H.; Rocamora, R.; Axmacher, N.; Verschure, P.F.M.J. Volitional Learning Promotes Theta Phase Coding in the Human Hippocampus. *Proc. Natl. Acad. Sci. USA* **2021**, *118*. [CrossRef]
132. Herzog, M.H.; Kammer, T.; Scharnowski, F. Time Slices: What Is the Duration of a Percept? *PLoS Biol.* **2016**, *14*, e1002433. [CrossRef] [PubMed]
133. Canolty, R.T.; Knight, R.T. The Functional Role of Cross-Frequency Coupling. *Trends Cogn. Sci.* **2010**, *14*, 506–515. [CrossRef]
134. Sweeney-Reed, C.M.; Zaehle, T.; Voges, J.; Schmitt, F.C.; Buentjen, L.; Borchardt, V.; Walter, M.; Hinrichs, H.; Heinze, H.-J.; Rugg, M.D.; et al. Anterior Thalamic High Frequency Band Activity Is Coupled with Theta Oscillations at Rest. *Front. Hum. Neurosci.* **2017**, *11*. [CrossRef]
135. Hassabis, D.; Kumaran, D.; Vann, S.D.; Maguire, E.A. Patients with Hippocampal Amnesia Cannot Imagine New Experiences. *Proc. Natl. Acad. Sci. USA* **2007**, *104*, 1726–1731. [CrossRef]
136. Schacter, D.L.; Addis, D.R. On the Nature of Medial Temporal Lobe Contributions to the Constructive Simulation of Future Events. *Philos. Trans. R. Soc. Lond. B. Biol. Sci.* **2009**, *364*, 1245–1253. [CrossRef] [PubMed]
137. MacKay, D.G. *Remembering: What 50 Years of Research with Famous Amnesia Patient H. M. Can Teach Us about Memory and How It Works*; Prometheus Books: Amherst, NY, USA, 2019; ISBN 978-1-63388-407-6.
138. Voss, J.L.; Cohen, N.J. Hippocampal-Cortical Contributions to Strategic Exploration during Perceptual Discrimination. *Hippocampus* **2017**, *27*, 642–652. [CrossRef]
139. Koster, R.; Chadwick, M.J.; Chen, Y.; Berron, D.; Banino, A.; Düzel, E.; Hassabis, D.; Kumaran, D. Big-Loop Recurrence within the Hippocampal System Supports Integration of Information across Episodes. *Neuron* **2018**, *99*, 1342–1354.e6. [CrossRef]
140. Rodriguez-Larios, J.; Faber, P.; Achermann, P.; Tei, S.; Alaerts, K. From Thoughtless Awareness to Effortful Cognition: Alpha - Theta Cross-Frequency Dynamics in Experienced Meditators during Meditation, Rest and Arithmetic. *Sci. Rep.* **2020**, *10*, 5419. [CrossRef]
141. Hasz, B.M.; Redish, A.D. Spatial Encoding in Dorsomedial Prefrontal Cortex and Hippocampus Is Related during Deliberation. *Hippocampus* **2020**, *30*, 1194–1208. [CrossRef] [PubMed]

142. Kunz, L.; Wang, L.; Lachner-Piza, D.; Zhang, H.; Brandt, A.; Dümpelmann, M.; Reinacher, P.C.; Coenen, V.A.; Chen, D.; Wang, W.-X.; et al. Hippocampal Theta Phases Organize the Reactivation of Large-Scale Electrophysiological Representations during Goal-Directed Navigation. *Sci. Adv.* **2019**, *5*, eaav8192. [CrossRef] [PubMed]
143. Hassabis, D.; Spreng, R.N.; Rusu, A.A.; Robbins, C.A.; Mar, R.A.; Schacter, D.L. Imagine All the People: How the Brain Creates and Uses Personality Models to Predict Behavior. *Cereb. Cortex* **2014**, *24*, 1979–1987. [CrossRef]
144. Zheng, A.; Montez, D.F.; Marek, S.; Gilmore, A.W.; Newbold, D.J.; Laumann, T.O.; Kay, B.P.; Seider, N.A.; Van, A.N.; Hampton, J.M.; et al. Parallel Hippocampal-Parietal Circuits for Self- and Goal-Oriented Processing. *bioRxiv* **2020**, 2020.12.01.395210. [CrossRef]
145. Ijspeert, A.J.; Crespi, A.; Ryczko, D.; Cabelguen, J.-M. From Swimming to Walking with a Salamander Robot Driven by a Spinal Cord Model. *Science* **2007**, *315*, 1416–1420. [CrossRef] [PubMed]
146. Di Lallo, A.; Catalano, M.G.; Garabini, M.; Grioli, G.; Gabiccini, M.; Bicchi, A. Dynamic Morphological Computation Through Damping Design of Soft Continuum Robots. *Front. Robot. AI* **2019**, *6*. [CrossRef]
147. Othayoth, R.; Thoms, G.; Li, C. An Energy Landscape Approach to Locomotor Transitions in Complex 3D Terrain. *Proc. Natl. Acad. Sci. USA* **2020**, *117*, 14987–14995. [CrossRef] [PubMed]
148. Clark, A. Whatever next? Predictive Brains, Situated Agents, and the Future of Cognitive Science. *Behav. Brain Sci.* **2013**, *36*, 181–204. [CrossRef] [PubMed]
149. Constant, A.; Ramstead, M.J.D.; Veissière, S.P.L.; Campbell, J.O.; Friston, K.J. A Variational Approach to Niche Construction. *J. R. Soc. Interface* **2018**, *15*. [CrossRef] [PubMed]
150. Merleau-Ponty, M. *The Visible and the Invisible: Followed by Working Notes*; Northwestern University Press: Evanston, IL, USA, 1968; ISBN 978-0-8101-0457-0.
151. Araya, J.M. Emotion and the predictive mind: Emotions as (almost) drives. *Revista de Filosofia Aurora* **2019**. [CrossRef]
152. Craig, A.D. A New View of Pain as a Homeostatic Emotion. *Trends Neurosci.* **2003**, *26*, 303–307. [CrossRef]
153. Critchley, H.D.; Garfinkel, S.N. Interoception and Emotion. *Curr. Opin. Psychol.* **2017**, *17*, 7–14. [CrossRef]
154. Seth, A.K.; Suzuki, K.; Critchley, H.D. An Interoceptive Predictive Coding Model of Conscious Presence. *Front. Psychol.* **2011**, *2*, 395. [CrossRef]
155. Parr, T.; Limanowski, J.; Rawji, V.; Friston, K. The Computational Neurology of Movement under Active Inference. *Brain J. Neurol.* **2021**. [CrossRef]
156. Damasio, A. *The Feeling of What Happens: Body and Emotion in the Making of Consciousness*, 1st ed.; Mariner Books: Boston, MA, USA, 2000; ISBN 0-15-601075-5.
157. Cappuccio, M.L.; Kirchhoff, M.D.; Alnajjar, F.; Tani, J. Unfulfilled Prophecies in Sport Performance: Active Inference and the Choking Effect. *J. Conscious. Stud.* **2019**, *27*, 152–184.
158. Sengupta, B.; Tozzi, A.; Cooray, G.K.; Douglas, P.K.; Friston, K.J. Towards a Neuronal Gauge Theory. *PLoS Biol.* **2016**, *14*, e1002400. [CrossRef]
159. Bartolomei, F.; Lagarde, S.; Scavarda, D.; Carron, R.; Bénar, C.G.; Picard, F. The Role of the Dorsal Anterior Insula in Ecstatic Sensation Revealed by Direct Electrical Brain Stimulation. *Brain Stimul. Basic Transl. Clin. Res. Neuromodulation* **2019**, *12*, 1121–1126. [CrossRef]
160. Belin-Rauscent, A.; Daniel, M.-L.; Puaud, M.; Jupp, B.; Sawiak, S.; Howett, D.; McKenzie, C.; Caprioli, D.; Besson, M.; Robbins, T.W.; et al. From Impulses to Maladaptive Actions: The Insula Is a Neurobiological Gate for the Development of Compulsive Behavior. *Mol. Psychiatry* **2016**, *21*, 491–499. [CrossRef]
161. Campbell, M.E.J.; Nguyen, V.T.; Cunnington, R.; Breakspear, M. Insula Cortex Gates the Interplay of Action Observation and Preparation for Controlled Imitation. *bioRxiv* **2021**. [CrossRef]
162. Rueter, A.R.; Abram, S.V.; MacDonald, A.W.; Rustichini, A.; DeYoung, C.G. The Goal Priority Network as a Neural Substrate of Conscientiousness. *Hum. Brain Mapp.* **2018**, *39*, 3574–3585. [CrossRef]
163. Park, H.-D.; Barnoud, C.; Trang, H.; Kannape, O.A.; Schaller, K.; Blanke, O. Breathing Is Coupled with Voluntary Action and the Cortical Readiness Potential. *Nat. Commun.* **2020**, *11*, 1–8. [CrossRef]
164. Zhou, Y.; Friston, K.J.; Zeidman, P.; Chen, J.; Li, S.; Razi, A. The Hierarchical Organization of the Default, Dorsal Attention and Salience Networks in Adolescents and Young Adults. *Cereb. Cortex N. Y. NY* **2018**, *28*, 726–737. [CrossRef] [PubMed]
165. Smigielski, L.; Scheidegger, M.; Kometer, M.; Vollenweider, F.X. Psilocybin-Assisted Mindfulness Training Modulates Self-Consciousness and Brain Default Mode Network Connectivity with Lasting Effects. *NeuroImage* **2019**, *196*, 207–215. [CrossRef] [PubMed]
166. Lutz, A.; Mattout, J.; Pagnoni, G. The Epistemic and Pragmatic Value of Non-Action: A Predictive Coding Perspective on Meditation. *Curr. Opin. Psychol.* **2019**, *28*, 166–171. [CrossRef] [PubMed]
167. Deane, G.; Miller, M.; Wilkinson, S. Losing Ourselves: Active Inference, Depersonalization, and Meditation. *Front. Psychol.* **2020**, *11*. [CrossRef] [PubMed]
168. Block, N. Phenomenal and Access Consciousness Ned Block and Cynthia MacDonald: Consciousness and Cognitive Access. *Proc. Aristot. Soc.* **2008**, *108*, 289–317.
169. O'Regan, J.K.; Noë, A. A Sensorimotor Account of Vision and Visual Consciousness. *Behav. Brain Sci.* **2001**, *24*, 939–973; discussion 973–1031. [CrossRef]

170. van den Heuvel, M.P.; Sporns, O. Rich-Club Organization of the Human Connectome. *J. Neurosci.* **2011**, *31*, 15775–15786. [CrossRef] [PubMed]
171. Tononi, G.; Edelman, G. Consciousness and Complexity. *Science* **1998**, *282*, 1846–1851. [CrossRef] [PubMed]
172. Baars, B.J. *In the Theater of Consciousness: The Workspace of the Mind*, Reprint edition; Oxford University Press: New York, NY, USA, 2001; ISBN 978-0-19-514703-2.
173. Tononi, G. An Information Integration Theory of Consciousness. *BMC Neurosci.* **2004**, *5*, 42. [CrossRef] [PubMed]
174. Kirchhoff, M.D.; Kiverstein, J. *Extended Consciousness and Predictive Processing: A Third Wave View*, 1st ed.; Routledge: New York, NY, USA, 2019; ISBN 978-1-138-55681-2.
175. Buzsáki, G. Neural Syntax: Cell Assemblies, Synapsembles, and Readers. *Neuron* **2010**, *68*, 362–385. [CrossRef]
176. Buzsáki, G.; Watson, B.O. Brain Rhythms and Neural Syntax: Implications for Efficient Coding of Cognitive Content and Neuropsychiatric Disease. *Dialogues Clin. Neurosci.* **2012**, *14*, 345–367.
177. Ramstead, M.J.D.; Kirchhoff, M.D.; Friston, K.J. A Tale of Two Densities: Active Inference Is Enactive Inference. Available online: http://philsci-archive.pitt.edu/16167/ (accessed on 12 December 2019).
178. Friedman, D.; Tschantz, A.; Ramstead, M.; Friston, K.; Constant, A. Active Inferants The Basis for an Active Inference Framework for Ant Colony Behavior. *Front. Behav. Neurosci.* **2020**. [CrossRef]
179. LeDoux, J. *The Deep History of Ourselves: The Four-Billion-Year Story of How We Got Conscious Brains*; Penguin Books: London, UK, 2019.
180. Tsakiris, M. The Multisensory Basis of the Self: From Body to Identity to Others. *Q. J. Exp. Psychol.* **2017**, *70*, 597–609. [CrossRef]
181. Rudrauf, D.; Bennequin, D.; Granic, I.; Landini, G.; Friston, K.J.; Williford, K. A Mathematical Model of Embodied Consciousness. *J. Theor. Biol.* **2017**, *428*, 106–131. [CrossRef]
182. Sauciuc, G.-A.; Zlakowska, J.; Persson, T.; Lenninger, S.; Madsen, E.A. Imitation Recognition and Its Prosocial Effects in 6-Month Old Infants. *PLoS ONE* **2020**, *15*, e0232717. [CrossRef] [PubMed]
183. Slaughter, V. Do Newborns Have the Ability to Imitate? *Trends Cogn. Sci.* **2021**, *25*, 377–387. [CrossRef]
184. Bouizegarene, N.; Ramstead, M.; Constant, A.; Friston, K.; Kirmayer, L. Narrative as active inference. *PsyArXiv* **2020**. [CrossRef]
185. Gentner, D. Bootstrapping the Mind: Analogical Processes and Symbol Systems. *Cogn. Sci.* **2010**, *34*, 752–775. [CrossRef] [PubMed]
186. Hofstadter, D.R. *Gödel, Escher, Bach: An Eternal Golden Braid*; 20 Anv.; Basic Books: New York, NY, USA, 1979; ISBN 0-465-02656-7.
187. Friston, K.J.; Frith, C. A Duet for One. *Conscious. Cogn.* **2015**, *36*, 390–405. [CrossRef] [PubMed]
188. Friston, K.J.; Frith, C.D. Active Inference, Communication and Hermeneutics. *Cortex J. Devoted Study Nerv. Syst. Behav.* **2015**, *68*, 129–143. [CrossRef] [PubMed]
189. De Jaegher, H. Embodiment and Sense-Making in Autism. *Front. Integr. Neurosci.* **2013**, *7*, 15. [CrossRef]
190. Tomasello, M.; Carpenter, M. Shared Intentionality. *Dev. Sci.* **2007**, *10*, 121–125. [CrossRef]
191. Tomasello, M. *The Cultural Origins of Human Cognition*; Harvard University Press: Cambridge, MA, USA, 2001; ISBN 0-674-00582-1.
192. Maschler, M. The Bargaining Set, Kernel, and Nucleolus. *Handb. Game Theory Econ. Appl.* **1992**, *1*, 591–667.
193. Kuhn, T.S. *The Structure of Scientific Revolutions*, 3rd ed.; University of Chicago Press: Chicago, IL, USA, 1962; ISBN 978-0-226-45808-3.
194. Blakeslee, S.; Blakeslee, M. *The Body Has a Mind of Its Own: How Body Maps in Your Brain Help You Do (Almost) Everything Better*; Random House Publishing Group: New York, NY, USA, 2008; ISBN 978-1-58836-812-6.
195. Cardinali, L.; Frassinetti, F.; Brozzoli, C.; Urquizar, C.; Roy, A.C.; Farnè, A. Tool-Use Induces Morphological Updating of the Body Schema. *Curr. Biol.* **2009**, *19*, R478–R479. [CrossRef]
196. Ehrsson, H.H.; Holmes, N.P.; Passingham, R.E. Touching a Rubber Hand: Feeling of Body Ownership Is Associated with Activity in Multisensory Brain Areas. *J. Neurosci. Off. J. Soc. Neurosci.* **2005**, *25*, 10564–10573. [CrossRef]
197. Metral, M.; Gonthier, C.; Luyat, M.; Guerraz, M. Body Schema Illusions: A Study of the Link between the Rubber Hand and Kinesthetic Mirror Illusions through Individual Differences. *BioMed Res. Int.* **2017**, *2017*. [CrossRef]
198. Ciaunica, A.; Petreca, B.; Fotopoulou, A.; Roepstorff, A. Whatever next and close to my self—the transparent senses and the 'second skin': Implications for the case of depersonalisation. *PsyArXiv* **2021**. [CrossRef]
199. Rochat, P. The Ontogeny of Human Self-Consciousness. *Curr. Dir. Psychol. Sci.* **2018**, *27*, 345–350. [CrossRef]
200. Bullock, D.; Takemura, H.; Caiafa, C.F.; Kitchell, L.; McPherson, B.; Caron, B.; Pestilli, F. Associative White Matter Connecting the Dorsal and Ventral Posterior Human Cortex. *Brain Struct. Funct.* **2019**, *224*, 2631–2660. [CrossRef] [PubMed]
201. O'Reilly, R.C.; Wyatte, D.R.; Rohrlich, J. Deep predictive learning: A comprehensive model of three visual streams. *ArXiv* **2017**, ArXiv170904654 Q-Bio. Available online: http://arxiv.org/abs/1709.04654 (accessed on 19 October 2019).
202. Heylighen, F.; Joslyn, C. Cybernetics and Second-Order Cybernetics. In *Proceedings of the Encyclopedia of Physical Science & Technology*, 3rd ed.; Academic Press: Cambridge, MA, USA, 2001.
203. Goekoop, R.; de Kleijn, R. How Higher Goals Are Constructed and Collapse under Stress: A Hierarchical Bayesian Control Systems Perspective. *Neurosci. Biobehav. Rev.* **2021**, *123*, 257–285. [CrossRef] [PubMed]
204. Whitehead, K.; Meek, J.; Fabrizi, L. Developmental Trajectory of Movement-Related Cortical Oscillations during Active Sleep in a Cross-Sectional Cohort of Pre-Term and Full-Term Human Infants. *Sci. Rep.* **2018**, *8*, 1–8. [CrossRef] [PubMed]
205. Williford, K.; Bennequin, D.; Friston, K.; Rudrauf, D. The Projective Consciousness Model and Phenomenal Selfhood. *Front. Psychol.* **2018**, *9*. [CrossRef]

206. Barsalou, L.W. Grounded Cognition: Past, Present, and Future. *Top. Cogn. Sci.* **2010**, *2*, 716–724. [CrossRef]
207. Prinz, J. The Intermediate Level Theory of Consciousness. In *The Blackwell Companion to Consciousness*; John Wiley & Sons, Ltd.: Hoboken, NJ, USA, 2017; pp. 257–271. ISBN 978-1-119-13236-3.
208. Zhou, J.; Cui, G.; Zhang, Z.; Yang, C.; Liu, Z.; Wang, L.; Li, C.; Sun, M. Graph Neural Networks: A Review of Methods and Applications. *arXiv* **2019**, arXiv:1812.08434.
209. Battaglia, P.W.; Hamrick, J.B.; Bapst, V.; Sanchez-Gonzalez, A.; Zambaldi, V.; Malinowski, M.; Tacchetti, A.; Raposo, D.; Santoro, A.; Faulkner, R.; et al. Relational Inductive Biases, Deep Learning, and Graph Networks. *arXiv* **2018**, arXiv:1806.01261.
210. Bapst, V.; Keck, T.; Grabska-Barwińska, A.; Donner, C.; Cubuk, E.D.; Schoenholz, S.S.; Obika, A.; Nelson, A.W.R.; Back, T.; Hassabis, D.; et al. Unveiling the Predictive Power of Static Structure in Glassy Systems. *Nat. Phys.* **2020**, *16*, 448–454. [CrossRef]
211. Cranmer, M.; Sanchez-Gonzalez, A.; Battaglia, P.; Xu, R.; Cranmer, K.; Spergel, D.; Ho, S. Discovering Symbolic Models from Deep Learning with Inductive Biases. *arXiv* **2020**, arXiv:2006.11287.
212. Haun, A.; Tononi, G. Why Does Space Feel the Way It Does? Towards a Principled Account of Spatial Experience. *Entropy* **2019**, *21*, 1160. [CrossRef]
213. Haun, A. What Is Visible across the Visual Field? *Neurosci. Conscious.* **2021**, *2021*. [CrossRef]
214. Faul, L.; St. Jacques, P.L.; DeRosa, J.T.; Parikh, N.; De Brigard, F. Differential Contribution of Anterior and Posterior Midline Regions during Mental Simulation of Counterfactual and Perspective Shifts in Autobiographical Memories. *NeuroImage* **2020**, *215*, 116843. [CrossRef]
215. Hills, T.T.; Todd, P.M.; Goldstone, R.L. The Central Executive as a Search Process: Priming Exploration and Exploitation across Domains. *J. Exp. Psychol. Gen.* **2010**, *139*, 590–609. [CrossRef]
216. Kaplan, R.; Friston, K.J. Planning and Navigation as Active Inference. *Biol. Cybern.* **2018**, *112*, 323–343. [CrossRef]
217. Çatal, O.; Verbelen, T.; Van de Maele, T.; Dhoedt, B.; Safron, A. Robot Navigation as Hierarchical Active Inference. *Neural Netw.* **2021**, *142*, 192–204. [CrossRef] [PubMed]
218. Graziano, M.S.A. The Temporoparietal Junction and Awareness. *Neurosci. Conscious.* **2018**, *2018*. [CrossRef] [PubMed]
219. Edelman, G.; Gally, J.A.; Baars, B.J. Biology of Consciousness. *Front. Psychol.* **2011**, *2*, 4. [CrossRef] [PubMed]
220. Tononi, G.; Boly, M.; Massimini, M.; Koch, C. Integrated Information Theory: From Consciousness to Its Physical Substrate. *Nat. Rev. Neurosci.* **2016**, *17*, 450. [CrossRef]
221. Luppi, A.I.; Mediano, P.A.M.; Rosas, F.E.; Allanson, J.; Pickard, J.D.; Carhart-Harris, R.L.; Williams, G.B.; Craig, M.M.; Finoia, P.; Owen, A.M.; et al. A Synergistic Workspace for Human Consciousness Revealed by Integrated Information Decomposition. *bioRxiv* **2020**, 2020.11.25.398081. [CrossRef]
222. Luppi, A.I.; Mediano, P.A.M.; Rosas, F.E.; Holland, N.; Fryer, T.D.; O'Brien, J.T.; Rowe, J.B.; Menon, D.K.; Bor, D.; Stamatakis, E.A. A Synergistic Core for Human Brain Evolution and Cognition. *bioRxiv* **2020**, 2020.09.22.308981. [CrossRef]
223. Betzel, R.F.; Fukushima, M.; He, Y.; Zuo, X.-N.; Sporns, O. Dynamic Fluctuations Coincide with Periods of High and Low Modularity in Resting-State Functional Brain Networks. *NeuroImage* **2016**, *127*, 287–297. [CrossRef] [PubMed]
224. Madl, T.; Baars, B.J.; Franklin, S. The Timing of the Cognitive Cycle. *PLoS ONE* **2011**, *6*, e14803. [CrossRef]
225. Tomasi, D.; Volkow, N.D. Association between Functional Connectivity Hubs and Brain Networks. *Cereb. Cortex N. Y. NY* **2011**, *21*, 2003–2013. [CrossRef] [PubMed]
226. Battiston, F.; Guillon, J.; Chavez, M.; Latora, V.; de Vico Fallani, F. Multiplex core–periphery organization of the human connectome. *J. R. Soc. Interface* **2018**, *15*, 20180514. [CrossRef]
227. Castro, S.; El-Deredy, W.; Battaglia, D.; Orio, P. Cortical Ignition Dynamics Is Tightly Linked to the Core Organisation of the Human Connectome. *PLoS Comput. Biol.* **2020**, *16*, e1007686. [CrossRef] [PubMed]
228. Davey, C.G.; Harrison, B.J. The Brain's Center of Gravity: How the Default Mode Network Helps Us to Understand the Self. *World Psychiatry* **2018**, *17*, 278–279. [CrossRef]
229. Deco, G.; Cruzat, J.; Cabral, J.; Tagliazucchi, E.; Laufs, H.; Logothetis, N.K.; Kringelbach, M.L. Awakening: Predicting External Stimulation to Force Transitions between Different Brain States. *Proc. Natl. Acad. Sci. USA* **2019**, *116*, 18088–18097. [CrossRef] [PubMed]
230. Wens, V.; Bourguignon, M.; Vander Ghinst, M.; Mary, A.; Marty, B.; Coquelet, N.; Naeije, G.; Peigneux, P.; Goldman, S.; De Tiège, X. Synchrony, Metastability, Dynamic Integration, and Competition in the Spontaneous Functional Connectivity of the Human Brain. *NeuroImage* **2019**. [CrossRef]
231. Marshall, P.J.; Meltzoff, A.N. Body Maps in the Infant Brain. *Trends Cogn. Sci.* **2015**, *19*, 499–505. [CrossRef] [PubMed]
232. Smith, G.B.; Hein, B.; Whitney, D.E.; Fitzpatrick, D.; Kaschube, M. Distributed Network Interactions and Their Emergence in Developing Neocortex. *Nat. Neurosci.* **2018**, *21*, 1600–1608. [CrossRef] [PubMed]
233. Wan, Y.; Wei, Z.; Looger, L.L.; Koyama, M.; Druckmann, S.; Keller, P.J. Single-Cell Reconstruction of Emerging Population Activity in an Entire Developing Circuit. *Cell* **2019**, *179*, 355–372.e23. [CrossRef] [PubMed]
234. Ramachandran, V.S.; Blakeslee, S.; Sacks, O. *Phantoms in the Brain: Probing the Mysteries of the Human Mind*; William Morrow Paperbacks: New York, NY, USA, 1999; ISBN 978-0-688-17217-6.
235. Valyear, K.F.; Philip, B.A.; Cirstea, C.M.; Chen, P.-W.; Baune, N.A.; Marchal, N.; Frey, S.H. Interhemispheric Transfer of Post-Amputation Cortical Plasticity within the Human Somatosensory Cortex. *NeuroImage* **2020**, *206*, 116291. [CrossRef]
236. Muller, L.; Chavane, F.; Reynolds, J.; Sejnowski, T.J. Cortical Travelling Waves: Mechanisms and Computational Principles. *Nat. Rev. Neurosci.* **2018**, *19*, 255–268. [CrossRef]

237. Roberts, J.A.; Gollo, L.L.; Abeysuriya, R.G.; Roberts, G.; Mitchell, P.B.; Woolrich, M.W.; Breakspear, M. Metastable Brain Waves. *Nat. Commun.* **2019**, *10*, 1–17. [CrossRef]
238. Zhang, H.; Watrous, A.J.; Patel, A.; Jacobs, J. Theta and Alpha Oscillations Are Traveling Waves in the Human Neocortex. *Neuron* **2018**, *98*, 1269–1281.e4. [CrossRef]
239. Atasoy, S.; Deco, G.; Kringelbach, M.L. Playing at the Edge of Criticality: Expanded Whole-Brain Repertoire of Connectome-Harmonics. In *The Functional Role of Critical Dynamics in Neural Systems*; Tomen, N., Herrmann, J.M., Ernst, U., Eds.; Springer Series on Bio- and Neurosystems; Springer International Publishing: Cham, Switzerland, 2019; pp. 27–45. ISBN 978-3-030-20965-0.
240. Atasoy, S.; Deco, G.; Kringelbach, M.L.; Pearson, J. Harmonic Brain Modes: A Unifying Framework for Linking Space and Time in Brain Dynamics. *Neurosci. Rev. J. Bringing Neurobiol. Neurol. Psychiatry* **2018**, *24*, 277–293. [CrossRef]
241. Deco, G.; Kringelbach, M.L. Metastability and Coherence: Extending the Communication through Coherence Hypothesis Using A Whole-Brain Computational Perspective. *Trends Neurosci.* **2016**, *39*, 125–135. [CrossRef]
242. Lord, L.-D.; Expert, P.; Atasoy, S.; Roseman, L.; Rapuano, K.; Lambiotte, R.; Nutt, D.J.; Deco, G.; Carhart-Harris, R.L.; Kringelbach, M.L.; et al. Dynamical Exploration of the Repertoire of Brain Networks at Rest Is Modulated by Psilocybin. *NeuroImage* **2019**, *199*, 127–142. [CrossRef]
243. Seth, A.K. A Predictive Processing Theory of Sensorimotor Contingencies: Explaining the Puzzle of Perceptual Presence and Its Absence in Synesthesia. *Cogn. Neurosci.* **2014**, *5*, 97–118. [CrossRef]
244. Drew, P.J.; Winder, A.T.; Zhang, Q. Twitches, Blinks, and Fidgets: Important Generators of Ongoing Neural Activity. *The Neuroscientist* **2019**, *25*, 298–313. [CrossRef] [PubMed]
245. Musall, S.; Kaufman, M.T.; Juavinett, A.L.; Gluf, S.; Churchland, A.K. Single-Trial Neural Dynamics Are Dominated by Richly Varied Movements. *Nat. Neurosci.* **2019**, *22*, 1677–1686. [CrossRef]
246. Benedetto, A.; Binda, P.; Costagli, M.; Tosetti, M.; Morrone, M.C. Predictive Visuo-Motor Communication through Neural Oscillations. *Curr. Biol.* **2021**. [CrossRef]
247. Graziano, M.S.A. *The Spaces Between Us: A Story of Neuroscience, Evolution, and Human Nature*; Oxford University Press: Oxford, UK, 2018; ISBN 978-0-19-046101-0.
248. Safron, A. What Is Orgasm? A Model of Sexual Trance and Climax via Rhythmic Entrainment. *Socioaffective Neurosci. Psychol.* **2016**, *6*, 31763. [CrossRef] [PubMed]
249. Miller, L.E.; Fabio, C.; Ravenda, V.; Bahmad, S.; Koun, E.; Salemme, R.; Luauté, J.; Bolognini, N.; Hayward, V.; Farnè, A. Somatosensory Cortex Efficiently Processes Touch Located Beyond the Body. *Curr. Biol.* **2019**. [CrossRef] [PubMed]
250. Bergouignan, L.; Nyberg, L.; Ehrsson, H.H. Out-of-Body–Induced Hippocampal Amnesia. *Proc. Natl. Acad. Sci. USA* **2014**, *111*, 4421–4426. [CrossRef]
251. St. Jacques, P.L. A New Perspective on Visual Perspective in Memory. *Curr. Dir. Psychol. Sci.* **2019**, *28*, 450–455. [CrossRef]
252. Graziano, M.S.A. *Consciousness and the Social Brain*; Oxford University Press: Oxford, UK, 2013; ISBN 978-0-19-992865-1.
253. Guterstam, A.; Kean, H.H.; Webb, T.W.; Kean, F.S.; Graziano, M.S.A. Implicit Model of Other People's Visual Attention as an Invisible, Force-Carrying Beam Projecting from the Eyes. *Proc. Natl. Acad. Sci. USA* **2019**, *116*, 328–333. [CrossRef]
254. Corbetta, M.; Shulman, G.L. Spatial neglect and attention networks. *Annu. Rev. Neurosci.* **2011**, *34*, 569–599. [CrossRef]
255. Blanke, O.; Mohr, C.; Michel, C.M.; Pascual-Leone, A.; Brugger, P.; Seeck, M.; Landis, T.; Thut, G. Linking Out-of-Body Experience and Self Processing to Mental Own-Body Imagery at the Temporoparietal Junction. *J. Neurosci. Off. J. Soc. Neurosci.* **2005**, *25*, 550–557. [CrossRef] [PubMed]
256. Guterstam, A.; Björnsdotter, M.; Gentile, G.; Ehrsson, H.H. Posterior Cingulate Cortex Integrates the Senses of Self-Location and Body Ownership. *Curr. Biol.* **2015**, *25*, 1416–1425. [CrossRef] [PubMed]
257. Saxe, R.; Wexler, A. Making Sense of Another Mind: The Role of the Right Temporo-Parietal Junction. *Neuropsychologia* **2005**, *43*, 1391–1399. [CrossRef]
258. Dehaene, S. *Consciousness and the Brain: Deciphering How the Brain Codes Our Thoughts*; Viking: New York, NY, USA, 2014; ISBN 978-0-670-02543-5.
259. Ramstead, M.J.D.; Veissière, S.P.L.; Kirmayer, L.J. Cultural Affordances: Scaffolding Local Worlds Through Shared Intentionality and Regimes of Attention. *Front. Psychol.* **2016**, *7*. [CrossRef]
260. Veissière, S.P.L.; Constant, A.; Ramstead, M.J.D.; Friston, K.J.; Kirmayer, L.J. Thinking Through Other Minds: A Variational Approach to Cognition and Culture. *Behav. Brain Sci.* **2019**, 1–97. [CrossRef]
261. Frith, C.D.; Metzinger, T.K. How the Stab of Conscience Made Us Really Conscious. In *The Pragmatic Turn: Toward Action-Oriented Views in Cognitive Science*; MIT Press: Cambridge, MA, USA, 2015.
262. Chang, A.Y.C.; Biehl, M.; Yu, Y.; Kanai, R. Information Closure Theory of Consciousness. *arXiv* **2019**, arXiv:1909.13045.
263. Barsalou, L.W. Simulation, Situated Conceptualization, and Prediction. *Philos. Trans. R. Soc. B Biol. Sci.* **2009**, *364*, 1281–1289. [CrossRef]
264. Elton, M. Consciousness: Only at the Personal Level. *Philos. Explor.* **2000**, *3*, 25–42. [CrossRef]
265. Dennett, D.C. The self as the center of narrative gravity. In *Self and Consciousness*; Psychology Press: East Sussex, UK, 2014; pp. 111–123.
266. Haken, H. Synergetics. *Phys. Bull.* **1977**, *28*, 412. [CrossRef]
267. Butterfield, J. Reduction, Emergence and Renormalization. *arXiv* **2014**, arXiv:1406.4354. [CrossRef]

268. Carroll, S. *The Big Picture: On the Origins of Life, Meaning, and the Universe Itself*; Dutton: Boston, MA, USA, 2016; ISBN 978-0-698-40976-7.
269. Albarracin, M.; Constant, A.; Friston, K.; Ramstead, M. A Variational Approach to Scripts. *PsyArXiv* **2020**. [CrossRef]
270. Hirsh, J.B.; Mar, R.A.; Peterson, J.B. Personal Narratives as the Highest Level of Cognitive Integration. *Behav. Brain Sci.* **2013**, *36*, 216–217. [CrossRef] [PubMed]
271. Harari, Y.N. *Sapiens: A Brief History of Humankind*, 1st ed.; Harper: New York, NY, USA, 2015; ISBN 978-0-06-231609-7.
272. Henrich, J. *The Secret of Our Success: How Culture Is Driving Human Evolution, Domesticating Our Species, and Making Us Smarter*; Princeton University Press: Princeton, NJ, USA, 2017; ISBN 978-0-691-17843-1.
273. Fujita, K.; Carnevale, J.J.; Trope, Y. Understanding Self-Control as a Whole vs. Part Dynamic. *Neuroethics* **2018**, *11*, 283–296. [CrossRef]
274. Mahr, J.; Csibra, G. Why Do We Remember? The Communicative Function of Episodic Memory. *Behav. Brain Sci.* **2017**, 1–93. [CrossRef]
275. Ainslie, G. Précis of Breakdown of Will. *Behav. Brain Sci.* **2005**, *28*, 635–650; discussion 650–673. [CrossRef]
276. Lewis, M. *The Biology of Desire: Why Addiction Is Not a Disease*; Public Affairs Books: New York, NY, USA, 2015; ISBN 978-1-61039-437-6.
277. Peterson, J.B. *Maps of Meaning: The Architecture of Belief*; Psychology Press: East Sussex, UK, 1999; ISBN 978-0-415-92222-7.
278. Shiller, R.J. *Narrative Economics: How Stories Go Viral and Drive Major Economic Events*; Princeton University Press: Princeton, NJ, USA, 2019; ISBN 978-0-691-18229-2.
279. Edelman, G.J. *Neural Darwinism: The Theory OF Neuronal Group Selection*, 1st ed.; Basic Books: New York, NY, USA, 1987; ISBN 0-465-04934-6.
280. Minsky, M. *Society of Mind*; Simon and Schuster: New York, NY, USA, 1988; ISBN 978-0-671-65713-0.
281. Ainslie, G. *Picoeconomics: The Strategic Interaction of Successive Motivational States within the Person*, Reissue edition; Cambridge University Press: Cambridge, MA, USA, 2010; ISBN 978-0-521-15870-1.
282. Traulsen, A.; Nowak, M.A. Evolution of Cooperation by Multilevel Selection. *Proc. Natl. Acad. Sci. USA* **2006**, *103*, 10952–10955. [CrossRef]
283. Carhart-Harris, R.L.; Friston, K.J. The Default-Mode, Ego-Functions and Free-Energy: A Neurobiological Account of Freudian Ideas. *Brain J. Neurol.* **2010**, *133*, 1265–1283. [CrossRef]
284. Barrett, L.F. *How Emotions Are Made: The Secret Life of the Brain*; Houghton Mifflin Harcourt: Boston, MA, USA, 2017.
285. Damasio, A. *Self Comes to Mind: Constructing the Conscious Brain*, Reprint edition; Vintage: New York, NY, USA, 2012; ISBN 978-0-307-47495-7.
286. Elston, T.W.; Bilkey, D.K. Anterior Cingulate Cortex Modulation of the Ventral Tegmental Area in an Effort Task. *Cell Rep.* **2017**, *19*, 2220–2230. [CrossRef]
287. Luu, P.; Posner, M.I. Anterior Cingulate Cortex Regulation of Sympathetic Activity. *Brain* **2003**, *126*, 2119–2120. [CrossRef]
288. Talmy, L. Force Dynamics in Language and Cognition. *Cogn. Sci.* **1988**, *12*, 49–100. [CrossRef]
289. Baumeister, R.F.; Tierney, J. *Willpower: Rediscovering the Greatest Human Strength*; Penguin: London, UK, 2012; ISBN 978-0-14-312223-4.
290. Bernardi, G.; Siclari, F.; Yu, X.; Zennig, C.; Bellesi, M.; Ricciardi, E.; Cirelli, C.; Ghilardi, M.F.; Pietrini, P.; Tononi, G. Neural and Behavioral Correlates of Extended Training during Sleep Deprivation in Humans: Evidence for Local, Task-Specific Effects. *J. Neurosci. Off. J. Soc. Neurosci.* **2015**, *35*, 4487–4500. [CrossRef]
291. Hung, C.-S.; Sarasso, S.; Ferrarelli, F.; Riedner, B.; Ghilardi, M.F.; Cirelli, C.; Tononi, G. Local Experience-Dependent Changes in the Wake EEG after Prolonged Wakefulness. *Sleep* **2013**, *36*, 59–72. [CrossRef]
292. Tononi, G.; Cirelli, C. Sleep and Synaptic Homeostasis: A Hypothesis. *Brain Res. Bull.* **2003**, *62*, 143–150. [CrossRef]
293. Wenger, E.; Brozzoli, C.; Lindenberger, U.; Lövdén, M. Expansion and Renormalization of Human Brain Structure During Skill Acquisition. *Trends Cogn. Sci.* **2017**, *21*, 930–939. [CrossRef]
294. Che, X.; Cash, R.; Chung, S.W.; Bailey, N.; Fitzgerald, P.B.; Fitzgibbon, B.M. The Dorsomedial Prefrontal Cortex as a Flexible Hub Mediating Behavioral as Well as Local and Distributed Neural Effects of Social Support Context on Pain: A Theta Burst Stimulation and TMS-EEG Study. *NeuroImage* **2019**, *201*, 116053. [CrossRef] [PubMed]
295. Marshall, T.R.; O'Shea, J.; Jensen, O.; Bergmann, T.O. Frontal Eye Fields Control Attentional Modulation of Alpha and Gamma Oscillations in Contralateral Occipitoparietal Cortex. *J. Neurosci.* **2015**, *35*, 1638–1647. [CrossRef] [PubMed]
296. Santostasi, G.; Malkani, R.; Riedner, B.; Bellesi, M.; Tononi, G.; Paller, K.A.; Zee, P.C. Phase-Locked Loop for Precisely Timed Acoustic Stimulation during Sleep. *J. Neurosci. Methods* **2016**, *259*, 101–114. [CrossRef]
297. Clancy, K.J.; Andrzejewski, J.A.; Rosenberg, J.T.; Ding, M.; Li, W. Transcranial Stimulation of Alpha Oscillations Upregulates the Default Mode Network. *bioRxiv* **2021**, 2021.06.11.447494. [CrossRef]
298. Evans, D.R.; Boggero, I.A.; Segerstrom, S.C. The Nature of Self-Regulatory Fatigue and "Ego Depletion": Lessons From Physical Fatigue. *Personal. Soc. Psychol. Rev. Off. J. Soc. Personal. Soc. Psychol. Inc.* **2015**. [CrossRef] [PubMed]
299. Dennett, D. *Freedom Evolves*, Illustrated edition; Viking Adult: New York, NY, USA, 2003; ISBN 0-670-03186-0.
300. Dennett, D. Real Patterns. *J. Philos.* **1991**, *88*, 27–51. [CrossRef]
301. Fry, R.L. Physical Intelligence and Thermodynamic Computing. *Entropy* **2017**, *19*, 107. [CrossRef]
302. Kiefer, A.B. Psychophysical Identity and Free Energy. *J. R. Soc. Interface* **2020**, *17*, 20200370. [CrossRef] [PubMed]

303. Ao, P. Laws in Darwinian Evolutionary Theory. *Phys. Life Rev.* **2005**, *2*, 117–156. [CrossRef]
304. Haldane, J.B.S. Organisers and Genes. *Nature* **1940**, *146*, 413. [CrossRef]
305. Sir, R.A.F.; Fisher, R.A. *The Genetical Theory of Natural Selection: A Complete Variorum Edition*; OUP Oxford: Oxford, UK, 1999; ISBN 978-0-19-850440-5.
306. Wright, S. The Roles of Mutation, Inbreeding, Crossbreeding, and Selection in Evolution. *J. Agric. Res.* **1921**, *20*, 557–580.
307. Tinbergen, N. On Aims and Methods of Ethology. *Z. Tierpsychol.* **1963**, *20*, 410–433. [CrossRef]
308. Campbell, J.O. Universal Darwinism As a Process of Bayesian Inference. *Front. Syst. Neurosci.* **2016**, *10*, 49. [CrossRef]
309. Friston, K.J.; Wiese, W.; Hobson, J.A. Sentience and the Origins of Consciousness: From Cartesian Duality to Markovian Monism. *Entropy* **2020**, *22*, 516. [CrossRef]
310. Kaila, V.; Annila, A. Natural Selection for Least Action. *Proc. R. Soc. Math. Phys. Eng. Sci.* **2008**, *464*, 3055–3070. [CrossRef]
311. Gazzaniga, M.S. The Split-Brain: Rooting Consciousness in Biology. *Proc. Natl. Acad. Sci. USA* **2014**, *111*, 18093–18094. [CrossRef]
312. Gazzaniga, M.S. *The Consciousness Instinct: Unraveling the Mystery of How the Brain Makes the Mind*; Farrar, Straus and Giroux: New York, NY, USA, 2018; ISBN 978-0-374-12876-0.
313. Rovelli, C. *The Order of Time*; Penguin: London, UK, 2018; ISBN 978-0-7352-1612-9.
314. Ismael, J. *How Physics Makes Us Free*; Oxford University Press: Oxford, UK, 2016; ISBN 978-0-19-026944-9.
315. Hoel, E.P.; Albantakis, L.; Marshall, W.; Tononi, G. Can the Macro Beat the Micro? Integrated Information across Spatiotemporal Scales. *Neurosci. Conscious.* **2016**, *2016*. [CrossRef] [PubMed]
316. Hume, D. *An Enquiry Concerning Human Understanding: With Hume's Abstract of A Treatise of Human Nature and A Letter from a Gentleman to His Friend in Edinburgh*, 2nd ed.; Steinberg, E., Ed.; Hackett Publishing Company, Inc.: Indianapolis, IN, USA, 1993; ISBN 978-0-87220-229-0.
317. Baars, B.J. Global Workspace Theory of Consciousness: Toward a Cognitive Neuroscience of Human Experience. *Prog. Brain Res.* **2005**, *150*, 45–53. [CrossRef]
318. Brang, D.; Teuscher, U.; Miller, L.E.; Ramachandran, V.S.; Coulson, S. Handedness and Calendar Orientations in Time-Space Synaesthesia. *J. Neuropsychol.* **2011**, *5*, 323–332. [CrossRef]
319. Jaynes, J. *The Origin of Consciousness in the Breakdown of the Bicameral Mind*; Houghton Mifflin Harcourt: Boston, MA, USA, 1976; ISBN 978-0-547-52754-3.
320. Balduzzi, D.; Tononi, G. Qualia: The Geometry of Integrated Information. *PLoS Comput. Biol.* **2009**, *5*, e1000462. [CrossRef]
321. Brown, R.; Lau, H.; LeDoux, J.E. Understanding the Higher-Order Approach to Consciousness. *Trends Cogn. Sci.* **2019**, *23*, 754–768. [CrossRef]
322. Modha, D.S.; Singh, R. Network Architecture of the Long-Distance Pathways in the Macaque Brain. *Proc. Natl. Acad. Sci. USA* **2010**, *107*, 13485–13490. [CrossRef]
323. Preuss, T.M. The Human Brain: Rewired and Running Hot. *Ann. N. Y. Acad. Sci.* **2011**, *1225* (Suppl. 1), E182–E191. [CrossRef]
324. Abid, G. Deflating Inflation: The Connection (or Lack Thereof) between Decisional and Metacognitive Processes and Visual Phenomenology. *Neurosci. Conscious.* **2019**, *2019*. [CrossRef] [PubMed]
325. Dennett, D.C. Facing up to the Hard Question of Consciousness. *Philos. Trans. R. Soc. B Biol. Sci.* **2018**, *373*. [CrossRef] [PubMed]
326. Noë, A. Is the Visual World a Grand Illusion? *J. Conscious. Stud.* **2002**, *9*, 1–12.
327. Tversky, B. *Mind in Motion: How Action Shapes Thought*, 1st ed.; Basic Books: New York, NY, USA, 2019; ISBN 978-0-465-09306-9.
328. Morgan, A.T.; Petro, L.S.; Muckli, L. Line Drawings Reveal the Structure of Internal Visual Models Conveyed by Cortical Feedback. *bioRxiv* **2019**, 041186. [CrossRef]
329. Sutterer, D.W.; Polyn, S.M.; Woodman, G.F. α-Band Activity Tracks a Two-Dimensional Spotlight of Attention during Spatial Working Memory Maintenance. *J. Neurophysiol.* **2021**, *125*, 957–971. [CrossRef] [PubMed]
330. Chater, N. *Mind Is Flat: The Remarkable Shallowness of the Improvising Brain*; Yale University Press: New Haven, CT, USA, 2018; ISBN 978-0-300-24061-0.
331. Coupé, C.; Oh, Y.M.; Dediu, D.; Pellegrino, F. Different Languages, Similar Encoding Efficiency: Comparable Information Rates across the Human Communicative Niche. *Sci. Adv.* **2019**, *5*, eaaw2594. [CrossRef] [PubMed]
332. Buonomano, D. *Your Brain Is a Time Machine: The Neuroscience and Physics of Time*; W. W. Norton & Company: New York, NY, USA, 2017; ISBN 978-0-393-24795-4.
333. Wittmann, M. *Felt Time: The Science of How We Experience Time*, Reprint edition; The MIT Press: Cambridge, MA, USA, 2017; ISBN 978-0-262-53354-6.
334. Whyte, C.J.; Smith, R. The Predictive Global Neuronal Workspace: A Formal Active Inference Model of Visual Consciousness. *Prog. Neurobiol.* **2020**, 101918. [CrossRef]
335. Cellai, D.; Dorogovtsev, S.N.; Bianconi, G. Message Passing Theory for Percolation Models on Multiplex Networks with Link Overlap. *Phys. Rev. E* **2016**, *94*, 032301. [CrossRef]
336. Bianconi, G. Fluctuations in Percolation of Sparse Complex Networks. *Phys. Rev. E* **2017**, *96*, 012302. [CrossRef]
337. Kryven, I. Bond Percolation in Coloured and Multiplex Networks. *Nat. Commun.* **2019**, *10*, 1–16. [CrossRef]
338. Arese Lucini, F.; Del Ferraro, G.; Sigman, M.; Makse, H.A. How the Brain Transitions from Conscious to Subliminal Perception. *Neuroscience* **2019**, *411*, 280–290. [CrossRef]
339. Kalra, P.B.; Gabrieli, J.D.E.; Finn, A.S. Evidence of Stable Individual Differences in Implicit Learning. *Cognition* **2019**, *190*, 199–211. [CrossRef]

340. Hills, T.T. Neurocognitive Free Will. *Proc. Biol. Sci.* **2019**, *286*, 20190510. [CrossRef]
341. Ha, D.; Schmidhuber, J. World Models. *arXiv* **2018**. [CrossRef]
342. Wang, J.X.; Kurth-Nelson, Z.; Kumaran, D.; Tirumala, D.; Soyer, H.; Leibo, J.Z.; Hassabis, D.; Botvinick, M. Prefrontal Cortex as a Meta-Reinforcement Learning System. *Nat. Neurosci.* **2018**, *21*, 860. [CrossRef] [PubMed]
343. Peña-Gómez, C.; Avena-Koenigsberger, A.; Sepulcre, J.; Sporns, O. Spatiotemporal Network Markers of Individual Variability in the Human Functional Connectome. *Cereb. Cortex* **2018**, *28*, 2922–2934. [CrossRef] [PubMed]
344. Toro-Serey, C.; Tobyne, S.M.; McGuire, J.T. Spectral Partitioning Identifies Individual Heterogeneity in the Functional Network Topography of Ventral and Anterior Medial Prefrontal Cortex. *NeuroImage* **2020**, *205*, 116305. [CrossRef]
345. James, W. Are We Automata? *Mind* **1879**, *4*, 1–22. [CrossRef]
346. Libet, B.; Gleason, C.A.; Wright, E.W.; Pearl, D.K. Time of Conscious Intention to Act in Relation to Onset of Cerebral Activity (Readiness-Potential). The Unconscious Initiation of a Freely Voluntary Act. *Brain J. Neurol.* **1983**, *106 Pt 3*, 623–642. [CrossRef]
347. Fifel, K. Readiness Potential and Neuronal Determinism: New Insights on Libet Experiment. *J. Neurosci.* **2018**, *38*, 784–786. [CrossRef] [PubMed]
348. Maoz, U.; Yaffe, G.; Koch, C.; Mudrik, L. Neural Precursors of Decisions That Matter-an ERP Study of Deliberate and Arbitrary Choice. *eLife* **2019**, *8*. [CrossRef]
349. Seth, A.K.; Tsakiris, M. Being a Beast Machine: The Somatic Basis of Selfhood. *Trends Cogn. Sci.* **2018**, *22*, 969–981. [CrossRef]
350. Bastos, A.M.; Lundqvist, M.; Waite, A.S.; Kopell, N.; Miller, E.K. Layer and Rhythm Specificity for Predictive Routing. *Proc. Natl. Acad. Sci. USA* **2020**, *117*, 31459–31469. [CrossRef]
351. Pezzulo, G.; Rigoli, F.; Friston, K.J. Hierarchical Active Inference: A Theory of Motivated Control. *Trends Cogn. Sci.* **2018**, *22*, 294–306. [CrossRef] [PubMed]
352. Travers, E.; Khalighinejad, N.; Schurger, A.; Haggard, P. Do Readiness Potentials Happen All the Time? *NeuroImage* **2020**, *206*, 116286. [CrossRef]
353. Brunia, C.H.M.; van Boxtel, G.J.M.; Böcker, K.B.E. Negative Slow Waves as Indices of Anticipation: The Bereitschaftspotential, the Contingent Negative Variation, and the Stimulus-Preceding Negativity. Available online: https://www.oxfordhandbooks.com/view/10.1093/oxfordhb/9780195374148.001.0001/oxfordhb-9780195374148-e-008 (accessed on 24 December 2020).
354. Darby, R.R.; Joutsa, J.; Burke, M.J.; Fox, M.D. Lesion Network Localization of Free Will. *Proc. Natl. Acad. Sci. USA* **2018**, *115*, 10792–10797. [CrossRef]
355. Hesp, C.; Tschantz, A.; Millidge, B.; Ramstead, M.; Friston, K.; Smith, R. Sophisticated Affective Inference: Simulating Anticipatory Affective Dynamics of Imagining Future Events. In Proceedings of the Active Inference; Verbelen, T., Lanillos, P., Buckley, C.L., De Boom, C., Eds.; Springer International Publishing: Cham, Switzerland, 2020; pp. 179–186.
356. Dohmatob, E.; Dumas, G.; Bzdok, D. Dark Control: The Default Mode Network as a Reinforcement Learning Agent. *Hum. Brain Mapp.* **2020**, *41*, 3318–3341. [CrossRef]
357. Travers, E.; Friedemann, M.; Haggard, P. The Readiness Potential Reflects Planning-Based Expectation, Not Uncertainty, in the Timing of Action. *Cogn. Neurosci.* **2021**, *12*, 14–27. [CrossRef]
358. Hamilos, A.E.; Spedicato, G.; Hong, Y.; Sun, F.; Li, Y.; Assad, J.A. Dynamic Dopaminergic Activity Controls the Timing of Self-Timed Movement. *bioRxiv* **2020**. [CrossRef]
359. Kay, K.; Chung, J.E.; Sosa, M.; Schor, J.S.; Karlsson, M.P.; Larkin, M.C.; Liu, D.F.; Frank, L.M. Constant Sub-Second Cycling between Representations of Possible Futures in the Hippocampus. *Cell* **2020**, *180*, 552–567.e25. [CrossRef] [PubMed]
360. Frith, C.D.; Haggard, P. Volition and the Brain—Revisiting a Classic Experimental Study. *Trends Neurosci.* **2018**, *41*, 405–407. [CrossRef]
361. Sinnott-Armstrong, W. Contrastive Mental Causation. *Synthese* **2019**. [CrossRef]
362. Khachouf, O.T.; Poletti, S.; Pagnoni, G. The Embodied Transcendental: A Kantian Perspective on Neurophenomenology. *Front. Hum. Neurosci.* **2013**, *7*. [CrossRef]
363. Ramstead, M.J.D.; Wiese, W.; Miller, M.; Friston, K.J. Deep Neurophenomenology: An Active Inference Account of Some Features of Conscious Experience and of Their Disturbance in Major Depressive Disorder. Available online: http://philsci-archive.pitt.edu/18377/ (accessed on 30 April 2021).
364. Varela, F. Neurophenomenology: A Methodological Remedy for the Hard Problem. *J. Conscious. Stud.* **1996**, *3*, 330–349.
365. Damasio, A. *Looking for Spinoza: Joy, Sorrow, and the Feeling Brain*, 1st ed.; Houghton Mifflin Harcourt: Boston, MA, USA, 2003; ISBN 978-0-15-100557-4.
366. Fields, C.; Levin, M. How Do Living Systems Create Meaning? *Philosophies* **2020**, *5*, 36. [CrossRef]
367. Levin, M. Life, Death, and Self: Fundamental Questions of Primitive Cognition Viewed through the Lens of Body Plasticity and Synthetic Organisms. *Biochem. Biophys. Res. Commun.* **2020**. [CrossRef]
368. Sandrone, S.; Safron, A. Pain and (e) Motion in Postural Responses. *Front. Hum. Neurosci.* **2013**, *7*, 286. [CrossRef] [PubMed]
369. LeDoux, J. *Anxious: Using the Brain to Understand and Treat Fear and Anxiety*, Reprint edition; Penguin Books: London, UK, 2016; ISBN 978-0-14-310904-4.
370. Ocaña, F.M.; Suryanarayana, S.M.; Saitoh, K.; Kardamakis, A.A.; Capantini, L.; Robertson, B.; Grillner, S. The Lamprey Pallium Provides a Blueprint of the Mammalian Motor Projections from Cortex. *Curr. Biol.* **2015**, *25*, 413–423. [CrossRef] [PubMed]
371. Suryanarayana, S.M.; Robertson, B.; Wallén, P.; Grillner, S. The Lamprey Pallium Provides a Blueprint of the Mammalian Layered Cortex. *Curr. Biol. CB* **2017**, *27*, 3264–3277.e5. [CrossRef]

372. Kirchhoff, M.; Parr, T.; Palacios, E.; Friston, K.J.; Kiverstein, J. The Markov Blankets of Life: Autonomy, Active Inference and the Free Energy Principle. *J. R. Soc. Interface* **2018**, *15*. [CrossRef]
373. Stolyarova, A. Solving the Credit Assignment Problem With the Prefrontal Cortex. *Front. Neurosci.* **2018**, *12*. [CrossRef] [PubMed]
374. Joffily, M.; Coricelli, G. Emotional Valence and the Free-Energy Principle. *PLoS Comput. Biol.* **2013**, *9*, e1003094. [CrossRef] [PubMed]
375. Schultz, W. Dopamine Signals for Reward Value and Risk: Basic and Recent Data. *Behav. Brain Funct. BBF* **2010**, *6*, 24. [CrossRef] [PubMed]
376. Schultz, W. Dopamine Reward Prediction Error Coding. *Dialogues Clin. Neurosci.* **2016**, *18*, 23–32. [PubMed]
377. Miller, M.; Kiverstein, J.; Rietveld, E. Embodying Addiction: A Predictive Processing Account. *Brain Cogn.* **2020**, *138*, 105495. [CrossRef] [PubMed]
378. Berridge, K.C.; Kringelbach, M.L. Building a Neuroscience of Pleasure and Well-Being. *Psychol. Well-Being* **2011**, *1*, 1–3. [CrossRef] [PubMed]
379. Berridge, K.C.; Kringelbach, M.L. Pleasure Systems in the Brain. *Neuron* **2015**, *86*, 646–664. [CrossRef]
380. Safron, A. Rapid Anxiety Reduction (RAR): A Unified Theory of Humor. *arXiv* **2019**, arXiv:1911.02364.
381. Dawkins, R. *River Out Of Eden: A Darwinian View Of Life*; Basic Books: New York, NY, USA, 1996; ISBN 0-465-06990-8.
382. de Abril, I.M.; Kanai, R. A Unified Strategy for Implementing Curiosity and Empowerment Driven Reinforcement Learning. *arXiv* **2018**, arXiv:1806.06505.
383. Friston, K.J.; Lin, M.; Frith, C.D.; Pezzulo, G.; Hobson, J.A.; Ondobaka, S. Active Inference, Curiosity and Insight. *Neural Comput.* **2017**, *29*, 2633–2683. [CrossRef]
384. Gottlieb, J.; Oudeyer, P.-Y. Towards a Neuroscience of Active Sampling and Curiosity. *Nat. Rev. Neurosci.* **2018**, *19*, 758–770. [CrossRef]
385. Koelsch, S.; Vuust, P.; Friston, K.J. Predictive Processes and the Peculiar Case of Music. *Trends Cogn. Sci.* **2019**, *23*, 63–77. [CrossRef] [PubMed]
386. Schmidhuber, J. POWERPLAY: Training an Increasingly General Problem Solver by Continually Searching for the Simplest Still Unsolvable Problem. *arXiv* **2012**, arXiv:1112.5309. [CrossRef]
387. Crespi, L.P. Quantitative Variation of Incentive and Performance in the White Rat. *Am. J. Psychol.* **1942**, *55*, 467–517. [CrossRef]
388. Cooper, J.C.; Hollon, N.G.; Wimmer, G.E.; Knutson, B. Available Alternative Incentives Modulate Anticipatory Nucleus Accumbens Activation. *Soc. Cogn. Affect. Neurosci.* **2009**, *4*, 409–416. [CrossRef] [PubMed]
389. Friston, K.; Da Costa, L.; Hafner, D.; Hesp, C.; Parr, T. Sophisticated Inference. *arXiv* **2020**, arXiv:2006.04120.
390. Dalege, J.; Borsboom, D.; van Harreveld, F.; Maas, H.L.J. van der The Attitudinal Entropy (AE) Framework as a General Theory of Individual Attitudes. *Psychol. Inq.* **2018**, *29*, 175–193. [CrossRef]
391. Hirsh, J.B.; Mar, R.A.; Peterson, J.B. Psychological Entropy: A Framework for Understanding Uncertainty-Related Anxiety. *Psychol. Rev.* **2012**, *119*, 304–320. [CrossRef] [PubMed]
392. Panksepp, J. *Affective Neuroscience: The Foundations of Human and Animal Emotions*, Illustrated edition; Oxford University Press: Oxford, UK, 1998; ISBN 0-19-509673-8.
393. Panksepp, J. Neuroevolutionary Sources of Laughter and Social Joy: Modeling Primal Human Laughter in Laboratory Rats. *Behav. Brain Res.* **2007**, *182*, 231–244. [CrossRef]
394. Csikszentmihalyi, M. *Finding Flow: The Psychology of Engagement with Everyday Life*; Basic Books: New York, NY, USA, 1997; ISBN 978-0-465-02411-7.
395. Kiverstein, J.; Miller, M.; Rietveld, E. The Feeling of Grip: Novelty, Error Dynamics, and the Predictive Brain. *Synthese* **2019**, *196*, 2847–2869. [CrossRef]
396. Vasileva, O.; Balyasnikova, N. (Re)Introducing Vygotsky's Thought: From Historical Overview to Contemporary Psychology. *Front. Psychol.* **2019**, *10*, 1515. [CrossRef]
397. Kauffman, S.; Clayton, P. On Emergence, Agency, and Organization. *Biol. Philos.* **2006**, *21*, 501–521. [CrossRef]
398. Kauffman, S.A. Prolegomenon to Patterns in Evolution. *Biosystems* **2014**, *123*, 3–8. [CrossRef]
399. Buchsbaum, D.; Bridgers, S.; Skolnick Weisberg, D.; Gopnik, A. The Power of Possibility: Causal Learning, Counterfactual Reasoning, and Pretend Play. *Philos. Trans. R. Soc. B Biol. Sci.* **2012**, *367*, 2202–2212. [CrossRef]
400. Dhawale, A.K.; Miyamoto, Y.R.; Smith, M.A.; Ölveczky, B.P. Adaptive Regulation of Motor Variability. *Curr. Biol.* **2019**, *29*, 3551–3562.e7. [CrossRef]
401. Friston, K.J.; Thornton, C.; Clark, A. Free-Energy Minimization and the Dark-Room Problem. *Front. Psychol.* **2012**, *3*. [CrossRef]
402. Allen, N.B.; Badcock, P.B.T. The Social Risk Hypothesis of Depressed Mood: Evolutionary, Psychosocial, and Neurobiological Perspectives. *Psychol. Bull.* **2003**, *129*, 887–913. [CrossRef]
403. Fauconnier, G.; Turner, M. *The Way We Think: Conceptual Blending And The Mind's Hidden Complexities*, Reprint edition; Basic Books: New York, NY, USA, 2003; ISBN 978-0-465-08786-0.
404. Brang, D.; Ramachandran, V.S. Survival of the Synesthesia Gene: Why Do People Hear Colors and Taste Words? *PLoS Biol.* **2011**, *9*, e1001205. [CrossRef]
405. Sievers, B.; Polansky, L.; Casey, M.; Wheatley, T. Music and Movement Share a Dynamic Structure That Supports Universal Expressions of Emotion. *Proc. Natl. Acad. Sci. USA* **2013**, *110*, 70–75. [CrossRef]

406. Sievers, B.; Lee, C.; Haslett, W.; Wheatley, T. A Multi-Sensory Code for Emotional Arousal. *Proc. R. Soc. B Biol. Sci.* **2019**, *286*, 20190513. [CrossRef] [PubMed]
407. Cuskley, C.; Dingemanse, M.; Kirby, S.; van Leeuwen, T.M. Cross-Modal Associations and Synesthesia: Categorical Perception and Structure in Vowel–Color Mappings in a Large Online Sample. *Behav. Res. Methods* **2019**, *51*, 1651–1675. [CrossRef]
408. Barwich, A.S. *Smellosophy: What the Nose Tells the Mind*; Harvard University Press: Cambridge, MA, USA, 2020; ISBN 978-0-674-98369-4.
409. Vecchiet, L.; Vecchiet, J.; Giamberardino, M.A. Referred Muscle Pain: Clinical and Pathophysiologic Aspects. *Curr. Rev. Pain* **1999**, *3*, 489–498. [CrossRef] [PubMed]
410. Bloom, P. *How Pleasure Works: The New Science of Why We Like What We Like*, 1st ed.; W. W. Norton & Company: New York, NY, USA, 2010; ISBN 0-393-06632-0.
411. Suzuki, K.; Garfinkel, S.N.; Critchley, H.D.; Seth, A.K. Multisensory Integration across Exteroceptive and Interoceptive Domains Modulates Self-Experience in the Rubber-Hand Illusion. *Neuropsychologia* **2013**, *51*, 2909–2917. [CrossRef] [PubMed]
412. Lush, P.; Botan, V.; Scott, R.B.; Seth, A.K.; Ward, J.; Dienes, Z. Trait Phenomenological Control Predicts Experience of Mirror Synaesthesia and the Rubber Hand Illusion. *Nat. Commun.* **2020**, *11*, 4853. [CrossRef] [PubMed]
413. Barrett, L.F.; Quigley, K.S.; Hamilton, P. An Active Inference Theory of Allostasis and Interoception in Depression. *Philos. Trans. R. Soc. Lond. B. Biol. Sci.* **2016**, *371*. [CrossRef]
414. Farshidian, F.; Hoeller, D.; Hutter, M. Deep Value Model Predictive Control. *arXiv* **2019**, arXiv:1910.03358.
415. Ikemoto, S.; Panksepp, J. The Role of Nucleus Accumbens Dopamine in Motivated Behavior: A Unifying Interpretation with Special Reference to Reward-Seeking. *Brain Res. Brain Res. Rev.* **1999**, *31*, 6–41. [CrossRef]
416. Toates, F. *How Sexual Desire Works: The Enigmatic Urge*; Cambridge University Press: Cambridge, UK, 2014; ISBN 978-1-107-68804-9.
417. FitzGerald, T.H.B.; Dolan, R.J.; Friston, K.J. Dopamine, Reward Learning, and Active Inference. *Front. Comput. Neurosci.* **2015**, *9*. [CrossRef] [PubMed]
418. Friston, K.J.; Schwartenbeck, P.; FitzGerald, T.; Moutoussis, M.; Behrens, T.; Dolan, R.J. The Anatomy of Choice: Dopamine and Decision-Making. *Philos. Trans. R. Soc. B Biol. Sci.* **2014**, *369*. [CrossRef]
419. Friston, K.J.; Shiner, T.; FitzGerald, T.; Galea, J.M.; Adams, R.; Brown, H.; Dolan, R.J.; Moran, R.; Stephan, K.E.; Bestmann, S. Dopamine, Affordance and Active Inference. *PLoS Comput. Biol.* **2012**, *8*, e1002327. [CrossRef]
420. Dabney, W.; Kurth-Nelson, Z.; Uchida, N.; Starkweather, C.K.; Hassabis, D.; Munos, R.; Botvinick, M. A Distributional Code for Value in Dopamine-Based Reinforcement Learning. *Nature* **2020**, 1–5. [CrossRef]
421. Leknes, S.; Tracey, I. A Common Neurobiology for Pain and Pleasure. *Nat. Rev. Neurosci.* **2008**, *9*, 314–320. [CrossRef]
422. Sacks, O. *Musicophilia: Tales of Music and the Brain, Revised and Expanded Edition*, Revised&enlarged edition; Vintage: New York, NY, USA, 2008; ISBN 978-1-4000-3353-9.
423. Sayette, M.A.; Loewenstein, G.; Griffin, K.M.; Black, J.J. Exploring the Cold-to-Hot Empathy Gap in Smokers. *Psychol. Sci.* **2008**, *19*, 926–932. [CrossRef]
424. Kahneman, D. *Thinking, Fast and Slow*, 1st ed.; Farrar, Straus and Giroux: New York, NY, USA, 2011; ISBN 0-374-27563-7.
425. Zajchowski, C.A.B.; Schwab, K.A.; Dustin, D.L. The Experiencing Self and the Remembering Self: Implications for Leisure Science. *Leis. Sci.* **2017**, *39*, 561–568. [CrossRef]
426. Jennings, J.R.; Allen, B.; Gianaros, P.J.; Thayer, J.F.; Manuck, S.B. Focusing Neurovisceral Integration: Cognition, Heart Rate Variability, and Cerebral Blood Flow. *Psychophysiology* **2015**, *52*, 214–224. [CrossRef]
427. Porges, S.W. The Polyvagal Theory: New Insights into Adaptive Reactions of the Autonomic Nervous System. *Cleve. Clin. J. Med.* **2009**, *76*, S86–S90. [CrossRef] [PubMed]
428. Gopnik, A. Explanation as Orgasm. *Minds Mach.* **1998**, *8*, 101–118. [CrossRef]
429. Chalmers, D.J. Facing Up to the Problem of Consciousness. *J. Conscious. Stud.* **1995**, *2*, 200–219.
430. Nagel, T. What Is It Like to Be a Bat? *Philos. Rev.* **1974**, *83*, 435–450. [CrossRef]
431. Chalmers, D.J. The Meta-Problem of Consciousness. *J. Conscious. Stud.* **2018**, *25*, 6–61.
432. Limanowski, J.; Friston, K.J. 'Seeing the Dark': Grounding Phenomenal Transparency and Opacity in Precision Estimation for Active Inference. *Front. Psychol.* **2018**, *9*. [CrossRef]
433. Hofstadter, D.R. *I Am a Strange Loop*; Basic Books: New York, NY, USA, 2007; ISBN 978-0-465-00837-7.
434. Lloyd, S. A Turing Test for Free Will. *Philos. Trans. R. Soc. Math. Phys. Eng. Sci.* **2012**, *370*, 3597–3610. [CrossRef] [PubMed]
435. Lau, H.; Michel, M. On the dangers of conflating strong and weak versions of a theory of consciousness. *PsyArXiv* **2019**. [CrossRef]
436. Smith, R.; Ramstead, M.J.D.; Kiefer, A. Active inference models do not contradict folk psychology. *PsyArXiv* **2021**. [CrossRef]

Concept Paper

Permutation Entropy as a Universal Disorder Criterion: How Disorders at Different Scale Levels Are Manifestations of the Same Underlying Principle

Rutger Goekoop [1,*] and Roy de Kleijn [2]

[1] Parnassia Group, PsyQ Parnassia Academy, Department of Anxiety Disorders, Early Detection and Intervention Team (EDIT), Lijnbaan 4, 2512 VA Den Haag, The Netherlands
[2] Cognitive Psychology Unit, Institute of Psychology & Leiden Institute for Brain and Cognition, Leiden University, Wassenaarseweg 52, 2333 AK Leiden, The Netherlands; kleijnrde@fsw.leidenuniv.nl
* Correspondence: r.goekoop@psyq.nl

Citation: Goekoop, R.; de Kleijn, R. Permutation Entropy as a Universal Disorder Criterion: How Disorders at Different Scale Levels Are Manifestations of the Same Underlying Principle. *Entropy* **2021**, *23*, 1701. https://doi.org/10.3390/e23121701

Academic Editors: Paul Badcock, Maxwell Ramstead, Zahra Sheikhbahaee and Axel Constant

Received: 4 July 2021
Accepted: 13 December 2021
Published: 20 December 2021

Publisher's Note: MDPI stays neutral with regard to jurisdictional claims in published maps and institutional affiliations.

Copyright: © 2021 by the authors. Licensee MDPI, Basel, Switzerland. This article is an open access article distributed under the terms and conditions of the Creative Commons Attribution (CC BY) license (https:// creativecommons.org/licenses/by/ 4.0/).

Abstract: What do bacteria, cells, organs, people, and social communities have in common? At first sight, perhaps not much. They involve totally different agents and scale levels of observation. On second thought, however, perhaps they share everything. A growing body of literature suggests that living systems at different scale levels of observation follow the same architectural principles and process information in similar ways. Moreover, such systems appear to respond in similar ways to rising levels of stress, especially when stress levels approach near-lethal levels. To explain such communalities, we argue that all organisms (including humans) can be modeled as hierarchical Bayesian controls systems that are governed by the same biophysical principles. Such systems show generic changes when taxed beyond their ability to correct for environmental disturbances. Without exception, stressed organisms show rising levels of 'disorder' (randomness, unpredictability) in internal message passing and overt behavior. We argue that such changes can be explained by a collapse of allostatic (high-level integrative) control, which normally synchronizes activity of the various components of a living system to produce order. The selective overload and cascading failure of highly connected (hub) nodes flattens hierarchical control, producing maladaptive behavior. Thus, we present a theory according to which organic concepts such as stress, a loss of control, disorder, disease, and death can be operationalized in biophysical terms that apply to all scale levels of organization. Given the presumed universality of this mechanism, 'losing control' appears to involve the same process anywhere, whether involving bacteria succumbing to an antibiotic agent, people suffering from physical or mental disorders, or social systems slipping into warfare. On a practical note, measures of disorder may serve as early warning signs of system failure even when catastrophic failure is still some distance away.

Keywords: permutation entropy; disorder; stress; allostatic (hub) overload; cascading failure; disease; hierarchical control systems; active inference; free energy principle; critical slowing down

1. A Short History on Stress Tolerance Studies in Different Organisms

For a long time, it was believed that different organisms respond in different ways to environmental challenges. This assumption is understandable, since stress responses in bacteria, fish, birds, or mammals involve totally different genetic and neural pathways. When ignoring the details of a particular stress response and observing the whole of system dynamics at a slightly more abstract level, however, such differences disappear. No matter what type of organism is studied, its response to unfavorable environmental conditions is essentially the same: the various components that constitute the organism (such as genes, proteins, metabolites, neurons, or brain regions) increasingly synchronize their responses and assume a larger number of different values [1,2]. In other words, the strength of correlations between system components increases, as so does the variance. Meanwhile, system components remain within the same state for longer periods of time, causing the values of these components to correlate more strongly with their previous values ('autocorrelations'). This happens up to a discrete point, after which synchronization decreases but variance remains high. Such 'tipping points' usually correspond to the onset of disease or the death of the organism (Figure 1). This peculiar phenomenon has been rediscovered many times since the 1980s. Examples include an impressive range of organisms and types of stressors, from bacteria succumbing to antibiotic stressors and plants fighting conditions of severe drought to insects, reptiles, birds, and mammals that struggle under all sorts of unfavorable conditions [1]. In humans, the same dynamics can be observed in cardiac muscle cells prior to myocardial infarction, asthmatic attacks in patients with obstructive pulmonary disease, and neuronal activity prior to cardiac arrhythmias and epileptic seizures [2]. In addition to physical disorders, similar changes have been observed in self-reported mental states of patients with different forms of acute mental illness, such as major depression, bipolar disorders, or psychosis [3–5]. This generic response to environmental challenges seems to be independent of the spatial scale level of observation. It has been observed to govern the dynamics of molecules, genes, different cell types, tissues, organs and whole organisms, food webs, stock markets, and entire ecosystems [2]. Typically, just before the tipping point occurs, the system becomes slow to recover from environmental perturbations, which is why this phenomenon is sometimes referred to as 'critical slowing down' (CSD) [6,7]. CSD has been confirmed in different fields of science, although knowledge of this phenomenon still seems to be largely restricted to the physical rather than biological sciences [8,9]. There may be several factors that contribute to CSD, but a generic mechanism that underlies CSD at multiple scale levels so far remains elusive. Critical slowing down may be due to a gradual increase in the number and strength of recurrent connections between system components (e.g., computers, genes, neurons, or people) [10]. Such components continuously enforce each other's activity, for which reason it will take longer for the system to quiet down after initial perturbation ('hysteresis' or slowing down: this would explain the increase in autocorrelations). A gradual increase in the number and strength of local connections decreases the number of network clusters (communities of connected nodes) until, at some discrete point, only a few additional connections are required to link all network clusters together into one giant connected component [11]. At that point, only a small increase in local connectivity is sufficient to produce an abrupt change in global network activity: a phase transition [12]. Despite such valuable insights, however, it has so far remained unclear what causes the connectivity and variance of system components to increase prior to a tipping point or to decrease after the tipping point has been reached.

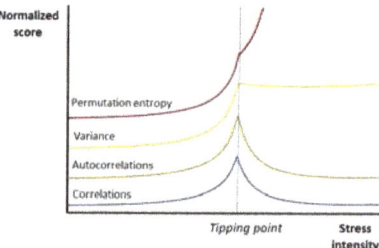

Figure 1. Universal changes in signal transduction of living systems under rising levels of stress. *Just before living systems undergo a sudden phase transition (a tipping point, e.g., disease or death), they show characteristic changes in internal signal transduction that may serve as early warning signs for system failure. As can be observed from this schematic figure, (auto)correlations between system components increase prior to the tipping point and decrease afterward, whereas variance increases and remains high (after [13]). A generic cause of such changes has so far remained unclear. In this paper, we argue that these changes are incorporated by a single variable (permutation entropy, see below), which may provide insights into a universal mechanism that underlies critical transitions in living systems.*

Rising levels of stress do not only cause universal changes in internal signal transduction of living systems. The content of their behavior also changes in an apparently universal way. When stress levels approach near-lethal levels, organisms shift their behavior from so called 'slow' to 'fast' behavioral policies [14]. This means they are less prone to spending time and energy on caring for each other and future generations (e.g., reproduction and parental investment). Instead, they become more focused on energy economy and self-preservation (e.g., aggression and maternal cannibalism). Behavior also shifts from long-term strategies (e.g., storing food, stacking fat) toward more short-term strategies (e.g., eating food, burning fat). Physiologically, such changes coincide with a shift back from more sophisticated, 'goal-directed' forms of behavior (such as navigating mazes in order to locate a food source) to relatively simple, habitual forms behavior (such as feeding, fighting, or fleeing) [15,16]. In other words, the organism's behavior becomes more focused on managing basic challenges that are currently at hand, rather than considering complex and possibly long-term scenarios. Such changes have previously been explained by a need of organisms to redistribute scarce amounts of energy and resources to their most primary processes [17,18]. In this view, organisms can be modeled as regulatory systems with a hierarchical structure, in which higher and lower systems work together to produce stability [19]. When a lower-level system fails to stabilize the organism, a higher-level system will take over to nonetheless secure stability. The lower regulatory levels are called 'homeostatic' systems, since they are concerned with the relatively simple task of maintaining some state of the system within some narrowly defined limits (e.g., raising insulin or glucagon levels to keep glucose levels within certain limits). Higher-level systems are called 'allostatic' systems, since they are concerned with maintaining "stability through change" [19]. This usually involves more elaborate forms of behavior that will secure stability via a detour (e.g., navigating a complex environment to locate a food source, the ingestion of which will eventually raise glucose levels) [20]. To explain the observed changes in behavioral policies of organisms under stress, it has been proposed that stress induces an 'allostatic overload', i.e., a failure of higher-level (allostatic) systems that require a lot of energy to secure stability, leaving the more energy-efficient lower-level (homeostatic) systems to fend for themselves. Although this sounds intuitively appealing, the mechanism behind allostatic overload, as well as the way in which this mechanism relates to the observed changes in behavioral policies, has so far remained unclear. In this paper, we offer an explanation of these changes that has its footings in first principles in biophysics and control theory. Below, we first discuss the common stress response in somewhat more detail. After that, we discuss a consensus view on the structure and function of living systems that results from the integration of network theory, systems biology, and the free energy principle [21]. Departing from this framework, we then propose a generic mechanism that explains the characteristic changes in signal transduction and overt behavior of living systems under high levels of stress.

2. Disorder as a Common Response of Organisms to High Levels of Stress

In a seminal study, Zhu et al. showed that bacteria of different species respond in a similar fashion to antibiotic stressors [22]. Although bacterial stress responses include many different genetic pathways that depend on the type of stressor and the bacterial species involved, a generic stress response could nonetheless be observed when considering the whole system dynamics (i.e., when observing the whole gene transcription activity as measured in terms of differential mRNA expression in time). When antibiotic concentrations approach near-lethal levels, this causes a decrease in the number of statistical dependencies that normally exist between the genes of bacteria (correlations decrease, but variance remains high). This loss of coherence in gene expression was observed to increase the amount of randomness of the timeseries that describe differential gene expression in time. Such 'disorder' can be expressed in terms of a statistical quantity called permutation entropy, which is a measure of the amount of randomness that can be observed in the covariance patterns the describe the relationships between the various components of a system (Box 1).

Zhu et al. noted that the observed rise in disorder scores resulted from large-amplitude changes that were produced by independently responding genes, and that this independence may result from of a loss of regulatory connections that normally synchronize gene activity to produce order (Figure 2) [22]. As it turns out, permutation entropy levels in the timeseries of bacterial gene expression predict bacterial fitness (defined as the growth and survival rates of bacteria). Such predictions can be made with superior accuracy when compared to standard techniques that rely on the expression profiles of specific genetic pathways. This allows doctors to select antibiotics that are effective in treating certain types of bacterial infections, even when the specific genetic pathways involved in a particular bacterial stress response are not fully known.

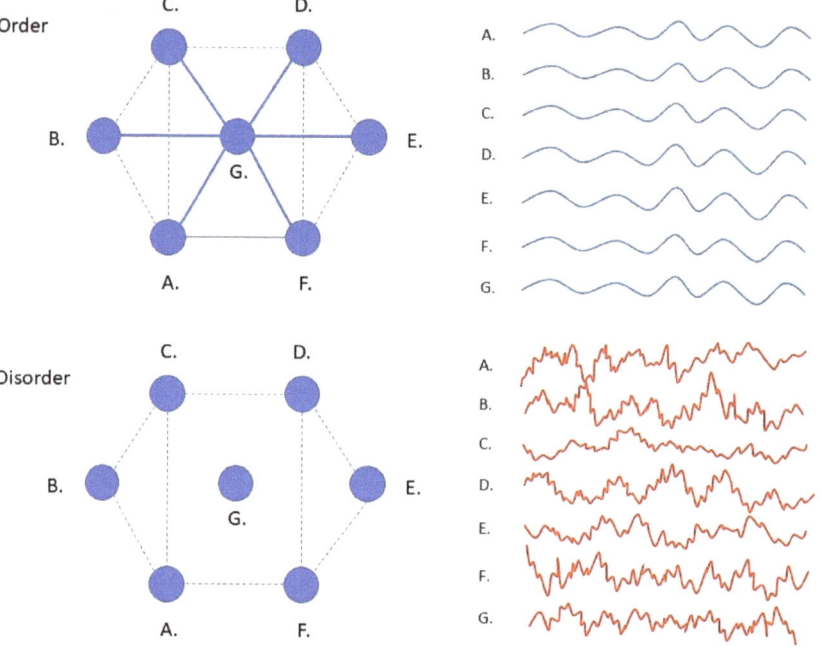

Figure 2. Increased disorder (permutation entropy) may be due to a loss of regulatory connections. *The emergence of disorder in timeseries may be due to the loss of regulatory connections that normally synchronize system components (e.g., genes, neurons) to produce order. In this figure, G is a regulatory (hub) node with many connections that synchronize the timeseries of node A–F. The loss of regulatory connections may cause nodes A–F to show autonomous (unsynchronized and, hence, disordered) behavior. The reason for this loss of regulatory connections has so far remained unclear.*

Box 1. Permutation entropy explained.

> Permutation entropy is a measure of the amount of disorder, unpredictability, randomness, or information content of a timeseries [23]. In calculating this measure, the values of successive timepoints are examined for predictable patterns by ordering them in partitions of prespecified length n (e.g., in case $n = 3$, the timeseries (1 9 3 5 2 7) will yield the partitions [1 9 3], [9 3 5], [3 5 2], etc.). The values of each partition are then placed in ascending order (e.g., for [1 9 3], the ascending order is [1 3 9]), and each value of the ordered partition is then assigned the logical code [0 1 2], depending on its position in the ascending sequence (e.g., 1 = 0, 3 = 1, 9 = 2). The full timeseries is then recoded according to this code table (e.g., the partition [1 9 3] is recoded into [0 2 1], [9 3 5] is recoded into [2 0 1], [3 5 2] is recoded into [1 2 0], etc.). Such logical reorderings of numbers are called permutations. The relative frequency $p(\pi)$ of all $n!$ permutations π of order n is then calculated, which expresses the probability of occurrence of some permutation with respect to all others in the timeseries. The permutation entropy is then calculated, which is a measure of the amount of patternlessness or randomness in the timeseries. This is done as follows:
>
> $$H(n) = -\sum p(\pi) \ln p(\pi),$$
>
> where the sum is run across all $n!$ permutations π of order n. From this formula, it can be seen that $H(n)$ lies in between 0 and 1, with the value 0 indicating a completely logically ordered timeseries of either ascending or descending values and the value 1 meaning complete randomness.
>
> The calculation of permutation entropy scores requires only few parameters and can be done quickly. A single score can be calculated for a single timeseries or set of timeseries at once, enabling a study of global signal intensity changes within organisms (e.g., differential mRNA expression in time, or activity changes in brain regions), as well as their overt behavior as a function of stress levels [22]. To study a set of timeseries at once, PE can be expressed as the natural logarithm of a glasso-regularized empirical correlation matrix M, which contains the partial correlation coefficients of all statistical relationship between the components of a system [22]. PE is then expressed as follows:
>
> $$H = \ln |M_\rho|,$$
>
> where | | denotes the regularization, and ρ signifies the regularization strength. Crucially, permutation entropy can be calculated not only for timeseries, but also for a single timepoint (stp), in which case the cross-sectional (snapshot) level of disorder of the system can be expressed as a single value [22,24].
>
> $$H_{stp} = \ln(\sigma^2),$$
>
> where σ^2 denotes the variance of the distribution across all measured variables.
>
> The traditional PE measure as explained above does not take the amplitude (or weight) of signal changes into account. Additionally, it is insensitive to signal changes at different temporal scale levels (i.e., high- versus low-frequency components) and highly sensitive to differences in the length of a timeseries and noise artefacts. For this reason, several refinements have been proposed of the original PE measure, which involve calculating weighted PE scores that are compared to white noise (pure randomness) across multiple (coarse grained) temporal scale levels. This refined multiscale reverse weighted (RMSRW) permutation entropy measure can handle noisy timeseries of different lengths, as well as signal changes at different scale levels [25]. By incorporating amplitude, variance, and temporal autocorrelations into a single value, RMSRW-PE covers all aspects that are considered typical hallmarks of critical slowing down (CSD). This means that living systems become increasingly 'disordered' prior to their failure, which we argue results from a loss of integrative regulatory connections that normally synchronize system components to produce order (see text). Throughout the rest of this paper, we use the terms PE and 'disorder' interchangeably as a more parsimonious term to refer to signal changes in stressed systems prior to their collapse.

Since (weighted) permutation entropy is a measure of global system dynamics, it incorporates the previously observed changes in correlation strength, variance, and (auto)correlations that are considered typical hallmarks of critical slowing down (Box 1). The permutation entropy measure appears to have comparable usability to the traditional measures of CSD. For instance, rising levels of permutation entropy are observed in living systems across all scale levels of biological organization, from genes and individual cells to tissues, organs, organisms, and social communities [26]: the death of a single bacterium follows the same dynamics as the collapse of a multicellular organism, populations of organisms, or entire ecosystems [27]. The increase in disorder levels affects both internal signal transduction and the outwardly observable behavior of organisms. For instance, fruit flies show erratic flying patterns when air pollution levels are high [28]. Water fleas, mussels, fish, dolphins, and whales show increasingly disordered swimming patterns when water quality deteriorates [29–31]. Human locomotion patterns show signs of increased randomness when stressed [32]. Like traditional measures of CSD, permutation entropy is able to predict the onset of tipping points in living systems, which signal the sudden onset of disease (or death). For example, bacteria succumbing to an antibiotic stressor, plants dying from a lengthy drought, or the bleaching of coral in deteriorating environments are typically discrete events that can be predicted by elevated levels of PE. Such findings have inspired ideas to use permutation entropy as part of an early warning system to monitor plant and animal welfare [29–31,33]. In humans, early warning signs of system failure typically precede the (sudden) onset of physical or mental illness [3–5,26]. Such knowledge is gradually making its way to medical practice. Permutation entropy levels can predict the onset of blood infections [34] and the spread of infectious disease throughout human populations [35]. In cardiology, neurology, and psychiatry, early warning signs for epileptic seizures, cardiac arrhythmias, and major depressive or psychotic disorders may allow for timely countermeasures [5,26]. Such observations underscore the practical value of 'disorder' as an early warning sign and warrants a further look into optimal descriptors of this phenomenon, as well as its possible causes.

The idea that permutation entropy can be used as a single parsimonious measure of signal changes in struggling systems has practical consequences in the sense that it reduces the complexity of calculations. More importantly, however, this conceptual step may help to gain a better understanding of the possible mechanisms that underlie CSD. On the one hand, the presence of generic early warning signs in struggling systems may just be a coincidence, with many different causes of disorder loading onto a single quantity (permutation entropy) that is so generic that it fails to say anything useful about living systems. On the other hand, such similarities may suggest a common biophysical principle that underlies disorder at different scale levels of organization [27,36]. Below, we argue for the latter position by showing that similar biophysical rules govern the structure and function of living systems at different scale levels of organization. We show that living systems are hierarchically organized network structures in which highly connective components (hubs) maintain high-level allostatic control. We then show that stress can be equated to variational free energy under the free-energy principle [37,38] and that high levels of stress (free energy) specifically cause the most connective nodes in a network (hubs) to overload and fail, since these are the first to reach their limits of free-energy dissipation. Since hubs keep the various components of a system together and synchronized (like horse cart drivers keeping a team of horses in check), the failure of such structures produces desynchronization and disorder, including the generic early warning signs as described above. We argue that a loss of (allostatic) control by key connective structures is not necessarily restricted to living systems, but may reflect a universal feature of open dissipative systems that are loaded up with free energy beyond their capacity to dissipate it back to the environment. We conclude by showing how the proposed disorder concept may apply to disease processes in general and to the human situation in particular.

3. Organisms as Control Systems

Woodlice keep on running around erratically until the air that surrounds them approaches a humidity level near 100%. Only then do they truly come to rest, which is why we find these creatures in all sorts of nooks and crannies. Woodlice do not know exactly where to find a nice and wet place in which they can safely retreat from the dangers of desiccation: they just keep on running around until they stumble across a suitable spot, after which the 'running faucet' is screwed shut. This mechanism has much in common with the way in which a central heating system works. Such systems have thermostats that indicate the desired temperature (e.g., 22 °C, a 'setpoint'), sensors that indicate the actual temperature (e.g., 18 °C) and heating elements that produce heat. The difference (4 °C) between the desired and the actual temperature is sent to the heater that heats up the environment until room temperature reaches the preset value. At that very moment, the difference ('error') is zero, and the heater shuts down. All organisms, including humans, turn out to follow this same principle: we are 'control systems' that try to minimize the difference between our 'setpoints' and the actual state of the environment [39]. It is just that our setpoints are more elaborate and describe several more desirable states than just ambient temperature (e.g., partners, jobs, and social positions). Together, the total collection of our setpoints describes our preferential 'econiches': spots on the planet and in our society where we like to be and where we will eventually end up provided these niches are encoded correctly and the right actions are performed in order to reach these places (Figure 3).

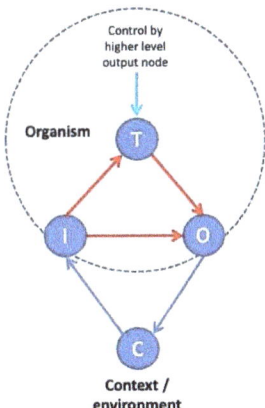

Figure 3. Organisms as control systems. *In a very simple model, organisms can be seen as controls systems with an input (I), throughput (T, reference value), and output compartment that interacts with the environment (context, C). The difference between the input (e.g., temperature) and reference value (e.g., the thermostat) is called the 'error', which is transferred onto the output module to generate an action that changes the environment. This in turn changes the input to the organism, and the cycle repeats. Thus, organisms iteratively seek out (or create) environments that fit their reference values. Complex (sets of) reference values are called 'world models'. These encode a complex set of environmental circumstances representing an optimal econiche (see text).*

4. Active Inference

In reality, things are a bit more complicated: our thermostats do not merely indicate which states we like to experience. They indicate which states we *expect to occur* at some point in the future. That means they encode predictions, or predictive models of our environment. This still resembles a thermostat in some way, since one may wonder whether such devices actually indicate what temperature we like, or whether the preset value of 22 °C actually represents a prediction of what room temperature will be, provided the system will keep on running indefinitely. In fact, all setpoints can be construed as predictions, and many setpoints together as predictive models of our inner and outer worlds or preferential niches. Such multifaceted models are called 'world models' [40]. The difference between the world that we perceive and our predictive models of that world is called a 'prediction error' [41,42]. This is a measure that indicates how 'surprising' a certain observation or outcome is, given that outcomes may deviate from predictions. For instance, a frog that is suddenly thrown into a pool of hot water will show a lot of prediction error. Such error provides an estimate of the degree to which its predictive models deviate from the way it perceives the world. In living systems, prediction errors trigger actions that are aimed at reducing the prediction error itself (e.g., the frog will start a struggle to escape its unpleasant surroundings and return to safer grounds). This happens because such actions change the external world (e.g., ambient temperature drops when the frog moves out of the pool), which in turn changes the organism's perception of that world, which then reduces or increases prediction errors that induce actions, after which the cycle repeats (Figure 3). Action is, therefore, a way to vary prediction errors and test the 'fitness' of a world model.

It turns out that prediction errors are not only used to induce action (as in central heating systems), but also to adjust the models (thermostat settings) themselves: a process called 'belief updating'. This involves a process where the 'weights' of the connections between the various elements that constitute the predictive system are altered as a function of prediction error [43]. Thus, belief updating is a form of learning or adaptation, which allows organisms to meet environmental conditions halfway. For instance, the same frog will show less prediction error and remain exactly where it is when put in a pool of cool water that is gradually warmed to unpleasant levels, since it now has the time to adjust its predictive models. The iterative loop of trial (action) and learning from prediction error (belief updating) is called 'active inference' [42,44]. This is a process by which organisms are actively foraging their environments for novel experiences that may be counterfactual to (or falsify) their conjectures of the world, after which the most unrefuted model is selected as the most plausible explanation of the observed events [37]. This is sometimes compared to organisms as little scientists [45], although active inference more generally refers to a circular process of inference (niche modeling) and action (niche exploration and active niche construction) [46,47].

In a seminal paper, Karl Friston used insights from Bayesian information theory to show that prediction error (under some circumstances) is equal to the mean amount of 'variational free energy' across time of a living system, such as a cell or a brain [48]. This means that when organisms try to iteratively reduce their prediction errors through active inference, they are actually trying to reduce their free-energy levels across longer timespans. In this respect, they are not much different from crystals in which ions arrange themselves into highly ordered patterns, despite the fact that all objects in this universe need to obey the second law of thermodynamics (which states that they must seek a state of maximum disorder, i.e., high entropy). For quite some time, it was thought that crystals violated the second law of thermodynamics, until it was discovered that crystallization produces heat that dissipates into the environment, producing a global increase in entropy (and free energy) levels [49]. Additionally, the ordering of ions into neatly arranged lattices in many cases allows water molecules to move more freely through the system, which adds to the global amount of disorder (and free energy) of the universe. Thus, scholars realized that objects may arrange themselves *locally* into more ordered (low-entropy) states as long as this allows for a *global* increase in entropy and free energy. Despite the necessity that everything in nature eventually needs to revert to a state of high disorder, living systems have found a way in which they can maintain their circumscribed form and stable state (i.e., order) at least for some period of time, by having found the most efficient way of losing (dissipating) their free energy to the environment, which is to reduce prediction error [37,50,51]. Similarly, an organism can be compared to a ping-pong ball that rolls into a pit in order to keep its potential (free) energy as low as possible: that ball simply has no choice, since it needs to obey the second law of thermodynamics, which states that any object may seek a local state of low free energy and entropy (the bottom of the pit) as long as this leads to a global increase in entropy levels of the universe (in this case, the act of rolling into the pit increases the global freedom of the individual molecules of the ball in the form of heat, which subsequently dissipates into the environment [52]). In living systems, the basin of the pit corresponds to a state of low entropy (prediction error or variational free energy) that is called 'homeostasis' [37]. Active inference can, therefore, be seen as a walk across a free-energy landscape, in which organisms actively try to roll into pits of low variational free energy that represent high levels of niche model 'fitness' (homeostasis) (Figure 4). In most cases, such low-energy states correspond to organisms occupying their locally optimal econiches. The whole process of seeking stability through change thus follows from the basic laws of thermodynamics [51]. Friston has found a series of equations with which to describe this process that do not only apply to life in general, but to all objects in this universe that are required to dissipate their free-energy levels as efficiently as possible [53]: a true 'Theory of Every Thing' [54]. In a way, this theory says something we already knew for quite some time: by actively searching for optimal niches (minimizing prediction error), living systems can reach homeostasis (a stable state of low mean variational free energy) and survive (remain intact). The novelty is that we now have mathematical equations with which to describe this process, which may apply to any object in this universe.

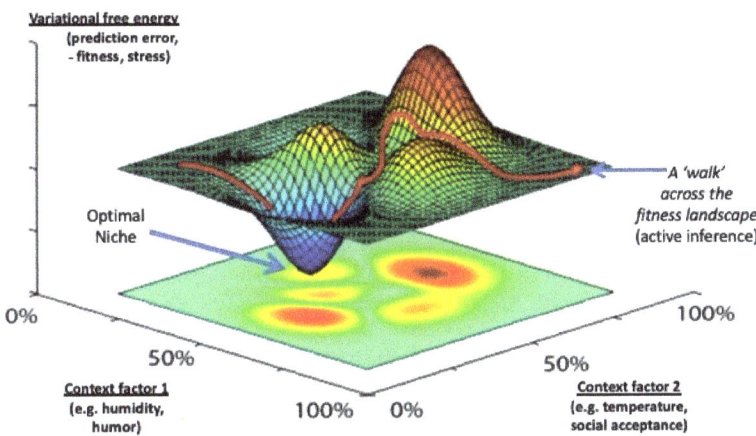

Figure 4. Active inference pictured as organisms exploring a free-energy (model fitness) landscape. *In biology, organisms are said to be involved in niche exploration and active niche construction to occupy econiches that optimize their chances of survival and reproduction (niche exploitation). Active inference theory can be seen as a way to describe this process in biophysical terms. According to this theory, organisms use action to change their environments (e.g., digging in or building a shelter), which in turn alters their perception of the world (e.g., a rise in humidity levels). This altered perception produces a different fit with the organism's predictive models of the world (alters prediction error), which can be expressed as a change in the theoretical quantity of (variational) free energy. According to the free-energy principle, action (niche exploration and construction) and belief updating (model adjustment) serve to minimize mean variational free energy (produce high average model fitness), allowing organisms to find a low-energy stable state that corresponds to the concept of 'homeostasis' in biology. Approaching or occupying optimal econiches, therefore, ensures thermodynamic stability (survival). In this respect, organisms that seek optimal econiches are like ping-pong balls that actively try to roll into pits that correspond to the lowest possible levels of free energy across time (this is called a 'gradient descent' on a free-energy plot [55]). In this figure, the vertical axis represents the free energy levels of some organism (prediction error, negative model fitness). The horizontal axes represent environmental conditions (i.e., econiches), which are limited to only two conditions in this example, since we have difficulty imagining organisms navigating multidimensional state spaces (i.e., complex econiches). The various peaks and valleys together form an energy 'landscape' (although 'seascape' might be more appropriate, since environmental conditions change continuously). Valleys in this seascape represent areas with relatively low (variational) free-energy levels, which correspond to more optimal environmental niches. Active inference is a process by which organisms are continuously improving their internal map of the sea (inference) by actively exploring its surface (niche exploration) and making some ripples of their own (niche construction) to eventually make for the shallowest waters (econiches) where they can remain intact (survive) and reproduce (exploit their niche). In evolutionary biology, similar diagrams are used in which the vertical axis represents 'reproductive fitness', which is often defined in terms of the (relative) number of offspring or copies of some gene. In contrast, local or 'instantaneous fitness' (prediction error) may be a more proximal measure of biological fitness than gene frequencies or the number of offspring, since the latter measures are counted post hoc. The two can easily be converted into each other,* e.g., *by defining reproductive fitness as the integral of local model fitness (prediction error, homeostasis) across all econiches encountered by the organism and its offspring across some period of time (e.g., the lifespan).*

5. Organisms as Hierarchical Bayesian Control Systems

In a recent paper [21], we proposed a consensus view on the 'plumbing' that makes active inference possible. The approach taken involves combining current knowledge on the structure of living systems with recent insights into their function. First, we show that all living systems follow the same architectural principles, i.e., they are *small world* network systems with a nested modular structure [56]. These are networks in which most elements (nodes) have few connections, but some have many. These highly connected units (hubs) ensure that the network as a whole has a small average 'pathlength', which is the average distance between any two nodes in the network when moving along the shortest paths. This causes signal transmission across small world networks to be highly efficient even in very large networks (e.g., in social networks, only six degrees of separation lie in between any two people on this world, making it 'a small world after all'). Hubs contract parts of the network into so-called communities or clusters [57]. Such clusters may themselves serve as nodes at a higher spatial scale level of observation and so on. For example, organelles form cells that are a part of larger modules (tissues), which in turn are a part of supermodules (organs), etcetera, until one reaches the level of the organism itself. Thus, a hierarchy of part–whole relationships is formed (a 'mereology'), in which one scale level of biological organization cannot exist without the other (e.g., [58]). The topological structure of such networks is the same across scale levels, which is why such networks are called scale-invariant or 'scale-free' [59,60]. We then show that all organisms appear to follow the same principles of network function (internal signal transduction, dynamics). This involves a combination of hierarchical message passing and predictive coding that has seen diverse representations and for which a consensus view has been proposed by Karl Friston [61,62]. In this view, all living systems are involved in some form of hierarchical Bayesian inference, i.e., modeling the latent (hidden) common causes behind observed events in their inner and outer worlds and updating these models using new evidence. In order to accomplish this, organisms have nodes that function either as prior (prediction) units or as prediction error units (Figure 5). Whereas prior units encode some predictive model of the world, prediction error units encode the difference between the model and newly obtained evidence. Such evidence initially enters at the bottom of the hierarchy in the form of excitatory input from the senses (bottom left in Figure 5). These input signals update the values of prior units, which in turn suppress the activity of prediction error units at the same hierarchical level by means of inhibitory connections. These prediction error units then try to update the values of prior units by means of excitatory connections, producing circularly causal dynamics (within-level oscillations). Since the suppression of prediction error by (updated) priors is rarely complete, a residual prediction error is produced that projects upward in the hierarchy to update the values of prior units at a higher level within the hierarchy. These units in turn project backward to suppress the same lower-level prediction error units by means of inhibitory connections, again producing circularly causal dynamics (between-level oscillations). Thus, each hierarchical level is involved in suppressing prediction error within that same level, as well as at a lower level. As observed above, the process of updating the values of priors by means of prediction errors is called '(Bayesian) belief updating'. The suppression of prediction errors by updated predictions is often referred to as 'evidence' that is 'explained away' by hierarchical Bayesian 'beliefs' [42]. Typically, prediction errors are fed forward until they are suppressed by a model of sufficient hierarchical depth, which is the model that best 'explains the observed evidence'. Note that only prediction errors are carried forward through the hierarchy and not the original input from the senses. Quite fundamentally, this means that organisms have no direct access to the external world, from which they are separated by a barrier. What they perceive is a hierarchical model of the world that best explains the observed evidence, rather than a direct representation of the world [51,63].

The above dynamics is thought to underlie hierarchical Bayesian inference in living systems [61–63]. When applying this principle to scale-free network structures, one can see that the process of generating and updating Bayesian beliefs occurs at all spatial scale levels of organization within the nested modular hierarchy. Each scale level has an 'input part' (a collection of prediction error units) that connects to a higher-level 'throughput part' (a smaller number of priors that try to suppress prediction error), after which the residual error is fed back down the hierarchy to an 'output part' (a larger number of prediction error units), to produce output sequences. Crucially, the various priors and prediction error units in this configuration may involve network nodes or clusters, depending on the spatial scale level of observation. Thus, a self-similar (scale free/fractal-like) network structure is obtained in which the same input–throughput–output motif (a 'feed-forward loop' [64]) can be observed at each spatial scale level of observation: from the smallest scale of only three nodes (e.g., a neural circuit within the visual cortex) to a global 'hierarchical Bayesian control system' comprising the global compartments of perception, goal setting, and action control, which constitutes the organism (Figure 5). At each level of observation, prediction errors converge while ascending in the input hierarchy and diverge while descending in the output hierarchy, giving the structure the overall shape of a dual hierarchical (nested modular) 'bowtie' network structure [60,65]. Note that predictions converge while ascending in the output hierarchy and diverge while descending in the input hierarchy, to form a global counterflow. Information flows can take shortcuts via skip-connections that run between input and output hierarchies at comparable levels within the hierarchy, effectively causing the bowtie structure to fold back onto itself (Figure 5).

In forming hierarchical Bayesian models, organisms need to solve the binding problem [66], i.e., they need to figure out whether a set of events that occur simultaneously share a single common cause that should be encoded by a single variable (e.g., by a single network node or cluster), or whether these events represent separate causes that should be encoded separately (e.g., by separate nodes or clusters). In solving the binding problem, an important role is played by highly connected elements in these networks (so-called 'hubs'). A hub can be pictured as a horse cart driver that needs to keep a team of horses in check, while using the reins to appreciate the general state of the team of horses as a whole (another example would be a middle manager that tries to get a sense of the general state of a team of employees). Every single horse keeps in touch with a part of the external world, but the driver itself tries to form a picture of the whole situation. This driver can in turn be seen as a horse that, together with other drivers, is kept in check by yet other drivers (directors), etc. The highest drivers (CEOs) thus try to get a sense of the global state of most horses in the hierarchy, through which they encode the most contextually integrated model of the experienced world, but only in a very compact and abstract sense. Similarly, living systems contain hub structures that converge onto hubs to form a nested modular network structure (a pyramidal shape), which encodes an increasingly integrated model of the world (Figure 5). Such nested modular collections of hubs are called 'rich clubs', since they are 'rich in connections' [67,68]. In Figure 5, a hierarchy of priors (black nodes) can be discerned that starts with the simplest of setpoints at the base of the hierarchy, to eventually involve only a few hub clusters at the top. Each subsequent level within this hierarchy encodes the hidden common causes behind a multitude of subordinate events using an increasingly small number of independent variables (degrees of freedom). Such integration takes place across multiple contextual cues in space (e.g., multiple horses influence the hub-driver at the same time), as well as time (e.g., the same horses show faster and slower dynamics, which are encoded vertically in the hierarchy) [69,70]. In other words, each subsequent level in the hierarchy encodes increasingly long-term predictions of increasingly complex econiches in an increasingly abstract and parsimonious way. Organisms, therefore, try to model their inner and outer environments using a shrinking number of variables but with minimal loss of information, meaning that some form of compression takes place while moving upward in the hierarchy [71]. In mathematical terms, information is funneled through an increasingly low-dimensional manifold (which has been compared to Occam's razor) [72]. The apex of the pyramid shown in Figure 5 (the 'knot' of the bowtie), therefore, serves as an 'information bottleneck' structure [73] that encodes econiches at the highest level of 'sophistication' that an organism can achieve [65,74,75]. The term sophistication is used on purpose here, since it has been proposed to refer to predictive models that are models of other models (i.e. recursive beliefs: having beliefs about beliefs) [75]. In nested modular network systems such as Figure 5, higher hierarchical levels integrate across a range of lower levels (by means of hub nodes). Such integration takes place across multiple contextual cues in space, as well as time, causing higher-level models to encode increasingly long-term predictions of increasingly complex econiches in increasingly parsimonious (and abstract) ways. In other words, information bottleneck structures are used by living systems to build hierarchical Bayesian models using a minimum number of parameters (i.e., while minimizing model complexity costs). For this reason, we prefer not to call higher-level models more 'complex', since that term is reserved for models with many parameters. Higher levels do convey more long-term, abstract, and symbolic representations (i.e., a joint probability distribution over a set of prior probabilities under a hierarchical model [76]). This causes higher hierarchical levels to be relatively disconnected from events at lower levels, i.e., they encode models that model latent causal structure behind lower-level events with some degree of autonomy and creativity. Such 'hierarchical generative models' are able to escape the limitations of scarce and noisy data samples and nonetheless reach high levels of predictive accuracy, e.g., [77]. In living systems, the highest hierarchical levels encode contextually rich econiches that are to be explored or rather avoided in the near or further future [40]. Another way to refer to such hierarchical predictive models of econiches is a 'goal hierarchy' [20,78]. Goal hierarchies encode the logical set of econiches (goals) and corresponding subniches (subgoals) that the organism needs to pursue in order to reach the global econiche (goal) encoded at the top of the hierarchy [72].

As mentioned, prediction errors with respect to goal hierarchies serve not only to update these hierarchies and produce optimally informed models of the world, but also to inspire action [37,42,51]. Hierarchical Bayesian control systems are dual-aspect hierarchies in which the input hierarchy continuously supplies the output hierarchy with residual prediction error to coordinate behavior. When a simple goal state at some hierarchical level of inference and corresponding policy is insufficient to explain the evidence, the residual error is passed onto a higher level within the goal hierarchy, where a more sophisticated world model (goal state) tries to suppress prediction error. Any residual error then crosses over to corresponding levels of the output hierarchy to produce action sequences of corresponding levels of sophistication. Thus, a hierarchy of red hub nodes can be observed in Figure 5 that encodes a hierarchy of evidence, which is contrasted with the hierarchy of priors within the goal hierarchy to produce prediction errors at matching hierarchical levels that are fed into the output hierarchy to induce behavioral responses of corresponding levels of sophistication. Such output then serves to change the environment and produce a different niche model fit [37,42,51]. A common example is walking: this (habitual) motor pattern can in itself be sufficient to solve the problem of getting to a food source without much effort. When the terrain becomes rough, however, the organism may encounter obstacles that lie between itself and its goal (the food source). Such encounters produce prediction errors, which ascend in the hierarchy until they are suppressed by a sufficiently sophisticated model of the econiche (goal state). Prediction errors relative to this goal state then induce behavioral policies at a higher level of sophistication. For instance, the organism will now reorient itself (sample the environment to infer a model that encodes a richer environmental context) and plan a detour. Thus, goals and corresponding subgoals are pursued in a logical order by means of matching action sequences until the organism reaches its preferential global econiche [79]. Organisms can, therefore, be seen as hierarchical problem-solving machines that infer ever more sophisticated goal states and corresponding action–perception sequences until prediction errors are suppressed and the problem is solved. Since the level of sophistication of each behavioral response matches the sophistication of its corresponding goal state, which in turn matches the organism's optimal perceptive model of the world, organisms automatically produce 'adaptive' behavior that is flexibly tuned to fit the level of complexity of their actual environments [21,80].

Interestingly, the output hierarchy is also involved in some form of inference [80,81]. In output hierarchies, the sensory states of output organs (such as muscles or endocrine glands) are used to model the actual actions that are taking place, whereas prediction errors with respect to such models are used as output signals to these organs to make on-the-fly corrections (Figure 5). Thus, hierarchical Bayesian control systems have input hierarchies that try to figure out "what the world is doing" (perception), output hierarchies that try to infer "what the organism is doing" (action control), and throughput hierarchies that try to infer "what the organisms *should* be doing" (goal setting) [21]. These domains enter in a closed (feedforward-feedback) loop with the environment to allow for active inference.

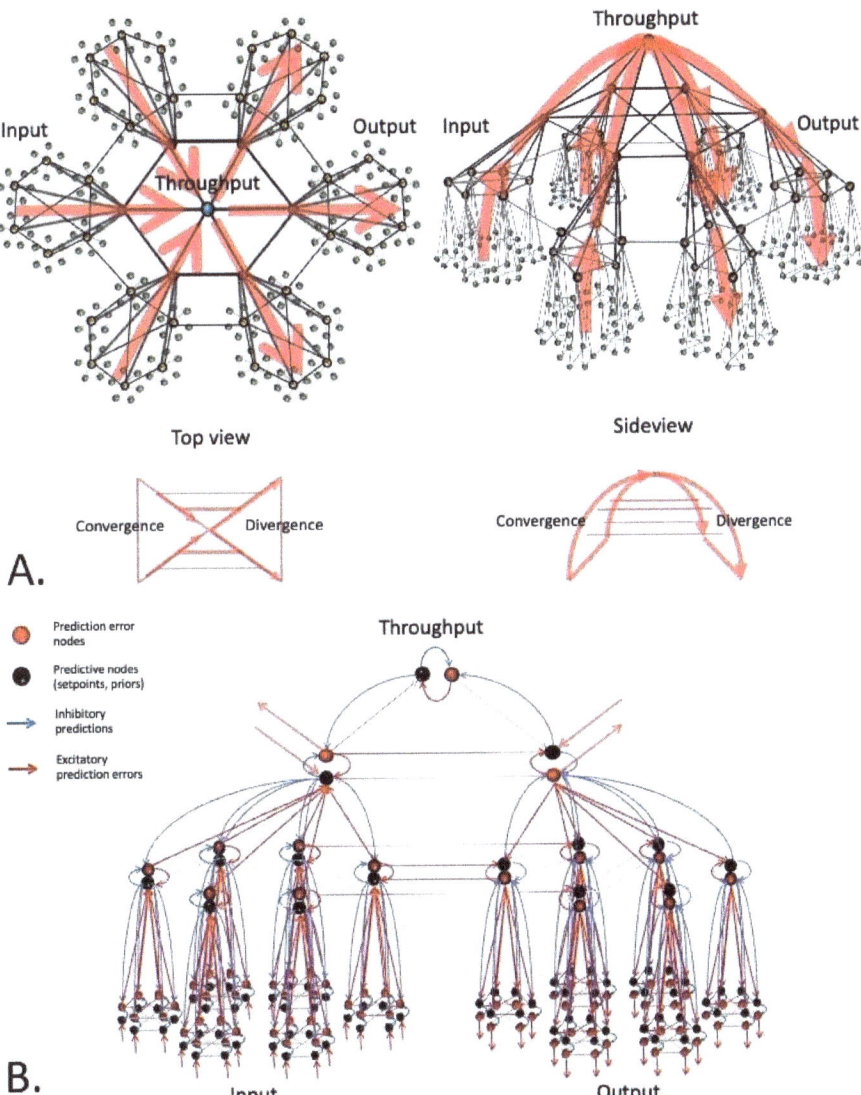

Figure 5. Consensus network structure that is proposed to support the process of active inference in all living systems. *Organisms can be conceived of as dual hierarchical Bayesian control systems that consist of an input hierarchy (left side), throughput hierarchy (top of the pyramidical structure), and output hierarchy (right side). Hierarchical message passing through these structures is thought*

to underlie hierarchical Bayesian inference in living systems. (**Panel A**). The structure shown in this figure integrates current ideas on hierarchical predictive coding [61,62] with key findings from network science [56,59] and systems biology [60,65]. (**Panel B**). This panel shows a cutout of the structure shown in panel A for closer inspection. Black nodes: priors (setpoints or predictions), red nodes: prediction error units. Blue arrows: inhibitory predictions, red arrows: excitatory prediction errors. Hierarchy of black nodes: a goal hierarchy (encoding world models). Hierarchy of red nodes: a hierarchy of evidence. At the base of the input hierarchy, input is compared to predictions (priors), and the residual error is projected upward in the hierarchy, where it is compared to higher-level priors (world models), and the process repeats. Prediction errors at some level of organization are used to both update priors ('belief updating') and inspire action. Predictions suppress prediction errors ('explain away the evidence'). Note that prediction errors are escalated upward in the input hierarchy to update the goal hierarchy and downward in the output hierarchy to inspire action (**panel A**, top image, large red arrows). Predictions follow the opposite path to form a global counterstream, i.e., they are escalated upward in the output hierarchy and downward in the input hierarchy (not shown, but see **panel B**, small blue arrows). The entire structure has an information bottleneck or 'bowtie' structure, in which information (prediction errors and predictions) reaches maximum compression within the throughput hierarchy and is less compressed in input and output hierarchies (**panel A**). Note that local flows of prediction errors and predictions may deviate from the global flows (left to right, or right to left), i.e., counterflows may exist locally. Skip connections (horizontal red lines) allow for shortcuts between input and output hierarchies e.g., corticocortical connections), causing the bowtie to fold back onto itself (panel A, lower part).

6. How Information Processing in Living Systems Corresponds to Behavior

In order to understand how stress alters the behavior of organisms in a universal way, we need to understand how message passing at different levels within hierarchical Bayesian control systems correspond to different forms of behavior. In this view, the lowest levels within such systems produce basic stimulus–response patterns called reflexes (e.g., sweating or salivation or spinal reflexes such as locomotion). In control theory, low-level reflex arcs such as these are said to produce 'homeostatic' reflexes, i.e., the closest regulators of a low-energy stable state (homeostasis) [19]. When moving upward in the regulatory hierarchy, more sophisticated action–perception cycles are formed that consists of combinations of basic reflexes, e.g., fighting, fleeing, freezing, feeding, reproducing, resting, digesting, self-repairing, and (parental) caring in response to typical cues. Such complex reflexes are called instinct patterns in evolutionary psychology [82]. When moving further upward in the regulatory hierarchy, more sophisticated policies are formed, which are called 'habits' [83]. These are automated responses to typical stimuli that consists of a combination of reflexes and instinct patterns in response to more complex perceptual cues (e.g., taking a morning stroll involves combination of reflexes and instinct patterns such as walking, resting, and digesting). Lastly, the highest levels of the regulatory hierarchy produce 'goal-directed' behavior, which involves nonautomatic (i.e., effortful) actions based on explicit and often long-term predictions of the consequences (perceptual outcomes) of actions [84]. Such predictions take the form of 'simulations' of what might happen if some action is taken. The predicted outcome of certain actions is then a prerequisite for such actions to be selected as the policies that are most likely to suppress prediction errors across trials [20,80]. In control theory, goal-directed behavior is considered a form of 'allostatic' behavior, i.e., behavior that is produced by hierarchically higher regulators that are superposed onto lower-level regulators in order to secure stability by means of more sophisticated responses when lower levels and less sophisticated forms of behavior fail to do so (i.e., "stability through change") [19].

Together, these different forms of behavior develop over the course of many iterations of trial and learning from prediction error (active inference). In this context, learning refers to a process of Bayesian belief updating, where prior expectations are updated in response to novel evidence (prediction error). Such updating involves a change in the efficiency (or complete rewiring) of the connections between priors, which corresponds to the actual learning process [43]. Belief updating may occur at any level within the hierarchy of priors shown in Figure 5. At the lowest (reflexive) levels of the hierarchy, belief updating produces a form of associative (stimulus–stimulus) learning that is called 'Pavlovian learning' (classic conditioning). During Pavlovian learning, organisms gradually associate one (familiar) stimulus with a new one and produce the same behavior to either of these stimuli (e.g., dogs learn to associate the ringing of a bell with food, causing anticipatory salivation).

Belief updating at 'intermediate' and 'higher' levels within the hierarchy of priors is referred to as 'habit learning' and 'goal-directed learning', respectively. Pavlovian learning and habit learning have been observed in a wide variety of species, including bacteria. Although goal-directed learning is usually associated with 'higher' species, many aspects of behavior in 'lower' species (including bacteria) resemble goal-directed behavior [84]. This means that similar forms of learning and behavior are present to different degrees in different species, depending on the sophistication of their goal hierarchies. Similarly, within-species individual differences in inferential abilities and behavior are thought to be due to differences in the outgrowth (maturation) of goal hierarchies during the lifetime of the organism. The next paragraph examines what types of world models are encoded at the top of goal hierarchies and to what kind of behavior they give rise. After that, we examine how changes in hierarchical Bayesian control systems correspond to shifts in behavioral policies under rising levels of stress.

Organisms are known to construct at least two distinct types of world (econiche) models at the top of their goal hierarchies: models of their external environments and models of their internal environments [85]. Such models inspire behavior that purports some sense of agency, i.e., the ability to distinguish between events that are generated by the organism itself versus events that have their origin outside of the organism [86,87]. The former include signals that arise within the body of the organism, as well as signals out of the body that have been produced by the organism itself, such as sounds or vibrations due to its own movement [86]. Basic forms of self (versus non-self) encoding have been observed even at the level of bacteria and may take more elaborate forms in higher mammals [88]. Such models increase in contextual richness when they gain in complexity and hierarchical depth, which appears to underlie the distinction between 'higher' and 'lower' species [37,51]. Self-models may include any form of self-representation, such as a body image and a psychological self-image [89]. Such models encode self-referential (personal) goals that the organisms would like to occupy or sample. Prediction errors with respect to such global goals inspire behavior that is aimed at achieving these goals through a logical series of subgoals and corresponding behavioral policies [72]. For instance, the global goal of catching food requires the global policy of hunting, which consists of subpolicies such as hiding, freezing, fighting, and eating. Reaching such goals involves the mastery of personal skills that vary from hunting and gathering and building nests to finding shelter and mastering survival skills (or occupational skills in humans). The growing mastery of such skills is referred to as self-actualization or the development of agency [87,90–93]. Especially in higher social mammals, models of the external world include social models ('theories of mind') [92,94]. Such models try to infer the hidden common causes behind multiple signals in the external world that are produced by other organisms, i.e., the intentions and motives of friends, rivals, mates, or kin [92]. Prediction errors relative to such models inspire behavior that is aimed at achieving personal or interpersonal (social) goals by taking these motives into account. Such actions may involve e.g., offensive or defensive actions, courtship rituals, parental investment, or nursing behavior. The increasing mastery of social skills is called social learning [95]. Note that even some forms of antisocial behavior (e.g., deceit or fraud) require the presence of social models, since such behavior requires some degree of knowledge of the intentions of others, which is used to one's own advantage. Regardless of the type of species, self-models and social models involve more integrative (goal-directed) forms of inference that occur at higher levels within a goal hierarchy (see previous section and Figure 5). In our recent paper [21], we showed that external (social) models are likely to form the top of the input hierarchy, since these are involved in inferring 'what the outside world is doing'. Following the same line of reasoning, internal (self) models are thought form the top of the output hierarchy, since these are involved in inferring 'what the organism is doing'. These assumptions are confirmed in the human brain [21], but require confirmation in other species. Since the timescale of events is encoded vertically in hierarchical networks [69,70], the vertical outgrowth of self and social models allows organisms to incorporate increasingly long-term predictions with respect to increasingly abstract personal or interpersonal goals. For instance, self-models and social models in higher primates have reached a level of sophistication that allows them to imagine and work toward complex social positions across many years of time.

For a long time, it was thought that organisms only construct these two global models, i.e., internal (self) models and external (social) models. In our recent paper [21], we demonstrated that the principle of hierarchical Bayesian inference logically (and necessarily) dictates that there must exist a third, highest level of inference, whose job it is to infer the hidden common causes behind events that involve both the internal and the external world of the organism, across multiple context factors in both space and time. In short, there must be an overarching model that integrates across self and social models to encode a commonly held world model (a common econiche) (Figure 6). Prediction errors relative to such models inspire actions that are aimed at affecting this common econiche rather than the local, internal, or external (social) niches of the organism itself. Although in theory, knowledge of a 'common ground' can be used solely to the advantage of an individual organism or local group, such knowledge is unlikely to produce strictly selfish policies since any type of behavior that favors a global goal (i.e., promotes global stability) eventually also favors individual organisms and local groups (i.e., promote local stability). Especially in higher social species, the vertical outgrowth of overarching models allows organisms to produce increasingly sophisticated models of common econiches across increasingly lengthy periods of time. Prediction errors relative to such models inspire behavior that is aimed at promoting long-term collective stability, such as an equal sharing of energy and resources across multiple stakeholders (e.g., collaboration, food sharing, and other forms of distributive justice), resolving conflict situations (e.g., mediation or arbitration), or holding each other responsible when goals are violated that apply to all members of the community (punishment for norm violation and other forms of justice). Normative or law-abiding behavior of this kind (including altruistic behavior) has been observed in some form or another in a wide range of organisms, from unicellular organisms and invertebrates to higher vertebrates and mammals [96–100]. Whereas a clear self–other dichotomy seems to mark the distinction between kinship selection (i.e., the favoring of kin over others, nepotism) and reciprocal altruism (i.e., investing in unknown individuals) [101], the hierarchical expansion of overarching world models seems to soften the self–other dichotomy by pushing behavior toward an increasingly inclusive (social) space and toward ever larger (transgenerational) timescales, i.e., devoting time and energy to improve the stability of unknown future individuals and species [102–107]. Such overarching world models allow organisms to escape the polarization or nepotism that is inherent to local self-referential or interpersonal goals by appealing to commonly held niche models that are invariant across generations. Especially in social organisms where regulatory hierarchies have reached high levels of sophistication, such shared setpoints may take the form of community norms or values [106–110]. Such goals promote social cohesion between large numbers of individuals across substantial individual differences and substantial spatial and temporal boundaries [111]. Even the ability to see all of life as connected under such common laws and insights (which includes religious insights and corresponding feelings) may be caused by this highest level of inference (e.g., [112]). In this respect, it is interesting to note that 'religare' originally means 'to reconnect' in Latin (across individual differences and timeframes, under a common highest law), that Catholicism means '(moving) toward a whole', Islam means 'order/peace through submission (to a higher law)', and 'hierarchy' refers to 'holy ordination' in ancient Greek. In short, organisms are likely to be engaged in a highest level of inference at the top of their goal hierarchies, which tries to infer what the organism "should be doing". Such overarching (normative) world models are not restricted to higher organisms, although organisms with more sophisticated goal hierarchies do tend to show more sophisticated forms of behavior (see previous section for a definition).

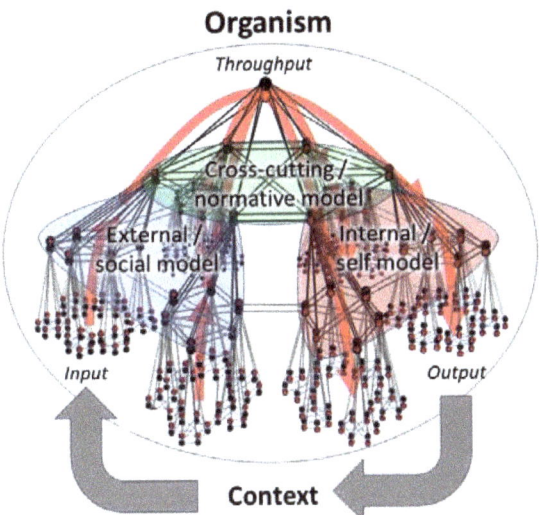

Figure 6. The putative positions of different world models in living systems.

7. Disorder: A Collapse of Hierarchical Control

We now turn to the point of explaining the apparently universal stress response of organisms in terms of the actions of hierarchical Bayesian control systems, as laid down in the previous sections. To summarize, this generic response is composed of the following elements: as a first rule, rising levels of stress produce characteristic changes in internal message passing of living systems. These involve an increase in the strength of (auto)correlations and variance observed between the various components of a living system. This happens up to a discrete 'tipping point' (or bifurcation), after which (auto)correlations drop but variance remains high. Such changes are captured by a single variable of permutation entropy, which shows that the dynamics of signal transduction within organisms turns increasingly disorderly until a tipping point is reached (Figure 1). Such changes coincide with the phenomenon of critical slowing down (CSD): a delayed recovery after perturbation of the system. When systems move beyond the tipping point, correlations decrease but variance and entropy levels remain high until the system fails completely. As a second rule, the timeseries of overt behavior of organisms follows the same pattern as internal signal transduction: disorder levels gradually rise until a tipping point is reached. Thirdly, rising levels of stress change the content of an organism's behavior in an apparently universal way: low levels of stress induce routine (reflexive or habitual) behavioral policies, whereas moderately high levels cause organisms to show more sophisticated (goal-directed) forms of behavior. When exposed to extreme (near-lethal) levels of stress, behavior shifts from 'slow' to 'fast' behavioral policies [14], i.e., organisms shift their focus from a long-term commitment to fellow organisms and reproductive activity to behavior that is focused largely on the preservation of self and/or kin. This corresponds to a shift back from goal-directed to habitual forms of behavior. Lastly, when living systems remain challenged after having passed the tipping point, they willfully disintegrate (i.e., lose their independence from the environment). The state of the system will now linearly follow that of the environment, amounting to a loss of homeostasis (i.e., an unstable, high entropy state). Such tipping points usually correspond to malfunction, disease, or the death of a system.

The sum of these observations can be explained by looking at the actions of hierarchical Bayesian controls systems, as shown in Figure 5. We argue that 'prediction error' can be read as 'stress' and 'action' can be read as the 'stress response', such that the theory of active inference can be applied to stress research [21]. In this view, any change in environmental conditions may alter an organism's perception of the world, which produces a different fit with the organism's predictive models of the world (goal states). This prediction error ('stress') is used to adjust the predictive model (i.e., belief updating, learning) and converted into action (a stress response). Hence, when we feel stressed, we actually perceive the mental and bodily changes that constitute a stress response to a prediction error. Incidentally, this means that stress can be reduced in two fundamentally different ways: either by performing an action or by changing expectations or beliefs. This view has been highly influential in the psychological literature and is applied worldwide, for instance, during cognitive behavioral therapy (CBT) [113,114].

As mentioned in Section 5, the ascent of prediction error in goal hierarchies adds levels to a hierarchical model of the world up to a level of sophistication that sufficiently explains the observed effects. Prediction errors relative to this model are then used to inspire behavior of corresponding levels of sophistication, starting from simple, low-level reflexive (e.g., walking) or instinctive forms of behavior (e.g., foraging) to habitual (e.g., take a morning stroll) and goal-directed forms of behavior (e.g., finding the shortest route to a food source in a complex environment). When prediction error (stress) ascends in information bottleneck structures such as Figure 5, this causes an increasingly large number of lower-level systems (horses) to be 'enslaved' by an increasingly small number of high-level hub regions (drivers). Rising levels of prediction error, therefore, initially increase the amount of centrally coherent governance (top-down hierarchical control), causing the subordinate systems to become increasingly synchronized (coherent). Thus, we propose that the observed increase in correlations between the various components of systems that are stressed in the mild-to-moderate range is due to an increase in central governance exerted by high-level hub structures (Figure 5). Similarly, we propose that the observed increase in the total variance of such systems may be due to the recruitment of increasing numbers of subordinate systems. This is because each of these subsystem produces its own within-level and between-level oscillations between prediction and prediction error units, which correspond to unique amplitudes and variances (frequencies). Since the increased involvement of hub structures raises the connectivity between system components, the number of recurrent connections between such components is also likely to rise. Subsystems will, therefore, increasingly reinforce each other's activity through circularly causal connections to the point where it takes longer for stressed systems to recover from initial perturbation. This may explain the phenomenon of hysteresis or 'slowing down', as quantified by rising autocorrelations (see Section 1). Together, these changes are likely to affect the permutation entropy of the system (Box 1). On the one hand, the increase in central integrative governance exerted by hub structures synchronizes signal transduction between lower-level (subordinate) domains, which imposes some degree of order and decreases the permutation entropy of the system. On the other hand, however, every level that is added to a hierarchical model increases the number of microstates (and microvariances) required to describe the total state and evolution of the system. Since the amount of information required to describe the total state and evolution of a system is equal to its (weighted) permutation entropy [23], the recruitment of additional systems will raise entropy scores. Thus, an equilibrium will ensue between 'order through synchronization' by hub units and 'disorder through recruitment of additional subsystems'. This balance may at times favor either order or disorder at different trajectories within the mild-to-moderate range, but empirical studies show that rising levels of stress eventually cause a *net* rise in permutation entropy levels (see Section 1).

Although organisms can recruit ever higher (allostatic) levels of control to enhance the sophistication of their (stress) responses, this cannot go on indefinitely. Since any hierarchy is finite, there must be some limit to the modeling and problem-solving capabilities of an organism, i.e., some prediction errors cannot be suppressed even by the most sophisticated models an organism can produce. Such models are encoded at the top of the goal hierarchy (the knot of a bowtie), which contains some of the most central hub structures of the system. When prediction errors reach the top of a goal hierarchy, these high-level hub structures are continuously triggered by prediction errors (stimuli) that originate from any direction within the network structure. In order to respond to such excessive stimulation, hubs require more metabolic energy than they have access to. When energy demand exceeds energy supply, this causes hub units to congest and shut down: a phenomenon called 'hub overload and failure' [115]. This can be compared to a high-level horse cart driver that is overpowered by the sheer number of horses that need to be restrained. In biophysical terms, hub units reach the limits of their capacity to dissipate energy back into the environment. Studies show that the most connected nodes in a network (hubs) are most sensitive to such overload [116]. This means that high levels of stress cause a selective targeting of hub structures in living systems. Although *small world* network systems are known to be robust to random attacks of nodes and links, they are very sensitive to targeted attacks of hub nodes [117]. Since hub nodes maintain the global connectivity of living network systems, the selective targeting of such units will cause such systems to fall apart in a top-down fashion, as a function of node degree: the loss of only a few high-level hubs will cause information flows to be relayed to hub structures in subordinate parts of the network, which may subsequently get overloaded, etc., until the system is only capable of low-level performance (Figure 7). Cascading failures such as these have been described in power grids, transportation networks, and stock markets [118,119], as well as in biological systems [51,52] and social networks [120,121]. Since the most sophisticated models are produced at the top of a goal hierarchy, the top-down collapse of a regulatory hierarchy forces organisms to move from allostatic (more sophisticated and goal-directed) to homeostatic (less sophisticated and habitual) levels of control. To our knowledge, this is the first mechanistic account of the phenomenon of 'allostatic overload', which can be read as a process theory for shifts in behavioral policies toward 'survival mode' under severe levels of stress (e.g., [18]). It is important to note that this loss of hubs is initially of a functional nature, i.e., they become unresponsive to stimulation, but retain their structural connections, causing a loss of functional but not structural connectivity. When hub overload persists (i.e., when stress is chronic), hubs may become permanently unresponsive, causing a loss of structural connectivity and permanent damage to system integrity [122].

Cascading failures typically involve the occurrence of tipping points [123]. The abruptness of the change seems to be due to the fact that, at some critical point, only a small change (e.g., the overload of a single hub node) may be sufficient to cause a chain reaction that leads to the collapse of a large part of a hierarchy [118,119]. The collapse of goal hierarchies will leave subordinate structures of the network without central guidance, causing the balance between functional integration (order) and segregation (disorder) of states to tip over toward desynchronization and 'disorder' (e.g., the horses will panic and start running wild when the driver falls away) (Figures 2 and 8). This may explain the sudden rise in permutation entropy that is universally observed in the timeseries of severely struggling systems. Hub overload and cascading failure may similarly explain the decrease in number and strength of correlations between system components in terms of the loss of central integrative connections (reins) maintained by hubs. In contrast, variance remains high since lower-level systems are no longer coupled and suppressed by higher-level priors, yet they are continuously excited by incoming prediction error. This overexcitation of subordinate systems is called 'disinhibition' in the psychological sciences [124]. The massive involvement of independently responding and disinhibited microstates is likely to make an important contribution to rising permutation entropy scores (see Section 1) [22].

Since failing systems are characterized by low levels of (auto)correlations and high levels of variance, this means that the amplitude-to-error (signal-to-noise) ratio of the system decreases. In active inference theory, the signal-to-noise ratio is called the 'precision' of the signal (i.e., a quantity that expresses the level of confidence that the information conferred by the signal is correct). Thus, allostatic overload is a process where model complexity costs are reduced at the expense of long-term precision (see [125] for a mathematical description of this tradeoff). This makes sense from an evolutionary perspective, where stressed organisms may become quick to respond but less precise in their actions, as long as this saves energy and resources. An advantage of this mechanism is that organisms will have to spend less time and energy on the integration of large amounts of complex information (i.e., a reduction in model complexity costs). Prediction errors can now pass from input to output areas across skip-connections while avoiding much processing in higher-level throughput areas (goal hierarchies) (Figure 7). This allows organisms to respond more quickly and strongly to certain situations (disinhibition), providing them with just the edge needed to escape from a dire situation. As a disadvantage, however, goal hierarchies may become so shallow and noisy (i.e., unsophisticated and imprecise) that the corresponding behavioral policies will lack hierarchical correspondence with the environment and fail to suppress prediction errors in an effective way. In other words, overly flattened goal hierarchies will produce 'maladaptive' behavior. Such inefficient problem solving will cause the system to require more time to quiet down after initial perturbation, which adds to the phenomenon of (critical) slowing down. In addition to changes in internal message passing (such as circular causal loops between system components that keep re-exciting the system as discussed above), critical slowing down can, therefore, be explained by an insufficient suppression of prediction error through maladaptive action.

In summary, we expect that low-to-moderate levels of stress produce a net shift of the balance between functional segregation and integration of message passing in living systems in favor of functional integration by hub structures, corresponding to a gradual rise in (auto)correlations, variance, and permutation entropy scores. When stress levels increase further, a tipping point is reached at which central coherence by hub structures is suddenly lost, causing a steep rise in permutation entropy scores. These conclusions are in line with experimental data that show how changes in network topology may contribute to the formation of tipping points [10]. Our model seems to explain several generic changes in internal message passing of living systems under rising levels of stress. The next paragraph focuses on changes in the overt behavior of struggling organisms.

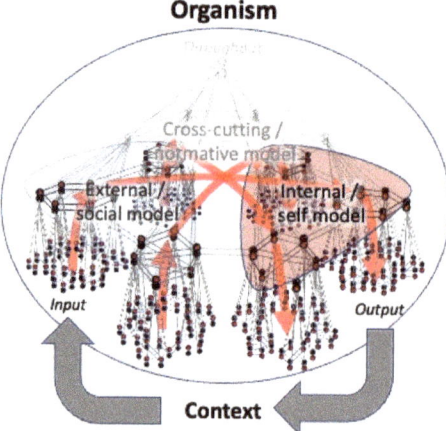

Figure 7. The top-down collapse of a goal hierarchy under severe levels of stress. *The vertical escalation of free energy (model error) in bowtie network structures causes hub structures within the top of the hierarchical pyramid (the knot of the folded bowtie) to overload and fail as a function of node degree (the number of connections per node). Since such hubs maintain global (functional) connectivity within the network structure, their failure causes a top-down collapse or 'flattening' of hierarchical structure (i.e., a loss of nested modularity). Prediction errors (large red arrows) and predictions (not shown) then seek the shortest path from input to output (or vice versa) via horizontal skip connections, effectively 'bypassing' integrative processing at higher (allostatic) areas within the hierarchy, to produce less well-informed (homeostatic) forms of behavior. This is a biophysical model of 'allostatic overload', which is a dominant theory that explains physiological changes and shifts in behavioral policies in organisms under extremely stressful conditions. See text for further details.*

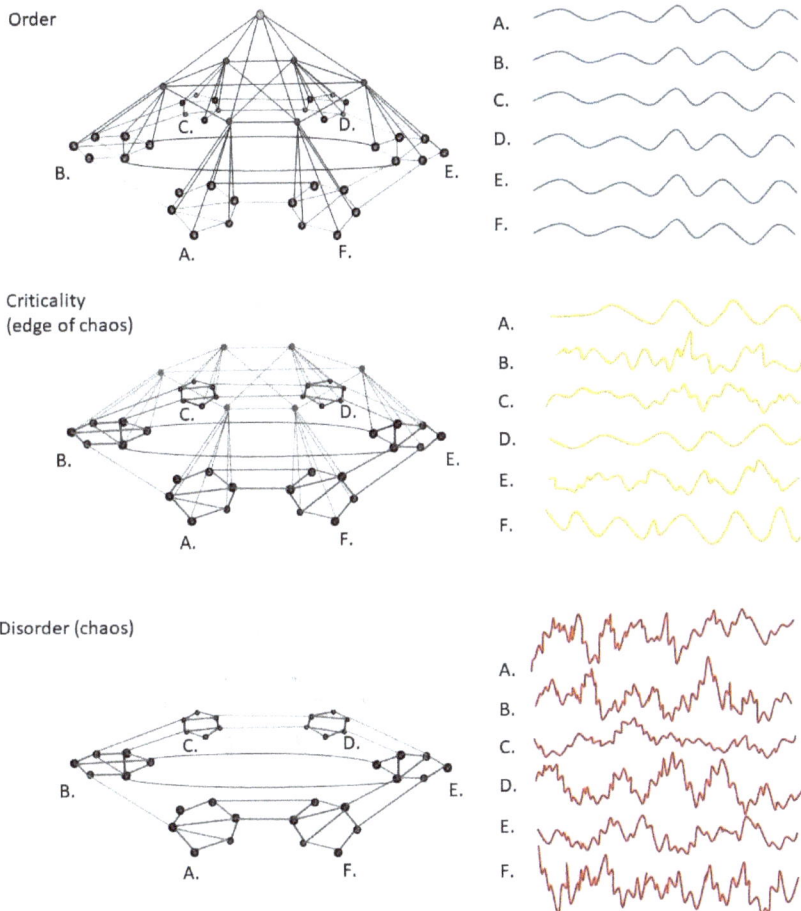

Figure 8. Explaining disorder and tipping points in stressed systems. *The balance between order and disorder of a system is at last partially controlled by the coupling of subsystems by central connectors (hub units). Disorder (including disease) may result from a loss of centralized and integrative coupling that is caused by a top-down collapse of hierarchical control systems, due to hub overload and failure. This causes a loss of coherence and increased variance at lower levels within the hierarchy that translate into increased levels of permutation entropy scores (see text). Organisms self-organize toward a dynamic state in between complete order (i.e., perfect synchrony of timeseries A–F; upper picture) and complete disorder (i.e., perfect randomness of timeseries A–F; lower picture). This equilibrium state is called self-organized criticality (SOC; 'the edge of chaos'; middle picture). A loss of higher (integrative) hierarchical levels of control may shift this equilibrium toward the disordered side of the spectrum. Although stress levels may rise gradually, the loss of high-level central control by a cascading failure of high-level hubs structures is a discrete process, causing discrete transitions from order to disorder. A stress-induced loss of hub structures may, therefore, explain sudden phase transitions that mark the onset of physical or mental dysfunction, disease, or death. See text for further details.*

As observed, the various form of behavior that are produced by an organism reflect the level of sophistication of its internal states. Changes that affect internal message passing of stressed organisms will, therefore, produce behavioral changes that can be observed externally. To explain the shift away from *slow* to *fast* behavioral policies in stressed organisms, we propose that the top-down collapse of goal hierarchies causes organisms to shift from high-level goal-directed (allostatic) to lower-level habitual or even reflexive (homeostatic) forms of behavior (see Section 5). Since high-level goal states are responsible for factoring in all kinds of context factors in both space and time (past, current, and future scenarios of increasing complexity), the collapse of such models will cause organisms to pursue less sophisticated and more short-term goals: a 'decontextualization' of behavior (see Section 6). Since the top of the goal hierarchy encodes world models at the highest levels of sophistication (i.e., contextual integration in both space and time), this may explain why long-term and socially inclusive (normative) goals are often the first to go. Organisms will instead move toward more short-term and socially selective forms of behavior, which may include a shift from transgenerational and reciprocal altruism toward kinship selection ('nepotism') and self-preservation, potentially at the cost of other organisms and kin (e.g., maternal cannibalism in rodents). In the words of Brecht, 'Zuerst kommt das Fressen, dann kommt die Moral' (fodder comes first, then comes morality). The collapse of normative goal states may sharpen the self–other dichotomy, which may manifest as increased ingroup–outgroup behavior (polarization). When stress persists, external (social) and internal (self) models may be next to collapse. When external models disintegrate, individuals will make less sophisticated models of the goals or intentions of others, for which reason behavior will appear to become increasingly asocial in nature. This means that even some forms of antisocial behavior (e.g., deceit) are likely to diminish, since these require some insight into the motives and intentions of others (see below). Behavioral signs of collapsing social goal hierarchies may include lesser amounts of (long term) kinship-promoting activities such as parental or grandparental investment. With the possible exception of (grand)parents that sacrifice themselves for their offspring and admirable individual differences, it can be stated that severe and prolonged stress levels will generally cause organisms to economize on long-term and socially inclusive policies to focus on self-preservation, to the point where even self-preservation is at stake. When internal (self) models disintegrate, this causes fragmented and aimless behavior. Together, such changes may translate into rising levels of permutation entropy in behavioral timeseries, including constituent elements such as decreased (auto)correlations and high levels of variance (see below). When goal hierarchies collapse further, the decoupling between system components may become so severe that the system as a whole disintegrates. The internal state of a system will then linearly follow that of its environment (i.e., a complete loss of homeostasis), which usually corresponds to disease or the death of the system. In short, the overload and cascading failure of central integrative control may explain several of the generic behavioral features of living systems under rising levels of stress.

8. Permutation Entropy as a Universal Disorder Criterion

In the previous section, we showed that living systems can be modeled as hierarchical Bayesian control systems in which central integrative (allostatic) control falls apart in a top-down manner as a result of rising levels of stress, which can be defined as prediction error or variational free energy. Given the multitude of observations that similar behavior can be observed in nonliving systems, one may wonder whether more general laws exist that underlie such changes in living and nonliving systems. In this paper, we argue for the latter position by showing that living systems are a special class of open dissipative systems, for which general rules apply. Open dissipative systems are collections of coupled nodes that receive a constant flux of energy or matter from their surroundings, which they need to get rid of (dissipate) in the most efficient way possible [126]. Experimental studies and in vivo experiments have shown that the most efficient way in which networks can dissipate energy back into their environments is when their nodes organize themselves into nested modular (hierarchical) structures [127] and start to oscillate [116]. Apparently, the short pathlength and nested modular structure of small world networks (e.g., living systems) result from the necessity to dissipate energy back into the environment as efficiently as possible. The same can be said for the emergence of oscillations, e.g., in gene activity, insulin secretion, neuronal firing rates, or social rhythms. The simple necessity for efficient energy dissipation apparently causes the spontaneous emergence of ordered patterns in both structure and function of coupled systems: a phenomenon called 'self-organization' [11,128,129]. As observed in Section 3, the *local* emergence of ordered patterns (e.g., crystals) is allowed as long as this leads to a *global* increase in the entropy of the universe. Similarly, living systems have found a way to temporarily maintain their local form and order, by being able to dissipate energy as efficiently as possible back into the environment (which is to reduce variational free energy). This means that living systems will lose their internal coherence and fall apart when free energy (stress) is not dissipated quickly enough into the environment. We argue that this is essentially what happens in any system that is loaded up with free energy (stress) beyond its capacity to dissipate it back to the environment: the accumulation of such energy will cause a disintegration of system components and system failure (i.e., malfunction and death), causing a rise in permutation entropy scores. This is explained further below.

In lifeless open dissipative systems, the flow of energy through a system is mediated by its components that engage in some form of coupling. For instance, granular media such as water molecules, snowflakes, grains of sand, or pieces of the Earth's crust act as coupled components that distribute chemical or mechanical energy across a network of similar components [49]. As observed, the simple need for optimal energy dissipation causes such systems to self-organize toward a network structure with an optimal level of (nested) modularity [49]. Such structural characteristics are in turn thought to influence the dynamics of such systems, producing a dynamic interplay between the structure and function of the system [130]. Since the various scale levels of a nested modular network system correspond to different levels of segregation and integration of energy flows [127], this means that open dissipative systems automatically arrive at an optimal balance between the integration and segregation of energy flows. Whereas functional integration corresponds to some degree of predictability through synchronization (order), functional segregation corresponds to a state of relative randomness through desynchronization (chaos). Thus, systems of coupled oscillators self-organize toward an equilibrium state in between order and chaos that is called 'self-organized criticality' (SOC) [131]. This *'edge of chaos'* [132,133] is a special place where the level of coupling between system components is such that energy flows are able to propagate through the network with enough freedom to cause 'cascades' of node activity of some size and duration before dying out; too much coupling will cause such cascades to die out quickly (when coupling is inhibitive) or rather produce massive synchronization (when excitatory); both phenomena involve a state of high predictability or 'order'. Too little coupling, on the other hand, will cause a lack of synchronization and 'disorder'. Studies show that the transitional zone between ordered and disordered states of network systems is a discrete one, i.e., such zones are referred to as 'phase transitions' or 'tipping points' ('bifurcations', 'catastrophes', 'percolation points', or 'regime shifts') [123]. Tipping points describe a situation where only a small amount of energy is sufficient to push a system from one global (integrated, ordered) state into another (segregated, disordered) state [123]. Examples of such states in nonliving systems are melting or boiling points, where, e.g., ice represents a highly ordered state with strong connections between water molecules and only a small increase in temperature is sufficient to cause a cascading failure of hydrogen bonds (i.e., melting), allowing all water molecules to move around more freely as water. The exact origins of tipping points are still unknown, but network topology appears to be an important factor [10,130]. In systems of coupled oscillators, the flow of energy may arrange system components in such a way that it will arrive at a point where only a few central nodes are responsible for connecting all of the system's nodes into one giant 'connected component' [11]. The removal of only a few of such nodes due to energy overload may then trigger a cascading failure [119], causing the system to lose global connectivity and move from a state of relative order to a state of relative disorder. Such transitions may occur in any (randomly wired) open dissipative network system, but are especially prevalent in nonrandomly wired ('nonegalitarian') systems where a few key connectors (hubs) are responsible for maintaining global connectivity [134] (Figure 8).

Since living systems in most cases tend to be of the nested modular and nonegalitarian type [135], this may explain why critical phenomena are frequently observed in struggling organisms. We believe that the nonegalitarian nature of living systems has been insufficiently incorporated in today's models of tipping points or critical slowing down, and that doing this may significantly improve those models.

In living systems, information processing takes the form of hierarchical Bayesian inference, which can be equated to free-energy dissipation in nested modular systems (a gradient descent on free energy, see above). The need for efficient energy dissipation (information processing) will cause living systems to automatically tune toward a level of nested modularity and corresponding equilibrium between integration (order) and segregation (chaos) that allows for optimal message passing. This means that the *edge of chaos* is a place where conditions for hierarchical Bayesian inference are optimal: too much coupling (functional integration, order) will interfere with the articulation of hidden causal factors (and, hence, model formation), but so does too little coupling (functional segregation, disorder). Instead, organisms automatically produce world models of optimal hierarchical depth (sophistication, see above). A simple need to get rid of an excess of free energy will cause living systems to automatically tune toward a point where information processing is optimal and (consequently) where the stress adaptation mechanism of organisms can operate most effectively. In other words, the basic laws of thermodynamics appear to cause living systems to automatically produce adaptive behavior in response to environmental fluctuations, to the best of their abilities. Of course, this is only true up to a certain (tipping) point. When the influx of free energy (stress) exceeds the dissipation capacity of the organism, a point will be reached where only a few key connectors are responsible for maintaining global network connectivity. At that point, even a small increase in free-energy levels (stress) will cause such structures to shut down, triggering a cascade that causes to the system to fall apart into disconnected components. This pushes system dynamics over the edge of chaos, toward disorder and system failure (Figure 8). The overflattening of a goal hierarchy therefore produces Bayesian models of suboptimal sophistication that cause the organisms to show maladaptive behavior (i.e., dysfunction or disease; see below).

This concludes our discussion of the emergence of disorder in living systems under conditions of severe stress. We showed that severe stress can be defined as an influx of (free) energy beyond the capacities of open systems to dissipate energy back to the environment. This causes a selective targeting of hub structures that maintain a nested modular hierarchy. The subsequent collapse of hierarchical structure involves a transition from a relatively ordered (synchronized, integrated, adaptive) state to a relatively disordered (desynchronized, segregated, maladaptive) state. The top-down collapse of goal hierarchies in living systems appears to be a special case of cascading failure in open dissipative systems that overload with free energy. Losing control and the sudden emergence of disorder may, therefore, be a universal feature of any open system that disintegrates as a result of a free-energy overload. As a result, permutation entropy (or any other suitable measure of disorder for that matter) may serve as a universal disorder criterion.

9. Disorder as a Universal Measure of Disease

In living systems, the term 'disorder' is often used as a way to describe dysfunction or disease of such systems. Whereas the Anglo-Saxon scientific literature often speaks of 'disorder', Dutch and German literature tends to use words such as 'disturbance' or 'dysregulation' when referring to dysfunction or disease. Such use of words speaks to a general intuition that disease and other forms of maladaptive behavior somehow involve a problem of control and a loss of 'order'. In the previous section, we showed that the emergence of disorder may be a generic feature of open dissipative systems that overload with free energy and reflect a loss of central integrative governance [27,36]. The ubiquitous presence of rising disorder levels, tipping points, and other critical phenomena in living systems under difficult conditions suggests that many forms of malfunction and disease involve a generic mechanism (see Section 1). We therefore propose that any physical, mental, or social disorder eventually involves a loss of integrative control due to an excess of free energy (stress, prediction error). The ensuing overflattening of goal hierarchies then causes suboptimal inference and maladaptive behavior (see above). The cascading failure of hub structures is a key element in our theory and is increasingly being recognized as an important factor in the emergence of physical and mental disorders. Examples involve a cascading failure of hub genes in metabolic disease [136] and cancers [137], hub cells in diabetes mellitus [116], and hub brain regions in neurological disease [115] and mental disorders [138]. Studies have shown that similar processes govern the collapse of social hierarchies and the emergence of social disorder in animal and human societies (see below). Nevertheless, this theory remains to be tested by systematically examining (permutation) entropy scores and other hallmarks of critical slowing down as a function of the hierarchical depth of goal hierarchies in a diverse range of living systems under severe levels of stress. Due to the ethical difficulties of such studies, a valuable approach is to test these assumptions in silico, by systematically examining changes in signal transduction and overt behavior of hierarchical Bayesian control systems, e.g., using hierarchical machine learning techniques. In our recent paper, we made several recommendations for such studies [21].

Although disordered states tend to be undesirable in organisms, this does not mean that order is always good and disorder is always bad. As stated above, signal transduction in organisms is normally poised on the edge between order and disorder, reflecting optimal information processing. Some level of chaos (disorder) is, therefore, required for organisms to respond in a lively and creative fashion to environmental challenges [133]. Overly ordered states may on the other hand produce malfunction, e.g., when overly controlling hierarchies exert too much influence over hierarchical message passing at lower hierarchical systems and cause inflexible states of low adaptability. Eventually, however, any problem in the balance between order and disorder is likely to produce high levels of prediction error that cause organisms to 'lose control' and system dynamics to tilt heavily toward 'disorder'.

Since prediction error (stress) can be defined as the difference between a prediction and an actual perception, it is fundamentally a relative measure. This means that the cause of stress may lie either with the individual, since it expresses some rare or extreme setpoints (encoding rare or extreme niches that are difficult to occupy), or with the environment, which may itself be so rare or extreme that that it does not fit otherwise frequently expressed setpoints. In both cases, stress may increase to such levels as to cause goal hierarchies to collapse and disorder to emerge. For example, thermophilic or acidophilic bacteria may thrive in hot-water springs or extremely acid conditions, but fail to thrive under more common conditions that would otherwise be considered favorable for most organisms. Conversely, most organisms that encode quite common environmental niches as world models will express high levels of prediction error in response to evolutionary 'unfamiliar' stressors such as toxins or ultrahigh temperatures. This shows that the concepts of stress and disorder that we propose are fundamentally relative: one set of priors (thermostats, goals, world models) may cause an individual to have a nice fit with its current environment and remain stable, whereas the same set of priors may produce stress and disorder in some other niche. The relativity of stress and disorder, however, does not detract from the objectivity with which their presence can be established.

Since a loss of integrative control may explain the emergence of disorder across scale levels, we will now examine how it applies to the specifically human perspective, by discussing how stress may produce disorder at intraindividual, interpersonal, and population levels. These scale levels are the main focus of psychiatry as a medical discipline, with its traditional focus on biological, psychological, and social determinants of mental illness [139]. This represents a novel approach, and the examples that are given can be read as avenues for further research.

10. The Human Perspective: Disorder at the Individual Level

Just like woodlice, humans can be modeled as hierarchical Bayesian control systems with goal hierarchies that encode the econiches they wish to explore. The major difference is that human world models are more sophisticated, which allows them to encode complex econiches at high levels of parsimony and abstraction (see above). Since humans are a highly social species, their goal hierarchies often encode social goals (e.g., partners, jobs, and social positions), and stress often involves social stress (e.g., not finding a suitable partner or job, or not reaching some social position in time). Where people fail in the pursuit of such goals, stress and disorder may emerge.

Within the field of psychiatry, is has been known for some time that there are at least two distinct types of mental disorders. One involves episodic disorders, which represent a temporary decline in mental abilities with respect to a previously attained level of functioning (e.g., panic attacks, major depression, or psychotic episodes). Such disorders typically emerge and resolve at relatively discrete moments (e.g., within hours or days), indicating the presence of tipping points [4,5]. Another type of psychiatric problems involves trait disorders, in which patients exhibit a series of stable mental traits that together increase the risk of episodic disorders across longer timeframes (e.g., avoidant, dependent, or borderline personality profiles). With respect to acute or episodic disorders, is has been proposed that such disorders represent various forms of 'false inference', i.e., a suboptimal balance between top-down predictions and bottom-up belief updating by prediction errors [140]. Interestingly, this overall balance between predictions and prediction errors is controlled by the 'precision' of such signals, i.e., their signal-to-noise ratio, which expresses the overall level of 'confidence' that the information conveyed by the signal is correct (see above). On the one hand, such problems of inference may involve the emergence of 'hyperprecise priors', which are models that are overly dominant in suppressing prediction errors and leave little room for alternative explanations of the observed events (this could explain the occurrence of e.g., hallucinations, delusions, phobias, and other anxiety disorders). On the other hand, prediction errors may become overly precise, signaling high confidence that some signal carries consistent uncertainty and leaving little room for systems to converge upon a suitable explanation of observed events (this may explain, e.g., feelings of dissatisfaction, emptiness, pathological doubt, and obsessive–compulsive behavior) [140]. Note that the same mental problems can be explained by presuming *hypo*precise priors and hyperprecise prediction errors: all such variants are likely to exist in the form of (epi)genetic variations in neurotransmission and cytoarchitecture, which may explain different subtypes of mental disorders [141]. As observed, high levels of stress cause a net decrease in precision levels in living systems, which may modulate the precision balance and cause suboptimal inference. In the human brain, the precision of signals is controlled by neuromodulatory neurotransmitters such as serotonin, noradrenaline, dopamine, and acetylcholine [140]. Most neurotropic drugs that are used in psychiatry modulate the release of such neurotransmitters, which may be beneficial in correcting the precision balance and reducing symptoms [142].

A problem of the precision balance provides a likely explanation for various forms of psychopathology, but does not in itself explain the episodic versus chronic nature of such phenomena [21]. We, therefore, propose that episodic disorders result from a (temporary) collapse of goal hierarchies in response to stress, whereas trait disorders result from a failure of such hierarchies to develop normally. In episodic disorders, a cascading failure of a goal hierarchy may reduce integrative control until the system passes the edge of chaos, producing tipping points and disorder. This can be compared to a cascading failure of a multilevel thermostat which then gives off the wrong values, causing problems with heating the house (producing maladaptive behavior). In trait disorders, on the other hand, people may inherit or acquire a set of priors (thermostat settings) that encode a predilection for certain (social) econiches. When such prior settings do not match the actual state of the environment, prediction error (stress) and disorder may emerge. For example, people may differ with respect to their desire to explore new surroundings or to avoid negative outcomes. When the environment matches such predilections (e.g., the adrenaline seeker at the edge of the Grand Canyon, or the couch potato in front of the TV), prediction error and 'stress' are minimal, and disorder is some distance away. When the opposite is true (i.e., the adrenaline seeker sitting on a couch and the couch potato living on the edge), fitness is poor, and disorder may emerge. People with extreme prior settings ('temperaments') can in this respect be compared to extremophile bacteria that thrive in extreme environments but not in others or to central heating systems with high thermostat values. Such systems perform well in hot climates but overheat and break down in colder climates, since they are unable to reach some extremely high goal temperature. The more rare or extreme such prior settings are, the more difficult it will be for an individual to find econiches that are equally rare or extreme. Niche exploration may, therefore, take a long time and, consequently, chronic prediction error will occur (i.e., chronic stress). This increases the chances of collapsing goal hierarchies and episodic disorders.

Fortunately, people do not simply inherit a fixed set of priors which they have to deal with throughout the rest of their lives. The innate set of priors is tuned by a continuous process of belief updating, which allows them to meet environmental conditions halfway. Moreover, people may gain additional (allostatic) levels of control over their innate priors through the vertical outgrowth of their goal hierarchies. This involves the addition of hierarchical layers to a hierarchical control system over the course of individual development [143]. Belief updating within these successive hierarchical layers globally corresponds to Pavlovian, habit- and goal-directed learning [20]. Thus, people 'grow' a set of world models that encode increasingly sophisticated (social) econiches, which globally involve internal (self), external (social), and crosscutting (normative) models. Together, such high-level models may be referred to as 'character', and the combination of temperament and character maturation is called 'personality development' [144,145]. Character development may allow people to find a suitable (social) niche after all, even when their innate set of priors (temperament) is rare or otherwise extreme. When character development fails for any particular reason, this results in less sophisticated world models that will cause people to seek out suboptimal (social) econiches (i.e., show maladaptive behavior). Such shallow world models are more likely to collapse during stress and reach a hierarchical depth below which the system tips toward an undercontrolled state of disorder. This would be a testable model of the emergence of episodic disorders or 'crises' in patients with traits disorders such as ADHD, autism spectrum, or personality disorders.

The specific phenomenology that ensues in various mental disorders can be further explained by observing the general architecture of hierarchical Bayesian control systems (Figures 5 and 6). Depending on the location and depth of the collapse of such structures under stress, different symptoms may be produced [21,140,146]. Since stress preferentially affects the integrative top of a goal hierarchy, a top-down collapse from goal-directed to habitual, instinctual, or even reflexive behavior may generally be observed in episodic disorders (Section 6). This may explain why a decline in self-functioning, interpersonal functioning, and/or normative functioning (a collapse of high-level goal-directed functions) is a common hallmark in different forms of mental illness, whether involving episodic or trait disorders (Figure 7, Section 7) [147,148]. Since the functional integration of specialized brain regions is important for maintaining a sense of awareness and proper cognition [149,150], the functional segregation produced by collapsing hierarchies may explain a loss of awareness with respect to self-referential, social, or transpersonal goals. When internal (self)models become less sophisticated or precise, people report difficulties experiencing a coherent sense of self. Depending on the depth of such a deficit, this may involve symptoms that vary from a lack of agency or autonomy to a sense of depersonalization, disintegration, or dissociative disorder [151–153]. When external (social) models are involved, people may become unaware of the needs and intentions of others (have difficulty mentalizing). This may cause frequent misunderstandings, inspire paranoid interpretations of events, or prevent individuals from experiencing a sense of communion (i.e., showing interest in others, caring for and trusting other people). When crosscutting (normative) models are involved, people may show a reduced ability to feel connected across larger individual differences and timeframes (generations) or have the experience that life lacks inherent meaning: a state that is called 'demoralization'. Demoralization appears to be present in nearly all forms of mental illness and is arguably the most important reason for people to seek treatment [154]. This could be explained by the fact that stress causes the highest regions of a goal hierarchy to collapse first, which we propose harbors a crosscutting (normative) hierarchy that is responsible for generating our 'highest goals'. A collapse of such high-level structures may then produce problems further down the hierarchy. For instance, a failure or disinhibition of input (perceptive) hierarchies may produce hallucinations and other perceptual distortions, and a disinhibition of affective hierarchies may produce anxiety or mood disorders, whereas, when output (action control) hierarchies are involved, this may produce problems with executive functions (e.g., a loss of praxis and disorders of motor or endocrine planning).

To summarize, a hierarchical taxonomy of psychiatric disorders can be drafted that can be linked to suboptimal inference at different scale levels and locations within a hierarchical Bayesian control system. This idea relates strongly to one of the leading alternatives to the traditional (categorical) taxonomy of psychopathology as formulated in the Diagnostic and Statistical Manual for Mental Disorders (DSM-5): the hierarchical taxonomy of psychopathology (HiToP) [155]. The firm rooting of active inference in neuroscience and biology holds promise for integrating another alternative classification system (RDoc) into clinical practice, which puts more emphasis on the neurobiological underpinnings of psychiatric disorders [156]. According to DSM-5, a set of mental states and traits qualifies as a disorder if a certain set of mental states interferes 'in a significant way' with everyday personal functioning (e.g., maintaining relationships, managing a job, or performing activities of daily living). This introduces a degree of subjectivity to the definition of 'disorder' that is quite valuable, since objective measures may ignore aspects of subjective experience that may be crucial for determining the level of personal suffering. On the other hand, such subjectivity makes it difficult to quantify and compare mental states. We, therefore, propose to use permutation entropy as an objective disorder criterion, which can be used to link 'disorder' at different levels of biological organization to subjective experience and personal suffering. This may include the calculation of permutation entropy scores at level genetic, neurophysiological, psychometric, social, or demographic scales in order to quantify disorder at various levels (see Section 1).

At this point, it is important to note that disorder cannot always be measured within the individual itself, but rather within the environment that surrounds the individual: so-called 'internalizing individuals' have a tendency to model the hidden cause of experienced prediction errors within themselves and to engage in self-corrective activity in order to solve such errors (e.g., through a revision of their assumptions or by acting in response to the presumed internal deficit) [157]. In such a case, any stress or disorder is more likely to accumulate within the individual itself and take the form of a psychiatric disorder. In contrast, externalizing people tend to project the hidden cause of experienced errors outside of themselves and to reduce prediction errors by performing actions that are aimed at correcting the presumed external problem (with relatively little belief updating of their self-models). In that case, stress and disorder are more likely to accumulate in the environment rather than in the individual itself [157]. Our model, therefore, shows that people may still 'have a problem' even if they themselves do not show any signs of stress or disorder, since they induce a lot of disorder in their environments. This departs from the current disorder criterion as formulated in the DSM-5, which states that, in order to qualify as a disorder, a mental phenotype must occur "within an individual" and cause "clinically significant distress or disability" [158]. A more relative definition of mental disorder would, therefore, include 'stable people' that always sleep well but meanwhile produce unsophisticated models and corresponding actions that leave their environments in a state of complete uproar. This example illustrates the fact that the maladaptive behavior of one individual may pass on to other individuals, corresponding to a scale transition. This is discussed in the next section.

11. The Human Perspective: Disorder at the Interpersonal Level

Recent studies have shown that the free-energy principle can be used to model information transfer in social networks of animals and humans (i.e., communication patterns) [159,160]. A model has been proposed in which one individual monitors the behavioral output of another in order to infer the hidden common causes behind the observed behavior (i.e., its meaning or intentions). In order to read their mutual intentions, organisms must synchronize their responses, which in this view defines a social tie. Predicting the intentions behind another person's behavior becomes increasingly difficult when the observed behavior becomes increasingly unpredictable. This may happen when a subject's world model flattens to the point where the corresponding behavior of the individual loses its hierarchical correspondence with the actual state of the world. Such 'maladaptive behavior' is marked by high levels of permutation entropy (disinformation, low levels of predictability, see Section 1). This can be the case, e.g., in psychiatric patients with affective or psychotic disorders, in which the connection between the outside world and observed behavior does not seem to make sense (i.e., is unpredictable). When the behavioral output of some individual is sufficiently unpredictable (maladaptive), this may raise prediction error (stress) levels in another individual to the point where it causes the goal hierarchy of this new individual to collapse and the individual to show unpredictable (maladaptive) behavior of his own. Such 'disorder' may consequently be conveyed upon yet other individuals or feed back to the first individual to form a closed loop. Thus, disorder (disinformation) may spread through social networks (Figure 9). In an extreme example, individual 1 may be highly annoyed by the loud music produced by individual 2 (their stressed-out neighbor). This raises stress levels to the point where it causes a collapse of hierarchical control in individual 1, who is subsequently unable to factor in the needs of individual 2 (e.g., pay them a visit when they need help). Based on their decontextualized models, individual 1 then decides to make some noise of their own, keeping individual 2 (and perhaps some others) awake and removing any residual levels of control that individual 2 might have. Individual 2 then gets back at individual 1, etc. Thus, people may hold each other captive in complex webs of underregulated reflex arcs that are self-sustaining and difficult to extinguish, since they are insufficiently suppressed by more sophisticated (contextualized and socially inclusive) world models (Figure 9A). This can be compared to a neurological clonus, which is a disinhibited reflex that sustains itself by means of its own motor response, which serves as a trigger for a novel response. Such pathological reflexes are caused by the disappearance of higher-order regulatory functions (e.g., by a tumor or an infarction) that normally suppress the primary reflex arc. Similarly, the 'social clonus' may cause strong loops in social relationships (such as intense interpersonal conflict or symbiotic relationships) due to a lack of top-down regulatory constraint. Indeed, several studies have shown that emotional states such as (un)happiness and loneliness or mental illness such as major depression may spread through social networks in ways that are analogous to infectious disease, although a general mechanism for such 'social contagion' seems to be lacking [161]. The free-energy principle may explain such effects in terms of the spread of (dis)information through social networks in the context of insufficient hierarchical control.

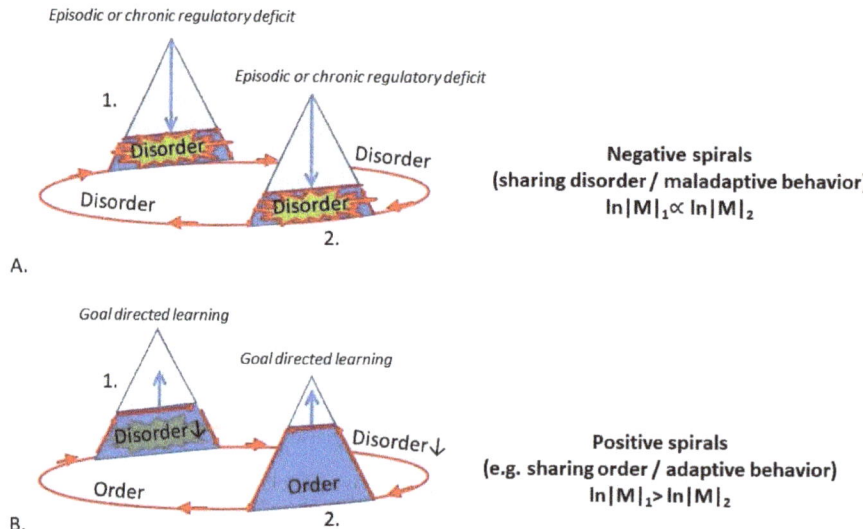

Figure 9. The spread of disorder through social networks as a function of hierarchical control. *Disorder may spread through social networks as a function of the amount of hierarchical control. Two special cases of mutually reinforcing social interactions are shown.* (**Panel A**) *The social clonus. This is a self-propagating (circularly causal) action–perception cycle between people (or communities of people) that is caused by a loss (or lack) of central integrative processing, e.g., during episodic disorders or in personality disorders. The unpredictable responses (maladaptive behavior) produced by individual/population 1 serve as input to individual/population 2 that similarly lacks the ability to view such behavior in a broader context. This results in a maladaptive response that feeds back to individual 1, which raises stress and disorder levels within individual 1, and the cycle repeats. Social clonuses may generalize to larger social communities via collateral connections, producing disorder at a population level. Ln|M| = whole system permutation entropy.* (**Panel B**) *Improving hierarchical control (e.g., by recovering from an episodic disorder or promoting the outgrowth of sophisticated goal hierarchies (personality development)) puts an intrinsic break on the spread of maladaptive behavior (disorder) though social networks. See text for details.*

The above is an extreme example of how a collapse of goal hierarchies may cause disorder or disinformation to spread through social networks (either in tight social loops or in wider social communities). A more delicate transmission of disinformation may take place in less extreme situations, e.g., when goal hierarchies are only mildly underdeveloped, as in personality disorders or intellectual deficits. Such 'shallow' world models may produce subtle forms of maladaptive behavior, which may only slightly raise disorder (disinformation) levels in other individuals, causing social networks to become slightly noisier. In short, the transmission of disorder (unpredictability) through social networks, as well as the emergence of vicious cycles between people, is a function of the hierarchical depth of all goal hierarchies that lie along the traveled path. A natural resistance to such spread would, therefore, be to encourage individuals to develop mature and contextually rich goal hierarchies (i.e., by recovering from acute mental illness, or through education or psychotherapy; Figure 9B). The fact that people form social ties that are based on the predictability of their responses highlights the importance of a shared normative set in the form of an overarching predictive model, which promotes social connectivity across large individual differences by emphasizing communalities between people [106,107,159]. Without such high-level constraint, self-propagating patterns of disorder may eventually generalize to population levels, where large groups of individuals enter into a collective state of disorder (e.g., lingering conflicts or war). This is discussed in the next section.

12. The Human Perspective: Disorder at a Population Level

By now, many studies have shown that the 'scale-free' principles of network architecture and function that govern living systems at different scale levels of organization also apply to social networks. Scientists have long been fascinated by the *small world* structure of social networks that allow any two persons on this earth to be connected through an average of only six degrees of separation [162]. Just like living systems at smaller spatial scales, social communities are held together by a limited number of hub individuals such as kings and queens, presidents, CEOs, pop idols, influencers, news readers, professors, schoolteachers, and social workers. Large social networks consistently show a nested modular (hierarchical) information bottleneck structure, just like network systems at a molecular and cellular levels [163,164]. This suggests that some parts of social networks are dedicated to input (perception), throughput (goal setting), and output (action) of whatever messages are passed between individuals. Social networks also display dynamic phenomena that resemble features of hierarchical message passing in living systems, such as oscillations, bursts, and tipping points that define the spread of infections, mass psychosis, mass hysteria, or riots [161,165–167]. Such processes are increasingly studied from a biophysical perspective, sparking the existence of a new field called computational sociology [168–170]. The many parallels that exist between signal transduction within single organisms and information transfer within social networks have led scholars to reserve the term 'superorganism' for some of these collectives (such as ant and termite colonies, beehives, and communities of blind mole rats). Although humans generally show a larger level of individual autonomy than the individual agents of a superorganism, it has been argued that human collectives can flexibly behave as superorganisms under certain conditions (e.g., [171]).

Despite such findings, however, the question remains whether the analogy with multicellular organisms ends here, or whether social systems are indeed involved in some form of active hierarchical Bayesian inference. In order to answer such questions, future studies may want to examine whether a division of labor exists between individuals that act primarily as priors (e.g., issuing hypotheses) and those that act as prediction error units (issuing deviations from these hypotheses). For instance, scientists or defense lawyers may be engaged in circularly causal dynamics of hypothesis generation and falsification. When compared to other living systems, however, human individuals are more likely able to flexibly shift their social roles as priors or prediction error units depending on the topic discussed. At a larger spatial scale level, the bowtie structure of social networks suggests a global division of labor across collective perception, goal setting, and action control. It may, therefore, be worthwhile to study the distribution of social roles and professions across these global domains of the social network. For instance, global perception may be shaped by journalists, scientists, and other influencers that feed the collective with novel information and facts (input). Collective goal setting may involve a legislative power that processes such information at a more abstract level to draft new laws (i.e., a hierarchy of priors). These are then criticized and updated by a house of representatives (i.e., a hierarchy of prediction errors), after which a judiciary power applies these updated laws to issue out policies (action control). The executive branch (output) then enforces these laws onto the environment (e.g., soldiers and police). In this model, the departments of internal and external affairs are involved in generating self-models and social models at the level of nation states, whereas crosscutting (or normative) models may be formed by some philosophical or religious institute of power.

Studies show that social networks may display cascading failures of social hierarchies in response to high levels of interpersonal traffic (e.g., a collapse of the social chain of command) [120,121,165]. In stressful situations, a mild flatting of a social hierarchy may be an adaptive response of social systems in times of crisis. This may speed up response times of collective decision making by bypassing elaborate processing at the top of social hierarchies (e.g., throughout history, a 'strong man' was appointed in times of crisis to force certain decisions through parliament). However, an overflattening of a social hierarchy may produce a state of disinhibited disorder within its lower ranks [120,121,165]. At a higher-scale level of social organization, a collapse of integrative government may cause the functional segregation of social communities and individuals, leading to increased polarization and interpersonal conflict [172]. This corresponds to a state of suboptimal inference of collective goal states and the production of maladaptive behavior at group level. As anywhere else in living nature, such changes should translate into rising levels of permutation entropy in hierarchical message passing (e.g., Twitter messages or other social media). We, therefore, argue that 'losing control' is basically the same process anywhere, whether involving bacteria succumbing to antibiotics, people developing physical or mental disorders, or social systems slipping into civil war. Permutation entropy may be a universal way to quantify disorder in timeseries at each of these scale levels of biological organization and to take the necessary precautions.

13. Conclusions

We reviewed the concept of permutation entropy as a universal disorder criterion. The allostatic overload and cascading failure of living systems and the emergence of disorder in response to stress appears to be a special case of the functional or structural disintegration of open dissipative systems as a universal response to a free energy overload. When confirmed in experimental studies, physical, mental, and social disorders can be described, predicted, and understood using the same mathematical language. This unifying principle may help to promote collaboration amongst a diverse range of disciplines and urge scientists to push forward a common research agenda that may speed up discoveries in all relevant fields.

Author Contributions: Conceptualization, R.G. and R.d.K.; writing—original draft preparation, R.G.; writing—review and editing, R.d.K. All authors have read and agreed to the published version of the manuscript.

Funding: This research received no external funding.

Institutional Review Board Statement: Not applicable.

Acknowledgments: We thank the reviewers for their constructive comments.

Conflicts of Interest: The authors declare no conflict of interest.

References

1. Gorban, A.; Tyukina, T.; Pokidysheva, L.; Smirnova, E. Dynamic and thermodynamic models of adaptation. *Phys. Life Rev.* **2021**, *37*, 17–64. [CrossRef] [PubMed]
2. Gorban, A.N.; Smirnova, E.V.; Tyukina, T.A. Correlations, risk and crisis: From physiology to finance. *Phys. A Stat. Mech. Appl.* **2010**, *389*, 3193–3217. [CrossRef]
3. van de Leemput, I.A.; Wichers, M.; Cramer, A.O.; Borsboom, D.; Tuerlinckx, F.; Kuppens, P.; van Nes, E.H.; Viechtbauer, W.; Giltay, E.J.; Aggen, S.H.; et al. Critical slowing down as early warning for the onset and termination of depression. *Proc. Natl. Acad. Sci. USA* **2014**, *111*, 87–92. [CrossRef]
4. Wichers, M.; Schreuder, M.J.; Goekoop, R.; Groen, R.N. Can we predict the direction of sudden shifts in symptoms? Transdiagnostic implications from a complex systems perspective on psychopathology. *Psychol. Med.* **2019**, *49*, 380–387. [CrossRef]
5. Schreuder, M.J.; Hartman, C.A.; George, S.V.; Menne-Lothmann, C.; Decoster, J.; van Winkel, R.; Delespaul, P.; De Hert, M.; Derom, C.; Thiery, E. Early warning signals in psychopathology: What do they tell? *BMC Med.* **2020**, *18*, 269. [CrossRef]
6. Strogatz, S.H. *Nonlinear Dynamics and Chaos with Student Solutions Manual: With Applications to Physics, Biology, Chemistry, and Engineering*; CRC Press: Boca Raton, FL, USA, 2018.
7. Van Nes, E.H.; Scheffer, M. Slow recovery from perturbations as a generic indicator of a nearby catastrophic shift. *Am. Nat.* **2007**, *169*, 738–747. [CrossRef]
8. Veraart, A.J.; Faassen, E.J.; Dakos, V.; van Nes, E.H.; Lürling, M.; Scheffer, M. Recovery rates reflect distance to a tipping point in a living system. *Nature* **2012**, *481*, 357–359. [CrossRef]
9. Dai, L.; Vorselen, D.; Korolev, K.S.; Gore, J. Generic indicators for loss of resilience before a tipping point leading to population collapse. *Science* **2012**, *336*, 1175–1177. [CrossRef] [PubMed]
10. Peng, X.; Small, M.; Zhao, Y.; Moore, J.M. Detecting and predicting tipping points. *Int. J. Bifurc. Chaos* **2019**, *29*, 1930022. [CrossRef]
11. Kauffman, S. *At Home in the Universe: The Search for the Laws of Self-Organization and Complexity*; Oxford University Press: Oxford, UK, 1996.

12. Scheffer, M. *Critical Transitions in Nature and Society*; Princeton University Press: Princeton, NJ, USA, 2020.
13. Dakos, V.; Carpenter, S.R.; van Nes, E.H.; Scheffer, M. Resilience indicators: Prospects and limitations for early warnings of regime shifts. *Philos. Trans. R. Soc. B Biol. Sci.* **2015**, *370*, 20130263. [CrossRef]
14. Del Giudice, M. Rethinking the fast-slow continuum of individual differences. *Evol. Hum. Behav.* **2020**, *41*, 536–549. [CrossRef]
15. Schwabe, L.; Wolf, O.T.; Oitzl, M.S. Memory formation under stress: Quantity and quality. *Neurosci. Biobehav. Rev.* **2010**, *34*, 584–591. [CrossRef] [PubMed]
16. Schwabe, L.; Wolf, O.T. Stress-induced modulation of instrumental behavior: From goal-directed to habitual control of action. *Behav. Brain Res.* **2011**, *219*, 321–328. [CrossRef] [PubMed]
17. Wingfield, J.C. Control of behavioural strategies for capricious environments. *Anim. Behav.* **2006**, *66*, 807–816. [CrossRef]
18. McEwen, B.S.; Wingfield, J.C. The concept of allostasis in biology and biomedicine. *Horm. Behav.* **2003**, *43*, 2–15. [CrossRef]
19. Seth, A.K. Causal connectivity of evolved neural networks during behavior. *Netw. Comput. Neural Syst.* **2005**, *16*, 35–54. [CrossRef]
20. Pezzulo, G.; Rigoli, F.; Friston, K. Active Inference, homeostatic regulation and adaptive behavioural control. *Prog. Neurobiol.* **2015**, *134*, 17–35. [CrossRef]
21. Goekoop, R.; de Kleijn, R. How higher goals are constructed and collapse under stress: A hierarchical Bayesian control systems perspective. *Neurosci. Biobehav. Rev.* **2021**, *123*, 257–285. [CrossRef]
22. Zhu, Z.; Surujon, D.; Ortiz-Marquez, J.C.; Huo, W.; Isberg, R.R.; Bento, J.; van Opijnen, T. Entropy of a bacterial stress response is a generalizable predictor for fitness and antibiotic sensitivity. *Nat. Commun.* **2020**, *11*, 4365. [CrossRef]
23. Bandt, C.; Pompe, B. Permutation entropy: A natural complexity measure for time series. *Phys. Rev. Lett.* **2002**, *88*, 174102. [CrossRef]
24. Lazo, A.V.; Rathie, P. On the entropy of continuous probability distributions (corresp.). *IEEE Trans. Inf. Theory* **1978**, *24*, 120–122. [CrossRef]
25. Li, Y.; Geng, B.; Jiao, S. Refined Composite Multi-Scale Reverse Weighted Permutation Entropy and Its Applications in Ship-Radiated Noise. *Entropy* **2021**, *23*, 476. [CrossRef]
26. Zanin, M.; Zunino, L.; Rosso, O.A.; Papo, D. Permutation entropy and its main biomedical and econophysics applications: A review. *Entropy* **2012**, *14*, 1553–1577. [CrossRef]
27. Drake, J.M.; Griffen, B.D. Early warning signals of extinction in deteriorating environments. *Nature* **2010**, *467*, 456–459. [CrossRef] [PubMed]
28. Eom, H.-J.; Liu, Y.; Kwak, G.-S.; Heo, M.; Song, K.S.; Chung, Y.D.; Chon, T.-S.; Choi, J. Inhalation toxicity of indoor air pollutants in Drosophila melanogaster using integrated transcriptomics and computational behavior analyses. *Sci. Rep.* **2017**, *7*, 46473. [CrossRef] [PubMed]
29. Asher, L.; Collins, L.M.; Ortiz-Pelaez, A.; Drewe, J.A.; Nicol, C.J.; Pfeiffer, D.U. Recent advances in the analysis of behavioural organization and interpretation as indicators of animal welfare. *J. R. Soc. Interface* **2009**, *6*, 1103–1119. [CrossRef]
30. Bae, M.-J.; Park, Y.-S. Biological early warning system based on the responses of aquatic organisms to disturbances: A review. *Sci. Total. Environ.* **2014**, *466*, 635–649. [CrossRef] [PubMed]
31. Eguiraun, H.; López-de-Ipiña, K.; Martinez, I. Application of entropy and fractal dimension analyses to the pattern recognition of contaminated fish responses in aquaculture. *Entropy* **2014**, *16*, 6133–6151. [CrossRef]
32. Qumar, A.; Aziz, W.; Saeed, S.; Ahmed, I.; Hussain, L. Comparative study of multiscale entropy analysis and symbolic time series analysis when applied to human gait dynamics. In Proceedings of the 2013 International Conference on Open Source Systems and Technologies, Lahore, Pakistan, 16–18 December 2013; pp. 126–132.
33. Maria, G.; Escós, J.; Alados, C.L. Complexity of behavioural sequences and their relation to stress conditions in chickens (Gallus gallus domesticus): A non-invasive technique to evaluate animal welfare. *Appl. Anim. Behav. Sci.* **2004**, *86*, 93–104. [CrossRef]
34. Shashikumar, S.P.; Li, Q.; Clifford, G.D.; Nemati, S. Multiscale network representation of physiological time series for early prediction of sepsis. *Physiol. Meas.* **2017**, *38*, 2235. [CrossRef] [PubMed]
35. Scarpino, S.V.; Petri, G. On the predictability of infectious disease outbreaks. *Nat. Commun.* **2019**, *10*, 898. [CrossRef]
36. Scheffer, M.; Bascompte, J.; Brock, W.A.; Brovkin, V.; Carpenter, S.R.; Dakos, V.; Held, H.; Van Nes, E.H.; Rietkerk, M.; Sugihara, G. Early-warning signals for critical transitions. *Nature* **2009**, *461*, 53–59. [CrossRef]
37. Friston, K. A free energy principle for biological systems. *Entropy* **2012**, *14*, 2100–2121.
38. Friston, K.; Kilner, J.; Harrison, L. A free energy principle for the brain. *J. Physiol.-Paris* **2006**, *100*, 70–87. [CrossRef] [PubMed]
39. Fortier, M.; Friedman, D.A. Of Woodlice and Men. 2018. Available online: https://www.aliusresearch.org/uploads/9/1/6/0/91600416/alius_bulletin_n%C2%B02__2018_.pdf#page=27 (accessed on 4 July 2021).
40. Ha, D.; Schmidhuber, J. World models. *arXiv* **2018**, arXiv:1803.10122.
41. Friston, K. Does predictive coding have a future? *Nat. Neurosci.* **2018**, *21*, 1019–1021. [CrossRef] [PubMed]
42. Friston, K. The free-energy principle: A unified brain theory? *Nat. Rev. Neurosci.* **2010**, *11*, 127–138. [CrossRef] [PubMed]
43. Friston, K.; FitzGerald, T.; Rigoli, F.; Schwartenbeck, P.; Pezzulo, G. Active inference and learning. *Neurosci. Biobehav. Rev.* **2016**, *68*, 862–879. [CrossRef] [PubMed]
44. Friston, K.; FitzGerald, T.; Rigoli, F.; Schwartenbeck, P.; Pezzulo, G. Active inference: A process theory. *Neural Comput.* **2017**, *29*, 1–49. [CrossRef]
45. Bruineberg, J.; Kiverstein, J.; Rietveld, E. The anticipating brain is not a scientist: The free-energy principle from an ecological-enactive perspective. *Synthese* **2018**, *195*, 2417–2444. [CrossRef]

46. Bruineberg, J.; Rietveld, E.; Parr, T.; van Maanen, L.; Friston, K.J. Free-energy minimization in joint agent-environment systems: A niche construction perspective. *J. Theor. Biol.* **2018**, *455*, 161–178. [CrossRef]
47. Constant, A.; Ramstead, M.J.; Veissiere, S.P.; Campbell, J.O.; Friston, K.J. A variational approach to niche construction. *J. R. Soc. Interface* **2018**, *15*, 20170685. [CrossRef]
48. Friston, K.J.; Stephan, K.E. Free-energy and the brain. *Synthese* **2007**, *159*, 417–458. [CrossRef]
49. Frenkel, D. Order through entropy. *Nat. Mater.* **2015**, *14*, 9–12. [CrossRef] [PubMed]
50. Ramstead, M.J.D.; Badcock, P.B.; Friston, K.J. Answering Schrödinger's question: A free-energy formulation. *Phys. Life Rev.* **2018**, *24*, 1–16. [CrossRef] [PubMed]
51. Friston, K. Life as we know it. *J. R. Soc. Interface* **2013**, *10*, 20130475. [CrossRef] [PubMed]
52. Jeffery, K.; Pollack, R.; Rovelli, C. On the Statistical Mechanics of Life: Schrödinger Revisited. *Entropy* **2019**, *21*, 1211. [CrossRef]
53. Edlund, J.A.; Chaumont, N.; Hintze, A.; Koch, C.; Tononi, G.; Adami, C. Integrated information increases with fitness in the evolution of animats. *PLoS Comput. Biol.* **2011**, *7*, e1002236. [CrossRef]
54. Friston, K. A free energy principle for a particular physics. *arXiv* **2019**, arXiv:1906.10184.
55. Friston, K. The free-energy principle: A rough guide to the brain? *Trends Cogn. Sci.* **2009**, *13*, 293–301. [CrossRef]
56. Watts, D.J.; Strogatz, S.H. Collective dynamics of "small-world" networks. *Nature* **1998**, *393*, 440–442. [CrossRef]
57. Newman, M.E.J. Modularity and community structure in networks. *Proc. Natl. Acad. Sci. USA* **2006**, *103*, 8577–8582. [CrossRef]
58. Palacios, E.R.; Razi, A.; Parr, T.; Kirchhoff, M.; Friston, K. On Markov blankets and hierarchical self-organisation. *J. Theor. Biol.* **2020**, *486*, 110089. [CrossRef] [PubMed]
59. Barabasi, A.L. Scale-free networks: A decade and beyond. *Science* **2009**, *325*, 412–413. [CrossRef] [PubMed]
60. Oltvai, Z.N.; Barabasi, A.L. Systems biology. Life's complexity pyramid. *Science* **2002**, *298*, 763–764. [CrossRef]
61. Constant, A.; Clark, A.; Friston, K.J. Representation wars: Enacting an armistice through active inference. *Front. Psychol.* **2020**, *11*, 3798. [CrossRef]
62. Friston, K. Waves of prediction. *PLoS Biol.* **2019**, *17*, e3000426. [CrossRef] [PubMed]
63. Friston, K.; Kiebel, S. Predictive coding under the free-energy principle. *Philos. Trans. R. Soc. B Biol. Sci.* **2009**, *364*, 1211–1221. [CrossRef]
64. Gorochowski, T.E.; Grierson, C.S.; Di Bernardo, M. Organization of feed-forward loop motifs reveals architectural principles in natural and engineered networks. *Sci. Adv.* **2018**, *4*, eaap9751. [CrossRef] [PubMed]
65. Kitano, H. Biological robustness. *Nat. Rev. Genet.* **2004**, *5*, 826. [CrossRef] [PubMed]
66. Rohe, T.; Ehlis, A.-C.; Noppeney, U. The neural dynamics of hierarchical Bayesian causal inference in multisensory perception. *Nat. Commun.* **2019**, *10*, 1907. [CrossRef]
67. Colizza, V.; Flammini, A.; Serrano, M.A.; Vespignani, A. Detecting rich-club ordering in complex networks. *Nat. Phys.* **2006**, *2*, 110–115. [CrossRef]
68. van den Heuvel, M.P.; Sporns, O. Rich-club organization of the human connectome. *J. Neurosci.* **2011**, *31*, 15775–15786. [CrossRef] [PubMed]
69. Kiebel, S.J.; Daunizeau, J.; Friston, K.J. A hierarchy of time-scales and the brain. *PLoS Comput. Biol.* **2008**, *4*, e1000209. [CrossRef]
70. Friston, K.; Buzsáki, G. The functional anatomy of time: What and when in the brain. *Trends Cogn. Sci.* **2016**, *20*, 500–511. [CrossRef] [PubMed]
71. Hafez-Kolahi, H.; Kasaei, S. Information Bottleneck and its Applications in Deep Learning. *arXiv* **2019**, arXiv:1904.03743.
72. Maisto, D.; Donnarumma, F.; Pezzulo, G. Divide et impera: Subgoaling reduces the complexity of probabilistic inference and problem solving. *J. R. Soc. Interface* **2015**, *12*, 20141335. [CrossRef]
73. Tishby, N.; Zaslavsky, N. Deep learning and the information bottleneck principle. In Proceedings of the 2015 IEEE Information Theory Workshop (ITW), Jeju Island, Korea, 11–15 October 2015; pp. 1–5.
74. Shwartz-Ziv, R.; Tishby, N. Opening the black box of deep neural networks via information. *arXiv* **2017**, arXiv:1703.00810.
75. Friston, K.; Da Costa, L.; Hafner, D.; Hesp, C.; Parr, T. Sophisticated inference. *Neural Comput.* **2021**, *33*, 713–763.
76. Kingma, D.P.; Welling, M. Auto-encoding variational bayes. *arXiv* **2013**, arXiv:1312.6114.
77. Tenenbaum, J.B.; Kemp, C.; Griffiths, T.L.; Goodman, N.D. How to grow a mind: Statistics, structure, and abstraction. *Science* **2011**, *331*, 1279–1285. [CrossRef] [PubMed]
78. Verschure, P.F.M.J.; Pennartz, C.M.A.; Pezzulo, G. The why, what, where, when and how of goal-directed choice: Neuronal and computational principles. *Philos. Trans. R. Soc. London. Ser. B Biol. Sci.* **2014**, *369*, 20130483. [CrossRef]
79. Pezzulo, G.; Rigoli, F.; Friston, K.J. Hierarchical active inference: A theory of motivated control. *Trends Cogn. Sci.* **2018**, *22*, 294–306. [CrossRef] [PubMed]
80. Friston, K.J.; Daunizeau, J.; Kilner, J.; Kiebel, S.J. Action and behavior: A free-energy formulation. *Biol. Cybern.* **2010**, *102*, 227–260. [CrossRef] [PubMed]
81. Adams, R.A.; Shipp, S.; Friston, K.J. Predictions not commands: Active inference in the motor system. *Brain Struct. Funct.* **2013**, *218*, 611–643. [CrossRef] [PubMed]
82. Cannon, W.B. *Bodily Changes in Pain, Hunger, Fear, and Rage*; Appleton-Century-Crofts: New York, NY, USA, 1929.
83. O'Doherty, J.P.; Cockburn, J.; Pauli, W.M. Learning, reward, and decision making. *Annu. Rev. Psychol.* **2017**, *68*, 73–100. [CrossRef] [PubMed]
84. Lyon, P. The cognitive cell: Bacterial behavior reconsidered. *Front. Microbiol.* **2015**, *6*, 264. [CrossRef] [PubMed]

85. Moutoussis, M.; Fearon, P.; El-Deredy, W.; Dolan, R.J.; Friston, K.J. Bayesian inferences about the self (and others): A review. *Conscious. Cogn.* **2014**, *25*, 67–76. [CrossRef] [PubMed]
86. Friston, K.; Schwartenbeck, P.; Fitzgerald, T.; Moutoussis, M.; Behrens, T.; Dolan, R. The anatomy of choice: Active inference and agency. *Front. Hum. Neurosci.* **2013**, *7*. [CrossRef]
87. Haggard, P. Sense of agency in the human brain. *Nat. Rev. Neurosci.* **2017**, *18*, 196. [CrossRef] [PubMed]
88. Crapse, T.B.; Sommer, M.A. Corollary discharge across the animal kingdom. *Nat. Rev. Neurosci.* **2008**, *9*, 587–600. [CrossRef]
89. Badoud, D.; Tsakiris, M. From the body's viscera to the body's image: Is there a link between interoception and body image concerns? *Neurosci. Biobehav. Rev.* **2017**, *77*, 237–246. [CrossRef] [PubMed]
90. Talevich, J.R.; Read, S.J.; Walsh, D.A.; Iyer, R.; Chopra, G. Toward a comprehensive taxonomy of human motives. *PLoS ONE* **2017**, *12*, e0172279. [CrossRef]
91. Schurz, M.; Radua, J.; Aichhorn, M.; Richlan, F.; Perner, J. Fractionating theory of mind: A meta-analysis of functional brain imaging studies. *Neurosci. Biobehav. Rev.* **2014**, *42*, 9–34. [CrossRef]
92. Ondobaka, S.; Kilner, J.; Friston, K. The role of interoceptive inference in theory of mind. *Brain Cogn.* **2017**, *112*, 64–68. [CrossRef]
93. Koltko-Rivera, M.E. Rediscovering the later version of Maslow's hierarchy of needs: Self-transcendence and opportunities for theory, research, and unification. *Rev. Gen. Psychol.* **2006**, *10*, 302–317. [CrossRef]
94. Gallagher, H.L.; Frith, C.D. Functional imaging of 'theory of mind'. *Trends Cogn. Sci.* **2003**, *7*, 77–83. [CrossRef]
95. Olsson, A.; Knapska, E.; Lindström, B. The neural and computational systems of social learning. *Nat. Rev. Neurosci.* **2020**, *21*, 197–212. [CrossRef] [PubMed]
96. Hamilton, W.D. The evolution of altruistic behavior. *Am. Nat.* **1963**, *97*, 354–356. [CrossRef]
97. Van Dyken, J.D.; Wade, M.J. Origins of altruism diversity I: The diverse ecological roles of altruistic strategies and their evolutionary responses to local competition. *Evol. Int. J. Org. Evol.* **2012**, *66*, 2484–2497. [CrossRef]
98. Kreft, J.-U. Biofilms promote altruism. *Microbiology* **2004**, *150*, 2751–2760. [CrossRef]
99. Bekoff, M.; Pierce, J. *Wild Justice: The Moral Lives of Animals*; University of Chicago Press: Chicago, IL, USA, 2009.
100. Fehr, E.; Fischbacher, U. Third-party punishment and social norms. *Evol. Hum. Behav.* **2004**, *25*, 63–87. [CrossRef]
101. Nowak, M.A.; Tarnita, C.E.; Wilson, E.O. The evolution of eusociality. *Nature* **2010**, *466*, 1057–1062. [CrossRef]
102. Lehmann, L. The evolution of trans-generational altruism: Kin selection meets niche construction. *J. Evol. Biol.* **2007**, *20*, 181–189. [CrossRef]
103. Van Dyken, J.D.; Wade, M.J. Origins of altruism diversity II: Runaway coevolution of altruistic strategies via "reciprocal niche construction". *Evol. Int. J. Org. Evol.* **2012**, *66*, 2498–2513. [CrossRef] [PubMed]
104. Rendell, L.; Fogarty, L.; Laland, K.N. Runaway cultural niche construction. *Philos. Trans. R. Soc. B Biol. Sci.* **2011**, *366*, 823–835. [CrossRef]
105. Lehmann, L. The adaptive dynamics of niche constructing traits in spatially subdivided populations: Evolving posthumous extended phenotypes. *Evol. Int. J. Org. Evol.* **2008**, *62*, 549–566. [CrossRef]
106. Veissière, S.P.; Constant, A.; Ramstead, M.J.; Friston, K.J.; Kirmayer, L.J. Thinking through other minds: A variational approach to cognition and culture. *Behav. Brain Sci.* **2020**, *43*, e90. [CrossRef] [PubMed]
107. Constant, A.; Ramstead, M.J.; Veissière, S.P.; Friston, K. Regimes of expectations: An active inference model of social conformity and human decision making. *Front. Psychol.* **2019**, *10*, 679. [CrossRef]
108. Sarma, G.P.; Hay, N.J.; Safron, A. AI Safety and Reproducibility: Establishing Robust Foundations for the Neuropsychology of Human Values. In Proceedings of the International Conference on Computer Safety, Reliability, and Security, Västerås, Sweden, 19–21 September 2018; Spriner: Berlin/Heidelberg, Germany, 2018; pp. 507–512.
109. Safron, A. The Radically Embodied Conscious Cybernetic Bayesian Brain: From Free Energy to Free Will and Back Again. *Entropy* **2021**, *23*, 783. [CrossRef] [PubMed]
110. De Waal, F.; Macedo, S.E.; Ober, J.E. *Primates and Philosophers: How Morality Evolved*; Princeton University Press: Princeton, NJ, USA, 2006.
111. Taylor, J.; Davis, A. Social cohesion. In *The International Encyclopedia of Anthropology*; John Wiley & Sons: Hoboken, NJ, USA, 2018; pp. 1–7.
112. Purzycki, B.G.; Apicella, C.; Atkinson, Q.D.; Cohen, E.; McNamara, R.A.; Willard, A.K.; Xygalatas, D.; Norenzayan, A.; Henrich, J. Moralistic gods, supernatural punishment and the expansion of human sociality. *Nature* **2016**, *530*, 327–330. [PubMed]
113. Beck, J.S.; Beck, A.T. *Cognitive Therapy: Basics and Beyond*; Guilford Press: New York, NY, USA, 1995.
114. Smith, R.; Moutoussis, M.; Bilek, E. Simulating the computational mechanisms of cognitive and behavioral psychotherapeutic interventions: Insights from active inference. *Sci. Rep.* **2021**, *11*, 10128. [CrossRef]
115. Stam, C.J. Modern network science of neurological disorders. *Nat. Rev. Neurosci.* **2014**, *15*, 683–695. [CrossRef]
116. Gosak, M.; Stožer, A.; Markovič, R.; Dolenšek, J.; Marhl, M.; Slak Rupnik, M.; Perc, M. The relationship between node degree and dissipation rate in networks of diffusively coupled oscillators and its significance for pancreatic beta cells. *Chaos Interdiscip. J. Nonlinear Sci.* **2015**, *25*, 073115. [CrossRef]
117. Albert, R.; Jeong, H.; Barabasi, A.L. Error and attack tolerance of complex networks. *Nature* **2000**, *406*, 378–382. [CrossRef] [PubMed]
118. Crucitti, P.; Latora, V.; Marchiori, M. Model for cascading failures in complex networks. *Phys. Rev. E* **2004**, *69*, 045104. [CrossRef]

119. Schäfer, B.; Witthaut, D.; Timme, M.; Latora, V. Dynamically induced cascading failures in power grids. *Nat. Commun.* **2018**, *9*, 1975. [CrossRef]
120. Yi, C.; Bao, Y.; Jiang, J.; Xue, Y.; Dong, Y. Cascading failures of social networks under attacks. In Proceedings of the 2014 IEEE/ACM International Conference on Advances in Social Networks Analysis and Mining (ASONAM 2014), Beijing, China, 17–20 August 2014; pp. 679–686.
121. Yi, C.; Bao, Y.; Jiang, J.; Xue, Y. Modeling cascading failures with the crisis of trust in social networks. *Phys. A Stat. Mech. Appl.* **2015**, *436*, 256–271. [CrossRef]
122. McEwen, B.S.; Bowles, N.P.; Gray, J.D.; Hill, M.N.; Hunter, R.G.; Karatsoreos, I.N.; Nasca, C. Mechanisms of stress in the brain. *Nat. Neurosci.* **2015**, *18*, 1353–1363. [CrossRef]
123. Kuehn, C. A mathematical framework for critical transitions: Bifurcations, fast–slow systems and stochastic dynamics. *Phys. D Nonlinear Phenom.* **2011**, *240*, 1020–1035. [CrossRef]
124. Gorenstein, E.E.; Newman, J.P. Disinhibitory psychopathology: A new perspective and a model for research. *Psychol. Rev.* **1980**, *87*, 301. [CrossRef]
125. Sajid, N.; Ball, P.J.; Parr, T.; Friston, K.J. Active inference: Demystified and compared. *Neural Comput.* **2021**, *33*, 674–712. [CrossRef] [PubMed]
126. Prigogine, I.; Stengers, I. *The End of Certainty*; Simon and Schuster: New York, UK, USA, 1997.
127. Jarman, N.; Steur, E.; Trengove, C.; Tyukin, I.Y.; van Leeuwen, C. Self-organisation of small-world networks by adaptive rewiring in response to graph diffusion. *Sci. Rep.* **2017**, *7*, 13158. [CrossRef] [PubMed]
128. Kauffman, S.A. *The Origins of Order: Self-Organization and Selection in Evolution*; OUP USA: Oxford, UK, 1993.
129. Camazine, S.; Deneubourg, J.-L.; Franks, N.R.; Sneyd, J.; Theraula, G.; Bonabeau, E. *Self-Organization in Biological Systems*; Princeton University Press: Princeton, NJ, USA, 2020.
130. Hoffmann, H. Impact of network topology on self-organized criticality. *Phys. Rev. E* **2018**, *97*, 022313. [CrossRef]
131. Bak, P.; Tang, C.; Wiesenfeld, K. Self-organized criticality. *Phys. Rev. A* **1988**, *38*, 364. [CrossRef]
132. Packard, N.H. *Adaptation Toward the Edge of Chaos*; University of Illinois at Urbana-Champaign, Center for Complex Systems Research: Chicago, IL, USA, 1988.
133. Waldrop, M.M. *Complexity: The Emerging Science at the Edge of Order and Chaos*; Simon and Schuster: New York, UK, USA, 1993.
134. Wang, X.F.; Xu, J. Cascading failures in coupled map lattices. *Phys. Rev. E* **2004**, *70*, 056113. [CrossRef]
135. Broido, A.D.; Clauset, A. Scale-free networks are rare. *Nat. Commun.* **2019**, *10*, 1017. [CrossRef] [PubMed]
136. Smart, A.G.; Amaral, L.A.; Ottino, J.M. Cascading failure and robustness in metabolic networks. *Proc. Natl. Acad. Sci. USA* **2008**, *105*, 13223–13228. [CrossRef]
137. Zhang, Y.; Zhao, M.; Su, J.; Lu, X.; Lv, K. Novel model for cascading failure based on degree strength and its application in directed gene logic networks. *Comput. Math. Methods Med.* **2018**, *2018*, 8950794. [CrossRef]
138. van den Heuvel, M.P.; Sporns, O. A cross-disorder connectome landscape of brain dysconnectivity. *Nat. Rev. Neurosci.* **2019**, *20*, 435–446. [CrossRef]
139. Engel, G.L. The need for a new medical model: A challenge for biomedicine. *Science* **1977**, *196*, 129–136. [CrossRef] [PubMed]
140. Friston, K.J.; Stephan, K.E.; Montague, R.; Dolan, R.J. Computational psychiatry: The brain as a phantastic organ. *Lancet Psychiatry* **2014**, *1*, 148–158. [CrossRef]
141. The Network and Pathway Analysis Subgroup of the Psychiatric Genomics Consortium. Psychiatric genome-wide association study analyses implicate neuronal, immune and histone pathways. *Nat. Neurosci.* **2015**, *18*, 199–209. [CrossRef] [PubMed]
142. Friston, K.J. Precision psychiatry. *Biol. Psychiatry Cogn. Neurosci. Neuroimaging* **2017**, *2*, 640–643. [CrossRef] [PubMed]
143. Oldham, S.; Ball, G.; Fornito, A. Early and late development of hub connectivity in the human brain. *Curr. Opin. Psychol.* **2021**, *44*, 321–329. [CrossRef]
144. Cloninger, C.R.; Svrakic, D.M.; Przybeck, T.R. A psychobiological model of temperament and character. *Arch. Gen. Psychiatry* **1993**, *50*, 975–990. [CrossRef]
145. Cloninger, C.R. The science of well-being: An integrated approach to mental health and its disorders. *World Psychiatry* **2006**, *5*, 71–76.
146. Corlett, P.R.; Fletcher, P.C. Computational psychiatry: A Rosetta Stone linking the brain to mental illness. *Lancet Psychiatry* **2014**, *1*, 399–402. [CrossRef]
147. Brunner, R.; Henze, R.; Parzer, P.; Kramer, J.; Feigl, N.; Lutz, K.; Essig, M.; Resch, F.; Stieltjes, B. Reduced prefrontal and orbitofrontal gray matter in female adolescents with borderline personality disorder: Is it disorder specific? *Neuroimage* **2010**, *49*, 114–120. [CrossRef]
148. Sleep, C.E.; Lynam, D.R.; Widiger, T.A.; Crowe, M.L.; Miller, J.D. An evaluation of DSM–5 Section III personality disorder Criterion A (impairment) in accounting for psychopathology. *Psychol. Assess.* **2019**, *31*, 1181. [CrossRef]
149. Tononi, G.; Boly, M.; Massimini, M.; Koch, C. Integrated information theory: From consciousness to its physical substrate. *Nat. Rev. Neurosci.* **2016**, *17*, 450–461. [CrossRef]
150. Safron, A. An Integrated World Modeling Theory (IWMT) of consciousness: Combining integrated information and global neuronal workspace theories with the free energy principle and active inference framework; Toward solving the hard problem and characterizing agentic causation. *Front. Artif. Intell.* **2020**, *3*, 30. [PubMed]
151. Deane, G. Dissolving the self: Active inference, psychedelics, and ego-dissolution. *Philos. Mind Sci.* **2020**, *1*, 1–27. [CrossRef]

152. Ciaunica, A.; Seth, A.; Limanowski, J.; Hesp, C. I Overthink—Therefore I Am Not: Altered Sense of Self and Agency in Depersonalisation Disorder. Available online: https://psyarxiv.com/k9d2n/download/?format=pdf (accessed on 4 July 2021).
153. Limanowski, J.; Friston, K. Attenuating oneself: An active inference perspective on "selfless" experiences. *Philos. Mind Sci.* **2020**, *1*, 1–16. [CrossRef]
154. Clarke, D.M.; Kissane, D.W. Demoralization: Its phenomenology and importance. *Aust. N. Z. J. Psychiatry* **2002**, *36*, 733–742. [CrossRef] [PubMed]
155. Kotov, R.; Krueger, R.F.; Watson, D.; Achenbach, T.M.; Althoff, R.R.; Bagby, R.M.; Brown, T.A.; Carpenter, W.T.; Caspi, A.; Clark, L.A. The Hierarchical Taxonomy of Psychopathology (HiTOP): A dimensional alternative to traditional nosologies. *J. Abnorm. Psychol.* **2017**, *126*, 454. [CrossRef] [PubMed]
156. Insel, T.R. The NIMH Research Domain Criteria (RDoC) Project: Precision Medicine for Psychiatry. *Am. J. Psychiatry* **2014**, *171*, 395–397. [CrossRef]
157. Carragher, N.; Krueger, R.F.; Eaton, N.R.; Slade, T. Disorders without borders: Current and future directions in the meta-structure of mental disorders. *Soc. Psychiatry Psychiatr. Epidemiol.* **2015**, *50*, 339–350. [CrossRef] [PubMed]
158. *DSM 5*; American Psychiatric Association: Washington, DC, USA, 2013.
159. Vasil, J.; Badcock, P.B.; Constant, A.; Friston, K.; Ramstead, M.J. A world unto itself: Human communication as active inference. *Front. Psychol.* **2020**, *11*, 417. [CrossRef]
160. Friston, K.J.; Frith, C.D. Active inference, communication and hermeneutics. *Cortex* **2015**, *68*, 129–143. [CrossRef]
161. Christakis, N.A.; Fowler, J.H. Social contagion theory: Examining dynamic social networks and human behavior. *Stat. Med.* **2013**, *32*, 556–577. [CrossRef]
162. Milgram, S. The small world problem. *Psychol. Today* **1967**, *2*, 60–67.
163. Italiano, G.F.; Parotsidis, N.; Perekhodko, E. What's Inside a Bow-Tie: Analyzing the Core of the Web and of Social Networks. In Proceedings of the 2017 International Conference on Information System and Data Mining, Denpasar, Indonesia, 26–29 September 2017; pp. 39–43.
164. Broder, A.; Kumar, R.; Maghoul, F.; Raghavan, P.; Rajagopalan, S.; Stata, R.; Tomkins, A.; Wiener, J. Graph structure in the web. In *The Structure and Dynamics of Networks*; Princeton University Press: Princeton, NJ, USA, 2011; pp. 183–194.
165. Pruitt, J.N.; Berdahl, A.; Riehl, C.; Pinter-Wollman, N.; Moeller, H.V.; Pringle, E.G.; Aplin, L.M.; Robinson, E.J.; Grilli, J.; Yeh, P. Social tipping points in animal societies. *Proc. R. Soc. B Biol. Sci.* **2018**, *285*, 20181282. [CrossRef]
166. Barzel, B.; Barabasi, A.L. Universality in network dynamics. *Nat. Phys.* **2013**, *9*, 673–681. [CrossRef]
167. Vazquez, A.; Oliveira, J.G.; Dezso, Z.; Goh, K.I.; Kondor, I.; Barabasi, A.L. Modeling bursts and heavy tails in human dynamics. *Phys. Rev. E* **2006**, *73*, 036127. [CrossRef] [PubMed]
168. Edelmann, A.; Wolff, T.; Montagne, D.; Bail, C.A. Computational social science and sociology. *Annu. Rev. Sociol.* **2020**, *46*, 61–81. [CrossRef]
169. Barabasi, A.L. Sociology. Network theory—the emergence of the creative enterprise. *Science* **2005**, *308*, 639–641. [CrossRef]
170. Lazer, D.; Pentland, A.; Adamic, L.; Aral, S.; Barabasi, A.L.; Brewer, D.; Christakis, N.; Contractor, N.; Fowler, J.; Gutmann, M.; et al. Social science. Computational social science. *Science* **2009**, *323*, 721–723. [CrossRef]
171. Kesebir, S. The superorganism account of human sociality: How and when human groups are like beehives. *Personal. Soc. Psychol. Rev.* **2012**, *16*, 233–261. [CrossRef] [PubMed]
172. Rotberg, R.I. One. The Failure and Collapse of Nation-States: Breakdown, Prevention, and Repair. In *When States Fail*; Princeton University Press: Princeton, NJ, USA, 2010; pp. 1–50.

Article

An Active Inference Model of Collective Intelligence

Rafael Kaufmann [1], Pranav Gupta [2] and Jacob Taylor [3,4,*]

1 Independent Researcher, Brooklyn, NY 11215, USA; rkauf@google.com
2 Tepper School of Business, Carnegie Mellon University, Pittsburgh, PA 15213, USA; pranavgu@andrew.cmu.edu
3 Institute of Cognitive & Evolutionary Anthropology, University of Oxford, Oxford OX2 6PN, UK
4 Crawford School of Public Policy, Australian National University, Canberra, ACT 2601, Australia
* Correspondence: jacob.taylor@anu.edu.au

Citation: Kaufmann, R.; Gupta, P.; Taylor, J. An Active Inference Model of Collective Intelligence. *Entropy* **2021**, *23*, 830. https://doi.org/10.3390/e23070830

Academic Editors: Paul Badcock, Maxwell Ramstead, Zahra Sheikhbahaee and Axel Constant

Received: 1 April 2021
Accepted: 12 June 2021
Published: 29 June 2021

Publisher's Note: MDPI stays neutral with regard to jurisdictional claims in published maps and institutional affiliations.

Copyright: © 2021 by the authors. Licensee MDPI, Basel, Switzerland. This article is an open access article distributed under the terms and conditions of the Creative Commons Attribution (CC BY) license (https://creativecommons.org/licenses/by/4.0/).

Abstract: Collective intelligence, an emergent phenomenon in which a composite system of multiple interacting agents performs at levels greater than the sum of its parts, has long compelled research efforts in social and behavioral sciences. To date, however, formal models of collective intelligence have lacked a plausible mathematical description of the relationship between local-scale interactions between autonomous sub-system components (individuals) and global-scale behavior of the composite system (the collective). In this paper we use the Active Inference Formulation (AIF), a framework for explaining the behavior of any non-equilibrium steady state system at any scale, to posit a minimal agent-based model that simulates the relationship between local individual-level interaction and collective intelligence. We explore the effects of providing baseline AIF agents (Model 1) with specific cognitive capabilities: Theory of Mind (Model 2), Goal Alignment (Model 3), and Theory of Mind with Goal Alignment (Model 4). These stepwise transitions in sophistication of cognitive ability are motivated by the types of advancements plausibly required for an AIF agent to persist and flourish in an environment populated by other highly autonomous AIF agents, and have also recently been shown to map naturally to canonical steps in human cognitive ability. Illustrative results show that stepwise cognitive transitions increase system performance by providing complementary mechanisms for alignment between agents' local and global optima. Alignment emerges endogenously from the dynamics of interacting AIF agents themselves, rather than being imposed exogenously by incentives to agents' behaviors (contra existing computational models of collective intelligence) or top-down priors for collective behavior (contra existing multiscale simulations of AIF). These results shed light on the types of generic information-theoretic patterns conducive to collective intelligence in human and other complex adaptive systems.

Keywords: collective intelligence; free energy principle; active inference; agent-based model; complex adaptive systems; multiscale systems; computational model

1. Introduction

Human collectives are examples of a specific subclass of complex adaptive system, the sub-system components of which—individual humans—are themselves highly autonomous complex adaptive systems. Consider that, subjectively, we perceive ourselves to be autonomous individuals at the same time that we actively participate in collectives. Families, organizations, sports teams, and polities exert agency over our individual behavior [1,2] and are even capable, under certain conditions, of intelligence that cannot be explained by aggregation of individual intelligence [3,4]. To date, however, formal models of collective intelligence have lacked a plausible mathematical description of the functional relationship between individual and collective behavior.

In this paper, we use the Active Inference Framework (AIF) to develop a clearer understanding of the relationship between patterns of individual interaction and collective intelligence in systems composed of highly autonomous subsystems, or "agents". We adopt a definition of collective intelligence established within organizational psychology, as groups of individuals capable of acting collectively in ways that seem intelligent and that cannot be explained by individual intelligence [5] (p.3). As we outline below, collective intelligence can be operationalized under AIF as a composite system's ability to minimize free energy or perform approximate Bayesian inference at the collective level. To demonstrate the formal relationship between local-scale agent interaction and collective behavior, we develop a computational model that simulates the behavior of two autonomous agents in state space. In contrast to typical agent-based models, in which agents behave according to more rudimentary decision-making algorithms (e.g., from game theory; see [6]), we model our agents as self-organizing systems whose actions are themselves dictated by the directive of free energy minimization relative to the "local" degrees of freedom accessible to them, including those that specify their embedding in the larger system [7–9]. We demonstrate that AIF may be particularly useful for elucidating mechanisms and dynamics of systems composed of highly autonomous interacting agents, of which human collectives are a prominent instance. But the universality of our formal computational approach makes our model relevant to collective intelligence in any composite system.

1.1. Motivation: The "Missing Link" between Individual-Level and System-Level Accounts of Human Collective Intelligence

Existing formal accounts of collective intelligence are predicated on composite systems whose sub-system components are subject to vastly fewer degrees of freedom than individuals in human collectives. Unlike ants in a colony or neurons in a brain, which appear to rely on comparatively rudimentary autoregulatory mechanisms to sustain participation in collective ensembles [10,11], human agents participate in collectives by leveraging an array of phylogenetic (evolutionarily) and ontogenetic (developmental) mechanisms and socio-culturally constructed regularities or affordances (e.g., language) [12–14]. Human agents' cognitive abilities and sociocultural niches create avenues for active participation in functional collective behavior (e.g., the pursuit of shared goals), as well as avenues to shirk global constraints in the pursuit of local (individual) goals. Mathematical models for collective intelligence of this subclass of system must not only seek to account for richer complexity of agent behavior at each scale of the system (particularly at the individual level), but also the relationship between local scale interaction between individual agents and global scale behavior of the collective.

Existing research of human collective intelligence is limited precisely by a lack of alignment between these two scales of analysis. On the one hand, accounts of local-scale interactions from behavioral science and psychology tend to construe individual humans as goal-directed individuals endowed with discrete cognitive mechanisms (specifically social perceptiveness or Theory of Mind and shared intentionality; see [15,16]) that allow individuals to establish and maintain adaptive connections with other individuals in service of shared goals [3–5,17–19] (Riedl and colleagues [19] report a recent analysis of 1356 groups that found social perceptiveness and group interaction processes to be strong predictors of collective intelligence measured by a psychometric test.). Researchers conjecture that these mechanisms allow collectives to derive and utilize more performance-relevant information from the environment than could be derived by an aggregation of the same individuals acting without such connections (for example, by facilitating an adaptive, system-wide balance between cognitive efficiency and diversity; see [4]). Empirical substantiation of such claims has proven difficult, however. Most investigations rely heavily on laboratory-derived summaries or "snapshots" of individual and collective behavior that flatten the complexity of local scale interactions [20] and make it difficult to examine causal relationships between individual scale mechanisms and collective behavior as they typically unfold in real world settings [21,22].

Accounts of global-scale (collective) behavior, by contrast, tend to adopt system-based (rather than agent-based) perspectives that render collectives as random dynamical systems in phase space, or equivalent formulations [23–26]. Only rarely deployed to assess the construct of human collective intelligence specifically (e.g., [27]), these approaches have been fruitful for identifying gross properties of phase-space dynamics (such as synchrony, metastability, or symmetry breaking) that correlate with collective intelligence or collective performance, more generally construed [28–32]. However, on their own, such analyses are limited in their ability to generate testable predictions for multiscale behavior, such as how global-scale dynamics (rendered in phase-space) translate to specific local-scale interactions between individuals (in state-space), or how local-scale interactions between individuals translate to evolution and change in collective global-scale dynamics [26].

In sum, the substantive differences between these two analytical perspectives (individual and collective) on collective intelligence in human systems make it difficult to develop a formal description of how local-scale interactions between autonomous individual agents relate to global-scale collective behavior and vice versa. Most urgent for the development of a formal model of collective intelligence in this subclass of system, therefore, is a common mathematical framework capable of operating between individual-level cognitive mechanisms and system-level dynamics of the collective [4].

1.2. The Free Energy Principle and an Active Inference Formulation of Collective Intelligence

FEP has recently emerged as a candidate for this type of common mathematical framework for multiscale behavioral processes [33–35]. FEP is a mathematical formulation of how adaptive systems resist a natural tendency to disorder [33,36]. FEP states that any non-equilibrium steady state system self organizes as such by minimizing variational free energy in its exchanges with the environment [37]. The key trick of FEP is that the principle of free energy minimization can be neatly translated into an agent-based process theory, AIF, of approximate Bayesian inference [38] and applied to any self-organizing biological system at any scale [39]. The upshot is that, in theory, any AIF agent at one spatio-temporal scale could be simultaneously composed of nested AIF agents at the scale below, and a constituent of a larger AIF agent at the scale above it [40–42]. In effect, AIF allows you to pick a composite system or agent A that you want to understand, and it will be generally true both that: A is an approximate, global minimizer of free energy at the scale at which that agent reliably persists; and A is composed of subsystems {A_i} that are approximate, local minimizers of free energy (which is composed of the remainder of A). Thus, under AIF, collective intelligence can conceivably be modelled as a case of individual AIF agents that interact within—or indeed, interact to produce—a superordinate AIF agent at the scale of the collective [9,43]. In this way, AIF provides a framework within which a multiscale model of collective intelligence could be developed. The aim of this paper is to propose a provisional AIF model of collective intelligence that can depict the relationship between local-scale interactions and collective behavior.

An AIF model of collective intelligence begins with the depiction of a minimal AIF agent. Specifically, an AIF agent denotes any set of states enclosed by a "Markov blanket"— a statistical partition between a system's internal states and external states [44]—that infers beliefs about the causes of (hidden) external states by developing a probabilistic *generative model* of external states [37]. A Markov blanket is composed of sensory states and active states that mediate the relationship between a system's internal states and external states: external states (ψ) act on sensory states (s), which influence, but are not influenced by internal states (b). Internal states couple back through active states (a), which influence but are not influenced by external states. Through conjugated repertoires of perception and action, the agent embodies and refines (learns) a generative model of its environment [45] and the environment embodies and refines its model of the agent (akin to a circular process of environmental niche construction; see [12]).

Having established the notion of an AIF agent, the next step in developing an AIF model of collective intelligence is to consider the existence of multiple nested AIF agents across individual and collective scales of organization. Existing multiscale treatments of AIF provide a clear account of "downward reaching" causation, whereby superordinate AIF agents like brains or multicellular organisms systematically determine [46] the behavior of subordinate AIF agents (neurons or cells), limiting their behavioral degrees of freedom [9,40,47,48]. Consistent with this account of downward-reaching causation, existing toy models that simulate the emergence of collective behavior under AIF do so by simply using the statistical constraints from one scale to drive behavior at another, e.g., by explicitly endowing AIF agents with a genetic prior for functional specialization within a superordinate system [9] or by constructing a scenario in which the emergence of a superordinate agent at the global scale is predestined by limiting an agent's model of the environment to sensory evidence generated by a counterpart agent [7,8].

While perhaps useful for depicting the behavior of cells within multicellular organisms [9] or exact behavioral synchronization between two or more agents [7,8], these existing AIF models are less well-suited to explain collective intelligence in human systems, for two reasons. First, humans are relatively autonomous individual agents whose statistical boundaries for self-evidencing appear to be transient, distributed, and multiple [49–52]. Therefore, human collective intelligence cannot be explained simply by the way in which global-level system regularities constrain individual interaction from the "top-down". Second, the behavior of the collective in these toy models reflects the instructions or constraints supplied exogenously by the "designer" of the system, not a causal consequence of individual agents' autonomous problem-solving enabled by AIF. In this sense, extant models of AIF for collectives bear a closer resemblance to Searle's [53] "Chinese Room Argument" than to what we would recognize as emergent collective intelligence.

In sum, currently missing from AIF models of composite systems are specifications for how a system's emergent global-level cognitive capabilities causally relate to individual agents' emergent cognitive capabilities, and how local-scale interactions between individual AIF agents give rise, *endogenously*, to a superordinate AIF agent that exhibits (collective) intelligence [43]. Specifically, existing approaches lack a description of the key cognitive mechanisms of AIF agents that might provide a functional "missing link" for collective intelligence. In this paper, we initiate this line of inquiry by exploring whether some basic information-theoretic capabilities of individual AIF agents, motivated by analogies with human social capabilities, create opportunities for collective intelligence at the global scale.

1.3. Our Approach

To operationalize AIF in a way that is useful for investigating this question, we begin by examining what minimal features of autonomous individual AIF agents are required to achieve collective intelligence, operationalized as active inference at the level of the global-scale system. We conjecture that very generic information theoretic patterns of an environment in which individual AIF agents exploit other AIF agents as affordances of free energy minimization should support the emergence of collective intelligence. Importantly, we expect that these patterns emerge under very general assumptions and from the dynamics of AIF itself—without the need for exogenously imposed fitness or incentive structures on local-scale behavior, contra extant computational models of collective intelligence (that rely on cost or utility functions; e.g., [54,55]) or other common approaches to reinforcement learning (that rely on exogenous parameters of the Bellman equation; see [56,57]).

To justify our modelling approach, we draw upon recent research that systematically maps the complex adaptive learning process of AIF agents to empirical social scientific evidence for cognitive mechanisms that support adaptive human social behavior. In line with this research, we posit a series of stepwise progressions or "hops" in the individual cognitive ability of any AIF agent in an environment populated by other self-similar AIF agents. These hops represent evolutionarily plausible "adaptive priors" [42] (p.109) that would likely guide action-perception cycles of AIF agents in a collective toward unsurprising states:

- **Baseline AIF**—AIF agents, to persist as such, will minimize immediate free energy by accurately sensing and acting on salient affordances of the environment. This will require a general ability for "perceptiveness" of the (physical) environment.
- **Folk Psychology**—AIF agents in an environment populated by other AIF agents would fare better by minimizing free energy not only relative to their physical en-

vironment, but also to the "social environment" composed of their peers [13]. The most parsimonious way for AIF agents to derive information from other agents would be to (i) assume that other agents are self-similar, or are "creatures like me" [58], and (ii) differentiate other-generated information by calculating how it diverges from self-generated information (akin to a process of "alterity" or self-other distinction). This ability aligns with the notion of a "folk psychological theory of society", in which humans deploy a combination of phylogenetic and ontogenetic modules to process social information [59,60].

- **Theory of Mind**—AIF agents that develop "social perceptiveness" or an ability to accurately infer beliefs and intentions of other agents will likely outperform agents with less social perceptiveness. Social perceptiveness, also commonly known in cognitive psychology as "Theory of Mind", would minimally require cognitive architecture for encoding the internal belief states of other agents as a source of self-inference (for game-theoretical simulations of this proposal, see [61,62]). As discussed above, experimental evidence suggests that social perceptiveness or Theory of Mind (measured using the "Reading the Mind in the Eyes" test; see [63]) is a significant predictor of human collective intelligence in a range of in-person and on-line collaborative tasks [4].
- **Goal Alignment**—It is possible to imagine scenarios in which the effectiveness of Theory of Mind would be limited, such as situations of high informational uncertainty (in which other agents hold multiple or unclear goals), or in environments populated by more agents than would be computationally tractable for a single AIF agent to actively theorize [64]. AIF agents capable of transitioning from merely encoding internal belief states of other AIF agents to recognizing shared goals and actively aligning goals with other AIF agents would likely enjoy considerable coordination benefits and (computational) efficiencies [16,65] that would also likely translate to collective-level performance [55,66].
- **Shared Norms**—Acquisition of capacities to engage directly with the reified signal of sharedness (a.k.a., "norms") between agents as a stand-in for (or in addition to) bottom-up discovery of mutually viable shared goals would also likely confer efficiencies to individuals and collectives [12]. Humans appear unique in their ability to leverage densely packaged socio-cultural installed affordances to cue regimes of perception and action that establish and stabilize adaptive collective behavior without the need for energetically expensive parsing of bottom-up sensory signals (a process recently described as "Thinking through Other Minds"; see [14]).

The clear resonance between generic information-theoretic patterns of basic AIF agents and empirical evidence of human social behavior is remarkable, and gives credence to the extension of seemingly human-specific notions such as "alterity", "shared goals", "alignment", "intention", and "meaning" to a wider spectrum of bio-cognitive agents [67]. In effect, the universality of FEP—a principle that can be applied to any biological system at any scale—makes it possible to strip-down the complex and emergent behavioral phenomenon of collective intelligence to basic operating mechanisms, and to clearly inspect how local-scale capabilities of individual AIF agents might enable global-scale state optimization of a composite system.

In the following section we use AIF to model the relationship between a selection of these hops in cognitive ability and collective intelligence. We construct a simple 1D search task based on [68], in which two AIF agents interact as they pursue individual and shared goals. We endow AIF agents with two key cognitive abilities—Theory of Mind and Goal Alignment—and vary these abilities systematically in four simulations that follow a 2 × 2 (Theory of Mind × Goal Alignment) progression: Model 1 (Baseline AIF, no social interaction), Model 2 (Theory of Mind without Goal Alignment), Model 3 (Goal Alignment without Theory of Mind), and Model 4 (Theory of Mind with Goal Alignment). We use a measure of free energy to operationalize performance at the local (individual) and global (collective) scales of the system [69]. While our goals in this paper are exploratory (these models and simulations are designed to be generative, not to test hypotheses), we do generally expect that increases in sophistication of cognitive abilities at the level of individual agents will correspond with an increase in local- and global-scale performance. Indeed, illustrative results of model simulations (Section 3) show that each hop in cognitive ability improves global system performance, particularly in cases of alignment between local and global optima.

2. Materials and Methods

2.1. Paradigm and Set-Up

Our AIF model builds upon the work of McGregor and colleagues, who develop a minimal AIF agent that behaves in a discrete one-dimensional time world [68]. In this set-up, a single agent senses a chemical concentration in the environment and acts on the environment by moving one of two ways until it arrives at its desired state, the position in which it believes the chemical concentration to be highest, denoting a food source. We adapt this paradigm by modelling two AIF agents (Agent A and Agent B) that occupy the same world and interact according to parameters described below (see Figure 1). The McGregor et al. paradigm and AIF model is attractive for its computational implementability and tractability as a simple AIF agent with minimum viable complexity. It is also accessible and reproducible; whereas most existing agent-based implementations of AIF are implemented in MATLAB, using the SPM codebase (e.g., [57]), an implementation of the McGregor et al. AIF model is widely available in the open-source programming language Python, using only standard open source numerical computing libraries [70]. For a comprehensive mathematical guide to FEP and a simple agent-based model implementing perception and action under AIF, see [36].

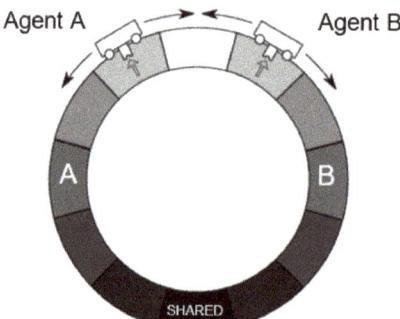

Figure 1. A minimal collective system of two AIF agents (adapted from McGregor et al.). We implement two agents (Agent A and Agent B) that have one common target position (Shared Target) and one individual target position (A's Target; B's Target). All targets are encoded with equal desirability. This figure is notional: our simulation environment contains 60 cells instead of the 12 depicted here. Note: we randomize the location of the shared target while preserving relative distances to unshared targets to ensure that the agents' behavior is not an artefact of its location in the sensory environment.

We extend the work of McGregor and colleagues to allow for interactions not only between an agent and the "physical" environment, but also between an agent and its "social" environment (i.e., its partner). Accordingly, we make minor simplifications to the McGregor et al. model that are intended to reduce the number of independent parameters and make interpretation of phenomena more straightforward (alterations to the McGregor et al. model are noted throughout).

2.2. Conceptual Outline of AIF Model

Our model consists of two agents. Descriptively, one can think of these as simple automata, each inhabiting a discrete "cell" in a one-dimensional circular environment where there are predefined targets (food sources). As agents aren't endowed with a frame of reference, an agent's main cognitive challenge is to situate itself in the environment (i.e., to infer its own position). Both agents have the following capabilities:

- **Physical capabilities:**
    - "Chemical sensors" able to pick up a 1-bit chemical signal from the food source at each time step;
    - "Actuators" that allow agents to "move" one cell at each time step;
    - "Position and motion sensors" that allow agents to detect each other's position and motion.
- **Cognitive capabilities:**
    - Beliefs about their own current position; we construe this as a "self-actualization loop" or Sense->Understand->Act cycle: (1) sense environment; (2) optimize belief distribution relative to sensory inputs (by minimizing free energy given by an adequate generative model); and (3) act to reduce FE relative to desired beliefs, under the same generative model.
    - Desires (also described as "desired beliefs") about their own position relative to their prescribed target positions;
    - Ability to select the actions that will best "satisfy" their desires;
    - "Theory of Mind": they possess beliefs about their partner's position, knowledge of their partner's desires, and therefore, the ability to imagine the actions that their partners are expected to take. We implement this as a "partner-actualization loop" that is formally identical to the self-actualization loop above;
    - "Goal Alignment": the ability to alter their own desires to make them more compatible with their partner's.

2.3. Model Preliminaries

Throughout, we use the following shorthand:

- $q^{superscript} \triangleq softmax(b^{superscript})$ for any superscript index, where $softmax(b)_i \triangleq \frac{e^{b_i - max(b)}}{\sum e^{b_i - max(b)}}$. This converts a belief represented as a vector in $\mathbb{R}^N$ to the equivalent probability distribution over [0..N-1]; the $max(b)$ offset is for numerical stability. We choose to convert back by $b_i = \ln q_i - \ln(max(q))$, to enforce $b_i \leq 0$.
- Beliefs are also implicitly constrained to $b_i \geq -10$, for numerical stability. This means $b_i \in \mathbf{B} = [-10, 0]$.
- $\varphi \triangleq \psi^{partner}$ when necessary, to disambiguate between it and ψ^{own}.
- $(v_{+x})_i \triangleq v_{i+x}$ to denote shifting a vector.
- $\Theta_\alpha(q) \triangleq \alpha q + \frac{1-\alpha}{N}$ to denote "re-ranging" a probability distribution, squishing its range from [0,1] to $[\frac{1-\alpha}{N}, \alpha + \frac{1-\alpha}{N}]$.
- All arithmetic in the space of positions (ψ or Δ) and actions (a) is considered to be mod N.

2.4. State Space

These capabilities are implemented as follows. Each agent A^i is represented by a tuple $A^i = (\psi^i, s^i, b^i, a^i)$. In what follows we'll omit the indices except where there is a relevant difference between agents. These tuples form the relevant state space (see Figure 2):

- $\psi \in [0..N-1]$ is the agent's external state, its position in a circular environment with period N. Crucially, the agent doesn't have direct access to its external state, but only to limited information about the environment afforded through the sensory state below.
- $s = (s^{own} \in \{0, 1\}, \Delta \in [0..N-1], a^{pp} \in \{-1, 0, 1\})$ is the agent's sensory state. s^{own} is a one-bit sensory input from the environment; Δ is the perceived difference between the agent's own position and its partner's; a^{pp} is the partner's last action.
- $b = (b^{own} \in \mathbf{B}^N, b^{*own} \in \mathbf{B}^N, b^{partner} \in \mathbf{B}^N, b^{*partner} \in \mathbf{B}^N)$ is the agent's internal or "belief" state. b^{own} and b^{*own} are, respectively, its actual and desired beliefs about

its own position; equivalently, $b^{partner}$ and $b^{*partner}$ are its actual and desired beliefs about its partner's position.
- $a = (a^{own} \in \{-1, 0, 1\}, a^{partner} \in \{-1, 0, 1\})$ is the partner's action state: a^{own} is its own action; $a^{partner}$ is the action it expects from the partner.

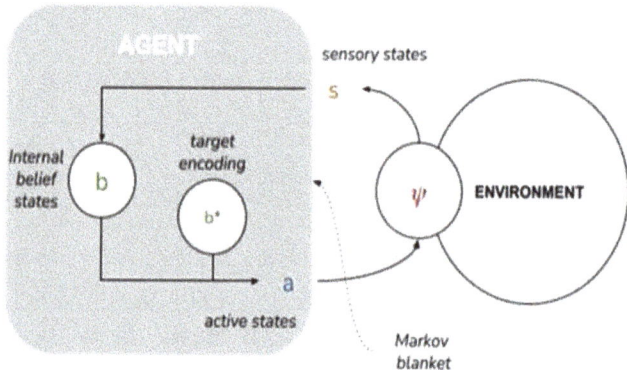

Figure 2. AIF agent based on McGregor et al. [68]. A Markov blanket defines conditional independencies between a set of internal belief states (b) and a set of environment states (ψ) with target encoding or "desires" (b*).

2.5. Agent Evolution

These states evolve according to a discrete-time free energy minimization procedure, extended from McGregor et al. (Figure 3). At each time step, each agent selects the action that will minimize the free energy relative to its target encoding (achieved by explicit computation of F for each of the 3 possible actions), and then updates its beliefs to best match the current sensory state (achieved by gradient descent on b').

2.6. Sensory Model

Let us recapitulate McGregor et al's definition of the free energy for a single-agent model:

$$F(b', b, s, a) = D_{KL}(q(\psi'|b') \| p(\psi', s|b, a)) \qquad (1)$$

where $q(b) = \text{softmax}(b)$ is the "variational (probability) density" encoded by b, and $p(\psi', s | b, a)$ is the "generative (probability) density" representing the agent's mental model of the world [37]. D_{KL} is the Kullback–Leibler (KL) divergence or relative entropy between the variational and generative densities [71].

To respect the causal relationships prescribed by the Markov blanket (see Figure 2), the generative density may be decomposed as:

$$p(\psi', s|b, a) = P(\psi'|s, b, a, \psi) \bullet P(s|b, a, \psi) \bullet P(\psi|b, a) \qquad (2)$$

where the three terms within the summation are arbitrary functions of their variables. In the single-agent model, where the only source of information is the environment, we follow McGregor's model, in a slightly simplified form:

1. $P(\psi' | s, b, a, \psi) = \delta(\psi', \psi + a)$: the agent's actions are always assumed to have the intended effect, δ being the discrete Kronecker delta.
2. $P(s | \psi) = k^s(1-k)^{1-s} e^{-\omega |\psi - \psi_{mid}|}$: the agent assumes the probability of s = 1 (sensoria triggered) is higher for regions near the "center" of the environment. This is identical to the real "physical" probability of chemical signals, meaning the agent's generative distribution is correct.
3. $P(\psi | b, a) = q(b)$, in agreement with the definition of b as encoding the belief distribution over ψ.

```
procedure simulate(ψ, b, b*)
    loop
        s^own i ← random value using P^i(s^own | ψ)
        a^i ← argmin_a F^i(b*, b, s^i, a)
        b'^i ← optimise(b^i, s^i, a^i)
        ψ' ← ψ + a                ◁ Unlike McGregor et al., we assume agents always act as intended
        Δ ← (ψ* - ψ*, ψ* - ψ*)    ◁ Agents' "position sensors" are assumed to be perfect
        a^pp ← (ψ'* - ψ*, ψ'* - ψ*)  ◁ Agents' "motion sensors" are assumed to be perfect
    end loop
end procedure


function optimize(b, s, a)
    b' = b                          ◁ starting from previous epoch's belief
    for i ∈ {1 ··· k} do
        b' ← b' - η ·∂/∂b' F(b', b, s, a)    ◁ gradient descent on b'
    end for
    return b'
end function
```

Figure 3. Pseudo code for agent evolution (adapted from [68]). Note that the loop is run for both agents in lockstep, but each agent selects actions and optimizes beliefs individually.

From list item 1 directly above, this generative density can also be read as a simple Bayesian updating plus a change of indexes to reflect the effects of the action: $p(\psi', s|b, a) = P(s|\psi' - a) P(\psi' - a|b)$ or even more simply, $p_{\psi'}^{posterior} = p_{\psi'-a}^{s} p_{\psi'-a}^{prior}$.

In our model, both agents implement their own copies of the generative density above (we leave it to the reader to add "$\square^{own}$" indices where appropriate). The parameter k, denoting the maximum sensory probability, is assumed agent-specific; we naturally identify it with an agent's "perceptiveness". ω and ψ_0, on the other hand, are environmental parameters.

2.7. Partner Model

In addition to the sensory model, we will define a new generative density implementing the agent's inference of its partner's behavior, or "Theory of Mind" (ToM; see Figure 6b). An agent with a sensory and partner model will adopt the following form:

$$p(\phi', \Delta, a^{pp}|b, a) = P(\phi'|a^{partner}, \phi) \bullet P(\Delta|b, \phi) \bullet P(a^{pp}|b, a^{partner}, \phi) \bullet P(\phi|b) \quad (3)$$

The first three terms on the right-hand side correspond to mechanistic models of the evolution of the variables ϕ', Δ, a^{pp}, whereas the last one, $P(\phi|b) = q_\phi^{partner}$, defines the "prior" and is analogous to $q(b)$ in the sensory model. To fully specify this density, we define these models as follows:

1. $P(\phi'|a^{partner}, \phi) = \delta(\phi', \phi + a^{partner})$ describes the expected results of the partner's observed action upon its inferred position. The Kronecker delta implies that the partner's actions are always effective, matching item #1 from Section 2.6.
2. $P(\Delta|b, \phi) = P(\psi = \phi + \Delta|b, \phi) = q_{\phi+\Delta}^{own}$: the agent (correctly) believes that Δ is a deterministic function of the two positions, and therefore the probability of observing a given Δ, given the partner's position ϕ, is equal to the probability the agent ascribes to itself being in the corresponding position $\psi = \phi + \Delta$.

3. $P(a^{pp}|b, a^{partner}, \phi) = P(a^{partner}|\phi - a^{pp}, b^{*partner})$: the agent determines its belief in the partner's previous action by "backtracking" to its previous state $\phi - a^{pp}$, and leveraging the following model of the partner's next action:

$$P(a^{partner} = \pm | \phi, b^{*partner}) = \{1 - P(a^{partner} = 0|\phi, b^{*partner})\} \frac{1}{p_{\phi-1}^{*partner} + p_{\phi+1}^{*partner}} q_{\phi - a^{partner}}^{*partner} \quad (4)$$

$$P(a^{partner} = 0|\phi, b^{*partner}) = \zeta \frac{1}{\max(q^{*partner})} q_{\phi}^{*partner}$$

This equation seems complex but its output and mechanical interpretation are quite simple (see Figure 4). To justify it, note that the agent must produce probabilities of the partner's actions without knowing their *actual* internal states at that time, but only their targets $q^{*partner}$. To do so, the agent assumes that the partner will act mechanistically according to those desires, i.e., the higher a partner's desire for its current location, the more likely it is to stay put. To eliminate spurious dependence on absolute values of $q^{*partner}$, we set $P(a^{partner} = 0)$ to be proportional to $q^{*partner}/\max(q^{*partner})$. The constant of proportionality ζ corresponds to the maximum probability of the partner standing still, when $q^{*partner}$ achieves its global maxima. This leaves the remaining probability mass to be allocated across the other actions (± 1), which we do by assuming the probability of moving in a given direction is proportional to the desires in the adjacent locations. For the purpose of this study, ζ is held constant at 0.9.

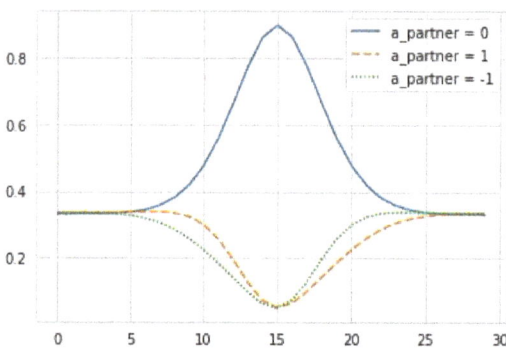

Figure 4. Illustrative plot of $P(a^{partner}|\phi, b^{*partner})$ for each possible value of $a^{partner}$ and ϕ, when $q^{*partner}$ follows a normal distribution centered on $\phi = 15$. At the valleys where $q^{*partner}$ is lowest and its gradient is small, the partner doesn't quite have strong incentives to go in any particular direction, and so is assigned roughly equal probabilities for the three actions. At the slopes, the action corresponding to the upward slope is more strongly expected. At peak $q^{*partner}$, $P(a^{partner} = 0) = \zeta$ and the probabilities of the two other actions are equal.

The combination of these three models results in a generative density has the same form as the original generative density from the baseline sensory model, $p_{\phi'}^{posterior} = p_{\phi'-a^{partner}}^{\Delta,a^{pp}} p_{\phi'-a^{partner}}^{prior}$. This is consistent with our modeling decision to make the "other-evidencing loop" functionally identical to the "self-actualization loop", as discussed above (Section 2.2).

As before, each agent implements its own copy of the partner model. ζ is assumed equal for both agents; they have the same capability to interpret the partner's actions.

2.8. Agent-Level Free Energy

We are finally ready to define the free energy for our individual-level model. For each agent:

$$F = D_{KL}\left(q'^{\ own} \parallel p^{own} \Theta_\alpha \left(p_{+\Delta'}^{partner}\right)\right) + D_{KL}\left(q'^{\ partner} \parallel p^{partner} \Theta_{\alpha^2}(p_{-\Delta'}^{own})\right) \quad (5)$$

where:

1. $p^{own}_{\psi'} = P(s^{own} \mid \psi' - a^{own}) \, q^{own}_{\psi' - a^{own}}$ is the sensory model (outlined above in Section 2.6).
2. $p^{partner}_{\phi'} = q^{own}_{\phi' - a^{partner} + \Delta} \, P(a^{partner} \mid \phi' - a^{partner} - a^{pp}, b^{\star partner}) \, q^{partner}_{\phi' - a^{partner}}$ is the partner model (outlined above in Section 2.7).
3. The "reranging" function, Θ_α, serves to moderate the influence of the partner model on the agent's own beliefs, and vice-versa. α is an agent-specific parameter, which, as we will see in Section 2.9, is identified with each agent's degree of "alterity".
4. The right-hand side of each KL divergence (i.e., the products of generative densities) is implicitly constrained to $[e^{-10}, 1]$, to ensure the resulting beliefs remain within their range **B**. This is interpreted as preventing overconfidence and is implemented as a simple maximum.

We interpret Equation (4) as follows: The agent's sensory and partner models jointly constrain its beliefs both about its own position and its partner's position. Thus, at each step, the agent: (a) refines its beliefs about both positions, in order to best fit the evidence provided by all of its inputs (i.e., its "chemical" sensor for the physical environment and "position and motion" sensor for its partner); and (b) selects the "best" next pair of actions (for self and partner), i.e., that which minimizes the "difference" (the KL divergence) between its present beliefs and the desired beliefs (For reasons of numerical stability, we follow McGregor et al. in implementing (b) before (a): The agent chooses the next actions based on current beliefs, then updates beliefs for the next time-step, based on the expected effects of those actions [68] (pp. 6–7)).

2.9. Theory of Mind

In this section we motivate the parameterization of an agent's Theory of Mind ability with α, or simply, its degree of *alterity*.

Note that when considered as a discrete-time dynamical system evolution, the process of refining beliefs about own and partner positions in the environment (step (a) in Section 2.8 above) potentially involves multiple recursive dependencies: the updated variational densities q'^{own} and $q'^{partner}$ both depend on the previous q^{own} (via both p^{own} and $p^{partner}$), as well as on the previous $q^{partner}$ (via $p^{partner}$). This is by design: the dependencies ensure that q'^{own} and $q'^{partner}$ are consistent with each other, as well as with their counterparts across time steps. However, too much of a good thing can be a problem. If left unconstrained, q'^{own} and $q'^{partner}$ can easily evolve towards spurious fixed points (Kronecker deltas), which can be interpreted as overfitting on prematurely established priors (In this case, it could be possible to observe scenarios such as *"the blind leading the blind"* in which a weak agent fixates on the movement trajectory of a strong agent who is overconfident about its final destination.). On the other hand, if q'^{own} were to depend only on q^{own}, it would eliminate the spurious fixed points: without the crossed dependence, the first term of the partner model (Section 2.7) only has fixed points at $(q'^{own} = \delta(\psi', argmax(q^{\star\,own})), a^{own} = 0)$, meaning that the agent has achieved a local desire optimum. Effectively, this "shuts down" the agent's ability to use the partner's information to shape its own beliefs, or its theory of mind, making it equivalent to MacGregor's original model.

Thus, there would appear to be no universal "best" value for an agent's Theory of Mind; an appropriate level of Theory of Mind would depend on a trade-off between the risk of overfitting and that of discarding valid evidence from the partner. The appropriate level of Theory of Mind would also depend on the agent's other capabilities (in this case, its perceptiveness, k).

This motivates the operationalization of α as a parameter for the intensity to which Theory of Mind shapes the agent's beliefs. α can be understood simply as an agent's degree of *alterity*, or propensity to see the "other" as an agent like itself. In simulations with values of α close to 0, we expect the partner's behavior to be dominated by its own "chemical" sensory input. Increasing α, we expect to see an agent's behavior being more heavily influenced by inputs from its partner, driving q^{own} to become sharper as soon as $q^{partner}$ does so. Past a certain threshold, this could spill over into premature overfitting.

Finally, note the α^2 in the second term of agent-level free energy (Equation (4)). This represents the notion that the agent is using "second-order theory of mind" or thinking about what its partner might be thinking about it (First-order ToM involves thinking about what some-one else is thinking or feeling; second-order ToM involves thinking about what someone is thinking or feeling about what someone else is thinking or feeling [72]). Here, p^{own} comes in as "my model of my partner's model of my behavior". It seems appropriate for the agent to believe the partner to possess the same level of alterity as itself; we then represent this as applying the rearranging function (the "squishing" of the probability distribution) twice, $\Theta_\alpha \bullet \Theta_\alpha = \Theta_{\alpha^2}$.

2.10. Goal Alignment

In this section we motivate the parameterization of the degree of goal alignment between agents.

Recall that $b^{\star\ own}$ is an arbitrary (exogenous) real vector; the implied desire distribution can have multiple maxima, leading to a generally challenging optimization task for the agent. Theory of Mind can help, but it can also make matters worse: if $b^{\star\ partner}$ also has multiple peaks, the partner's behavior can easily become *ambiguous*, i.e., it could appear coherent with multiple distinct positions. This ambiguity can easily lead the agent astray.

This problem is reduced if the agents can *align goals* with each other, that is, avoid pursuing targets that are not shared between them. We implement this as:

$$b^{\star\ own} \leftarrow b^{\star\ shared} + (1-\gamma)b^{\star\ own}_{private} \tag{6}$$

$$b^{\star\ partner} \leftarrow b^{\star\ shared} + (1-\gamma)b^{\star\ partner}_{private} \tag{7}$$

where γ is a parameter representing the degree of alignment between this specific agent pair, and we assume each agent has knowledge of what goals are shared vs private to itself or its partner. That is, with $\gamma = 0$, the agent is equally interested in its private goals and in the shared ones (and assumes the same for the partner); with $\gamma = 0$, the agent is solely interested in the shared goals (and assumes the same for the partner).

This operation may seem quite artificial, especially as it implies a "leap of faith" on the part of the agent to effectively change its expectations about the partner's behavior (Equation (6)). However, if we accept this assumption, we see that the task is made easier: in the general case, alignment reduces the agent-specific goal ambiguity, leading to better ability to focus and less positional ambiguity coming from the partner. Of course, one can construct examples where alignment does not help or even hurts; for instance, if both agents share all of their peaks, alignment not only will not help reduce ambiguity, but it can make the peaks sharper and hard to find. And as we will see, in the context of the system-level model, alignment becomes a natural capability.

In the present paper, for simplicity, we assume agents' shared goals are assigned exogenously. In light of the system-level model (Section 2.11), however, it is easy to see that such shared goals have a natural connection with the global optimum states. In this context, one can expect shared goals to emerge endogenously from the agents' interaction with their social environment over the "long run". This will be explored in future work.

2.11. System-Level Free Energy

Up until now, we have restricted ourselves to discussing our model at the level of individual agents and their local-scale interactions. We now take a higher vantage point and consider the implications of these local-scale interactions for global-scale system performance. We posit an ensemble of M identical copies of the two-agent subsystem above (i.e., 2M), each in its own independent environment, also assumed to be identical except for the position of the food source (see Figure 5).

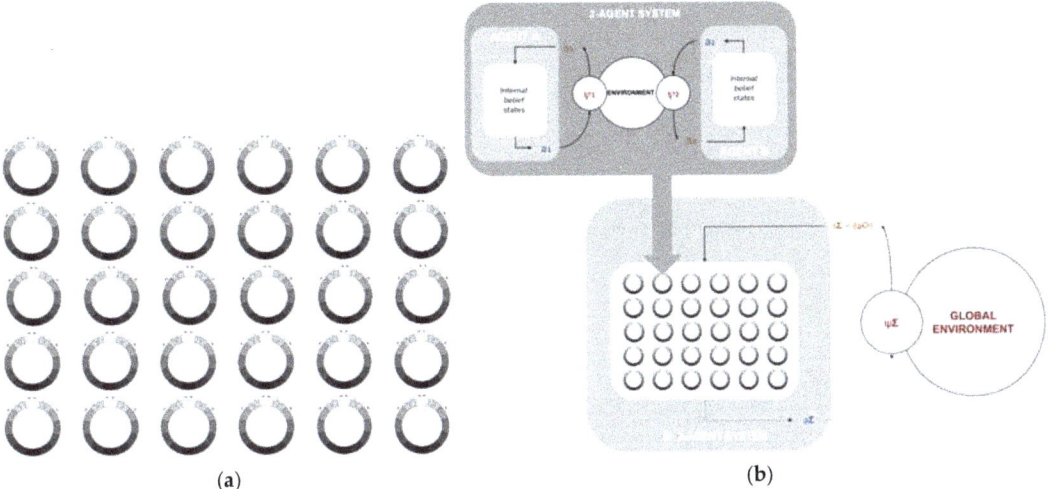

Figure 5. (a) M identical copies of the two-agent subsystem. (b) The M two-agent systems as internal states of a larger system, interacting with a global environment through the food sources (reinterpreted as sensory states) and some active mechanism (the dotted arrow lines for aΣ denote that this active mechanism is not defined in this paper).

From this vantage point, each of the 2M agents is now a "point particle", described only by its position ψ^i. The tuple $b^\Sigma = \left(\psi^i\right)_{i\in[1..2M]}$ is then the set of internal states of the system as a whole.

We will now assume that this set of internal states interacts with a global environment $\psi^\Sigma \in [0..N-1]$. We reinterpret the "food sources" as sensory states: $s^\Sigma = \left(\psi^i\right)_{i\in[1..2M]}$, where each ψ_0^i is assumed to correlate with ψ^Σ through some sensory mechanism. We further assume the system is capable to act back on the environment through some active mechanism a^Σ. This provides us with a complete system-level Markov blanket (Figure 5b), for which we can define a system-level free energy as

$$F^\Sigma = D_{KL}(q^{empirical}(\psi^{\Sigma'}|b^{\Sigma'}) \parallel p^\Sigma(\psi^{\Sigma'}, s^\Sigma|a^\Sigma, b^\Sigma)) \tag{8}$$

where $q^{empirical}(\psi^\Sigma|b^\Sigma) = \frac{1}{2M} \#\{\psi^i|\psi^i = \psi^\Sigma\}$, the system's "variational density", is simply the empirical distribution of the various agents' positions.

In this paper, we will not cover the "active" part of active inference at the global level—namely, the system action a^Σ remains undefined. We will instead consider a *single system-level inference step*, corresponding to fixed values of ψ^Σ, s^Σ. As we can see from the formulation above, this corresponds to optimizing ψ^i given ψ_0^i—that is, to the aggregate behavior of the 2M agents' over an *entire run* of the model at the individual level.

This in turn motivates defining the system's generative density as $p^\Sigma(\psi^{\Sigma'}, s^\Sigma|a^\Sigma, b^\Sigma) \propto exp\left\{-k\Sigma\left(\psi^i - \psi_0^i\right)^2\right\}$: given a set of internal states (agent positions), the system "expects" it to have been produced by the agents moving towards the corresponding sensory states (food source). Thus, to the extent that the agents perform their local active inference tasks well, the system performs approximate Bayesian inference over this generative density, and we can evaluate the degree to which this inference is effective, by evaluating whether, and how quickly, F^Σ is minimized. We return to the topic of system-level (active) inference in the discussion.

2.12. Simulations

We have thus defined this system at two altitudes, enabling us to perform simulations at the agent level and analyze their implied performance at the system level (as measured by system-level free energy). We can now use this framework to analyze the extent to which the two novel agent-level cognitive capabilities we introduced ("Theory of Mind" and "Goal Alignment") increase the system's ability to perform approximate inference at local and global scales. To explore the effects of agent-level cognitive capabilities on collective performance, we create four experimental conditions according to a 2 × 2 (Theory of Mind × Goal Alignment) matrix: Model 1 (Baseline), Model 2 (Theory of Mind), Model 3 (Goal Alignment), and Model 4 (Theory of Mind and Goal Alignment; see Table 1).

Table 1. 2 × 2 (Theory of Mind × Goal Alignment) permutations of our model.

	−Theory of Mind	+Theory of Mind
−Goal Alignment	Model 1 (Baseline)	Model 2 (Theory of Mind, No Goal Alignment)
+Goal Alignment	Model 3 (Goal Alignment, No ToM)	Model 4 (Theory of Mind × Goal Alignment)

Throughout, we use the same two agents, Agent A and Agent B. To establish meaningful variation in agent performance at the individual-scale, we parameterize an agent's perceptiveness to the physical environment (i.e., to the reliability of the information derived from its "chemical sensors"), by assigning one agent with "strong" perceptiveness (Agent A—Strong;) and the other agent with "weak" perceptiveness (Agent B—Weak).

We assign each agent with two targets, one shared (Shared Target) and one unshared (individual target or Target A and Target B). Accordingly, we assume each agent's desire distributions have both a shared peak (corresponding to a Shared Target) and an unshared peak (corresponding to Target A or Target B). Throughout, we measure both the collective performance (system-level free energy), as well as individual performance (distance from their closest target). In addition, we also capture their end-state desire distribution.

We implement simulations in Python (V3.7) using Google Colab (V1.0.0). As noted above, our implementation draws upon and extends an existing AIF model implementation developed in Python (V2.7) by van Shaik [70]. To ensure that the agent behavior is not an artefact of their specific location in the environment, we run 180 runs for each simulation for each experimental condition by randomizing their starting locations throughout the environment. The environment size was held constant at 60 cells. To ensure that the agent behavior is not an artefact of initial conditions, we perform 180 runs for each simulation for each experimental condition by uniformly distributing their starting locations throughout the environment (three times per location), while preserving the distance between starting locations and target. This uniform distribution of initial conditions across the environment also corresponds to the "worst-case scenario" in terms of system-level specification of sensory inputs for a two-agent system, discussed in Section 2.11.

2.13. Model Parameters

Our four models were created by setting physical perceptiveness for the strong and weak agent and varying their ability to exhibit social perceptiveness and align goals. The parameter settings are summarized at the individual agent level as follows (see Figure 6 and Table 2):

- Model 1 contains a self-actualization loop driven by physical perceptiveness. Physical perceptiveness (individual skill parameter; range [0.01, 0.99]) is varied such that Agent A is endowed with strong perceptiveness (0.99) and Agent B is endowed with weak perceptiveness (0.05).
- Model 2 is made up of a self-actualization loop and a partner-actualization loop (instantiating ToM). The other-actualization loop is implemented by setting the value

of alterity (ToM or social perceptiveness parameter; range [0.01, 0.99]) as 0.20 for the weak agent and 0 for the strong agent. This parameterization helps the weak agent use social information to navigate the physical environment. These two loops implement a single (non-separable) free energy functional: The weak agent's inferences from their stronger partner's behavior serve to refine its beliefs about its position in the environment.

- Model 3 entails a self-actualization loop (but no partner-actualization loop) as well as enforces the pursuit of a common goal (set alignment = 1) by fully suppressing their unshared goals (alignment parameter; range [0,1]). In this simplified implementation, we assume that goal alignment is a relational/dyadic property such that both partners exhibit the same level of alignment towards each other. This is akin to partners fully exploring each other's targets and agreeing to pursue their common goal. Setting alignment lower than 1 will increase the relative weighting of unshared goals and cause them to compete with their shared goals.
- Model 4 includes both cognitive features: self- and partner-actualization loops for the weak agent (instantiating ToM; alterity = 0.2) and complete goal alignment between agents.

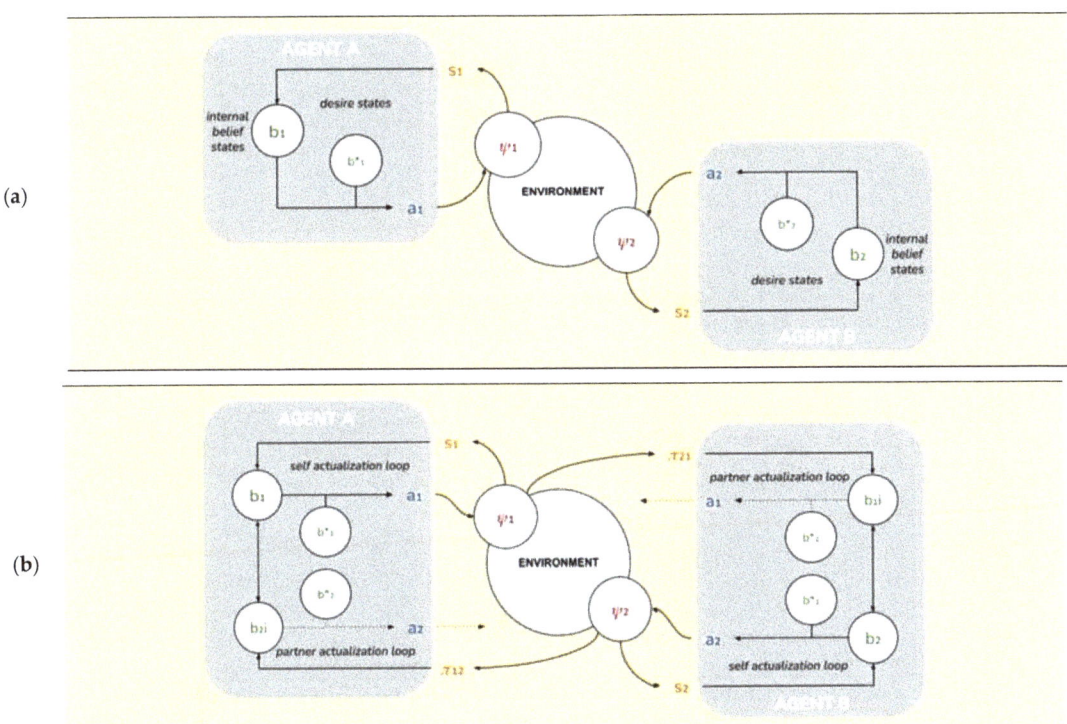

Figure 6. *Cont.*

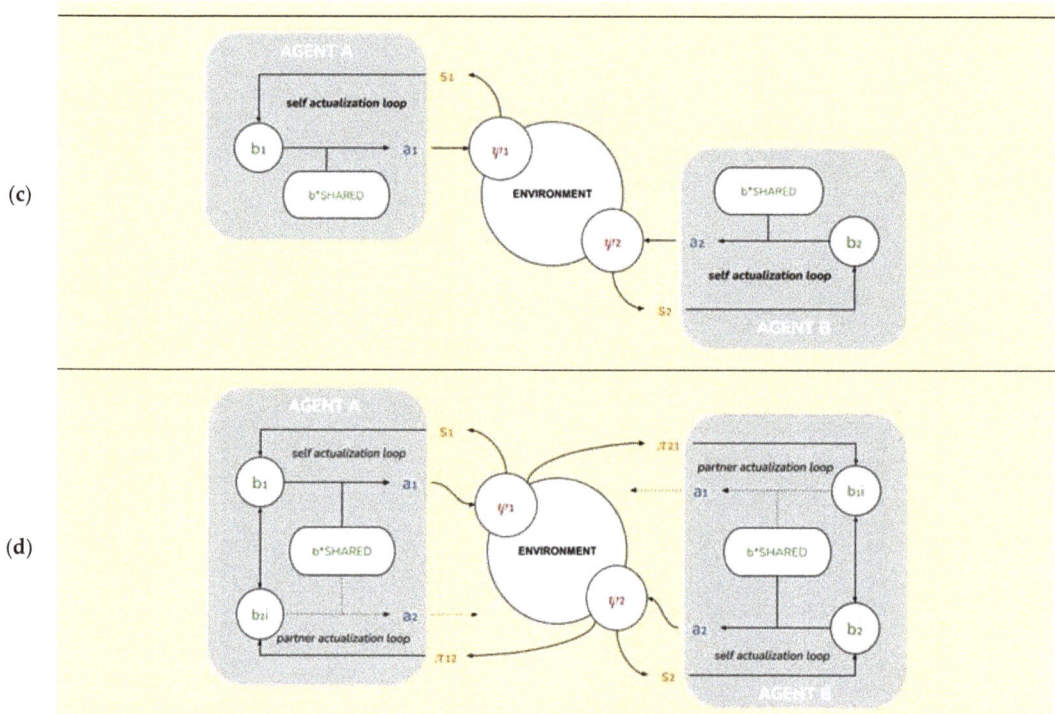

Figure 6. Models. (**a**) Model 1—Baseline with no direct interaction between agents; (**b**) Model 2—introduces "Theory of Mind" or a partner actualization loop; (**c**) Model 3—introduces Goal Alignment (b*SHARED); (**d**) Model 4—complete model with Theory of Mind with Goal Alignment.

Table 2. Parameterization of agent abilities Models 1–4.

	Model 1 Baseline		Model 2 Theory of Mind		Model 3 Goal Alignment		Model 4 ToM x Goal Alignment	
Parameter	Agent A	Agent B	Agent A	Agent B	Agent A	Agent B	Agent A	Agent B
Physical perceptiveness (0.01, 0.99)	0.99	0.05	0.99	0.05	0.99	0.05	0.99	0.05
Alterity, α (0.01, 0.99)	0.00	0.00	0.00	0.20 *	0.00	0.00	0.00	0.20 *
Goal Alignment, γ (0, 1)	0	0	0	0	1	1	1	1

* Alternative results for simulations with alterity set at $\alpha = 0.5$ exhibit a similar pattern of results for Model 2 and Model 4.

3. Results

3.1. Illustration of Agent-Level Behavior

In Figure 7, we show typical results from a single run of a single two-agent subsystem (Model 4: ToM with Goal Alignment) to illustrate qualitatively how the two cognitive capabilities introduced enable agent-level performance. In this example, Goal Alignment enters the picture at the outset; although each agent has two targets, they both only ever pursue their shared target.

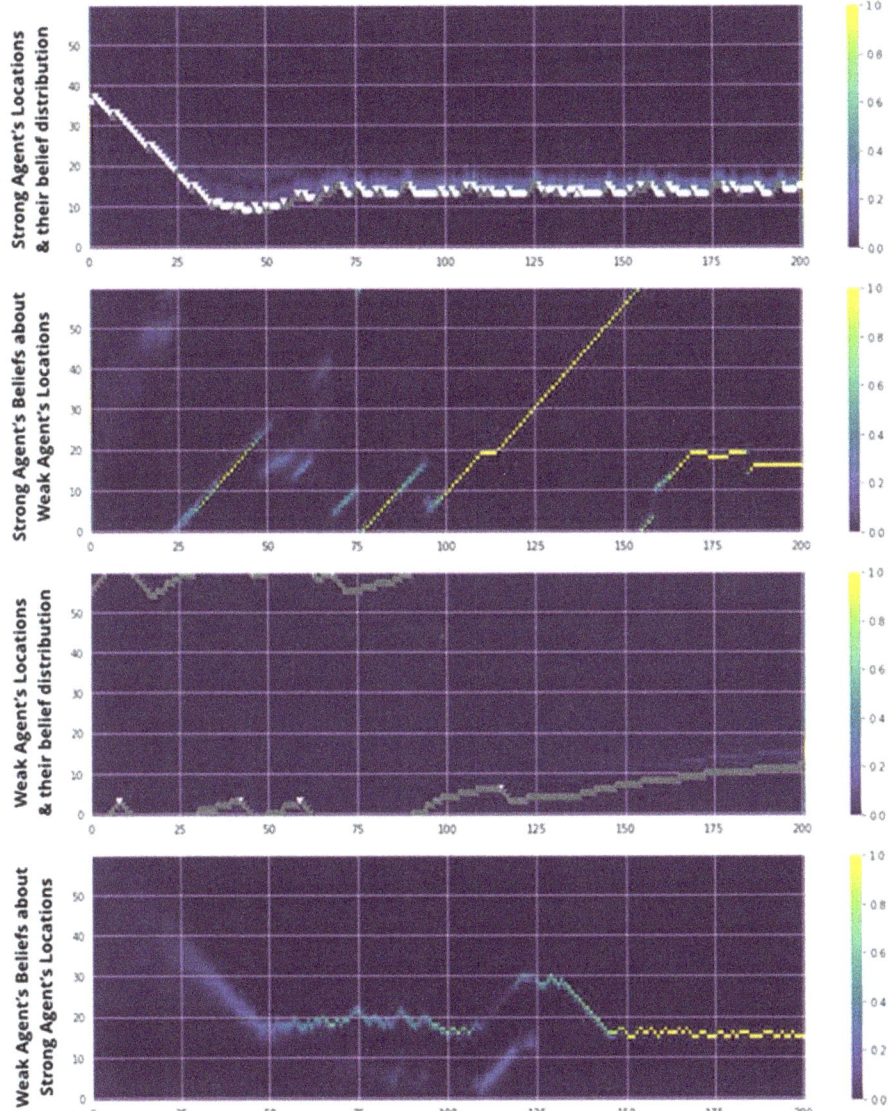

Figure 7. Results from a single run of Model 4 over 200 epochs. Agents' Shared Target position is set at location 15. Actual agent positions are illustrated as single dots for each epoch on the top graph, colored white when s = 1 and gray when s = 0. The background of the top graphs plots the agents' belief distribution of their own position, from dark blue (0) to bright yellow (1). The bottom graphs plot the agents' belief distribution of their partner's position, on the same scale.

The evolution of the two agents' behavior and beliefs over this run demonstrates the key features of interplay between sensory and partner inputs, and how ToM moderates the influence of partner inputs on an agent's behavior. Using its high perceptiveness, A identifies its own position around epoch 25–50, and quickly thereafter, directs itself towards the food position and remains stable there (top left). Meanwhile, for most of the run, B has no strong sense of its own position, and therefore its movement is highly random and undirected; at around epoch 150, it finally starts exhibiting a sharper (light blue) belief and converging to the target (top right). This is the same moment when B is finally able to disambiguate A's behavior (from green to yellow), which, via ToM, enables B's belief to become sharper (bottom right). Meanwhile, A can't make sense of B's random actions: the partner distribution it infers is unstable. But because A has ToM = 0, it doesn't take any of these misleading cues into account when deciding its own beliefs (bottom left).

3.2. Simulation Results

Model 1 lends face validity to the two-agent simulation setup. Figure 8 (Row 1, Model 1) demonstrates that, on average, the strong agent (endowed with high physical perceptiveness) converges to an end-state belief faster more accurately (closer to one of their individual targets) than the weak agent with severely diminished physical perceptiveness. This difference in individual performance can be attributed to the stark difference in agents' ability to form strong beliefs about the location of their target (see Figure 8: Row 2, Model 1). Agents show no clear preference for either shared or unshared targets (Figure 8: Row 3, Model 1).

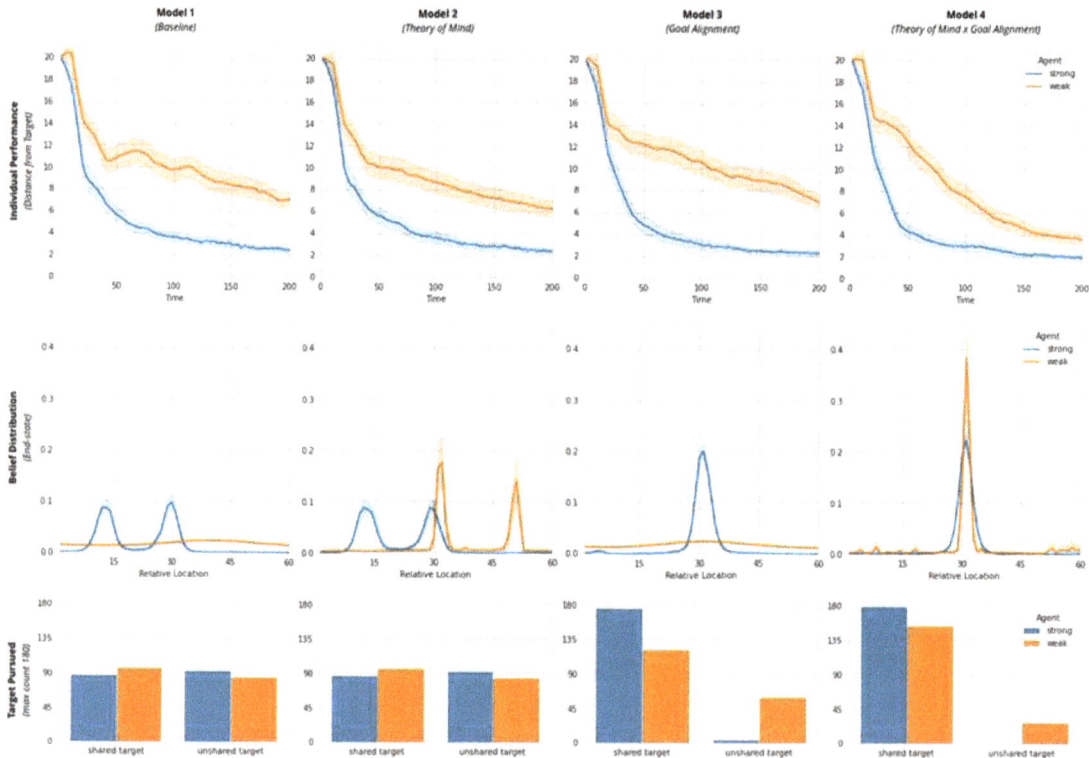

Figure 8. Simulation results of Agent A (strong; blue) and Agent B (weak; orange) in all four models. Row 1: Individual performance as time taken to reach a target position. Row 2: End state belief distribution of target location (Shared Target = 30; A's Target = 15; B's Target = 45). Row 3: Distribution of targets pursued in 180 runs.

In model 2, the weak agent possesses 'Theory of Mind'. This allows it to infer information about their own location in the environment by observing their partner's actions. This is evidenced by the emergence of two-sharp peaks in the weak agent's end-state belief distribution (Figure 8: Row 2, Model 2). Consequently, we see an improvement in the weak agent's individual performance (the agent converges faster on an end-state belief faster than in Model 1). Collective performance (Figure 9: System's free energy) does not appear to improve between Model 1 and Model 2. This may be because agents solely focus on achieving their individual goals (and do not understand any distinction between individual and system level goals). This is evidenced by the fact that of the 180 simulation runs each of Model 1 and Model 2, both agents end up pursuing their shared and unshared targets with roughly equal probability (Figure 8: Row 3, Model 1 and 2).

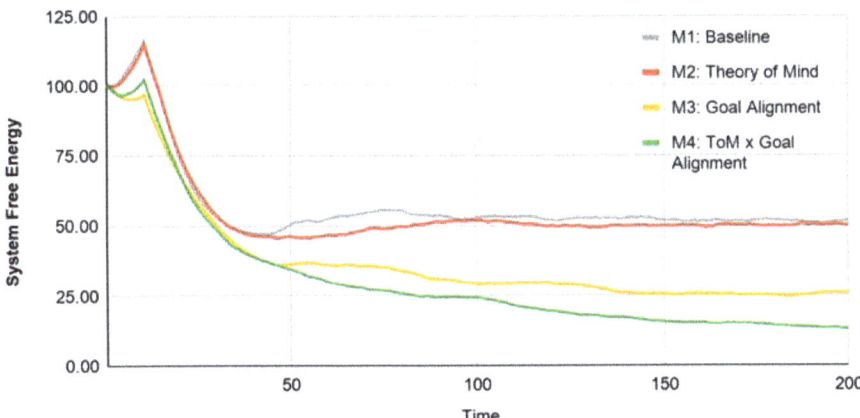

Figure 9. Actual system-level free energy F^Σ under each of the four models. Lower free energy denotes higher system performance. To the extent that the system is able to reduce its free energy over time (i.e., mimicking gradient descent on F^Σ), it can be interpreted as performing a single inference step of the active inference loop.

In Model 3, when both agents possess an ability for Goal Alignment, but the weak agent does not have the benefit of Theory of Mind, we see that both agents are biased towards pursuing the shared system goal (Figure 8: Row 3, Model 3). Accordingly, at the system level we see naturally higher collective performance—Model 3 clearly has lower system-level free energy compared to both Model 1 and Model 2 (see Figure 9). At the individual-level, however, the weak agent performs worse on average than it did in Model 2 and converges more slowly towards its goals (Figure 8: Row 1, Model 3). It appears that Goal Alignment helps improve system performance by reducing the ambiguity of multiple possible targets, but Goal Alignment does not help the weak agent compensate for low physical perceptiveness.

Finally, as expected, in Model 4, which combines Theory of Mind and Goal Alignment, we see a clear improvement in both individual and collective performance (Figure 8: Row 1, Model 4 and Figure 9: Model 4, respectively). The combination of Theory of Mind (for the weak agent) and Goal Alignment (for both agents) appears to enable the weak agent to overcome its poor physical perceptiveness and converge on a single unambiguous end-state belief. This achievement is illustrated by the sharp and overlapping single-peaked end-state belief structure achieved by both agents in model 4 (Figure 8: Row 2, Model 4) (We thank the anonymous reviewer for pushing us to consider the reasons why the end-state belief distribution for the weak agent is more sharply peaked. We didn't have any a priori expectation for this particular pattern of result. Our best guess is that this is an artefact of the weak agent iteratively engaging in 'Theory of Mind' based-estimation of its belief-distribution from the strong agent actions. From the perspective of the weak agent, the strong agent quickly converges near the goal state and spends more time in the vicinity of the peak. Thus, the weak agent is very likely to accrue higher levels of confidence within this relatively narrow vicinity. On the other hand, the stronger agent has no ToM and is only influenced by its direct perception of the environment.). This model suggests that collective performance is highest when individual agents' individual states align with the global system state.

4. Discussion

A formal understanding of collective intelligence in complex adaptive systems requires a formal description, within a single multiscale framework, of how the behavior of a composite system and its subsystem components co-inform each other to produce behavior that cannot be explained at any single scale of analysis. In this paper we make a contribution toward this type of formal grasp of collective intelligence, by using AIF to posit a computational model that connects individual-level constraints and capabilities of autonomous agents to collective-level behavior. Specifically, we provide an explicit, fully specified two-scale system where free energy minimization occurs at both scales, and where the aggregate behavior of agents at the faster/smaller scale can be rigorously identified with the belief-optimization (a.k.a. "inference") step at the slower/bigger scale. We introduce social cognitive capabilities at the agent level (Theory of Mind and Goal Alignment), which we implement directly through AIF. Further, illustrative results of this novel approach suggest that such capabilities of individual agents are directly associated with improvements in the system's ability to perform approximate Bayesian inference or minimize variational free energy. Significantly, improvements in global-scale inference are greatest when local-scale performance optima of individuals align with the system's global expected state (e.g., Model 4). Crucially, all of this occurs "bottom-up", in the sense that our model does not provide exogenous constraints or incentives for agents to behave in any specific way; the system-level inference emerges as a product of self-organizing AIF agents endowed with simple social cognitive mechanisms. The operation of these mechanisms improves agent-level outcomes by enhancing agents' ability to minimize free energy in an environment populated by other agents like it.

Of course, our account does not preclude or dismiss the operation of "top-down" dynamics, or the use of exogenous incentives or constraints to engineer specific types of individual and collective behavior. Rather, our approach provides a principled and mechanistic account of bio-cognitive systems in which "bottom-up" and "top-down" mechanisms may meaningfully interplay to inform accounts of behavior such as collective intelligence [4]. Our results suggest that models such as these may help establish a mechanistic understanding of how collective intelligence evolves and operates in real-life systems, and provides a plausible lower bound for the kind of agent-level cognitive capabilities that are required to successfully implement collective intelligence in such systems.

4.1. We Demonstrate AIF as a Viable Mathematical Framework for Modelling Collective Intelligence as a Multiscale Phenomenon

This work demonstrates the viability of AIF as a mathematical language that can integrate across scales of a composite bio-cognitive system to predict behavior. Existing multiscale formulations of AIF [39,40], while more immediately useful for understanding the behavior of docile subsystem components like cells in a multicellular organism or neurons in the brain, do not yet offer clear predictions about the behavior of collectives composed of highly autonomous AIF agents that engage in reciprocal self-evidencing with each other as well as with the physical (non-social) environment [43]. What's more, existing toy simulations of multiscale AIF engineer collective behavior as a predestination—either as a prior in an agent's generative model [9], or by default of an environment that consists solely of other agents [7,8]. We build upon these accounts by using AIF to first posit the minimal information-theoretical patterns (or "adaptive priors"; see [42]) that would likely emerge at the level of the individual agent to allow that agent to persist and flourish in an environment populated by other AIF agents [58]. We then examine the relationship between these local-scale patterns and collective behavior as a process of Bayesian inference across multiple scales. Our models show that collective intelligence can emerge endogenously in a simple goal-directed task from interaction between agents endowed with suitably sophisticated cognitive abilities (and without the need for exogenous manipulation or incentivization).

Key to our proposal is the suggestion that collective intelligence can be understood as a dynamical process of (active) inference at the global-scale of a composite system. We operationalize self-organization of the collective as a process of free energy minimization or approximate Bayesian inference based on sensory (but not active) states (for a previous attempt to operationalize collective behavior as both active and sensory inference, see [69]). In a series of four models, we demonstrate the responsiveness of this system-level measure to learning effects over time; the progression of each Model exhibits a pattern akin to a gradient descent on free energy, evoking the notion that a system that performs (active) Bayesian inference. Further, stepwise increases in cognitive sophistication at the individual level show a clear reduction in free energy, particularly between Model 1 (Baseline) and Model 4 (Theory of Mind x Goal Alignment). These illustrative results suggest a formal, causal link between behavioral processes across multiple scales of a complex adaptive system.

Going further, we can imagine an extension of this model where the collective system interacts with a non-trivial environment, but at a slower time scale, such that a complete simulation run of all 2M agents corresponds to a single belief optimization step for the whole system, after which it acts on the environment and receives sensory information from it (manifested, for example, as changes in the agents' food sources). In this extended model (see Figure 10), and if the agent-specific parameters (alterity/Theory of Mind (α), and Goal Alignment (γ)) could be made endogenous (either via selective mechanisms via some other learning mechanisms; see [48,73]) we would expect to see the system finding (non-zero) values of these parameters that optimize its free energy minimization. For example, it is likely that a system would select for higher values of γ (Goal Alignment) when both agents' end-state beliefs and actual target locations mutually cohere, or higher values of α for agents with weaker perceptiveness. Interestingly, this would show that degrees of Theory of Mind and Goal Alignment are capabilities that would be selected for or boosted at these longer time scales, providing empirical support for the heuristic arguments made for their existence in our model and in human collective intelligence research more generally [4].

4.2. AIF Sheds Light on Dynamical Operation of Mechanisms That Underwrite Collective Intelligence

In this way, AIF offers a paradigm through which to move beyond the methodological constraints associated with experimental analyses of the relationship between local interactions and collective behavior [21]. Even our very rudimentary 2-Agent AIF model proposed here offers insight into the dynamic operation and function of individual cognitive mechanisms for individual and collective level behavior. In distinct contrast to laboratory paradigms that usually rely on low-dimensional behavioral "snapshots" or summaries of behavior to verify linearly causal predictions about individual and collective phenomena, our computational model can be used to explore the effects of fine-grained, agent- and collective-level variations in cognitive ability on individual and collective behavior in real time.

For example, by parameterizing key cognitive abilities (Theory of Mind and Goal Alignment), our model shows that it is not necessarily a case of "more is better" when it comes to cognitive mechanisms underlying adaptive social behavior and collective intelligence. If an agent's level of social perceptiveness (Theory of Mind) were too low, it is likely that agents would miss vital performance-relevant information about the environment populated by other agents; if an agent's Theory of Mind were too high, it may instead over-index on partner belief states as an affordance for own beliefs (a scenario of "blind leading the blind"). We show that canonical cognitive abilities such as Theory of Mind and Goal Alignment can function across multiple scales to stabilize and reduce the computational uncertainty of an environment made up of other AIF agents, but only when these abilities are optimally tuned to a "goldilocks" level that is suitable to performance in that specific environment.

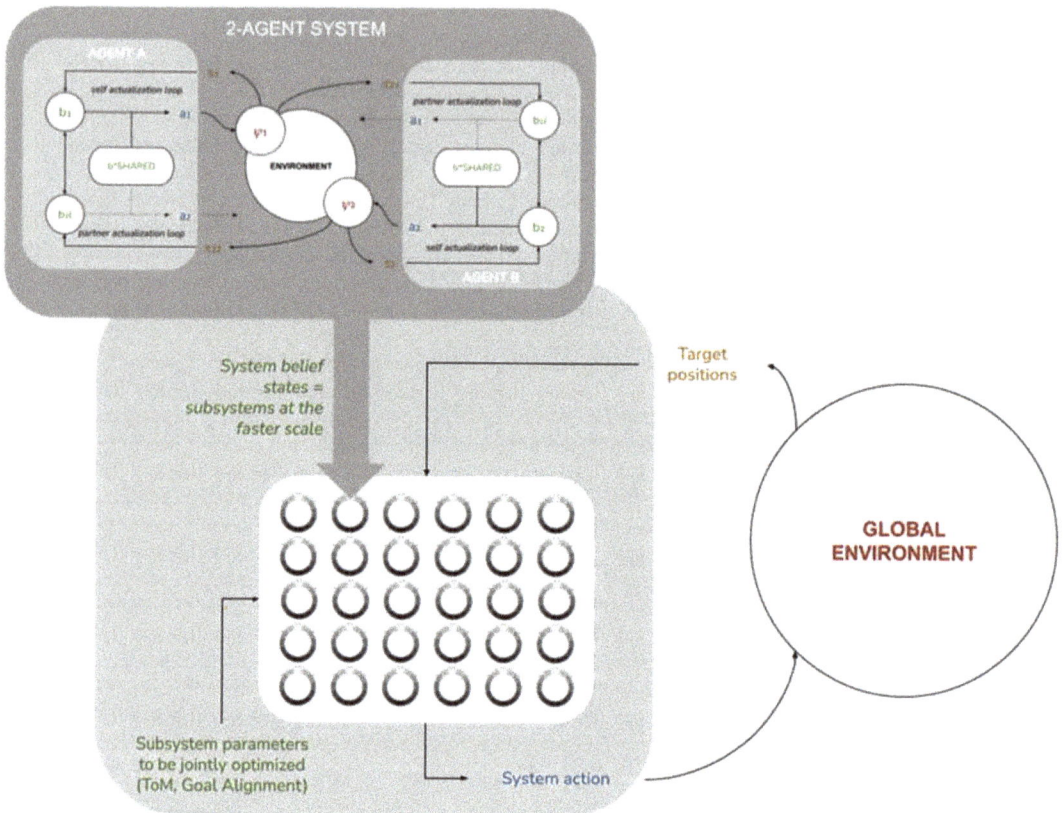

Figure 10. A notional complete two-scale model where agent-specific parameters are endogenized. This would entail parameters of subsystem components (Theory of Mind and Goal Alignment of each 2-agent system) being jointly optimized to inform a system action.

The essence of this proposal is captured by empirical research of attentional processes of human agents that engage in sophisticated joint action [74,75]. For instance, athletes in novice basketball teams are found to devote more attentional resources to tracking and monitoring their own teammates, while expert teams spend less time attending to each other and more time instead attending to the socio-technical task environment [76]. Viewed from the perspective of AIF, in both novice and expert teams alike, agents likely differentially deploy physical and social perceptiveness at levels that make sense for pursuing collective performance in a given situation; novices may stand to gain more from attending to (and therefore learning from) their teammates (recall our Agent B in Model 2 who leverages Theory of Mind to overcome weak physical perceptiveness, for example); while experts might stand to gain more from down-regulating social perceptiveness and redirecting limited attentional resources to physical perception of the task or (adversarial) social environment [77,78].

As evidence in organizational psychology and management suggests, (and outlined in the introduction), it is likely that social perceptiveness may indeed be an important factor (among many) that underwrites collective intelligence. But this may be especially the case in the context of unacquainted teams of "WEIRD" experimental subjects [79] who coordinate for a limited number of hours in a contrived laboratory setting [3]. If the experimental task were to be translated to a real-world performance setting (e.g., one involving high-stakes or elite performance requirements), or if that same team of experimental subjects were to persist over time beyond the lab in a randomly fluctuating environment, it is conceivable that a premium for social perceptiveness may give way to demands for other types of abilities needed to continue to gain performance-relevant information from the task environment (e.g., through physical perceptiveness of the task environment). Viewed from this perspective, the true "special sauce" of collective intelligence (and individual intelligence, for that matter; see [80]) may turn out not to be one or other discrete or reified individual or team level ability per se (e.g., social perceptiveness), but instead a collective ability to nimbly adjust the volumes of multiple parameters to foster specific information-theoretic patterns conducive to minimizing free energy across multiple scales and over specific, performance-relevant time periods.

In this spirit, the computational approach we adopt here under AIF affords a dynamical and situational perspective on team performance that may offer important insights into long-standing and nascent hypotheses concerning the causal mechanisms of collective intelligence. For instance, our model is well positioned to investigate the long-proposed (but hitherto unsubstantiated) claim that successful team performance, and by extension, collective intelligence, depends on balancing a tradeoff between cognitive diversity and cognitive efficiency [4] (p. 421). Likewise, our approach could help elucidate mechanisms and dynamics through which memory, attention, and reasoning capabilities become distributed through a collective, and the conditions in which these "transactive" processes [81] facilitate emergence of intelligent behavior [77,82,83]. In either case, our model would simply require specification with the appropriate individual-level cognitive abilities or priors. For example, to better understand the causal relationship between transactive knowledge systems and collective intelligence, our model could leverage recent empirical research that observes a connection between individual agents' metacognitive abilities (e.g., perception of others' skills, focus, and goals), the formation of transactive knowledge systems, and a collective's ability to adapt to a changing task environment [83]. On an important and related note to these opportunities for future research, efforts to simulate human collective intelligence should strive to develop models composed of two or more agents to better mimic human-like coordination dynamics [50,84].

4.3. Increases in System Performance Correspond with Alignment between an Agent's Local and Global Optima

A key insight from our models, and worthy of further investigation, is that the greatest improvement in collective intelligence (Model 4; measured by global-scale inference) occurs when local-scale performance optima of individuals align with the system's global expected state. This effect can be understood as individuals jointly implementing approximate Bayesian inference of the system's expectations. In effect, our model suggests that multi-scale alignment between lower- and higher-order states may contribute to the emergence of collective intelligence.

Alignment between local and global states might sound like an obvious prerequisite for collective intelligence, particularly for more docile AIF agents such as neurons or cells (it is near impossible to imagine a scenario in which a neuron or cell could meaningfully persist without being spatially aligned with a superordinate agent; see [9]). But our model exemplifies a more subtle form of alignment, based on a loose coupling between scales through a system's generative model (Section 2.11), enabling the extension of this idea to scenarios where the local and global optimizations may be taking place in arbitrarily distinct and abstract state spaces [49,51]. By now it is well understood in brain and behavioral sciences that coordinated human behavior relies for its stability and efficacy on an intricate web of biologically evolved physiological and cognitive mechanisms [85,86], as well as culturally evolved affordances of language, norms, and institutions [87]. But precisely how these various mechanisms and affordances—particularly those that are separated across scales—coordinate in real or evolutionary time to enable human collective phenomena remains poorly understood [39,73,88].

Computational models, such as the one we have presented here, that are capable of formally representing multiscale alignment may help reorganize and clarify causal relationships between the various hypothesized physiological, cognitive, and cultural mechanisms hypothesized to underpin human collective behavior [14]. For example, a computational model such as the one proposed here could conceivably be adapted to help more systematically test the burgeoning hypothesis that coordination between basal physiological, metabolic and homeostatic processes at one scale of organization and linguistically mediated processes of interaction and exchange at another scale determine fundamental dynamics of individual and collective behavior [88–90].

Future research should aspire to examine causal connections between a fuller range of meaningful scales of behavior. In the case of human collectives, meaningful scales of behavior could extend from the basal mechanisms of physiological energy, movement, and emotional regulation on the micro scale [91,92], to linguistically- (and now digitally-) mediated social informational systems at the meso scale [93] to global socio-ecological systems at the macro scale [94–97]. As we have demonstrated here, the key requirement for the development of such multiscale models under AIF is faithful construction of the appropriate generative models at each scale. These models provide the mechanistic "missing links" between AIF and the phenomena to be explained—a task that will require tremendously innovative and intelligent collective behavior on the part of a diverse range of agents.

The patterns that crop up again and again in successful space are there because they are in fundamental accord with characteristics of the human creature. They allow him to function as a human. They emphasize his essence—he is at once an individual and a member of a group. They deny neither his individuality nor his inclination to bond into teams. They let him be what he is.

- DeMarco and Lister [98] (1987, p.90)

Author Contributions: Conceptualization, R.K., J.T. and P.G.; methodology, R.K., P.G. and J.T.; software, R.K. and P.G.; validation, R.K., P.G.; formal analysis, R.K.; investigation, R.K., P.G. and J.T.; resources, R.K., J.T. and P.G.; data curation, P.G. and R.K.; writing—original draft preparation, J.T. & R.K.; writing—review and editing, and J.T, R.K. and P.G.; visualization, P.G., R.K. and J.T. All authors have read and agreed to the published version of the manuscript.

Funding: This research received no external funding.

Data Availability Statement: Model code can be found and implemented via this link to Google Colab: https://colab.research.google.com/drive/1CKdPTy8LD-Mpxc7kXy47m_fmCq44BT5u?usp=sharing (accessed on 15 June 2021).

Acknowledgments: The authors acknowledge the thoughtful and constructive feedback from all anonymous reviewers.

Conflicts of Interest: The authors declare no conflict of interest.

References

1. Kelso, J.A.S. *Dynamic Patterns: The Self-Organization of Brain and Behavior*; MIT Press: Cambridge, MA, USA, 1995; ISBN 0262611317.
2. Riley, M.A.; Richardson, M.J.; Shockley, K.; Ramenzoni, V.C. Interpersonal synergies. *Front. Psychol.* **2011**, *2*, 38. [CrossRef]
3. Woolley, A.W.; Chabris, C.F.; Pentland, A.; Hashmi, N.; Malone, T.W. Evidence for a Collective Intelligence Factor in the Performance of Human Groups. *Science* **2010**, *330*, 686. [CrossRef]
4. Woolley, A.W.; Aggarwal, I.; Malone, T.W. Collective Intelligence and Group Performance. *Curr. Dir. Psychol. Sci.* **2015**, *24*, 420–424. [CrossRef]
5. Malone, T.W.; Bernstein, M.S. Introduction. In *Handbook of Collective Intelligence*; MIT Press: Cambridge, MA, USA, 2015.
6. Bonabeau, E. Agent-based modeling: Methods and techniques for simulating human systems. *Proc. Natl. Acad. Sci. USA* **2002**, *99*, 7280–7287. [CrossRef]
7. Friston, K.J.; Frith, C.D. A Duet for one. *Conscious. Cogn.* **2015**, *36*, 390–405. [CrossRef] [PubMed]
8. Friston, K.J.; Frith, C.D. Active inference, Communication and hermeneutics. *Cortex* **2015**, *68*, 129–143. [CrossRef] [PubMed]
9. Palacios, E.R.; Razi, A.; Parr, T.; Kirchhoff, M.D.; Friston, K. On Markov blankets and hierarchical self-organisation. *J. Theor. Biol.* **2020**, *486*, 110089. [CrossRef] [PubMed]

10. Pratt, S.C.; Mallon, E.B.; Sumpter, D.J.; Franks, N.R. Quorum sensing, recruitment, and collective decision-making during colony emigration by the ant Leptothorax albipennis. *Behav. Ecol. Sociobiol.* **2002**, *52*, 117–127. [CrossRef]
11. Franks, N.R.; Dornhaus, A.; Fitzsimmons, J.P.; Stevens, M. Speed versus accuracy in collective decision making. *Proc. R. Soc. London. Ser. B Biol. Sci.* **2003**, *270*, 2457–2463. [CrossRef] [PubMed]
12. Constant, A.; Ramstead, M.J.D.; Veissière, S.P.L.; Friston, K. Regimes of expectations: An active inference model of social conformity and human decision making. *Front. Psychol.* **2019**, *10*. [CrossRef]
13. Ramstead, M.J.D.; Veissière, S.P.L.; Kirmayer, L.J. Cultural affordances: Scaffolding local worlds through shared intentionality and regimes of attention. *Front. Psychol.* **2016**, *7*, 1–21. [CrossRef]
14. Veissière, S.P.L.; Constant, A.; Ramstead, M.J.D.; Friston, K.J.; Kirmayer, L.J. Thinking Through Other Minds: A Variational Approach to Cognition and Culture. *Behav. Brain Sci.* **2019**. [CrossRef]
15. Baron-Cohen, S.; Tager-Flusberg, H.; Cohen, D.J. Understanding other Minds: Perspectives from autism. In *Most of the Chapters in This Book Were Presented in Draft form at a Workshop in Seattle*; Oxford University Press: Oxford, UK, 1994.
16. Tomasello, M.; Carpenter, M.; Call, J.; Behne, T.; Moll, H. Understanding and sharing intentions: The origins of cultural cognition. *Behav. Brain Sci.* **2005**, *28*, 675–691, discussion 691–735. [CrossRef] [PubMed]
17. Chikersal, P.; Tomprou, M.; Kim, Y.J.; Woolley, A.W.; Dabbish, L. Deep structures of collaboration: Physiological correlates of collective intelligence and group satisfaction. In Proceedings of the 2017 ACM Conference on Computer Supported Cooperative Work and Social Computing, Portland, OR, USA, 25 February 2017; pp. 873–888. [CrossRef]
18. Engel, D.; Malone, T.W. Integrated information as a metric for group interaction. *PLoS ONE* **2018**, *13*, 1–19. [CrossRef] [PubMed]
19. Riedl, C.; Kim, Y.J.; Gupta, P.; Malone, T.W.; Woolley, A.W. Quantifying Collective Intelligence in Human Groups. *Proc. Natl. Acad. Sci. USA* **2021**, *118*, e2005737118. [CrossRef] [PubMed]
20. Rozin, P. Social psychology and science: Some lessons from solomon asch. *Personal. Soc. Psychol. Rev.* **2001**, *5*, 2–14. [CrossRef]
21. Kozlowski, S.W.J.; Chao, G.T. Unpacking team process dynamics and emergent phenomena: Challenges, conceptual advances, and innovative methods. *Am. Psychol.* **2018**, *73*, 576–592. [CrossRef] [PubMed]
22. O'Bryan, L.; Beier, M.; Salas, E. How approaches to animal swarm intelligence can improve the study of collective intelligence in human teams. *J. Intell.* **2020**, *8*, 9. [CrossRef] [PubMed]
23. Richardson, M.J.; Schmidt, R.C.; Richardson, M.J. Dynamics of interpersonal coordination. *Coord. Neural. Behav. Soc. Dyn.* **2008**, 281–308.
24. Kelso, J.A.S. Coordination dynamics. In *Encyclopedia of Complexity and Systems Science*; Springer: Berlin/Heidelberg, Germany, 2009; pp. 1537–1565.
25. Coey, C.A.; Varlet, M.; Richardson, M.J. Coordination dynamics in a socially situated nervous system. *Front. Hum. Neurosci.* **2012**, *6*, 164. [CrossRef] [PubMed]
26. Gorman, J.C.; Dunbar, T.A.; Grimm, D.; Gipson, C.L. Understanding and modeling teams as dynamical systems. *Front. Psychol.* **2017**, *8*, 1–18. [CrossRef]
27. Reinero, D.A.; Dikker, S.; Van Bavel, J.J. Inter-brain synchrony in teams predicts collective performance. *Soc. Cogn. Affect. Neurosci.* **2021**, *16*, 43–57. [CrossRef]
28. Gorman, J.C.; Amazeen, P.G.; Crites, M.J.; Gipson, C.L. Deviations from mirroring in interpersonal multifrequency coordination when visual information is occluded. *Exp. Brain Res.* **2017**, *235*, 1209–1221. [CrossRef]
29. Wiltshire, T.J.; Butner, J.E.; Fiore, S.M. Problem-Solving Phase Transitions During Team Collaboration. *Cogn. Sci.* **2018**, *42*, 129–167. [CrossRef]
30. Wiltshire, T.J.; Steffensen, S.V.; Fiore, S.M. Multiscale movement coordination dynamics in collaborative team problem solving. *Appl. Ergon.* **2019**, *79*, 143–151. [CrossRef]
31. Zhang, M.; Kelso, J.A.S.; Tognoli, E. Critical diversity: Divided or united states of social coordination. *PLoS ONE* **2018**, *13*, e0193843. [CrossRef]
32. Demir, M.; Mcneese, N.J.; Gorman, J.C.; Cooke, N.J.; Myers, C.; Grimm, D.A. Exploration of Team Trust and Interaction in Human-Autonomy Teaming. *IEEE Trans. Hum. Mach. Syst.* **2017**. [CrossRef]
33. Friston, K.J. The free-energy principle: A unified brain theory? *Nat. Rev. Neurosci.* **2010**, *11*, 127–138. [CrossRef] [PubMed]
34. Friston, K.J. Life as we know it. *J. R. Soc. Interface* **2013**, *10*, 10. [CrossRef] [PubMed]
35. Friston, K.J. A free energy principle for a particular physics. *arXiv* **2019**, arXiv:1906.10184.
36. Buckley, C.L.; Kim, C.S.; McGregor, S.; Seth, A.K. The free energy principle for action and perception: A mathematical review. *J. Math. Psychol.* **2017**, *81*, 55–79. [CrossRef]
37. Friston, K.J.; Kilner, J.; Harrison, L. A free energy principle for the brain. *J. Physiol. Paris* **2006**, *100*, 70–87. [CrossRef]
38. Hohwy, J. The self-evidencing brain. *Nous* **2016**, *50*, 259–285. [CrossRef]
39. Ramstead, M.J.D.; Badcock, P.B.; Friston, K.J. Answering Schrödinger's question: A free-energy formulation. *Phys. Life Rev.* **2018**, *24*, 1–16. [CrossRef]
40. Kirchhoff, M.D.; Parr, T.; Palacios, E.; Friston, K.; Kiverstein, J. The markov blankets of life: Autonomy, active inference and the free energy principle. *J. R. Soc. Interface* **2018**, *15*. [CrossRef] [PubMed]
41. Hesp, C.; Ramstead, M.; Constant, A.; Badcock, P.; Kirchhoff, M.; Friston, K. A multi-scale view of the emergent complexity of life: A free-energy proposal. In *Evolution, Development and Complexity*; Springer: Berlin/Heidelberg, Germany, 2019; pp. 195–227.

42. Badcock, P.B.; Friston, K.J.; Ramstead, M.J.D. The hierarchically mechanistic mind: A free-energy formulation of the human psyche. *Phys. Life Rev.* **2019**, *31*, 104–121. [CrossRef]
43. Sims, M. How to count biological minds: Symbiosis, the free energy principle, and reciprocal multiscale integration. *Synthese* **2020**. [CrossRef]
44. Pearl, J. *Probabilistic Reasoning in Intelligent Systems: Networks of Plausible Inference*; Elsevier: Amsterdam, The Netherlands, 1988; ISBN 0080514898.
45. Friston, K.J. What is optimal about motor control? *Neuron* **2011**, *72*, 488–498. [CrossRef]
46. Haken, H. Synergetics. In *Self-Organizing Systems*; Springer: Berlin/Heidelberg, Germany, 1987; pp. 417–434.
47. Kirchhoff, M.D.; Kiverstein, J. How to determine the boundaries of the mind: A Markov blanket proposal. *Synthese* **2019**. [CrossRef]
48. Ramstead, M.J.D.; Constant, A.; Badcock, P.B.; Friston, K.J. Variational ecology and the physics of sentient systems. *Phys. Life Rev.* **2019**, *31*, 188–205. [CrossRef]
49. Clark, A. How to Knit Your Own Markov Blanket: Resisting the Second Law with Metamorphic Minds. *Philos. Predict. Coding* **2017**, 1–19. [CrossRef]
50. Zhang, M.; Beetle, C.; Kelso, J.A.S.; Tognoli, E. Connecting empirical phenomena and theoretical models of biological coordination across scales. *J. R. Soc. Interface* **2018**, *16*, 20190360. [CrossRef]
51. Krakauer, D.; Bertschinger, N.; Olbrich, E.; Flack, J.C.; Ay, N. The information theory of individuality. *Theory Biosci.* **2020**, *139*, 209–223. [CrossRef] [PubMed]
52. Ramstead, M.J.D. Have we lost our minds? An approach to multiscale dynamics in the cognitive sciences. Ph.D.'s Thesis, McGill University Libraries, Montréal, QC, Canada, 2019.
53. Searle, J.R. Minds and brains without programs. *Mindwaves* **1980**, *3*, 1–19.
54. Reia, S.M.; Amado, A.C.; Fontanari, J.F. Agent-based models of collective intelligence. *Phys. Life Rev.* **2019**, *31*, 320–331. [CrossRef]
55. Krafft, P.M. A Simple Computational Theory of General Collective Intelligence. *Top. Cogn. Sci.* **2019**, *11*, 374–392. [CrossRef] [PubMed]
56. Friston, K.J.; Daunizeau, J.; Kiebel, S.J. Reinforcement learning or active inference? *PLoS ONE* **2009**, *4*. [CrossRef]
57. Sajid, N.; Ball, P.J.; Parr, T.; Friston, K.J. Active Inference: Demystified and Compared. *Neural Comput.* **2021**, *44*, 1–39. [CrossRef]
58. Vasil, J.; Badcock, P.B.; Constant, A.; Friston, K.; Ramstead, M.J.D. A World Unto Itself: Human Communication as Active Inference. *Front. Psychol.* **2020**, *11*, 1–26. [CrossRef] [PubMed]
59. Hirschfeld, L.A. On a Folk Theory of Society: Children, Evolution, and Mental Representations of Social Groups. *Personal. Soc. Psychol. Rev.* **2001**, *5*, 107–117. [CrossRef]
60. Sperber, D. Intuitive and reflective beliefs. *Mind anguage* **1997**, *12*, 67–83. [CrossRef]
61. Yoshida, W.; Dolan, R.J.; Friston, K.J. Game theory of mind. *PLoS Comput. Biol.* **2008**, *4*. [CrossRef]
62. Press, W.H.; Dyson, F.J. Iterated Prisoner's Dilemma contains strategies that dominate any evolutionary opponent. *Proc. Natl. Acad. Sci. USA* **2012**, *109*, 10409–10413. [CrossRef]
63. Baron-Cohen, S.; Wheelwright, S.; Hill, J.; Raste, Y.; Plumb, I. The "Reading the Mind in the Eyes" Test revised version: A study with normal adults, and adults with Asperger syndrome or high-functioning autism. *J. Child Psychol. Psychiatry Allied Discip.* **2001**, *42*, 241–251. [CrossRef]
64. Dunbar, R.I.M. The Social Brain: Mind, Language, and Society in Evolutionary Perspective. *Annu. Rev. Anthropol.* **2003**, *32*, 163–181. [CrossRef]
65. Pesquita, A.; Whitwell, R.L.; Enns, J.T. Predictive joint-action model: A hierarchical predictive approach to human cooperation. *Psychol. Bull.* **2017**, *25*, 1751–1769. [CrossRef]
66. Angus, S.D.; Newton, J. Emergence of Shared Intentionality Is Coupled to the Advance of Cumulative Culture. *PLoS Comput. Biol.* **2015**, *11*, 1–12. [CrossRef] [PubMed]
67. Fields, C.; Levin, M. How Do Living Systems Create Meaning? *Philosophies* **2020**, *5*, 36. [CrossRef]
68. McGregor, S.; Baltieri, M.; Buckley, C.L. A Minimal Active Inference Agent. *arXiv* **2015**, arXiv:1503.04187.
69. Levchuk, G.; Pattipati, K.; Serfaty, D.; Fouse, A.; McCormack, R. *Active Inference in Multi-Agent Systems: Context-Driven Collaboration and Decentralized Purpose-Driven Team Adaptation*; 2018 AAAI Spring Symposium Series; AAAI: Menlo Park, CA, USA, 2018; pp. 157–165.
70. van Schaik, A. Python Implementation of a Minimal Active Inference Agent. 2018. Available online: https://github.com/vschaik/Active-Inference (accessed on 1 January 2021).
71. Friston, K. The free-energy principle: A rough guide to the brain? *Trends Cogn. Sci.* **2009**, *13*, 293–301. [CrossRef] [PubMed]
72. Westby, C.E. Social neuroscience and theory of mind. *Folia Phoniatr. Logop.* **2014**, *66*, 7–17. [CrossRef]
73. Badcock, P.B. Evolutionary systems theory: A unifying meta-theory of psychological science. *Rev. Gen. Psychol.* **2012**, *16*, 10–23. [CrossRef]
74. Sebanz, N.; Bekkering, H.; Knoblich, G. Joint action: Bodies and minds moving together. *Trends Cogn. Sci.* **2006**, *10*, 70–76. [CrossRef]
75. Vesper, C.; Abramova, E.; Bütepage, J.; Ciardo, F.; Crossey, B.; Effenberg, A.; Hristova, D.; Karlinsky, A.; McEllin, L.; Nijssen, S.R.R.; et al. Joint Action: Mental Representations, Shared Information and General Mechanisms for Coordinating with Others. *Front. Psychol.* **2017**, *07*, 1–7. [CrossRef] [PubMed]

76. Bourbousson, J.; R'Kiouak, M.; Eccles, D.W. The dynamics of team coordination: A social network analysis as a window to shared awareness. *Eur. J. Work Organ. Psychol.* **2015**, *24*, 742–760. [CrossRef]
77. Bourbousson, J.; Fortes-Bourbousson, M. How do Co-agents Actively Regulate their Collective Behavior States? *Front. Psychol.* **2016**, *7*, 1732. [CrossRef] [PubMed]
78. R'Kiouak, M.; Saury, J.; Durand, M.; Bourbousson, J. Joint action of a pair of rowers in a race: Shared experiences of effectiveness are shaped by interpersonal mechanical states. *Front. Psychol.* **2016**, *7*, 1–17. [CrossRef] [PubMed]
79. Henrich, J.; Heine, S.J.; Norenzayan, A. The weirdest people in the world? *Behav. Brain Sci.* **2010**, *33*, 61–83. [CrossRef]
80. Friston, K.; FitzGerald, T.; Rigoli, F.; Schwartenbeck, P.; O'Doherty, J.; Pezzulo, G. Active inference and learning. *Neurosci. Biobehav. Rev.* **2016**, *68*, 862–879. [CrossRef]
81. Wegner, D.M. Transactive memory: A contemporary analysis of the group mind. In *Theories of Group Behavior*; Springer: Berlin, Germany, 1987; pp. 185–208.
82. Semin, G.R.; Garrido, M.V. Socially Situated Cognition: Imagining New. In *Theory and Explanation in Social Psychology*; Guilford Press: New York, NY, USA, 2015; Volume 36, pp. 774–777.
83. Gupta, P.; Woolley, A.W. The Emergence of Collective Intelligence Behavior. In Proceedings of the Paper presented at the 8th ACM Collective Intelligence (CI) Conference, Virtual Event, Zurich, Switzerland, 18 June 2020.
84. Richardson, M.J.; Garcia, R.L.; Frank, T.D.; Gergor, M.; Marsh, K. Measuring group synchrony: A cluster-phase method for analyzing multivariate movement time-series. *Front. Physiol.* **2012**, *3*, 405. [CrossRef]
85. Frith, U.; Frith, C.D. The social brain: Allowing humans to boldly go where no other species has been. *Philos. Trans. R. Soc. B Biol. Sci.* **2010**, *365*, 165–176. [CrossRef]
86. Taylor, J.; Davis, A. Social Cohesion. In *The International Encyclopedia of Anthropology*; Wiley: Hoboken, NJ, USA, 2018; pp. 1–7.
87. Henrich, J. *The Secret of our Success: How Culture Is Driving Human Evolution, Domesticating Our Species, and Making Us Smarter*; Princeton University Press: Princeton, NJ, USA, 2015; ISBN 1400873290.
88. Taylor, J.; Cohen, E. Social bonding through joint action: When the team clicks. *OSF Pre Print* **2019**. [CrossRef]
89. Barrett, L.F.; Simmons, W.K. Interoceptive predictions in the brain. *Nat. Rev. Neurosci.* **2015**, *16*, 419–429. [CrossRef] [PubMed]
90. Krahé, C.; Springer, A.; Weinman, J.A.; Fotopoulou, A. The social modulation of pain: Others as predictive signals of salience-A systematic review. *Front. Hum. Neurosci.* **2013**, *7*, 386. [CrossRef]
91. Allen, M. Unravelling the Neurobiology of Interoceptive Inference. *Trends Cogn. Sci.* **2020**, *24*, 265–266. [CrossRef] [PubMed]
92. Barrett, L.F.; Quigley, K.S.; Hamilton, P. An active inference theory of allostasis and interoception in depression. *Philos. Trans. R. Soc. B* **2016**. [CrossRef]
93. Mesoudi, A. Cultural evolution: Integrating psychology, evolution and culture. *Curr. Opin. Psychol.* **2016**, *7*, 17–22. [CrossRef]
94. Doolittle, F.W.; Inkpen, A.S. Processes and patterns of interaction as units of selection: An introduction to ITSNTS thinking. *Proc. Natl. Acad. Sci. USA* **2018**, *115*, 4006–4014. [CrossRef]
95. Kaufmann, R. Gaianomics, or the self-designing Earth. In *The Great Redesign: Frameworks for the Future*; Schrader, M., Martens, V., Eds.; Edition NFO; Next Factory Ottensen: Hamburg, Germany, 2020; ISBN 9783948580841.
96. Rubin, S.; Parr, T.; Da Costa, L.; Friston, K. Future climates: Markov blankets and active inference in the biosphere: Future climates: Markov blankets and active inference in the biosphere. *J. R. Soc. Interface* **2020**, *17*, 13–16. [CrossRef]
97. Boik, J.C. Science-driven societal transformation, Part I: Worldview. *Sustainability* **2020**, *12*, 6881. [CrossRef]
98. Lister, T.R.; DeMarco, T. *Peopleware: Productive Projects and Teams*; Dorset House: New York, NY, USA, 1987; ISBN 0932633056.

Article

Equality and Freedom as Uncertainty in Groups

Jesse Hoey

David R. Cheriton School of Computer Science, Univeristy of Waterloo, Waterloo, ON N2L 3G1, Canada; jhoey@cs.uwaterloo.ca

Abstract: In this paper, I investigate a connection between a common characterisation of freedom and how uncertainty is managed in a Bayesian hierarchical model. To do this, I consider a distributed factorization of a group's optimization of free energy, in which each agent is attempting to align with the group and with its own model. I show how this can lead to equilibria for groups, defined by the capacity of the model being used, essentially how many different datasets it can handle. In particular, I show that there is a "sweet spot" in the capacity of a normal model in each agent's decentralized optimization, and that this "sweet spot" corresponds to minimal free energy for the group. At the sweet spot, an agent can predict what the group will do and the group is not surprised by the agent. However, there is an asymmetry. A higher capacity model for an agent makes it harder for the individual to learn, as there are more parameters. Simultaneously, a higher capacity model for the group, implemented as a higher capacity model for each member agent, makes it easier for a group to integrate a new member. To optimize for a group of agents then requires one to make a trade-off in capacity, as each individual agent seeks to decrease capacity, but there is pressure from the group to increase capacity of all members. This pressure exists because as individual agent's capacities are reduced, so too are their abilities to model other agents, and thereby to establish pro-social behavioural patterns. I then consider a basic two-level (dual process) Bayesian model of social reasoning and a set of three parameters of capacity that are required to implement such a model. Considering these three capacities as dependent elements in a free energy minimization for a group leads to a "sweet surface" in a three-dimensional space defining the triplet of parameters that each agent must use should they hope to minimize free energy as a group. Finally, I relate these three parameters to three notions of freedom and equality in human social organization, and postulate a correspondence between freedom and model capacity. That is, models with higher capacity, have more freedom as they can interact with more datasets.

Keywords: free energy; uncertainty; POMDP; active inference; emotion; affect control theory; sociology

Citation: Hoey, J. Equality and Freedom as Uncertainty in Groups. *Entropy* **2021**, *23*, 1384. https://doi.org/10.3390/e23111384

Academic Editors: Paul Badcock, Maxwell Ramstead, Zahra Sheikhbahaee and Axel Constant

Received: 16 August 2021
Accepted: 18 October 2021
Published: 22 October 2021

Publisher's Note: MDPI stays neutral with regard to jurisdictional claims in published maps and institutional affiliations.

Copyright: © 2021 by the author. Licensee MDPI, Basel, Switzerland. This article is an open access article distributed under the terms and conditions of the Creative Commons Attribution (CC BY) license (https://creativecommons.org/licenses/by/4.0/).

1. Introduction

My primary objective in this paper is to propose a computational model which may give insights into the deep level of cooperation observed in human groups. While much of economics and artificial intelligence have focussed on arbitrarily modifying a utility function (e.g., with incentives for "fairness" [1], "influence" [2], "envy" [3], or "altruism" [4,5]; see my review in [6]), this still requires an agent to solve an intractable social coordination problem:

"[...] a rational-choice model of collective action, in which individuals calculate that they will be better off cooperating with one another, vastly understates the degree of social cooperation that exists in human societies and misunderstands the motives that underlie it ([7], p. 439).

One possible explanation for how humans achieve this high level of cooperation is by figuring out who predicts, explains and generates what in a group, or how the epistemic labour is divided. While each individual can come up with some reasonable predictions, many of these will have flaws that can be uncovered by an opposing viewpoint, or will be invalidated by data. However, each individual will be overtaxed if asked to come up with, and compare, *every possible* solution. Therefore, the group will be more efficient if they spread out, each member trying to push a different viewpoint. The more viewpoints, the better. The search through epistemic space by the group to locate a position of minimal free energy will be handled by fanning out, but not so far apart that they cease to be a coherent group, as security is compromised. Intelligence, innovation, and learning therefore lie in diversity [8].

In this paper, I propose a computational model of this cooperation mechanism based on the management of uncertainty in a hierarchical Bayesian model. I show how agents that manage their uncertainty in the same way will have a "sweet spot" at which they best fit the group and the group best fits them. In order to make this more concrete, I use a two-level Bayesian model in which the "higher" level in the model represents *shared dynamic models of state and action based on cognitive social emotions*. These social emotional models are based on processual symbolic interactionist ideas arising in sociology [9]. I argue that these shared dynamics are useful to help a *group* of people find a free energy minimum, as they would be expected to do under the free energy principle (FEP) [10]. At this minimum, they are coordinated to the best degree possible: each individual fits the group and the group fits each individual as well as possible given variations in a huge variety of attributes across different group members. The inclusion of *action* (really, *policy*, or *strategy*) in these shared dynamic models means that not only is this alignment across states of belief, but it is also across *intents*, or what group members are planning to do in in the future. According to FEP, at equilibrium, each agent suffers the least surprise in its social interactions *with its own group* (which may have negative externality of an increase in free energy *outside the group*). In order to keep the free energy of each individual and that of the entire group to a minimum, a trade-off must be made, which is the primary subject of this paper.

I aim to show, in an upwards reduction, that a mathematical trade-off exists in the structure of multi-agent system cooperative action problems. This trade-off is conjectured in this paper to be externalized by people in their social econiches, in particular in their beliefs about equality and freedom. I will start this by looking at a single-dimensional space, and show that by factoring a free energy formulation of beliefs into two parts, an information asymmetry arises between individual agents (who act as "principals" here) and a group of agents (who act as "agent" here). The abstractions created in the mind, such as the conscious experience of language, necessarily discard information. A family of objects given a certain label must contain more information, or have higher capacity, than any individual object in the family. This creates a tension between top-down prediction, which is individually driven, and bottom up evidence, which is driven by a group. The individual favours simple models, as they require less cognitive effort, but these come with increased information hiding by the group. The group, on the other hand, favours more complex models, as these are more flexible to changing inputs (they can model more datasets). Therefore, a balance is sought in the complexity (or *"capacity"*) of the model selected.

I also conjecture that diversity in a group can be translated into model capacity in each agent's mind because of the good regulator theorem: every operational system has to be a model of its environment [11], which may be social (may include other agents). Thus, each agent is both defined by, and defines, the group it interacts with. If agents are defined by a group, yet agents must be diverse, this uncovers the trade-off. I make the simplifying assumption in this paper of a single group, while in practice, people are simultaneously in groups that span multiple scales of organization. Sitting with your friend in class is such a situation, as you are in two groups: friends and classmates.

There are two ways of organizing a social group, and of organizing each agent's model: precise and homogeneous, or uncertain and diverse. These two ways lead to solutions that are secure and static or insecure and innovative, respectively. Finally, I will claim that these methods correspond to one possible definition of equality and freedom, also respectively. They cannot be achieved at the same time, yet each has its advantages. The argument that the social structure is reflected in the human mind, and vice versa, lies at the heart of this conjecture. Beyond the good regulator theorem, the "social construction of reality" is precisely the idea that social structures (reality) are constructed in the mind, and vice versa [12]. Diversity in a society for example, leads to more liberal political structures emerging. It is precisely the increased uncertainty in each agent's mind that leads to this conclusion.

How will an agent choose between these two organizational methods? Being very certain about things is good because it allows decisions to be made, as an agent's certainty in something needs to be raised above a threshold for action. Being uncertain about things is also good because it allows an agent to be flexible towards changing situations and new and different people. However, these extreme values are difficult to sustain a social order over. The reason is that, in a state of perfect freedom, no cooperation is possible: there's just too much diversity. Similarly, a state of perfect equality will not succeed because everyone has to be identical. In this case, while everyone is very secure, the system has become very brittle to intrusions or exogenous changes, and remains stagnant (non-innovative).

I can plot a curve showing this trade-off by examining the free energy of the entire group, which splits into two terms. Figure 1 shows these two terms on a graph of the log(free energy) vs. this notion of equality and freedom I have explained in the previous paragraph. That is, to the left are systems where all group members are similar, so each individual has a minimal free energy (red curve), as it is really easy to predict everyone else since they are identical to everyone else, but the group's free energy (blue curve) is maximal, because they are inflexible to exogenous events. To the right are systems where all group members are diverse, which has minimal free energy for the group (blue curve), because they can manipulate the division of epistemic labour, but maximal free energy for the individual, because a more complex model is required. There is therefore a sweet spot in the sum of these free energies (black curve), shown with a star in Figure 1, that trades these two off optimally in the sense that each agent is able to accurately model the group and the group is able to accurately model each agent. At this sweet spot, agent and group share a model and are best able to predict and act cooperatively in the future world. The group as a whole is functioning according to the free energy principle. Smaller free energy configurations are better because they ensure there is less "surprise" for the group and its members. It is nevertheless true that any particular group may look very different to any other group, and so this sweet spot is only universal in an information theoretic way. The precise circumstances surrounding any group may result in a different, or non-decreasing, optimization.

This sweet spot is the configuration of both agent and group such that the free energy of the group is minimized, and it arises from the group leveraging the second law of thermodynamics for its own benefit by amassing orderly states (information) at the expense of externalities [13]. In some sense, the group has transferred as much energy as possible into maintaining a state of low entropy, that is, a state of as much order as is possible given the various circumstances surrounding the group. The group and the individual are aligned in this case, and the heightened collective consciousness, regardless of how it is implemented, allows individuals to be more free to think, be and do [14].

In the next section, I derive the curves in Figure 1 for a one-dimensional parameter space. I then generalize to three dimensions, by noting that three different (sets of) parameters are needed to implement a two-level (hierarchical or deep) Bayesian model. The minimum free energy, however, requires the "participation" of all three sets as a change by any one that increases free energy will have to be offset by a change in some other set. Thus, in three dimensions, the "sweet spot" is really a "sweet surface." The shape of this surface can be derived based on further assumptions covered in Section 2.6. Then, in Section 3, I discuss freedom and equality, and present a view of these quantities as being three dimensional and ternary, derived from social and political theorizing. Finally, in Section 4, I conjecture that the three dimensions of freedom and equality correspond to three settings of parameters in a two-level Bayesian model embedded in a multi-agent system in which agents do not have to be decision theoretically rational, but do have the capability to learn.

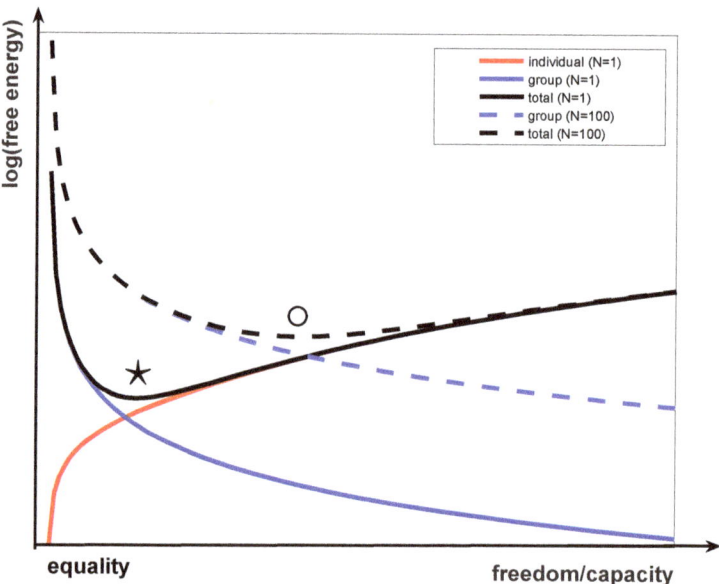

Figure 1. Free energy as a function of model capacity and/or freedom/equality. I plot the log(free energy) for clarity only. An arbitrary scaling of log(free energy) can be assumed, so only relative size matters. Lower free energy is a preferable situation, but the energy created by the group trying to match the individual (blue line) is balanced by that created by the individual trying to match the group (red line) to give an overall free energy which has a "sweet spot" (minimum) at ⋆. The black line shows the free energy if these are traded off equally. The dashed lines show the situation in which the group is much less flexible because it is larger (N = 100 times larger than the N = 1 group). Then, the "group" component of the free energy (individual stays fixed, group attempts to match, blue dashed line) is much higher, since the group's capacity is increased, and so plays a bigger role in the resulting free energy (black dashed line), and shifts the "sweet spot" outwards towards more freedom at ○.

2. Free Energy
2.1. One-Dimensional Derivation

I now derive the curves in Figure 1 from free energy principles. I will start with the free energy of the *whole group* of N agents. I will denote the ith agent's parameters as θ_i and the parameters of the whole group as $\theta \equiv \{\theta_1, \ldots, \theta_N\}$. Thus, the task of the group at time t, given data as observations ($D = \{o\}_t = \{o_1, o_2, \ldots, o_t\}$), is to compute

$$P(\theta|D, \mathcal{H}) = \frac{P(D|\theta, \mathcal{H}) P(\theta|\mathcal{H})}{P(D|\mathcal{H})}, \qquad (1)$$

where $\mathcal{H}$ is the hypothesis space (the modeling space as defined by a Bayesian hierarchical model, for example). The graphical model for these agents is shown in Figure 2a, with a single latent variable Z for the entire group. The difficult part here is the evaluation of $P(D|\mathcal{H})$ since it involves a summation over all values of θ. Further, each of these terms involves sums over the hidden variables Z.

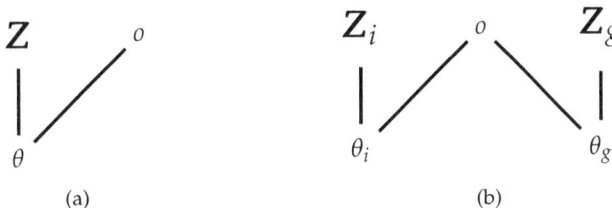

Figure 2. Simplified factor graph (Bayesian network) representing (a) a group with latent variables Z; and (b) the group without agent i with state Z_g, and one representing agent i with state Z_i.

The variational free energy, $\tilde{F}$, can be written as

$$\tilde{F} = \int d\theta Q(\theta) \log \frac{Q(\theta)}{P(D,\theta)}. \tag{2}$$

When the approximating distribution Q is chosen such that $\tilde{F}$ is minimized, then the minimum of this $\tilde{F}$ as θ is varied is obtained when θ is the parameters of the best predictor function for this domain and agent combination [15]. The minimization process may be approximated by choosing Q for some fixed (current best-guess) θ, and then optimizing θ with respect to that "discovered" Q, and repeating this process until convergence to a local minimum, as in the expectation-maximization algorithm. By choosing the Q function appropriately, a minimization over model parameters is possible, and this minimization will not leave the parameters any worse off as far as relationship (fit) with the data goes. In many cases, Q may be determined from the data, but in some it may only be possible over some parameterized subset of the space of Q. For example, Q can be factored into parts corresponding to each parameter, and then each such factored Q can be minimized analytically one at a time, while keeping the others constant.

In order to move beyond the group to each individual agent, I will split the group into two parts. One singleton set contains the ith agent, with parameters θ_i and latent variables Z_i, and the other set contains $N - 1$ agents $\{1, \ldots, N\} \backslash i$, with parameters θ_g and latent variables Z_g. I will consider this second set of agents as a single agent in what follows, and the network model looks as in Figure 2b. Equivalently, I assume each agent in the second set (the group) to be identical and act simultaneously and equally. In what follows, I will assume this group is *homogeneous and undifferentiated* in their overall parameter settings (which means they still may be using heterogeneous models), such that the group can be treated as an individual. At this point, I encourage the reader to think of this as a *dyadic* interaction, but it can also be viewed as an agent-group interaction, or even a group-group interaction. The role of this single "group" agent is, in fact, taken by a single individual from the group at any one time, but the statistics of interaction of the agent in question with the *whole* group is what matters. I am assuming here that this variation is sufficiently small, but in real human groups, I imagine it will be quite large.

I will now assume that the variational distribution for the group, Q, from the perspective of any agent i, can be factored into a piece for the agent, $Q_i(\theta_i)$ and a piece for the group, $Q_g(\theta_g)$, such that $Q(\theta) = Q_i(\theta_i)Q_g(\theta_g)$. As explained above, a variational solution will normally require some kind of iterative updating scheme like the expectation-maximization algorithm, which operates by optimising one parameter at a time, while holding the others fixed. This kind of iterative solution is achieved by factorizing the group into individuals optimizing their own Q functions, based on everyone else's Q functions, assuming they are fixed. For the entire group I am considering, I am assuming that each agent can separately and independently minimize some part of the variational free energy. However, the minimization is actually performed by the whole group at the same time.

If each agent attempts to perform this maximization separately, the resulting joint effort will result in a group pressure on each individual that reciprocates the pressure of the individual on the group, although magnified by the concentration of it. What this implies is that each agent in a group, in attempting to manage its social network, will tend towards solutions that combine the agent's own free energy, with the agent's contribution to the free energy of the groups in which it its nested (here I consider only one level of nesting). This means I can write

$$\tilde{F} = \int d\theta Q_i(\theta_i) Q_g(\theta_g) \log \frac{Q_i(\theta_i) Q_g(\theta_g)}{P_i(D|\theta_i) P_g(D|\theta_g)}. \quad (3)$$

Consider D, the total data "generated" (including actions performed) by the agent and group. I will break this into three non-overlapping sets, $D \equiv \{D_o, D_i, D_g\}$, where D_i is the data generated during the interaction by the agent, i, while D_g is the data generated by the group, g, and D_o is the data generated by both simultaneously (or neither). For example, such data may be spoken/written language, or facial expressions and gestures, some of which are normally only be jointly expressed (like sharing a hug). Such data may also include physical artifacts in a shared space. The goal of the optimization is to get D_i to be interpretable by the group, to get D_g to be interpretable by the agent, and to get D_o to be interpretable by both.

The denominator in Equation (3) is $P(D, \theta_i, \theta_g)$, but since D_i is being generated by i, and assuming $D_0 = \varnothing$, and constant priors $P(\theta_i)$ and $P(\theta_g)$, this is $P_i(D_i D_g|\theta_i) P_g(D_g D_i|\theta_g)$ (it is a "noisy or" or "mixture of experts" model) where P_i and P_g are the probabilistic models of the individual and of the group. Looking a little further, we note that the optimization in Equation (3) will favor P_i and P_g distributions with larger capacity, but that such a larger capacity P_i requires a more difficult optimization by i, but a simpler optimization for the group g. To see why, consider this exemplar based solution. Consider that for g to model what i does, it suffices to have one member of g who is very similar to i. If using a Monte-Carlo (sample-based) solver, this model's predictive samples would take most of the weight in the posterior distribution. The more diverse group with have larger capacity overall and will therefore be more likely to easily assimilate i. However, larger capacity agents work in the opposite way. For i to model what g does, it requires i to have a model for *every member of g*, or at least a sufficient abstraction (learned from) of all data from all group members. Should i not be able to do this, his free energy will increase very rapidly, as he struggles to figure out how everyone works. Individuals aim for the stability of homogeneity, while the group aims for the disorder of innovation. It is this asymmetry that is the primary focus of this paper. In the discussion, I will further elaborate on the connections between this and social and political freedom.

Agent and group will both be updating their models, θ_i and θ_g, respectively, during the interaction. I will therefore simplify by assuming that each agent generates "its" data, then observes D_i and D_g, and then generates the shared data D_0. Then I can factor

$$P_i(D|\theta_i) = \int_{\theta_i'} P_i(D_o, D_i, D_g, \theta_i'|\theta_i)$$
$$= \int_{\theta_i'} P_i(D_o|D_i, D_g, \theta_i', \theta_i) P_i(\theta_i'|D_g, D_i, \theta_i) P_i(D_i|D_g, \theta_i) P(D_g|\theta_i)$$
$$= \int_{\theta_i'} P_i(D_o|\theta_i') P_i(\theta_i'|D_g, D_i, \theta_i) P_i(D_i|\theta_i) P_i(D_g|\theta_i), \quad (4)$$

and

$$P_g(D|\theta_g) = \int_{\theta_g'} P_g(D_o, D_i, D_g, \theta_g'|\theta_g)$$
$$= \int_{\theta_g'} P_g(D_o|\theta_g') P_g(\theta_g'|D_i, D_g, \theta_g) P_g(D_g|\theta_g) P_g(D_i|\theta_g), \quad (5)$$

where I have assumed that D_o is generated from updated models in agent θ_i' and group θ_g' after seeing D_i and D_g. Further, I have assumed each agent computes its own $P(D|\theta)$

without considering the other's data. That is, $P_i(D_i|D_g, \theta_i) = P_i(D_i|\theta_i)$ and $P_g(D_i|D_g, \theta_g) = P_g(D_i|\theta_g)$. Putting Equations (4) and (5) into (3), and rearranging terms, I obtain:

$$\tilde{F} = \int Q_i(\theta_i) Q_g(\theta_g) \log \frac{Q_i(\theta_i)}{P_i(D_i|\theta_i) \int_{\theta_i'} P_i(D_o|\theta_i') P_i(\theta_i'|D_g, D_i, \theta_i)} \tag{6}$$

$$+ \int Q_i(\theta_i) Q_g(\theta_g) \log \frac{Q_g(\theta_g)}{P_i(D_g|\theta_i) P_g(D_i|\theta_g) P_g(D_g|\theta_g) \int_{\theta_g'} P_g(D_o|\theta_g') P_g(\theta_g'|D_i, D_g, \theta_g)}.$$

Now I will evaluate this free energy at a fixed point where $\theta_g' = \theta_g$ and $\theta_i' = \theta_i$, and in the particular case where $D_o = \varnothing$, ergo, the group and individual are at equilibrium and do not jointly generate data. This means neither agent nor group changes parameters based on the other's data. However, at equilibrium, it allows me to compute the integrals in closed form. Thus, in Equation (6), I can set $Q_g = P_g(D_g|\theta_g)$ and set the integrals over θ_i' and θ_g' in the denominators to identity (since one term picks out $\theta' = \theta$, and the other is $P(D_o = \varnothing|\theta) = 1$ they pick out the equilibrium point, which is the starting point).

With these assumptions in hand, I can rewrite Equation (6) as:

$$\tilde{F} = \int_{\theta_g} Q_g(\theta_g) \int_{\theta_i} Q_i(\theta_i) \log \frac{Q_i(\theta_i)}{P_i(D_i|\theta_i)} \tag{7}$$
$$- \int_{\theta_i} Q_i(\theta_i) \int_{\theta_g} Q_g(\theta_g) \log P_i(D_g|\theta_i) P_g(D_i|\theta_g).$$

The first term is the usual free energy for the agent, averaged over models of the group. However, assuming the group is stationary, then the free energy of the agent then resolves to its own free energy, which can be computed. The second term is the joint probability that agent i will be able to generate data D_i that are interpretable by the group, and that the group will be able to generate data D_g that are interpretable by the agent. This is taken in expectation over both models of agent and group parameters, Q_i and Q_g.

Note the symmetry in Equation (7), in which the dispersion of θ_i can be large if the dispersion of θ_g is small, and vice-versa, but both cannot be large or small at the same time. In fact, this symmetry is quite curious because it states that individuals operating in the first regime will be well suited to interact with individuals operating in the second. That is, although they are doing things differently, they in fact are complementary. There is a trade-off between the capacity of these parameters with insufficient density if the two are large, difficulty finding the other if the two are small, leaving the agents to find trade-offs in the middle. The exact location of this trade-off is then something that must be negotiated. It also determines the sets D_o, D_i, D_g defined above, since, e.g., if the dispersion of θ_g is small, most of the data will be generated by the group, so $D_o = D_g$. If the dispersion of θ_g is large, the dispersion of θ_i is small, and so $D_o = D_i$.

Focusing on the second term in Equation (7) only, I can expand out the logarithm and get two terms

$$- \int_{\theta_i} Q_i(\theta_i) \int_{\theta_g} Q_g(\theta_g) \log P_i(D_g|\theta_i) - \int_{\theta_g} Q_g(\theta_g) \int_{\theta_i} Q_i(\theta_i) \log P_g(D_i|\theta_g),$$

which I can optimize separately. Holding the agent fixed at θ_i^* and optimizing θ_g in the first, and holding the group fixed at θ_g^* and optimising θ_i in the second, then, this is

$$- \int_{\theta_g} Q_g(\theta_g) \log P_i(D_g|\theta_i^*) - \int_{\theta_i} Q_i(\theta_i) \log P_g(D_i|\theta_g^*).$$

Now, $D_g = \{d_{g0}, d_{g1}, \ldots, d_{gN}\}$ and $D_i = \{d_{i0}, d_{i1}, \ldots, d_{iN}\}$, which means, assuming all the data are independently and identically distributed given each model, we can write

$$-\sum_j \left[\int_{\theta_g} Q_g(\theta_g) \log P_i(D_{gj}|\theta_i^*) + \int_{\theta_i} Q_i(\theta_i) \log P_g(D_{ij}|\theta_g^*) \right].$$

I will assume that Q_g is a "hat" function which has constant probability over $[\mu_g^* - \sigma_g^*, \mu_g^* + \sigma_g^*]$ (so $\theta_g^* = \{\mu_g^*, \sigma_g^*\}$). Similarly for Q_i: replace all g subscripts with i. Next, I assume that P_i and P_g are normal distributions with parameters $\theta_i = \{\mu_i, \sigma_i\}$ and $\theta_g = \{\mu_g, \sigma_g\}$. The assumption of normality for P_i and P_g is only to ease exposition here. In fact, these distributions are more likely to be scalable, that is, operating similarly at very different scales (non-Gaussian). With these assumptions in place, the integrals can be done analytically to yield, for each data point, a contribution to the overall free energy of (note the extra negative sign that came from the log(*Normal*) distributions):

$$\frac{(\mu_g + \sigma_g - \mu_i^*)^3}{3\sigma_i^{*2}} - \frac{(\mu_g - \sigma_g - \mu_i^*)^3}{3\sigma_i^{*2}} + \frac{(\mu_i + \sigma_i - \mu_g^*)^3}{3\sigma_g^{*2}} - \frac{(\mu_i - \sigma_i - \mu_g^*)^3}{3\sigma_g^{*2}}. \quad (8)$$

Assuming equilibrium, set arbitrarily at $\mu_g^* = 0$ and $\sigma_g^* = 1$, I obtain two terms:

$$\left[\frac{(\sigma_g - \mu_i^*)^3}{3\sigma_i^{*2}} + \frac{(\sigma_g + \mu_i^*)^3}{3\sigma_i^{*2}} \right] + \left[\frac{(\mu_i + \sigma_i)^3}{3} - \frac{(\mu_i - \sigma_i)^3}{3} \right]. \quad (9)$$

Now, I will assume at equilibrium that $\sigma_i^* = \sigma_i$ and that $\mu_i^* = \mu_i = 1.0$. I deliberately choose $\mu_i^* \neq \mu_g^*$ because each individual is not necessarily at the group mean and I select unity arbitrarily. Holding all other parameters fixed (so $\mu_g = \mu_g^*$ and $\mu_i = \mu_i^*$), Equation (10) results.

$$\left[\frac{1}{\sigma_i^2} \right] + \left[\frac{(1+\sigma_i)^3}{3} - \frac{(1-\sigma_i)^3}{3} \right] = \left[\frac{1}{\sigma_i^2} \right] + \left[2\sigma_i + \frac{2\sigma_i^3}{3} \right]. \quad (10)$$

Equation (10) is plotted as a function of σ_i in Figure 1 (black solid line). Observe that the two terms work in opposite directions, leading to a minimum shown as a ⋆ in Figure 1. The first term is the negative log probability (free energy) that the group will align with the agent at fixed θ_i^*, which will be lower (more probable, lower free energy) if the agent is more "flexible" (can show a face the group will like, blue line in Figure 1). The second is the negative log probability the agent will align with the group, which will be lower if the agent is more precisely defined (i.e., more "findable," red line in Figure 1). Although in this case it is simply because I assumed we were at equilibrium, it will in general be true because the individuals are more homogeneous.

There are numerous assumptions and shortcuts in the above analysis, but my objective was to derive a first approximation to the free energy of a group. The assumption that group and agent are fixed are quite restrictive, and the analysis above simplifies the simultaneous change of agent to group and from group to agent by using the symmetry of the problem. This simplification allows me to hold one agent fixed and modulate the other (or hold the group fixed and modulate the agent). Nevertheless, any more complex and reciprocal change would be characterised by the same equations, except with perhaps a coordinate change. Thus, I have proceeded with loss of generality only in the assumptions made (such as $D_o = \emptyset$), but relaxing these assumptions would generate multiple interesting avenues for future work. Using non-Gaussian distributions may be informative.

Generality is also reduced by the fact that I left out external forces altogether. However, such forces could be added to the equations above, and would share responsibility for D (along with the agent and group). Adding such elements may skew the overall structures shown in Figure 1, but will not change the core ideas I am presenting. This does, however, remain for a topic of future research.

2.2. Bigger or Smaller Groups

Now I remind you that the first term in Equations (9) and (10) in fact represents the entire group of $N-1$ individuals. Therefore, by weighting the two terms equally (black line in Figure 1), I have made an implicit assumption that the group is fully connected, so that there are $N-1$ terms like the first in Equations (9) and (10), that is, the individual interacts with everyone. This is not likely to be the case, however. What is more likely is that the newcomer interacts with only a dozen colleagues and managers, so his influence on the group is small. If we approximate this linearly and weight the first term in Equation (10) arbitrarily by $N=100$, then the dashed curves in Figure 1 result. The optimal configuration of parameters for free energy minimizing agents has shifted *rightwards*, and more individual flexibility is called for in order to integrate the individual into the group. Note that there is an arbitrary scaling: N = 1 means the arbitrary scaling factor being applied to the group/individual trade-off.

Nevertheless, the individual may have to change more than the group, as the weight of the population is in their favour (he is outnumbered). However, if the individual's parameters are substantially mis-aligned in general with the group's but aligned with some sub-group's parameters, then if the social network is constructed in such a way that this individual is mostly interacting with the sub-group, then these models may be strengthened within the sub-group. Should the group become large enough, or socially organised enough, their skepticism may be able *"to offer a challenge to the upholders of the 'official' tradition"* ([12], p.121). This challenge may be handled by merger into the main institution (*internalization* by the sub-group of the primary group), which then enriches and differentiates this tradition, or by segregation of the skeptics, a process of *objectivation* that possibly includes dehumanization (change of their agreed upon assigned identity). Finally, the sub-group may gain sufficient strength to form a political party and trigger change, in which case the existing traditions are thrown away and replaced with the new ideology, and the sub-group *externalises* to the group, society is produced by this sub-group, who define the new reality [12]. The definition and recognition of official sub-groups may be able to steer this process from an institutional perspective (see Section 3.1).

2.3. Flashlight Allegory

I will present this balance problem using an allegory of two boys searching for each other in the dark with a flashlights, as shown in Figure 3. The flashlights have an adjustable beam width, from narrow and far to wide and close. The boys get rewarded for how much light the other records, or the **density** of light falling on him. One can see that for certain settings of flashlight beams, the boys have no hope. If one sets his beam on small and far, but the other does as well, they will have trouble finding each other. If both beams are wide, they can easily find each other, but the density of both together is low. Thus, they can either both use medium beams, or one can use a small beam and the other a large one.

In the flashlight allegory above, consider the targets for each boy (the other boy) are like the social world, and the flashlight is the boy's predictions of how the social world will behave on a level of "meaning." Thus, I am treating a group of agents as a single agent here, to simplify the presentation. The size of the target is the diversity of the social world, and represents the variance in expected behaviours. The size of the flashlight is the strength of the abstract social model the agent is building (his prior model). Therefore, the "allowable" settings are those that combine high diversity with strong abstract predictions and those that combine low diversity with weak abstract predictions. These settings may both work well in a network of agents with the same settings, but this does not mean that the agents are homogeneous. While their parameter settings may be the same, the parameter settings define the *space* of possible models and agent can take on, and are more of a measure of a social group's expansiveness. Granted, boys with wider flashlight beams will have settings that rely less on abstract meanings. Also, individuals may conflict when put in groups with different settings, as the existing models will necessarily break down (and not match). The process of learning the new "fit" will be one that may be individual dependent. Such "spotlight" metaphors have been deeply explored in the context of psychological (usually visual) attention [16].

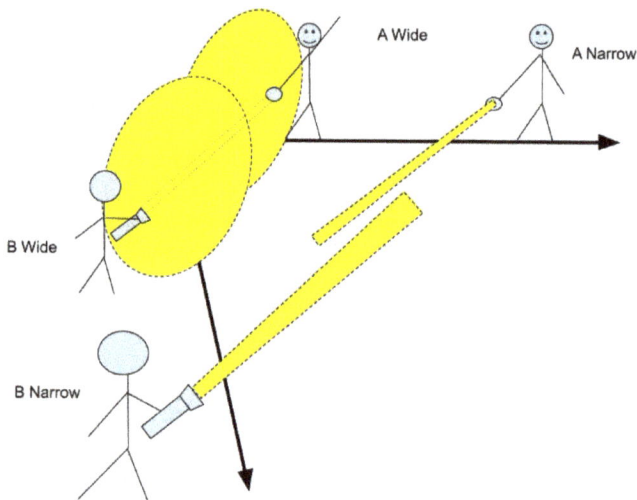

Figure 3. Allegorical example to demonstrate the uncertainty matching principle. Boy A (he can be A-narrow or A-wide) and boy B (B-narrow or B-wide) attempt to find each other's flashlights and are rewarded by the density of light falling on the other boy's flashlight.

If we also take into account how many connections link up the group members (the density of the network, or the effective group for any agent), then the group component becomes dominant and larger, it being harder for the whole group to shift towards the agent (blue dashed line in Figure 1), and the resulting free energy has a sweet spot that has shifted *rightwards*, towards more freedom, shown in Figure 1 with ∘. Such a shift may also be caused by the *intensity* of the relationship to the group. Those relations formed in primary socialization, for example, may have much more intensity, and therefore a much bigger effect, than those formed in secondary socialization ([12], p.152).

Work on latent structure learning of groups has shown that the assignment of a person to a group can be highly context dependent, as well as being dependent on dyadic similarity. That is, if Agent A meets Agent B, then how agent A categorizes agent B is dependent on how similar B is to each of A's prototypes of groups or identities (e.g., a "doctor" is an identity, part of the group "doctors," which is part of the group "medical professionals," etc.), but also whether or not agent C is present, and their similarity and group behaviour with B [17]. If group similarity is higher, then the group becomes more fixed in its relationship with the new agent, and the agent is more likely to assign other agents to the new group than to some other, more loosely defined group. That is, the larger, tighter groups will have more "gravity" pulling people towards them. Such groups are mobilizations of people into political parties, institutions embedded in the social fabric of the group and capable of swaying public policy.

Finally, the flashlight allegory ties back to the division of epistemic labour mentioned in the introduction. If we replace one of the boys with a group of boys, then we can see the value in this matching process. Each boy is simultaneously playing the same game, alone, trying to "match" the other $N-1$ boys. The places where their flashlights meet (the rewards they receive for playing the game properly) are in the innovations illuminated by their crossing beams. As the location from which the beam emanates in some degree represents which particular boy is standing there, the bigger the group, the broader the range of beams. A broader beam is easier for the group to find, but harder to make bright enough to solve the problem.

2.4. Two-Level Models

The one-dimensional analysis in the previous sections is somewhat simplistic, but I can generalize to a two-level model fairly easily, which is what this section will discuss. Generalizing beyond two levels, or beyond one group, requires further study. Throughout this section, do not lose sight of the fact that all probability distributions I refer to define the relative likelihoods of state *and of actions/behaviours*.

Multilevel systems are interesting because they are both neurologically plausible and information theoretically rich. Each level in such a model has a certain degree of uncertainty to it, where uncertainty is really a characterization of degree of belief, following a Bayesian view that puts the existentialism of the world into the mind itself [18]. Further, there must be uncertainty in the *connection* between the levels, which turns out to be important. That is, once we propose two different functional "levels" of processing in the brain, they must be combined in some way to produce, in the end, motor signals for purposeful action. The way this combination happens can be more or less precise, that is, the levels depend more or less on each other. I will call the three types of uncertainty denotative (objective model), connotative (subjective model), and connective (objective-subjective connection model). There is no constraint on what the model actually *is*, so long as it has a use for these three types of uncertainty. Further, since there are actually approximately five levels in the brain, I would expect at least nine types of uncertainty. I focus here on three primary ones as exemplary, where denotative corresponds roughly to language, while connotative to social emotions or sentiments.

This type of "dual-process" model is known to have parallels in human brain function and behaviour. However, it considers the role of abstract (some of it emotional) reasoning as a group-level process, and that of deliberative thought as an individual one. This is contrary to many modern views of deliberation and rationality as a group process (e.g., the "rational" economy), while emotion is individual and causes irrational behaviour. I make a distinction between *action* and *behaviour* in that the first describes linguistic labels (propositions) denoting actions, such as *give something to*, while the second describes the affective meanings of an action, say very positive and a bit powerful in this case.

Although these ideas generalize to other models, if using a probabilistic, two-level model, the state of the top level can be viewed as representing the *parameters* of the predictive model the next level down. Observations are then represented by the state at this next level down, and its dynamics are represented by the state one level up. Inference in this model is both state estimation and learning of the parameters of the low-level model, and is the definition of Bayesian machine learning. In what follows, I consider a particular type of two-level Bayesian model in which the "high" level is a continuous state parameter which is taken a priori to be the dynamics of sentiment as measured in population surveys, and the "low" level represents the dynamics of the objective, outside world. Such a model is restrictive, but gives me an easier way to relate to models of political freedom in Section 3.

2.5. Bayesact

BayesAct is a two-level model of human intelligence and affective reasoning (individual and social) that explicitly represents the three types of uncertainty in a simple and measurable way by leveraging the machinery of affect control theory (ACT) [9,19–22]. ACT is a model of emotional coherence based on language that was founded on the control principle of Powers [23], which states something very reminiscent of the free energy principle: that people try to minimise incongruencies by controlling their perceptions. Heise transposed this to the sentiment space of Osgood et al. [24], imposed a denotative structure from symbolic interactionism [25], and added affective dynamics [26]. ACT is a computational model that has been used to predict classes of human behaviour in a variety of settings [27]. ACT maintains a deterministic and static denotative model as an actor-behaviour-object-setting state (e.g., "doctor advises patient in clinic"), and an associated deterministic, but dynamic, connotative model. This connotative model is a a a dynamical system in Osgood's three-dimensional space of affective meaning: evaluation, potency and activity. This dynamical system represents *values*, or *evaluative knowledge*, which can be contrasted with *declarative* and *procedural* knowledge that are represented in the denotative model.

BayesAct combines these mechanics with a formal decision theoretic model, a partially observable Markov decision process, or POMDP [28,29], extensively used in operations research [30]. A POMDP instantiates a *temporal frame* or *structural representation* [31]. Frames, as schemas, are a classic structure used in early artificial intelligence (AI), Knowledge Discovery and Data Mining (KDD), and Information Retrieval (IR) research that assigns a label and interpretation to each object, fact, relation and event that constitute a particular situation. Such structures are typically logical and discrete-valued to enable ease of use in a computer program. For example, we might label the positions of pieces on a chess board, or predictions about how a game will turn out given a sequence of moves, or the bids in a negotiation. The inclusion of the connotative meanings of ACT means the model must be augmented with labels for identities and behaviours corresponding to ACT's denotative model, but with added noise modelling. These labels can then be interpreted as distributions in a sentiment space using a measured dictionary. This sentiment space thus complements the *denotative* state I have been describing so far, with a *connotative* state (which in fact is 18 dimensional). The model is fundamentally based on the symbolic interactionist idea that symbols (language) provide order for "the subjective apprehension of biographical experience" ([12], p.97). Symbols are then reified elements of exactly these same subjective apprehensions.

Thus, learning and being become one single experience. The combination of symbolic and affective interpretations is what enables *generalization*: once the symbol "doctor" is assigned to someone, expectations for her behaviour become defined as generally as possible with respect to her occupation. That is, I expect her to do something good and powerful, but I am open to a range of actual objective actions that could be in play in the current situation. For example, if the current situation is a court-room, I still expect her to do something good, such as testify honestly, and powerful, such as speak authoritatively. If she is coaching my son's hockey team, I also expect her to be honest, fair and caring. If my son's hockey coach is a policewoman, I may expect a more authoritarian and disciplinarian experience for my son. Note that both my assumptions may be wrong as this individual may be enacting a completely different identity while coaching.

Frames form the foundation of much knowledge representation work in AI, but have been efficiently implemented using Bayesian networks (BNs), which can be used to compute a distribution over all possible worlds modeled by a particular frame [18]. This probabilistic model then rests on the structural ontology and temporal logics that are proposed in the frame. Bayesian decision networks generalise the *goals* in frames as preference functions that rank all possible outcomes using a numeric scale, e.g., a utility function [32]. *BayesAct* complements this denotative model (the variance of which is called *invalidity*), with the ACT-based connotative model (the variance of which is called *coherence*), and a model of the relationship between them, the *somatic transform* (the variance of which is called *dependence*) [6,33]. For example, in a government policy decision, the facts may include the amount of money spent or saved, and long-term estimates from potentially complex predictive models, and the utility is financial or based on some index of social well-being. The denotative temporal dynamics may describe immediate and longer-term effects, enabled by adding more latent state, and allow for the construction of a policy that optimises over some definition of utility based on the same features. The denotative temporal dynamics may also encode *norms of behaviour* that indicate the normative choices to make for any given identity-behaviour combination (e.g., a "citizen" should not "free ride" on other "citizens").

The connotative dynamics are ACT-based, and will encode the relative freedom trade-offs for whatever group they are applied to. That is, for some particular configuration of the denotative state, including a definition of identities, a connotative distribution results that may be used to compute how emotionally coherent various behaviours are. This connotative coherence is one of "feeling" or "intuition," which may override any norms. I will call such coherence "prescriptive" rather than "normative." A striking example is a trolley problem, in which it is logical to throw the switch on a runaway trolley so that it kills only one person instead of five, a strong connotative prescription against "killing someone" may take over for many people and prevent this logical strategy. Another example is an ultimatum game, in which one player is given $10, and can give any amount he wishes to the other player. While logically the proper amount to give is $0 (or 1¢ if the game is repeated and the other player has a choice not to play), most humans will fork over approximately 20% to 40% of the amount they are given, with the amount being culturally dependent [34].

2.6. Three Types of Uncertainty

The two-level model discussed in the last section has three sets of parameters governing denotative, connective, and connotative elements. The three parameters are denoted δ, γ, and α, respectively. I therefore project the overall freedom-equality dimension from Figure 1 into a three-dimensional space.

Equation (9) is the free energy for a one-dimensional parameter space, under certain assumptions. In a three-dimensional space, we can imagine this free energy curve, as shown in Figure 1, varies along any ray emanating from the origin, and that the minimum point defines the surface of the "simplex," which is therefore revealed to be more of a "dome" shape (assuming radial symmetry). I therefore plot the simplex by seeking the minimum free energy along each ray from the origin. Plotting this as a function of $-\log\theta \propto \theta^{-1}$) yields Figure 4a, with an interpolated, smoothed version in (c). Figure 4b,d are the same plotting θ directly.

Since free energy increases with an increase in any parameter of the three, in order to be at equilibrium, it must decrease in at least one of the other two. What this implies is that the three-dimensional parameter space is in fact a two-dimensional surface of equilibrum, at each point of which the free energy is at a minimum. I have imposed a restriction here by assuming the decrease is the same; however, there may be some arbitrary scaling that may arise due to the physical nature of our environment. I make a radial assumption in Figure 4, which presents the information in three dimensions with as little added bias as possible (simply what this theoretical model is telling us). However, because of the assumed arbitrary (relative) scaling of parameter sets in the *BayesAct* model, viewing this surface as a simplex as in Figure 5 is easier to relate to theorizing about human freedom and equality, as in Section 3. The exact shape of this surface may not be as shown in Figure 4 or 5, but recall that a social system becomes increasingly difficult to arrange as you move out along any dimension of freedom, and thus the actual range of operation of these parameters is likely to be relatively small, centered around a region in center of the minimum free energy manifold.

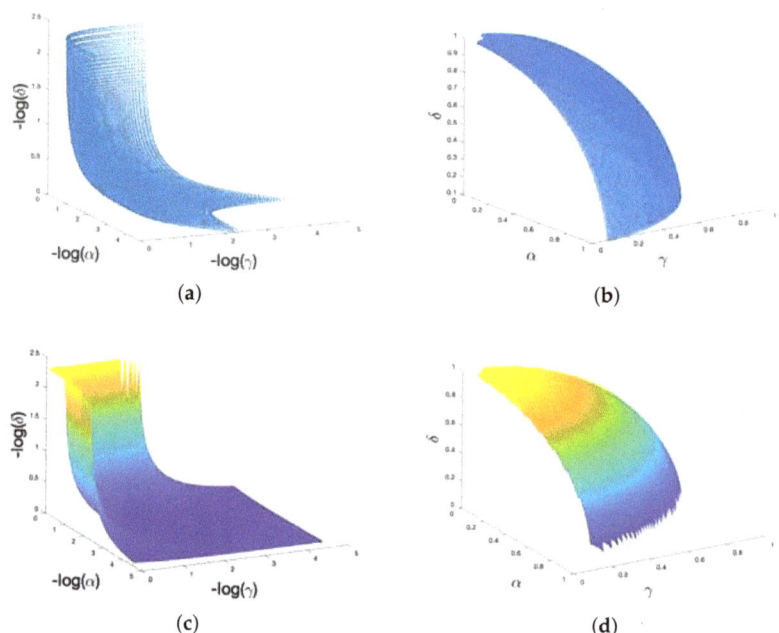

Figure 4. Views of the minimum free energy points along each ray from the origin. (**a,c**): Axes are -log(parameters), but correspond in scale to coherence ($-\log(\hat{\text{ff}})$), dependence ($-\log(\gamma)$), and validity ($-\log(\delta)$). I plotted the negative logarithm of each parameter, and colored the surface in (c), for visibility only. (**b,d**): Axes are the raw variance parameters (so larger is more dispersed, more freedom).

3. Freedom in Social Groups

While the model in the last section boils things down to three complementary sets of parameters, the non-determinism in social groups may be substantially more complex. However, as I will show in this section, they can also be boiled down to three complementary sets of parameters. First, consider what we mean by uncertainty. Often, non-determinism can be reduced to an estimate of how likely some outcome is to occur, given some policy of action: this is the *risk*. Risk is an important concept, because if one can define risk, and one has fixed preferences, then one can make a decision-theoretically optimal decision about behaviours that lead to this risky outcome. That is, an agent can rationally decide whether or not to do something, and be right about it, only when the risk is something she can estimate. However, if she cannot estimate the risk (perhaps she has never tried the behaviour so has no statistics to learn from about the likelihood of the outcomes), then her estimate of risk itself is uncertain, and we label this type of "meta-" uncertainty as "ambiguity," or the "unknown unknown" [35]. The reason ambiguity is important as a separate concept, is that it is a factor determining when people rely more on social than individual learning, alongside problem difficulty and learning cost ([36], p. 64).

There are two main reasons why an agent would no longer be able to estimate risk properly. The first is there may be some unknown (to the agent) factors that influence the outcome. These factors might be discovered should the agent try the behaviour, which it cannot do reliably without an estimate of risk. The second is the agent may lose the capacity to model an environment that has become too complex. There is a third reason risk may be hard to estimate, which is essentially the same as the first: the cost of a behaviour may be too high. This implies the agent cannot do the action, and so leaves the outcomes unknown as in the first reason for ambiguity. These three reasons are both known to be important in gauging if an agent will favour social learning (learning by imitating others, for example) over individual learning (e.g., learning by evaluating outcomes decision theoretically) ([36], p. 64). In either case, I will call the resulting environment *invalid* [37], which is synonymous with *ambiguous*, but less ambiguous.k

3.1. Three Freedoms

Ambiguity is handled by people in three complementary ways, which correspond to three things at play: the group, the individual, and the connection between the individual and the group. Another way of saying this is the objective (external, the group) the subjective (internal, the self) and the connective (membership in the group). The representations of the social context in an agent's brain or mind pervades reason and thought, and the way in which each agent in each context trades off the social and individual contexts will be defined by, and will define, the social order and thus reality: *"the relationship between the individual and the objective social world is like an ongoing balancing act"* ([12], p. 134). Therefore, these three locusses of ambiguity management lead to three concepts of freedom, *Republican*, *Positive*, and *Negative* which I now explore using the framework of Anderson [38].

Republican freedom means people are not subject to anyone's unaccountable will, and is also known as *independence*. As republican equality is increased, then everyone becomes equivalent and dependent. Normally this is done by making all dependent on a sovereign or a monarch, such that all independence is removed by subjugation to the monarch's unaccountable will. However, a smart and honest monarch gives his subjects lots of opportunities (positive freedoms) and lets them have free choices (negative freedoms) but can intervene at any time to impose an arbitrary will to ensure everyone is steering in the same direction.

Positive freedom implies opportunity, implemented by slackening constraints at the group level, meaning uncertainty must be managed at levels lower down (individual) and higher up (at the corporate or government level). Positive equality means that opportunity is more constrained. Positive equality is a place where everyone is exactly acting in the same way and the world is predictable and *valid* [37]. Therefore, if you could maximise positive equality, then everyone would act according to a single plan. One such plan could be a rational plan. By defining what is good and what is bad, a rational decision maker can be used to set policy. This definition also equates to the ontologies used to classify people and groups, as those considered "bad", e.g., those labeled "madmen and children" ([39], p. 33) can be excluded in order to preserve rationality. The power to make this definition may be abused by a despot for personal gain.

Negative freedom is defined by the freedom an agent has to choose its own actions, from whatever choices it is given. So moving towards negative equality means removing people's abilities to choose their own actions. One way to do this is by defining affective identities, and then making more stringent requirements on how actions should be coherent with these identities, as explored in Section 2.4. These culturally approved dynamics become institutionalised, and they remove negative freedom of individuals to act in whatever way their will directs them. Thus, an increase in emotional coherence between (seemingly self-imposed) actions and behaviours, in an emotionally stratified society, leads to a reduction in the space of actions under consideration, accompanied by a corresponding increase in negative equality in which actions are constrained by social prescriptions. A state of "world closedness," extracted from a state of "world openness," is a result ([12], p. 51). The classic imposition on negative freedom is private property. I can wall off a piece of ground for myself, and I have increased my negative freedom on my property. Although I still require the law, and an enforcement component of government to ensure this freedom is upheld, I have decreased the negative freedom of 7 billion people (realistically, only a few hundred co-citizens of my rural town), and therefore overall have increased negative equality.

Negative and positive freedom can be easily confused. The important difference is in *where* this freedom lies. Positive freedom is a property of the group of agents. The more open the group is to new ideas, for example, the more positive freedom it affords its members. Negative freedom is a property of the individual. As individuals are mostly constrained by the presence of others, negative freedom is decreased when positive freedom is increased through diversity, for example. Although I have the positive freedom in my country to stand outside and shout my opinions, I do not have the negative freedom to do that as I would be ashamed that my neighbors may see me. As more diverse preferences surround me, there are more of such things that will reduce my negative freedom further.

3.2. Social Capital

Defining "social capital" as the emotional bonds in a network of people [40], I find that it can be implemented in two ways. First, by restricting republican freedom but allowing negative and positive freedoms, one gets a tight-knit group of homogeneous, intolerant individuals devoted to the group. Such a group is rich in "bonding social capital" and have low tolerance, e.g., a "sectarian community" ([40], p. 355). Second, by restricting negative freedom but allowing positive and republican freedoms, one gets a highly diverse and tolerant group, but one that must be trusting of others. Such a group is rich in "bridging social capital" and has high tolerance for out-group members, e.g., a "civic community" ([40], p. 355). Putnam [40] also discusses two other forms of societies, those with high tolerance but low social capital (of either sort) are "individualistic" (every man for himself), and those with low tolerance and low social capital ("anarchic"). While the individualistic case implies no positive freedom but complete negative and republican freedom, the anarchic case implies complete freedom across the board, and is not workable as a societal solution given even natural diversity due to statistical fluctuations. Fukuyama has also written extensively on the idea of *trust* [41,42], which he equates with *social capital* [40] and *cultural values* ([41], p. 110).

3.3. Ternary "Simplex"

Anderson [38] presents these three freedoms as both *distinct* (in that they can be individually varied) and valuable (in that all are worth something). There is evidence that they vary inversely with respect to each other (e.g., gains in republican freedom are usually traded off against losses in negative freedom in a social democracy). If we make one assumption that an increase in one such freedom means an increase in overall freedom, then a group at an equilibrium of trading off freedom and equality would tend to increase equality in response, to restore equilibrium. What dimension is increased would not matter, but all cannot be increased (or decreased) at once. Thus, these three freedoms form a ternary structure (in which only one can be maximal at a time), and so I postulate three freedom-equality dimensions as shown in Figure 5, and so that it appears as a dashed green line in Figure 5. Freedoms increase down each axis towards the freedom pole at the origin (■) in Figure 5. Each type of equality (freedom) is increased by moving away from (towards) the origin along the corresponding axis.

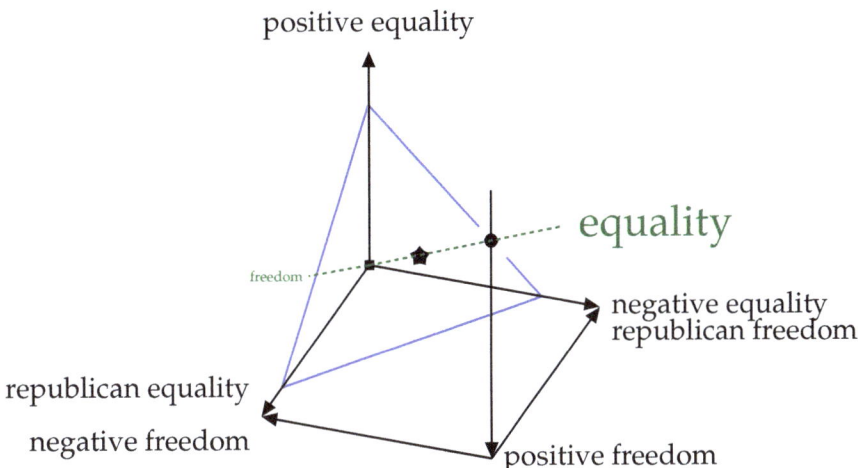

Figure 5. Simplex on the three dimensions of freedom and equality. Also shown are poles of perfect freedom ■ and perfect equality •, The star is in the most central position possible for a social agreement on the management of uncertainty.

4. Discussion

Politics, from the laws themselves to the people who make them, enforce them, and evaluate them, are based on some degree of balance between *freedom* and *equality*. As ([43], p. 96) points out, *"every system of law [has] two main objects, freedom and equality."* However, there are many ways to balance these two elements. For example, one group may value everyone's freedom to act (e.g., to carry a gun), while another may value everyone's equality of action. One can easily see that one cannot be free and be equal in a society of others. If everyone is free, then there will be inequality. If everyone is equal, then no one is free. In the words of ([44], p. 171): *"The liberty of some must depend on the restraint of others."* Freedom and equality are heavily discussed in the literature, of which I will barely skim the surface. My primary objective with this paper is to show that the different kinds of freedoms enjoyed by people are related in a non-trivial way to some information theoretic principles about the management of uncertainty.

I can represent this definition of freedom and equality on a single axis, as shown in Figure 1. On this figure, a society could be set up anywhere along the line between freedom and equality. However, using free energy principles on a one-dimensional model, I can show that there is a "sweet spot" at which the group functions most efficiently. This sweet spot, shown in Figure 1 with a ⋆, is a minimum of free energy for the group, and is defined by how uncertainty is managed in a group of agents (see Section 2). The natural equilibrium of the group is when the group and its members are in harmony. Another way to say this is that any group attempting to settle *away from* this sweet spot, will be less efficient, and may be dominated by groups who are at their own sweet spot. Learning where an agent should situate its own, internal model of the world is something non-self-interested that an agent does, but it is something that benefits the group as a whole. Due to a host of exogenous factors the group will be unlikely to be found at their "sweet spot," but rather would look like a small cloud in the three-dimensional space, with more density somewhere along this simplex. To get a sense just how much variation is found in such a cloud, one can consider how to implement collective intelligence through rewards, as in [45], but seeing collective intelligence as a property of the group, not of the individual, leads to a different interpretation in which the group prescription is the norm, and the individual's rational deliberations lead it astray.

I therefore conjecture that freedom is an estimate of the capacity of posterior belief distributions in a hierarchical model which includes agent policies. Different types of freedom express themselves at different levels. Similarly, I define equality as the inverse of this: an estimate of the precision of the same posterior belief distributions. Very precise distributions require people to be less diverse, more similar, more equal. This conjecture allows me to connect Figure 5, derived from social theory, to Figure 4, which is derived here analytically from information theoretic principles, but could potentially be derived from data by building artifacts that actually fit into and become members of a social group.

As a simple example, consider the diversity of a population. We can represent diversity as a distribution over a range of human attributes, plotted along the x-axis in Figure 1 as model capacity. Higher capacity allows a wider range of attributes, leading to a more diverse population with a lot of freedom. With reduced capacity (to the left) in Figure 1, comes reduced diversity, so people are spread across a smaller number of attributes, everybody is very much the same, and there is much more equality.

Those operating in the society of diversity are more often going to run into diverse views of things, and therefore they will learn a more uncertain or "spread out" view of their society. They will therefore be more free to choose their own actions as there will be less constraint from the group level (as it is more spread out). Agents that live in the homogeneous society are going to have very precise distributions over the other agents in their group since everyone is similar. Actions are constrained, but equality and security are guaranteed. Security is guaranteed because, if everyone is the same as you, then you can be very certain about things, you are in a state of pure equality, and you get pure security as a reward: you can predict what is going to happen next. If everyone is very different, then you will be very uncertain about how people will act but you can be free to act in any way you want because it will not stand out and people will know how to handle it.

Degrees of uncertainty are therefore intimately connected with freedom. What types of freedom are associated with each of these three type of uncertainty? Denotative uncertainty is the same as positive freedom, in that invalid environments are ones in which everyone is doing different things, and so positive freedom is maximised. When all are "forced" to behave in some way (e.g., rational), then positive equality is maximised (everyone is following the same plan), but of course, positive freedom is minimised.

Connotative uncertainty is the same as negative freedom, as it releases people from social norms and prescriptions that cause constraints on their actions. Note that I am making this association primarily on the basis of using ACT as a model for the connotative state. Seen from a strictly Bayesian model selection viewpoint, the connotative state is the *family* of models that are being used to make predictions about the effects of action on the world. Those using the same family of models, say Gaussian processes, will be solving problems represented the same way (same *perspectives* [8]). They may be using the same heuristics as well to solve their problems, at which point generating diverse solutions will be difficult, and negative freedom is reduced. They may also be using different heuristics, which gives them an advantage by allowing them to divide labour and act cooperatively. Those working from different model families (different perspectives) will find synchronization more difficult. However, they may also gain advantage from their diversity due to the "diversity trumps ability theorem" [46], which leads to two conclusions: "Diverse perspectives are more likely to lead to breakthroughs and to create communication problems. Diverse heuristics are more likely to lead to smaller, more iterative improvements" ([8], p. 239). In the first, putting together different models leads to an increase in negative freedom, whereas in the second, shared model families lead to a decrease in negative freedom, but may increase positive freedom.

Institutions, as a family of models, increase negative equality. An institution has an organizational "culture" that increases social norms and prescriptions, and decreases negative freedom. In my analysis above, I assume everything is in equilibrium, so that all model families are the same. However, there is much to be gained from studying how this system behaves out of equilibrium.

Finally, connective uncertainty is the same as republican freedom, as it releases people from adherence to some externally defined reference point. A great deal of connective certainty requires a leader, who, since positive and negative freedoms are maximised in this state, must be authoritarian. This leader must define what is "good" and "bad" for the group to be cooperative, since everyone within the group has so much freedom to follow their own definitions. Connotative certainty also requires a leader, but it can be defined as a social contract, since this configuration requires people to give up their negative freedoms to obtain this connotative security.

Therefore, the setting of parameters of uncertainty (variances) in a two-level Bayesian model of each agent corresponds to the setting of political belief in the resulting group and the placement on a three-dimensional simplex of freedoms. The primary insight is that all such settings are equivalent in terms of their trade-offs between equality and freedom *in general*, that is, along the dashed green axis in Figure 5, which is what we really should care about. The precise way in which this balance is achieved matters less, and conflicting mixtures of uncertainty management should be avoided. Narratives that can give justifications for actions in line with one group or the other may be important to guide marginalised groups towards fair solutions. Losses of republican freedom can be compensated for by underlining the associated gains in positive freedom, for example.

As with the single-dimensional (linear) version in Section 2, there are numerous different ways of achieving the same freedom-equality trade-off. The trade-off shown in Figure 1 happens along all three freedom axes. In order to handle this, I assumed that the trade-off in Figure 1 operates along any radial vector in this three-dimensional space. Variations on this assumption may yield different results. The simplex gives us a convenient way to discuss the manifold shown in Figure 4, so long as we remember that in practice it has this particular scaling. Note that the minimum free energy goes to ∞ as any parameter drops to zero, as Equation (9) blows up. It is therefore more difficult to plot the simplex as a function of the inverses of the parameters (Figure 4a,b). Regardless of how we talk about this space we have to end up on (or near to) this two-dimensional surface shown outlined in blue in Figure 5. This surface is a *simplex*, and represents the "sweet surface" of free energy. It may not actually be a plane, but rather a spherical shape or bowl shape, see Section 2.6, but this planar approximation sweeps arbitrary scaling under the rug and gives us a useful analytical tool.

The three freedoms that I have been describing can be related to the three different ways of managing uncertainty in a two-level Bayesian model. More generally, I believe these same three trade-offs in uncertainty will be happening across all levels of the brain, and may be generalizable using the approach of Gilead et al. [47], in which each level abstracts (is the "abstractum") from the level below (the complementary "concretum", which itself may be an "abstractum" of a further level). Such a hierarchy would vastly increase the modelling capacity of each agent, and thus of the group. The parameter space would, however, would have more dimensions, and so focussing on only two levels and three dimensions may give us insights in the construction of such a more complex model, while maintaining some explanatory validity.

5. Conclusions

In this paper, I have presented a highly abstracted model of a group optimization of free energy. I have shown how, under certain assumptions, a group of agents jointly minimizing free energy can be represented by a set of agents who learn from each other. Such agents will tend towards models with similar levels of dispersion, which is related to how much capacity for modelling the outside world they have. I further discuss a Bayesian hierarchical model with a hybrid state space that I relate to sociological theorizing about small group behaviours. I show how a trade-off in dispersion or capacity is present across the levels in this model, and discuss how these trade-offs relate to common notions of freedom in societies.

The model I am presenting is necessarily simplistic, and does not come close to approaching the complete gamut of tools and techniques used by humans to coordinate behaviour. In fact, one could view an entire society as a "cloud" of small distributions in this three-dimensional space, forming one large distribution. A cloud that is constantly moving as situations change and agents interact with one another and learn. A society can also likely be pulled forcefully into one or another configurations; however, their natural tendencies might operate clandestinely to provide a countervailing force.

Nevertheless, I find it compelling that the properties of the parameter space of this hierarchical Bayesian model seem to reflect some of the properties of people's understanding of freedom and uncertainty. This upwards reduction, if carried to its logical extreme, leads to a somewhat different philosophical view that denies primacy of individual states, or at least accords social states with equal status. In this view, everything is situational, although part of the situation is the agent itself, including all its strategies, planning, and decision making. However, these are not considered individual traits at all, but rather social constructs that are learned and applied in a given situation. In this view, "personality" is just a bag of tricks that a group has learned, and are not some inherent property of any given person. This philosophical view denies the primacy and stability of "personality" as a fixed and stable trait.

Individuals both try to make sense of the world they are in, and try to define it. They are faced, however, with an information asymmetry (principal agent problem), in which they cannot even represent, let alone understand, the complexity of their social groups. Thus, individuals, as principals, are forced to offload some of that computation onto other agents (as agents of the principal). The more they do this, the more similar to those other agents they become, and the more homogeneous the society becomes. However, if they do less of it, they become more independent, which the group favours as it leads to flexibility, the ability to handle the unforeseen (the "Black Swans" [48]) and the ability to assimilate new members. The derivation I have presented in this paper puts *learning* of "preferences" (as predictive distributions) as central to the collective decision making process, and does not assume individuals share predictive models (are all rational), violating two basic assumptions of economic theory [49]. While the analysis was simplistic, any number of the assumptions made could be lifted (such as radial symmetry) in order to see if and where the connection breaks down. Using normally distributed models in *BayesAct* is restrictive to allow for analysis, but I believe that using other distributions (e.g., with broader tails) would yield similar results, and the three-way trade-off would still show through.

A number of directions are currently being pursued, mostly directed at explaining a variety of so-called *heuristics and biases* in terms of this one unifying model. An initial paper shows how dissonance and fairness may be related to socio-emotional reasoning [50]. Work on confirmation and narrative biases is ongoing. Confirmation bias may function similarly to narrative bias in that both have sharpened denotative models as a result of further evidence (more other people opting for it, or more precise statements), and so these tend to be rated as more likely. Non-normal probability models are also under consideration.

Funding: This research was funded in part by a NSERC Discovery grant to Hoey, and by the THEMIS.COG project, jointly funded by the NSERC and the SSHRC through the Transatlantic Platform "Digging into Data" 2016 funding competition.

Data Availability Statement: Information about and supporting data for *BayesAct* can be found at bayesact.ca.

Acknowledgments: I thank the editor and reviewers for their insightful comments. I also thank David Heise, Neil MacKinnon, John Levi Martin, and Tobias Schröder for comments. Thanks to Angie Mercer for comments on early drafts.

Conflicts of Interest: The authors declare no conflict of interest.

References

1. Fehr, E.; Schmidt, K.M. A theory of fairness, competition, and cooperation. *Q. J. Econ.* **1999**, *114*, 817–868. [CrossRef]
2. Jaques, N.; Lazaridou, A.; Hughes, E.; Gulcehre, C.; Ortega, P.; Strouse, D.; Leibo, J.Z.; De Freitas, N. Social Influence as Intrinsic Motivation for Multi-Agent Deep Reinforcement Learning. In Proceedings of the 36th International Conference on Machine Learning, Long Beach, CA, USA, 9–15 June 2019; Chaudhuri, K.; Salakhutdinov, R., Eds.; Volume 97, pp. 3040–3049.
3. Ray, D.; King-Casas, B.; Montague, P.R.; Dayan, P. Bayesian Model of Behaviour in Economic Games. In Proceedings of the Neural Information Processing Systems, Vancouver, BC, Canada, 2–9 December 2008.
4. Kerkmann, A.M.; Rothe, J. Altruism in Coalition Formation Games. In Proceedings of the Twenty-Ninth International Joint Conference on Artificial Intelligence (IJCAI-20), Yokohama, Japan, 7–15 January 2020.
5. Loewenstein, G.; Lerner, J. The Role of Affect in Decision Making. In *Handbook of Affective Sciences*; Davidson, R., Sherer, K., Goldsmith, H., Eds.; Oxford University Press: Oxford, UK, 2003; pp. 619–642.
6. Hoey, J.; MacKinnon, N.; Schröder, T. Denotative and Connotative Control of Uncertainty: A Computational Dual-Process Model. *Judgm. Decis. Mak.* **2021**, *16*, 505–550.
7. Fukuyama, F. *The Origins of Political Order*; Farrar, Strauss and Giroux: New York, NY, USA, 2011.
8. Page, S. *The Difference: How the Power of Diversity Creates Better Groups, Firms, Schools, and Societies*; Princeton University Press: Princeton, NJ, USA, 2007.
9. Schröder, T.; Hoey, J.; Rogers, K.B. Modeling Dynamic Identities and Uncertainty in Social Interactions: Bayesian Affect Control Theory. *Am. Sociol. Rev.* **2016**, *81*, 828–855. [CrossRef]
10. Friston, K. The free-energy principle: A unified brain theory? *Nat. Rev. Neurosci.* **2010**, *11*, 127–138. [CrossRef] [PubMed]
11. Conant, R.C.; Ashby, W.R. Every good regulator of a system must be a model of that system. *Int. J. Syst. Sci.* **1970**, *1*, 89–97. [CrossRef]
12. Berger, P.L.; Luckmann, T. *The Social Construction of Reality*; Random House: New York, NY, USA, 1967.
13. Jeffery, K.; Pollack, R.; Rovelli, C. On the Statistical Mechanics of Life: Schrödinger Revisited. *Entropy* **2019**, *21*, 1211. [CrossRef]
14. Patterson, O. Making Sense of Culture. *Annu. Rev. Sociol.* **2014**, *40*, 1–30. [CrossRef]
15. MacKay, D.J.C. *Information Theory, Inference, and Learning Algorithms*; Cambridge University Press: Cambridge, UK, 2003.
16. Crick, F. Function of the thalamic reticular complex: The searchlight hypothesis. *Proc. Natl. Acad. Sci. USA* **1984**, *81*, 4568–4590.
17. Lau, T. Reframing social categorization as latent structure learning for understanding political behaviour. *Philos. Trans. B* **2021**, *376*, 20200136.
18. Pearl, J. *Probabilistic Reasoning in Intelligent Systems: Networks of Plausible Inference*; Morgan Kaufmann: San Mateo, CA, USA, 1988.
19. Heise, D.R. *Surveying Cultures: Discovering Shared Conceptions and Sentiments*; Wiley: Hoboken, NJ, USA, 2010.
20. Hoey, J.; Schröder, T.; Alhothali, A. Affect Control Processes: Intelligent Affective Interaction using a Partially Observable Markov Decision Process. *Artif. Intell.* **2016**, *230*, 134–172. [CrossRef]
21. Asghar, N.; Hoey, J. Monte-Carlo Planning for Socially Aligned Agents using Bayesian Affect Control Theory. In Proceedings of the Uncertainty in Artificial Intelligence (UAI), Amsterdam, NL, USA, 12–16 July 2015; pp. 72–81.
22. Hoey, J.; Schröder, T. Bayesian Affect Control Theory of Self. In Proceedings of the AAAI Conference on Artificial Intelligence, Austin, TX, USA, 2–9 February 2015; pp. 529–536.
23. Powers, W.T. *Behavior: The Control of Perception*; Aldine Publishing Co.: Chicago, IL, USA, 1973.
24. Osgood, C.E.; Suci, G.J.; Tannenbaum, P.H. *The Measurement of Meaning*; University of Illinois Press: Urbana, IL, USA, 1957.
25. Mead, G.H. *Mind, Self and Society*; University of Chicago Press: Chicago, IL, USA, 1934.
26. Gollob, H.F. The Subject-Verb-Object Approach to Social Cognition. *Psychol. Rev.* **1974**, *81*, 286–321. [CrossRef]
27. MacKinnon, N.J.; Heise, D.R. *Self, Identity and Social Institutions*; Palgrave and Macmillan: New York, NY, USA, 2010.
28. Åström, K.J. Optimal Control of Markov Decision Processes with Incomplete State Estimation. *J. Math. Anal. Appl.* **1965**, *10*, 174–205. [CrossRef]
29. Boutilier, C.; Dean, T.; Hanks, S. Decision Theoretic Planning: Structural Assumptions and Computational Leverage. *J. Artifical Intell. Res.* **1999**, *11*, 1–94. [CrossRef]
30. Puterman, M.L. *Markov Decision Processes: Discrete Stochastic Dynamic Programming*; Wiley: New York, NY, USA, 1994.
31. Russell, S.; Norvig, P. *Artificial Intelligence: A Modern Approach*, 3rd ed.; Prentice Hall: Hoboken, NJ, USA, 2009.
32. von Neumann, J.; Morgenstern, O. *Theory of Games and Economic Behavior*, 3rd ed.; Princeton University Press: Princeton, NJ, USA, 1953.
33. MacKinnon, N.J.; Hoey, J. On the Inextricability and Complementarity of Cognition and Affect: A Review and Model. *Emot. Rev.* **2021**, *13*.
34. Henrich, J.; Ensminger, J.; McElreath, R.; Barr, A.; Barrett, C.; Bolyanatz, A.; Cardenas, J.C.; Gurven, M.; Gwako, E.; Henrich, N.; et al. Markets, religion, community size, and the evolution of fairness and punishment. *Science* **2010**, *327*, 1480–1484. [CrossRef] [PubMed]
35. Taleb, N. *Skin in the Game: Hidden Asymmetries in Everyday Life*; Random House: New York, NY, USA, 2020.
36. Henrich, J. *The WEIRDest People in the World*; Farrar, Strauss and Giroux: New York, NY, USA, 2020.
37. Kahneman, D.; Klein, G. Conditions for intuitive expertise: A failure to disagree. *Am. Psychol.* **2009**, *64*, 515–526. [PubMed]
38. Anderson, E. *Private Government*; Princeton University Press: Princeton, NJ, USA, 2017.
39. Friedman, M. *Capitalism and Freedom*; University of Chicago Press: Chicago, IL, USA, 1962.

40. Putnam, R.D. *Bowling Alone: The Collapse and Revival of American Community*; Simon and Schuster: New York, NY, USA, 2000.
41. Fukuyama, F. *Political Order and Political Decay*; Farrar, Strauss and Giroux: New York, NY, USA, 2014.
42. Fukuyama, F. *Trust: The Social Virtues and the Creation of Prosperity*; Free Press: New York, NY, USA, 1995.
43. Rousseau, J.J. *The Social Contract*; Penguin Books: London, UK, 1968.
44. Berlin, I. *Liberty*; Oxford University Press: Oxford, UK, 2002.
45. Mann, R.P.; Helbing, D. Optimal incentives for collective intelligence. *Proc. Natl. Acad. Sci. USA* **2017**, *114*, 5077–5082. [PubMed]
46. Hong, L.; Page, S.E. Groups of diverse problem solvers can outperform groups of high-ability problem solvers. *Proc. Natl. Acad. Sci. USA* **2004**, *101*, 16385–16389. [CrossRef] [PubMed]
47. Gilead, M.; Trope, Y.; Liberman, N. Above and beyond the concrete: The diverse representational substrates of the predictive brain. *Behav. Brain Sci.* **2020**, *43*, 1–74. [CrossRef] [PubMed]
48. Taleb, N. *The Black Swan*; Random House: New York, NY, USA, 2007.
49. Arrow, K.J. *Social Choice and Individual Values*; John Wiley and Sons: New York, NY, USA, 1951.
50. Hoey, J. Structure is Management of Uncertainty in Groups. *SocArXiv* 2020. [CrossRef]

Article

How Active Inference Could Help Revolutionise Robotics

Lancelot Da Costa [1,2,*,†], Pablo Lanillos [3,†], Noor Sajid [2], Karl Friston [2] and Shujhat Khan [4]

1. Department of Mathematics, Imperial College London, London SW7 2AZ, UK
2. Wellcome Centre for Human Neuroimaging, University College London, London WC1N 3AR, UK; noor.sajid.18@ucl.ac.uk (N.S.); k.friston@ucl.ac.uk (K.F.)
3. Department of Artificial Intelligence, Donders Institute for Brain, Cognition and Behavior, Radboud University, 6525 XZ Nijmegen, The Netherlands; p.lanillos@donders.ru.nl
4. Milton Keynes Hospital, Oxford Deanery, Milton Keynes MK6 5LD, UK; shujhat.khan15@imperial.ac.uk
* Correspondence: l.da-costa@imperial.ac.uk
† These authors contributed equally to this work.

Abstract: Recent advances in neuroscience have characterised brain function using mathematical formalisms and first principles that may be usefully applied elsewhere. In this paper, we explain how active inference—a well-known description of sentient behaviour from neuroscience—can be exploited in robotics. In short, active inference leverages the processes thought to underwrite human behaviour to build effective autonomous systems. These systems show state-of-the-art performance in several robotics settings; we highlight these and explain how this framework may be used to advance robotics.

Keywords: free energy; model-based control; adaptive robots; generative model; Bayesian inference; filtering; neurotechnology

1. Active Inference

Active inference (AIF) is a unifying framework for describing and designing adaptive systems [1–4]. AIF emerged in the late 2000s as a unified theory of brain function [5,6] derived from statistical physics [2,7] and has since been used to simulate a wide range of behaviours in neuroscience [1,8], machine learning [9–13] and robotics [14]. AIF is an interesting framework for robotics because it unifies state-estimation, control and world model learning as inference processes that are solved by optimising a single objective functional: a free energy (also known as negative evidence lower bound), as used in variational Bayesian inference [15]. Furthermore, it endows robots with adaptive capabilities central to real world applications [14] (e.g., adaptation to internal and external parameter changes [16]). Additionally, its strong neuroscience foundation reduces the gap between engineering and the life sciences, thereby finessing human-centred robotic applications.

Although AIF has yet to be scaled—to tackle high dimensional problems—to the same extent as established approaches, such as deep reinforcement learning [17,18], numerical analyses generally show that active inference performs at least as well in simple environments [9,19–23], and better in environments featuring volatility, ambiguity and context sensitivity [21,22]. In this paper, we consider how AIF's features could help address key technical challenges in robotics and discuss practical robotic applications. Our exposition provides a broad perspective that suppresses mathematical details, which can be found in the references herein [1–4,14,24,25].

In AIF, a generative model encodes an agent's predictions (i.e., posterior beliefs), and preferred state and observation trajectories (i.e., prior beliefs) [2]. Behaviour realises the agent's preferences by matching posterior with prior beliefs. Specifically, state-estimation, control and learning are unified by minimising a free energy functional scoring the discrepancy between current beliefs and prior preferences under the state-space model. For continuous states, AIF filters incoming observations through variational inference in generalised coordinates of motion [26]. This enables flexible and scalable inference algorithms and extends Kalman filters by accommodating non-linear, non-Markovian time-series [26–28]. AIF generalises discrete and continuous optimal control [29], and planning to partially observed environments, similarly to model predictive control or control as inference [30,31]. However, a crucial difference is that the (expected) free energy optimised during planning combines exploitative and explorative behaviour [32] in a Bayes optimal fashion [2,7]. The agent's model—i.e., representations and goals—can then be learnt through few-shot learning [21], structure learning, imitation learning, and evolutionary approaches [1,33–35].

2. Solutions to Technical Challenges in Robotics

Current AIF models can help address challenges that require online adaptation, robustness and explainability, and may bring new perspectives to the state-of-the-art in estimation, control and planning—see Figure 1.

- **Accurate and robust state tracking.** Filtering schemes developed for neuroimaging time-series [26] enable accurate state-tracking in highly complex and volatile environments [27,36]. This allows for continuous refinement of past, present, future state-estimation and the estimated precision of sensors as new information arrives [37] (c.f., Bayes optimal estimators of Kalman gain [38]). Moreover, AIF fuses multiple sensory streams, by weighing incoming sensory information by their estimated precision [36,39]. This enables accurate and robust inferences.
- **Adaptive model-based and shared control.** Describing the agent's behaviour with a generative model—prescribing attracting states and trajectories—ensures robustness and adaptivity in the presence of noise, external fluctuations, and parameter changes. AIF humanoid robots [36] and industrial manipulators [40] show improved behaviour in the presence of internal and external parameter changes [16] and shared compliance control [41]. The robot's autonomy—in shared control—can also be dynamically tuned. In particular, the operator may be given high-level control and the robot low-level control.
- **Learning and grounding.** AIF agents learn from sparse and noisy observations by actively sampling informative data points, enabling few-shot learning. Learning latent structure by optimising model evidence, subject to prior preferences in the generative model, leads to organising knowledge in hierarchical, sparsely interconnected modular (i.e., factorised) representations with temporal depth, usually represented with a graphical model [2]. This offers a promising pathway for biologically plausible neurosymbolic technologies [42,43].
- **Operational specification, safety and explainability.** AIF behaviour is explainable as a mixture of information and goal-seeking policies that are explicitly encoded (and evaluated in terms of expected free energy) in the generative model as priors—which can be specified by the user. Planning, which proceeds by generating counterfactual actions and assessing their consequences [1], can be monitored online and control can be returned to the user if necessary (i.e., policy switching). Moreover, the generative model can be specified as a directed graph (i.e., a Bayesian network), which entails the causal relationships between agent's representations [44,45]. This affords an explicit and transparent explanation of sentient behaviour.

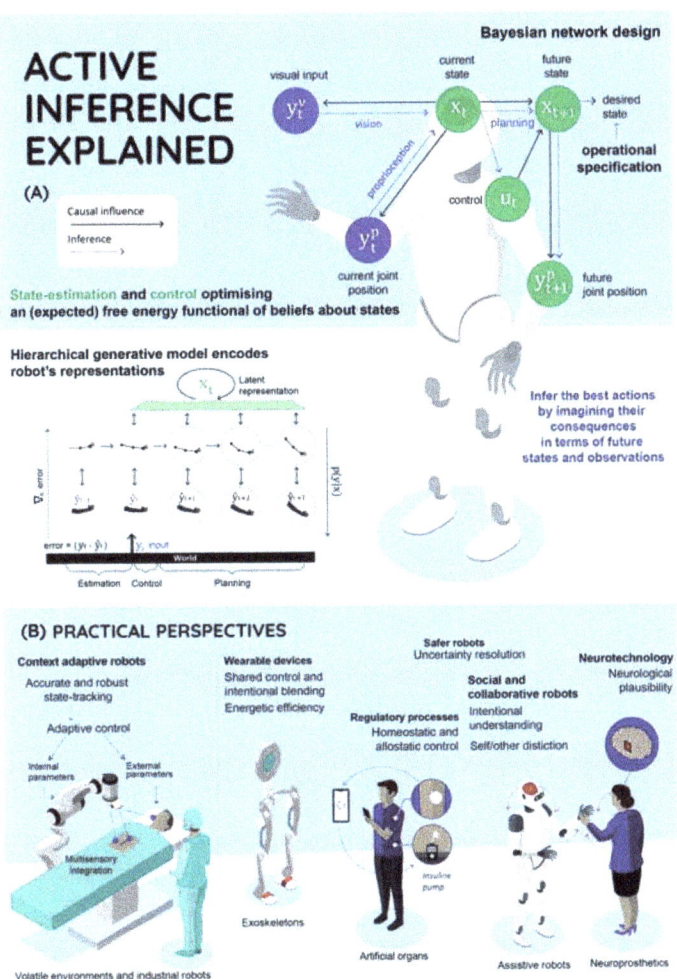

Figure 1. Active inference framework (AIF). AIF could engender important advances in estimation, control, planning and learning in robotics with applications including social, industrial and collaborative robotics, body prosthetics and neurotechnology. (**A**) AIF explained: Blue circles indicate observations while grey circles indicate random variables that need to be inferred. The black arrows indicate causal relationships implicit in a graphical model (e.g., a Bayesian network). The blue arrows indicate the process by which the agent infers future actions and observations. First, the agent infers the current states from available observation modalities (Bayesian fusion). Then, the agent infers the best available course of action by imagining the counterfactual consequences, in terms of future states and observations. These inferential processes are solved by optimising an (expected) free energy functional of beliefs about states and plausible action sequences. AIF generative models may be hierarchical and encode agent's representations at increasing levels of abstraction and temporal scales. Perception minimises the discrepancy between predictions and input at all levels. The top layer encodes the estimated (and preferred) states of the world—and the bottom layer encodes sensory input. (**B**) Practical perspectives: AIF can provide context sensitivity, online adaptivity, accurate state tracking, uncertainty resolution and shared control in a neurologically plausible fashion throughout a wide range of applications.

3. Practical Perspectives

Based on these properties, we envisage important applications of AIF in robotics.

- **Context adaptive robots**. AIF agents build generative (world) models by continuously optimising free energy with regard to incoming data. This optimisation process maximises model accuracy while minimising complexity, which enables generalisation and context-adaptivity [36]. Contrariwise, robots that solely optimise accuracy risk overfitting, which could lead to catastrophic outcomes when the context changes, such as when performing assistive surgery on a new patient. The ability to generalise and adapt is necessary for robotic skills such as scene understanding and adaptive control and should facilitate robots to operate in volatile (e.g., social) environments (e.g., hospitals) [36,46]. In industrial applications, this allows robots to operate freely while adapting to real world conditions—once the designer has specified preferences over the final outcome.
- **Safer robots**. AIF agents continuously resolve uncertainty by selecting informative actions that minimise risk [1], which is important for high-stakes, high-uncertainty tasks, such as human-robot interaction [41]. Actions are selected to minimise expected free energy, which minimises risk (expected cost) and ambiguity (expected inaccuracy) [1]. This allows for information seeking behaviour that is accompanied with an explicit and quantifiable measure of risk. Additionally, when uncertain about current states of affair, robots should automatically seek advice and guidance from the user, e.g., via shared control.
- **Social and collaborative robots**. AIF robots model others' intentions to predict others' actions, such as movements [47], enabling intentional understanding [48]. This allows robots to operate safely in social environments by constantly resolving uncertainty about others' intentions and implicit goals [42]. This embodiment [49] is crucial for social robots, such as personal aides, auxiliary robot nurses and companions, e.g., assisting the disabled and elderly. In collaborative robotics, AIF allows for imitation learning and intentional blending, whence robot goals and intentions can be guided by the user before and during the task [41,50].
- **Wearable devices**. The belief updating process that underwrites AIF is energetically efficient [51], which should aid the development of wearable devices with a degree of autonomy, such as exoskeletons [52]. This follows as optimising model free energy decreases the movement from prior to posterior, which corresponds to the computational (and hence energetic) cost of inference [1,2]. In addition, wearables directed by human intention [53] should benefit from AIF's intentional understanding [48], and adaptive and shared control capabilities [41].
- **Regulatory processes**. Generative models with temporal depth induce allostatic control, whence the robot acts on its environment to pre-empt homeostatic control [54,55]. This should benefit regulatory processes subject to strong external perturbations [16,36], such as closed-loop medical applications such as artificial organs (e.g., the artificial pancreas).
- **Neurotechnology**. The neurological functional plausibility of specific AIF algorithms [1,46,56] should facilitate integration with the nervous system. This opens new opportunities for neurotechnology, BCI-enabled sensorimotor restoration, perceptual body extension and brain or body enhancement using prosthetics and implants [57]. Currently, AIF provides testable hypotheses for optimising neural excitatory-inhibitory balance using deep brain stimulation to alleviate functional deficits induced by brain lesions [58]. Soon, monitoring of brain activity may predict aberrant neural responses, such as seizures, and anticipate the required intervention.

4. Discussion

In this perspective, we explained how active inference—a framework for describing and designing adaptive systems originating in computational neuroscience—can be exploited in robotics. In particular, we surveyed some key features of AIF that could provide solutions to current technical challenges in robotics, and how these could benefit human-centred robotic applications in the short-term.

In brief, the theoretical foundations of AIF suggest the potential for important advances in state-estimation, control, planning and learning that undergirds autonomous robots. This suggests a promising avenue for endowing robots with online adaptive strategies and context-sensitive and explainable decision-making. In turn, these advances could have several applications in robotics, spanning context-adaptive, safe and social robots, wearable devices, regulatory processes and neurotechnology. AIF brings several things to the table in this setting. Perhaps the most important aspects are: (i) a commitment to an explicit, explainable and interpretable world model—in the form of a forward or generative model—that underwrites inference and learning, (ii) framing state estimation, control and planning as different aspects of the same inverse or inference problem, whose solution affords context sensitivity and robustness (iii) and, finally, supplying a tractable objective function that subsumes different kinds of (Bayes) optimality: namely, an expected free energy that subsumes Bayesian decision theory and Bayesian optimal design [2,32]. The latter brings with it a quintessentially belief-based specification of sentient behaviour that can be read as equipping robots with the right kind of curiosity. These foundational features of AIF are, we suppose, also found in human subjects, and therefore place AIF robots in a potentially more empathetic relationship to their human operators. It will be interesting to see whether—or how—these features are leveraged over the next few years.

In short, AIF is generally considered to endow robots and artificial agents with adaptive capabilities. While promising, the application is in its early days and much work remains to be undertaken in order to resolve practical challenges and fulfil the framework's potential. Current endeavours include scaling AIF to handle high dimensional state-spaces in a variety of applications [10,12,13,59], effectively learning the generative model from data [2,34], and show its practicality in the real world, beyond the lab boundaries. While significant engineering challenges remain, the state-of-the-art laboratory experiments show AIF's potential as a powerful method in robotics [14].

Author Contributions: Conceptualization, L.D.C., P.L., N.S., K.F. and S.K.; writing—original draft preparation, L.D.C., P.L. and S.K.; writing—review and editing, N.S. and K.F.; visualization, P.L. and N.S.; supervision, K.F. All authors have read and agreed to the published version of the manuscript.

Funding: L.D.C. is supported by the Fonds National de la Recherche, Luxembourg (Project code: 13568875). P.L. is supported by Spikeference project, Human Brain Project Specific Grant Agreement 3 (ID: 945539). N.S. is funded by the Medical Research Council (MR/S502522/1) and 2021–2022 Microsoft PhD Fellowship. K.F. is supported by funding for the Wellcome Centre for Human Neuroimaging (Ref: 205103/Z/16/Z) and a Canada-UK Artificial Intelligence Initiative (Ref: ES/T01279X/1). This publication is based on work partially supported by the EPSRC Centre for Doctoral Training in Mathematics of Random Systems: Analysis, Modelling and Simulation (EP/S023925/1).

Data Availability Statement: Not applicable.

Acknowledgments: The authors thank Jeroen Infographics for designing the Figure. The authors thank Areeb Mian and Sima Al-Asad for helpful input on a previous version of the manuscript.

Conflicts of Interest: The authors declare no conflict of interest.

References

1. Da Costa, L.; Parr, T.; Sajid, N.; Veselic, S.; Neacsu, V.; Friston, K. Active inference on discrete state-spaces: A synthesis. *J. Math. Psychol.* **2020**, *99*, 102447. [CrossRef] [PubMed]
2. Barp, A.; Da Costa, L.; França, G.; Friston, K.; Girolami, M.; Jordan, M.I.; Pavliotis, G.A. Geometric Methods for Sampling, Optimisation, Inference and Adaptive Agents. In *Geometry and Statistics*; Academic Press: Cambridge, MA, USA, 2022.
3. Friston, K.J.; Daunizeau, J.; Kilner, J.; Kiebel, S.J. Action and behavior: A free-energy formulation. *Biol. Cybern.* **2010**, *102*, 227–260. [CrossRef] [PubMed]
4. Buckley, C.L.; Kim, C.S.; McGregor, S.; Seth, A.K. The free energy principle for action and perception: A mathematical review. *J. Math. Psychol.* **2017**, *81*, 55–79. [CrossRef]
5. Friston, K. The free-energy principle: A unified brain theory? *Nat. Rev. Neurosci.* **2010**, *11*, 127–138. [CrossRef] [PubMed]

6. Friston, K.; Kilner, J.; Harrison, L. A free energy principle for the brain. *J. Physiol.* **2006**, *100*, 70–87. [CrossRef] [PubMed]
7. Friston, K.; Da Costa, L.; Sajid, N.; Heins, C.; Ueltzhöffer, K.; Pavliotis, G.A.; Parr, T. The free energy principle made simpler but not too simple. *arXiv* **2022**, arXiv:2201.06387.
8. Parr, T. The Computational Neurology of Active Vision. Ph.D. Thesis, University College London, London, UK, 2019.
9. Millidge, B. Deep active inference as variational policy gradients. *J. Math. Psychol.* **2020**, *96*, 102348. [CrossRef]
10. Fountas, Z.; Sajid, N.; Mediano, P.A.M.; Friston, K. Deep active inference agents using Monte-Carlo methods. *arXiv* **2020**, arXiv:2006.04176.
11. Tschantz, A.; Millidge, B.; Seth, A.K.; Buckley, C.L. Reinforcement Learning through Active Inference. *arXiv* **2020**, arXiv:2002.12636.
12. Sajid, N.; Tigas, P.; Zakharov, A.; Fountas, Z.; Friston, K. Exploration and preference satisfaction trade-off in reward-free learning. *arXiv* **2021**, arXiv:2106.04316.
13. Mazzaglia, P.; Verbelen, T.; Dhoedt, B. Contrastive Active Inference. Available online: https://openreview.net/forum?id=5t5FPwzE6mq (accessed on 18 February 2022).
14. Lanillos, P.; Meo, C.; Pezzato, C.; Meera, A.A.; Baioumy, M.; Ohata, W.; Tschantz, A.; Millidge, B.; Wisse, M.; Buckley, C.L.; et al. Active Inference in Robotics and Artificial Agents: Survey and Challenges. *arXiv* **2021**, arXiv:2112.01871.
15. Blei, D.M.; Kucukelbir, A.; McAuliffe, J.D. Variational Inference: A Review for Statisticians. *J. Am. Stat. Assoc.* **2017**, *112*, 859–877. [CrossRef]
16. Meo, C.; Lanillos, P. Multimodal VAE Active Inference Controller. In Proceedings of the 2021 IEEE/RSJ International Conference on Intelligent Robots and Systems (IROS), Prague, Czech, 27 September–1 October 2021; pp. 2693–2699. [CrossRef]
17. Silver, D.; Huang, A.; Maddison, C.J.; Guez, A.; Sifre, L.; van den Driessche, G.; Schrittwieser, J.; Antonoglou, I.; Panneershelvam, V.; Lanctot, M.; et al. Mastering the game of Go with deep neural networks and tree search. *Nature* **2016**, *529*, 484–489. [CrossRef] [PubMed]
18. Vinyals, O.; Babuschkin, I.; Czarnecki, W.M.; Mathieu, M.; Dudzik, A.; Chung, J.; Choi, D.H.; Powell, R.; Ewalds, T.; Georgiev, P.; et al. Grandmaster level in StarCraft II using multi-agent reinforcement learning. *Nature* **2019**, *575*, 350–354. [CrossRef] [PubMed]
19. Van Der Himst, O.; Lanillos, P. Deep Active Inference for Partially Observable MDPs. In *Active Inference, IWAI 2020, Communications in Computer and Information Science*; Verbelen, T., Lanillos, P., Buckley, C.L., De Boom, C., Eds.; Springer: Cham, Switzerland, 2020; Volume 1326. [CrossRef]
20. Cullen, M.; Davey, B.; Friston, K.J.; Moran, R. Active Inference in OpenAI Gym: A Paradigm for Computational Investigations Into Psychiatric Illness. *Biol. Psychiatry Cogn. Neurosci. Neuroimaging* **2018**, *3*, 809–818. [CrossRef] [PubMed]
21. Sajid, N.; Ball, P.J.; Parr, T.; Friston, K.J. Active Inference: Demystified and Compared. *Neural Comput.* **2021**, *33*, 674–712. [CrossRef]
22. Marković, D.; Stojić, H.; Schwöbel, S.; Kiebel, S.J. An empirical evaluation of active inference in multi-armed bandits. *Neural Netw.* **2021**, *144*, 229–246. [CrossRef]
23. Paul, A.; Sajid, N.; Gopalkrishnan, M.; Razi, A. Active Inference for Stochastic Control. *arXiv* **2021**, arXiv:2108.12245.
24. Friston, K.; Da Costa, L.; Hafner, D.; Hesp, C.; Parr, T. Sophisticated Inference. *Neural Comput.* **2021**, *33*, 713–763. [CrossRef]
25. Smith, R.; Friston, K.J.; Whyte, C.J. A step-by-step tutorial on active inference and its application to empirical data. *J. Math. Psychol.* **2022**, *107*, 102632. [CrossRef]
26. Friston, K.; Trujillo-Barreto, N.; Daunizeau, J. DEM: A variational treatment of dynamic systems. *NeuroImage* **2008**, *41*, 849–885. [CrossRef] [PubMed]
27. Meera, A.A.; Wisse, M. Free Energy Principle Based State and Input Observer Design for Linear Systems with Colored Noise. In Proceedings of the 2020 American Control Conference (ACC), Denver, CO, USA, 1–3 July 2020; pp. 5052–5058. [CrossRef]
28. Baltieri, M.; Isomura, T. Kalman filters as the steady-state solution of gradient descent on variational free energy. *arXiv* **2021**, arXiv:2111.10530.
29. da Costa, L.; Sajid, N.; Parr, T.; Friston, K.; Smith, R. The relationship between dynamic programming and active inference: The discrete, finite-horizon case. *arXiv* **2020**, arXiv:2009.08111.
30. Imohiosen, A.; Watson, J.; Peters, J. Active Inference or Control as Inference? A Unifying View. *arXiv* **2020**, arXiv:2010.00262.
31. Millidge, B.; Tschantz, A.; Seth, A.K.; Buckley, C.L. On the Relationship Between Active Inference and Control as Inference. In *International Workshop on Active Inference*; Springer: Cham, Switzerland, 2020; pp. 3–11.
32. Sajid, N.; da Costa, L.; Parr, T.; Friston, K. Active inference, Bayesian optimal design, and expected utility. *arXiv* **2021**, arXiv:2110.04074.
33. Smith, R.; Schwartenbeck, P.; Parr, T.; Friston, K. An Active Inference Approach to Modeling Structure Learning: Concept Learning as an Example Case. *Front. Comput. Neurosci.* **2020**, *14*, 41. [CrossRef]
34. Çatal, O.; Wauthier, S.; De Boom, C.; Verbelen, T.; Dhoedt, B. Learning Generative State Space Models for Active Inference. *Front. Comput. Neurosci.* **2020**, *14*, 103. [CrossRef]
35. Friston, K.J.; Lin, M.; Frith, C.D.; Pezzulo, G.; Hobson, J.A.; Ondobaka, S. Active Inference, Curiosity and Insight. *Neural Comput.* **2017**, *29*, 2633–2683. [CrossRef]
36. Oliver, G.; Lanillos, P.; Cheng, G. An empirical study of active inference on a humanoid robot. *IEEE Trans. Cogn. Dev. Syst.* **2021**, *4*, 1–17. [CrossRef]
37. Meera, A.A.; Wisse, M. Dynamic Expectation Maximization Algorithm for Estimation of Linear Systems with Colored Noise. *Entropy* **2021**, *23*, 1306. [CrossRef]

38. Baltieri, M.; Buckley, C.L. PID Control as a Process of Active Inference with Linear Generative Models. *Entropy* **2019**, *21*, 257. [CrossRef] [PubMed]
39. Lanillos, P.; Cheng, G. Adaptive Robot Body Learning and Estimation Through Predictive Coding. In Proceedings of the 2018 IEEE/RSJ International Conference on Intelligent Robots and Systems (IROS), Madrid, Spain, 1–5 October 2018; pp. 4083–4090. [CrossRef]
40. Pezzato, C.; Ferrari, R.M.G.; Corbato, C.H. A Novel Adaptive Controller for Robot Manipulators Based on Active Inference. *IEEE Robot. Autom. Lett.* **2020**, *5*, 2973–2980. [CrossRef]
41. Chame, H.F.; Tani, J. Cognitive and motor compliance in intentional human-robot interaction. In Proceedings of the 2020 IEEE International Conference on Robotics and Automation (ICRA), Paris, France, 31 May–31 August 2020; pp. 11291–11297. [CrossRef]
42. Friston, K.; Moran, R.J.; Nagai, Y.; Taniguchi, T.; Gomi, H.; Tenenbaum, J. World model learning and inference. *Neural Netw.* **2021**, *144*, 573–590. [CrossRef] [PubMed]
43. Taniguchi, T.; Piater, J.; Worgotter, F.; Ugur, E.; Hoffmann, M.; Jamone, L.; Nagai, T.; Rosman, B.; Matsuka, T.; Iwahashi, N.; et al. Symbol Emergence in Cognitive Developmental Systems: A Survey. *IEEE Trans. Cogn. Dev. Syst.* **2018**, *11*, 494–516. [CrossRef]
44. Pearl, J. Graphical Models for Probabilistic and Causal Reasoning. In *Quantified Representation of Uncertainty and Imprecision*; Smets, P., Ed.; Springer: Dordrecht, The Netherlands, 1998; pp. 367–389. [CrossRef]
45. Friston, K.J.; Parr, T.; De Vries, B. The graphical brain: Belief propagation and active inference. *Netw. Neurosci.* **2017**, *1*, 381–414. [CrossRef]
46. Verbelen, T.; Lanillos, P.; Buckley, C.; Boom, C.D. (Eds.) Active Inference. In Proceedings of the First International Workshop, IWAI 2020, Co-Located with ECML/PKDD 2020, Ghent, Belgium, 14 September 2020; Springer: Berlin/Heidelberg, Germany, 2020. [CrossRef]
47. Wirkuttis, N.; Tani, J. Leading or Following? Dyadic Robot Imitative Interaction Using the Active Inference Framework. *IEEE Robot. Autom. Lett.* **2021**, *6*, 6024–6031. [CrossRef]
48. Horii, T.; Nagai, Y. Active Inference Through Energy Minimization in Multimodal Affective Human–Robot Interaction. *Front. Robot. AI* **2021**, *8*, 684401. [CrossRef]
49. Lanillos, P.; Pages, J.; Cheng, G. Robot Self/Other Distinction: Active Inference Meets Neural Networks Learning in a Mirror. In Proceedings of the ECAI 2020-24th European Conference on Artificial Intelligence, Compostela, Spain, 29 August–8 September 2020; IOS Press: Amsterdam, The Netherlands, 2020; pp. 2410–2416. [CrossRef]
50. Shin, J.Y.; Kim, C.; Hwang, H.J. Prior preference learning from experts: Designing a reward with active inference. *Neurocomputing* **2021**, *12*, 42. [CrossRef]
51. Friston, K. Complexity and Computation in the Brain: The Knowns and the Known Unknowns. Available online: https://direct.mit.edu/books/book/4588/chapter/204732/Complexity-and-Computation-in-the-Brain-The-Knowns (accessed on 18 February 2022).
52. Lanillos, P.; van Gerven, M. Neuroscience-inspired perception-action in robotics: Applying active inference for state estimation, control and self-perception. *arXiv* **2021**, arXiv:2105.04261.
53. Ajoudani, A.; Zanchettin, A.M.; Ivaldi, S.; Albu-Schäffer, A.; Kosuge, K.; Khatib, O. Progress and prospects of the human–robot collaboration. *Auton. Robot.* **2018**, *42*, 957–975. [CrossRef]
54. Çatal, O.; Verbelen, T.; Van de Maele, T.; Dhoedt, B.; Safron, A. Robot navigation as hierarchical active inference. *Neural Netw.* **2021**, *142*, 192–204. [CrossRef]
55. Tschantz, A.; Barca, L.; Maisto, D.; Buckley, C.L.; Seth, A.K.; Pezzulo, G. Simulating homeostatic, allostatic and goal-directed forms of interoceptive control using active inference. *Biol. Psychol.* **2022**, *169*, 108266. [CrossRef]
56. Friston, K.J.; Fitzgerald, T.H.B.; Rigoli, F.; Schwartenbeck, P.; Pezzulo, G. Active Inference: A Process Theory. *Neural Comput.* **2017**, *29*, 1–49. [CrossRef]
57. Cheng, G.; Ehrlich, S.K.; Lebedev, M.; Nicolelis, M.A.L. Neuroengineering challenges of fusing robotics and neuroscience. *Sci. Robot.* **2020**, *5*, eabd1911. [CrossRef]
58. Sajid, N.; Parr, T.; Gajardo-Vidal, A.; Price, C.J.; Friston, K.J. Paradoxical lesions, plasticity and active inference. *Brain Commun.* **2020**, *2*, fcaa164. [CrossRef]
59. Tschantz, A.; Baltieri, M.; Seth, A.K.; Buckley, C.L. Scaling active inference. *arXiv* **2019**, arXiv:1911.10601.

MDPI
St. Alban-Anlage 66
4052 Basel
Switzerland
Tel. +41 61 683 77 34
Fax +41 61 302 89 18
www.mdpi.com

Entropy Editorial Office
E-mail: entropy@mdpi.com
www.mdpi.com/journal/entropy

www.ingramcontent.com/pod-product-compliance
Lightning Source LLC
LaVergne TN
LVHW070744100526
838202LV00013B/1299